UNION GENERAL

UNION GENERAL

SAMUEL RYAN CURTIS AND VICTORY IN THE WEST

WILLIAM L. SHEA

Potomac Books

AN IMPRINT OF THE UNIVERSITY OF NEBRASKA PRESS

All rights reserved. Potomac Books is an imprint of the
University of Nebraska Press.
Manufactured in the United States of America.

Library of Congress Cataloging-in-Publication Data
Names: Shea, William L., author.
Title: Union General: Samuel Ryan Curtis and victory in the
West / William L. Shea.
Other titles: Samuel Ryan Curtis and victory in the West
Description: [Lincoln, Nebraska]: Potomac Books, an
imprint of the University of Nebraska Press, [2023] |
Includes bibliographical references and index.
Identifiers: LCCN 2022010736
ISBN 9781640125186 (hardback)
ISBN 9781640125582 (epub)
ISBN 9781640125599 (pdf)
Subjects: LCSH: Curtis, Samuel Ryan, 1805–1866. |
Generals—United States—Biography. | United States—
History—Civil War, 1861–1865—Campaigns. | West (U.S.)—
History—Civil War, 1861–1865—Campaigns. | United
States. Army—Biography. | Keokuk (Iowa)—Biography. |
BISAC: BIOGRAPHY & AUTOBIOGRAPHY / Military |
HISTORY / United States / Civil War Period (1850–1877)
Classification: LCC E467.1.C97 S54 2023 | DDC 355.0092
[B]—dc23/eng/20220527
LC record available at https://lccn.loc.gov/2022010736

Set in Questa by Laura Buis.

CONTENTS

ILLUSTRATIONS

PREFACE

SAMUEL RYAN CURTIS WAS THE MOST IMPORTANT FIGURE in the Civil War west of the Mississippi River. He was a West Point graduate, Mexican War veteran, and determined foe of secession who gave up his seat in Congress to fight for the Union. During his five years in uniform he rose to the rank of major general and served at various times as an army, district, and department commander. Curtis influenced the course of events in a half-dozen states and territories and personally led U.S. forces to victory in two remarkable campaigns. At Pea Ridge in 1862 and Westport in 1864 he overcame daunting logistical and geographical challenges, routed Confederate armies larger than his own, and reestablished government control over large swaths of rebel territory.

In addition to compiling an impressive record in the field, a record matched or exceeded by only a handful of other Union generals, Curtis dealt a heavy blow to slavery in the trans-Mississippi months before emancipation became the law of the land. His enlightened racial policies and practices freed thousands from bondage but also generated intense and underhanded opposition from a clique of conservative Union officers and politicians who sought to have him removed.

Before the war Curtis was a nationally recognized civil engineer and a prime mover of the transcontinental railroad. He was also an important figure in the emerging Republican Party and was thrice elected to the House of Representatives from Iowa. After Appomattox he participated in pioneering peacemaking efforts with Indians on the northern Great Plains and helped oversee the progress of the Union Pacific. Curtis was in the public eye for most of his life, but in the century and a half since his death he has faded from our collective memory. Few Americans recognize his name today. I hope this biography will help restore him to his rightful place in our history.

• • •

A project of this magnitude would not have been possible without the advice and assistance of dozens of archivists, curators, librarians, and fellow historians. I owe special thanks to Christopher Schnell at the Abraham Lincoln Presidential Library; Becki Plunkett and her colleagues at the State Historical Society of Iowa; Jeffrey L. Patrick and Alan P. Chilton at Wilson's Creek National Battlefield; Mark Flotow of Springfield, Illinois; and the staff of the Taylor Library at the University of Arkansas at Monticello.

UNION GENERAL

1

BEGINNINGS

ZARAH CURTIS WAS A NINETEEN-YEAR-OLD FARMER FROM Litchfield, Connecticut, when he joined the Continental Army in 1781. He served for two years in Colonel Elisha Sheldon's Second Connecticut Light Dragoons and rose to the rank of sergeant. He married Phally Yale of Hartford when the War of Independence ended and began to make his way in the new country he had helped create. Zarah and Phally moved first to Charlotte, Vermont, then to Champlain, New York, where they purchased a farm within sight of the Canadian border. They had nine children, seven of whom lived to adulthood. Their last, Samuel Ryan, made his appearance on the Champlain farm on February 3, 1805.[1]

In 1809 the Curtis family packed up and headed west to improve their fortunes. Their journey across the Appalachian Mountains took two and a half months and must have seemed a great adventure, at least to the younger children. Zarah and Phally finally called a halt near Newark, a promising village in central Ohio. They bought a farm on the South Fork of the Licking River and it was there, in a wooded, rolling landscape dotted with Indian mounds, that the Curtis children grew up. Educational opportunities were limited in Licking County, but the three boys— Hosmer, Henry, and Samuel—attended such schools as were available and received private lessons from local ministers and itinerant scholars. The financial burden must have been heavy but the results were impressive. Hosmer and Henry enjoyed distinguished careers in law, politics, business, and public service. Samuel also achieved success in those fields, but his life followed a more complicated trajectory.[2]

Hosmer, the oldest brother, left home in 1815 and moved to Mount Vernon in nearby Knox County. Within a remarkably short time he became a prosperous attorney and businessman. Henry followed two years later and, with his older brother's tutelage and support, opened his own legal practice in Mount Vernon. He, too, met with success and eventually surpassed his elder brother in prominence, wealth, and influence. Samuel, the youngest by six years, remained behind to help his parents, but like his brothers he had no interest in farming. In 1823 Hosmer and Henry convinced Amos H. Caffee, the Licking County clerk of court, to hire Samuel as a clerical assistant. Caffee probably needed little convincing. He supplemented his income by tutoring promising youngsters and was familiar with the Curtis boys and their intellectual gifts. At the age of eighteen Samuel left the family farm and moved to Newark, the county seat. It was a journey of only a few miles but Samuel never looked back. It was his first step onto a larger stage.[3]

Samuel received advice, encouragement, and criticism from his siblings throughout his life. Some brotherly comments were sharp. "I was much pleased to see the advancement you had made in writing, but disgusted with your carelessness in spelling," wrote Henry in 1824. "Pray be more careful in your spelling and you will succeed very well in penmanship." Others were platitudinous: "Be studious and acquire steady habits." Still others reflected fraternal concern about the temptations of life in Newark: "Be cautious you do not attend too many of those dances and routs you speak of for remember you spend both time and money at them which ought to be better employed, and above all avoid contracting licentious or vicious habits, and guard against falling in love." Samuel did not enjoy being lectured about his shortcomings, real or imagined, but he took to heart much of what his brothers had to say. Their achievements and their obvious concern for his welfare were lifelong sources of inspiration.[4]

After two years of scribbling in Caffee's office, Samuel wanted to try something different. Hosmer and Henry, as usual, were supportive. "I am in hopes I shall be able to get you into some other business before long," wrote Henry. "In the mean time lose no means within your grasp to acquire learning and information—this is all important." A few months later Samuel received an offer of employment in the "mercantile business" from Robert McComb, a prominent merchant in nearby Mansfield. The offer was arranged by Hosmer, who assured Samuel that McComb was an "agreeable man" and that a career in business might lead "to wealth and respectability which should be the aim of a young man of your age and situation." Samuel, however, expressed an interest in becoming an attorney. "The thing I am anxious to undertake [is] the studdy of the Law," he confided to Hosmer. Samuel believed his brothers would welcome him to the legal profession with open arms, but he was mistaken. "If wealth, ease, or pleasure is to be consulted I cannot advise any young man at this time to undertake the study of the law," replied Hosmer in his ponderous manner. "It will be essential that your whole life should be in a great measure devoted to close study and severe mental labour." Hosmer clearly did not think Samuel was ready to make such a commitment. Nevertheless, he offered to support Samuel should he undertake to "read the law" in Hosmer's Mount Vernon office, as Henry had done some years earlier. Faced with his brothers' disapproval, Samuel accepted McComb's offer.[5]

Samuel moved to Mansfield in March 1825 and began his business apprenticeship as a clerk in McComb's dry goods store. McComb was an energetic and forward-looking entrepreneur who had commercial interests across Ohio. He regularly traveled over the Appalachians to sell cattle in eastern cities, acquire inventory for his store, and explore emerging business opportunities. During these absences he left Samuel, barely twenty years old, in charge of affairs in Mansfield. McComb reminded Samuel to maintain regular hours, keep the books in order, and watch for counterfeit bills, no small matter in an era when there was no national currency. "You must be very much on your *guard*," he warned. McComb also stressed the importance of making a good impression: "There is *considerable* dust gets on the goods and *shelves*. Have that all *taken off*." Samuel soon mastered the mysteries of his new trade and established himself as McComb's right-hand man, more of a manager than a clerk.[6]

McComb clearly was impressed with Samuel, which makes it all the more puzzling why family and friends constantly exhorted him to abandon his supposedly frivolous ways. Hosmer desired Samuel to "form and persevere in such habits of industry strict temperance and fidelity as shall meet the approbation and advance the interest of Mr. McComb." Henry offered a mix of moral and practical advice: "I think there is one point (*particularly*) in your character in which you are not sufficiently circumspect, i.e., Economy." Henry emphasized that saving money and avoiding debt would "lay the foundation for a good and economical life, the sure road to wealth." Even Amos Caffee joined in. He exhorted his former clerk to develop a sound character and warned that "to devote too much time (at your age) to company and trivial amusement is in my opinion injurious."[7]

It is difficult to say what caused such concern, but repeated references to "strict temperance" and "trivial amusement" suggest that Samuel enjoyed good company. The Curtis family was of old New England stock and its Puritan sensibilities may have been offended by the frontier frolics Samuel found so congenial. A touching 1826 letter from Zarah and Phally urging their youngest son to maintain the moral standards of another time and place suggests a generational fissure within the family. If so, it is not surprising. Samuel was the only Curtis child born in the nineteenth century and the only one raised from infancy west of the Appalachians. To a greater degree than any of his brothers and sisters, he was a child of the antebellum Midwest.[8]

Toward the end of 1826, about eighteen months into his budding mercantile career in Mansfield, Samuel informed his brothers that he desired an appointment to the United States Military Academy at West Point, New York. The announcement was a complete surprise. "What has given rise to this notion," exclaimed Henry. After due consideration, however, Hosmer and Henry concluded that a formal education in a structured environment might be just the thing for their supposedly wayward younger brother. "By attention to your studies while at West Point you might, at your age, become one of the best scholars in our country," enthused Henry. "This would give you many, very many, advantages in society, it would make you respectable, and if not abused would give you character and influence in community." This passage reveals more about Henry's aspirations and values than anything else, but it also illuminates the exalted status of a college education in antebellum America. It was not lost on Hosmer and Henry that if Samuel succeeded he would be the first member of the family to acquire that status.[9]

The application process for the military academy in the 1820s favored candidates of modest means whose fathers were veterans of the War of Independence. Samuel was a perfect fit except that at age twenty-two he was two years older than the regulations allowed. Hosmer and Henry were men of unassailable integrity but they did not hesitate to fudge the truth on this occasion. "Your age perhaps may be an obstacle," Henry observed smoothly, "with management however you perhaps can be passed off for twenty." Samuel therefore declared 1807, not 1805, to be the year of his birth. This small lie made him twenty years old on paper and allowed his application to go forward. The three siblings conspired to keep Samuel's actual age a secret for the next forty years. The truth was not revealed until Samuel's death in 1866, when Henry made certain the monument marking his younger brother's grave displayed the correct birth date.[10]

When Henry assured Samuel that "I will do all in my power to further your wishes," he meant it. He and Hosmer launched a lobbying campaign in support of their brother's application. "It is best to proceed cautiously and endeavor to obtain sure footing," observed Henry in true lawyerly fashion. The brothers first asked McComb if he had any objections to losing his principal assistant. McComb expressed his enthusiastic support for Samuel's quest and even offered to help. The brothers then contacted congressmen from Ohio and neighboring states, some of whom they knew personally, and convinced most to write to Secretary of War James Barbour on Samuel's behalf. Their efforts were crowned with success. In early 1827 Samuel was notified of his acceptance into the military academy.[11]

Samuel had become fascinated with "internal improvements" during his years in Newark and Mansfield. The Industrial Revolution was well underway by this time and the country needed engineers to survey, map, design, build, operate, and maintain roads, canals, railroads, factories, bridges, dams, wharves, levees, breakwaters, sewers, and the like. McComb was an avid proponent of improved transportation—he later invested in and served on the board of an Ohio railroad—and his enthusiasm doubtless fueled Samuel's interest. The military academy was one of only two engineering schools in the world and the only one in the western hemisphere. Hosmer described it as "one of the best institutions in our country—where science and chivalry combine." Samuel had no discernible interest in a military career except as a means to an end. For him, West Point provided an opportunity to acquire a "scientific education" and embark on an extraordinary adventure.[12]

• • •

Samuel and another prospective Ohio cadet, William Hoyt of Wooster, set out together for West Point in June 1827. It is tempting to suggest that the pair traveled across New York on the newly completed Erie Canal, the engineering wonder of the age, but on this as on so much else the record is silent. Upon arrival at the military academy, the eighty-six freshmen or "plebes" took part in summer encampment, a boot camp that introduced them to the rigors of antebellum military service. Samuel quickly settled into a spartan routine of discipline, drill, and coursework, but not everyone made the adjustment. Hoyt departed for home within a week. "I am happy to see you possess more resolution," wrote Henry in a warm letter filled with praise, encouragement, and advice. The advice came from an unexpected source, Zarah Curtis, who hearkened back to his service in the Continental Army. "Father particularly desires you to be obedient and show due deference and submission to the rules and orders of your officers as the only means by which you will secure the confidence and esteem of your commanders and instructors."[13]

Academic competition at West Point was intense. Samuel told Henry that Colonel Sylvanus Thayer, the school's superintendent, said that "ours is the best class ever here—at any rate I find them hard fellows to contend with." Midway through his first year he reported that he was doing fairly well despite his sketchy frontier schooling: "If you take into consideration my [dis]advantages in comparison to most of my fellow Cadets you must know I stand *very* high in mathematics to be twenty-fifth in a class of about eighty." French was more of a struggle. Samuel ranked only forty-fifth in that subject, "owing initially to my not having studied the language before I came here," but he was satisfied with his standing: "I am yet low in it and most likely I will continue to. But I will know it is not for want of study for I have paid much more attention to French than mathematics and have moreover succeeded as well as could be expected." The ability to read French was vital because most books in science, engineering, and the military arts in the post-Napoleonic era were written in that language. Recognizing this, Samuel even subscribed to a French-language newspaper to improve his literary skills. "I am satisfied I shall not be wanting," he declared.[14]

Hosmer and Henry expressed their satisfaction with Samuel's progress. "Your arduous and incessant studies are as I hope amply requited by the very respectable standing you have attained in your Class," wrote Hosmer. "In truth you are not without your share of natural genius but even with this providential favor it was not to be expected you could keep pace with the choice spirits composing the cadets at West Point without an extraordinary effort on your part." Henry advised his brother not to feel sorry for himself but to get on with the task at hand. He noted with approval that Samuel's academic standing was "above all the other cadets from Ohio of your class." Bolstered by these votes of confidence from his staunchest supporters (and most persistent critics), Samuel mastered algebra, geometry, physics, chemistry, geology, history, drawing, cartography, and, of course, engineering, which he found "agreeable."[15]

Life at West Point was spartan. "I am deprived of . . . nearly *every* kind of amusement," Samuel complained. On the positive side, the strict regimen and busy schedule provided few opportunities for cadets to engage in what he termed "low vices." In his limited spare time, Samuel read novels and newspapers, painted watercolors, and joined several student organizations, including the prestigious Lyceum of Natural History. He developed a lifelong interest in botany. Predictably, Hosmer urged Samuel to ignore the "little inconveniences of confinement and hard study" and focus on the future.[16]

Samuel did not achieve academic distinction at the military academy. "I had gone to West Point with much unfavorable qualifications," he wrote many years later. "I had received a very indifferent western common school education, and had never devoted myself to any regular course of studies. I was exceedingly backward and ignorant of reading, writing, and arithmetic, and when I found my class mostly composed of regular students and many of them graduates of colleges, I saw my prospects were poor indeed." Samuel recognized that he had an opportunity to excel on the military side of the curriculum, where none of the cadets had an advantage: "I found myself therefore on equal footing in matters purely military and I did not fail to exert myself when I saw a prospect of distinction. In other studies I would only expect to retain a respectable standing, and I found often that I could not at all succeed, but in the matter of drill and science of war, I seldom if ever missed any part of the lesson." His diligence was rewarded.[17]

The commandant of the Corps of Cadets at that time was Major William J. Worth. "The whole army regarded him as the most accomplished soldier," gushed Samuel, "and I almost idolised him." Worth singled out Samuel for praise and promoted him to first corporal of his plebe class. The recognition made a deep impression on Samuel. Two decades later, as colonel of the Third Ohio Volunteers in the Mexican War, he recalled his first promotion with pride. "I have never received any appointment that so much flattered my vanity and satisfied my aspirations," he wrote. "My advancement was one of the most conspicuous in my class and in a military point of view gave me a distinction which I succeed[ed] in holding during my long course of four years." Samuel received additional promotions to first sergeant, first captain, and superintendent of the mess hall, a position that required him to wear a ceremonial sword and enforce proper decorum during meals.[18]

The Corps of Cadets was the most cosmopolitan collegiate student body in the United States. It was composed of young men from every section of the country and from many walks of life. Some were wealthy or well connected. Samuel discovered that Henry Clay Jr., son of the Kentucky senator, was a classmate. Meriwether Lewis Clark, son of one legendary explorer and namesake of another, was one class ahead, while Henry du Pont, son of the founder of the famous gunpowder works in Delaware, was one behind. Samuel also rubbed shoulders with a platoon of future Confederate generals, among them Robert E. Lee and Joseph E. Johnston.

It was a personal relationship of a very different sort that caused him considerable distress. While clerking in Mansfield, Samuel had become enamored of a blonde teenage girl named Belinda Buckingham. Mindful of Henry's warning to "guard against falling in love," he downplayed the seriousness of the relationship. By early 1828, however, Samuel could contain his feelings no longer. He told Hosmer that he wanted to return to Mansfield, marry Belinda, and become a lawyer. When Hosmer predictably urged him to continue his studies, Samuel responded with angry words that caused his brother "much unpleasant feeling and vexation." Holding his own temper in check, Hosmer urged Samuel to put the "idea of matrimony" aside for a while longer and complete the priceless education in which all three brothers had invested so much. Abashed, Samuel remained at the military academy. "I am surprised at my patience and endurance," he remarked later.[19]

Henry was closer to Samuel's age and a more congenial correspondent. Sometime after the flap with Hosmer, Samuel told Henry about Belinda. The letter has not survived but Henry's reply provides a hint of its contents: "I thank you Samuel for the plain and undisguised history, you have been pleased to confide to me, of your life in Mansfield. I can fully appreciate the happy, yet perplexing, scenes that you have so pleasantly described. . . . I highly approve your taste and judgment, and hope that . . . you will continue to deserve her." Henry added that Belinda recently had passed through Mount Vernon. "She has gone to learn music I am told." From this time forward there was an understanding between the Curtis and Buckingham families that Samuel and Belinda would wed as soon as Samuel completed his studies and acquired a regular income.[20]

Henry later heard a rumor that Belinda was to marry another man. Instead of looking into the matter, as he should have done, Henry rushed to inform his brother. He advised Samuel that if the story turned out to be true, Belinda "deserved your forgetfulness and will no longer be worthy [of] your regard. Stand therefore aloof, ready to be true if others remain true, independent if others prove false." There was nothing to the rumor; Samuel and Belinda remained happily engaged.[21]

No portraits of a youthful Samuel Curtis exist, but he was tall and trim with wavy brown hair and deep-set hazel eyes in a square face. He possessed a "robust constitution" and took part in the usual physical activities of his day. Open and lighthearted with family and friends, he was serious and undemonstrative in public and went about his business in a methodical manner. He carried himself in an erect military posture and was fastidious about his dress and appearance, traits that made him seem more reserved than he actually was. Other aspects of his personality were apparent only to those who knew him well. He was ambitious and thin-skinned. He was sensitive about his rustic upbringing and did not take criticism well. By the time he left West Point few traces remained of the carefree young man who had amused his friends and troubled his family.[22]

Samuel graduated from the military academy in July 1831. Nearly two-thirds of his entering class had fallen away and he ranked twenty-seventh in a class of thirty-three. Setting aside the less happy aspects of his time at West Point, he exuberantly declared that "four years have flown round like a day, and it will seem but yesterday that I bid adieu to my friends in Ohio." Samuel celebrated by taking a steamboat down the Hudson River to New York. "I am going to have most of my clothes made in the city," he informed Henry. "I am going to wait for the London fashions." Anxious to head off a fraternal lecture on fiscal responsibility, he quickly added, "I am not going to pay too much for clothes lest I may not have cash to last."[23]

Military academy graduates at that time were required to serve one year on active duty. Cadets at the top of the list were assigned to the elite technical branches of the army, primarily engineering and artillery. Everyone else ended up in the cavalry and infantry. Samuel found himself a brevet second lieutenant in the Seventh Infantry. It was hardly a choice assignment. The regiment was stationed at Fort Gibson in the northeast corner of the Indian Territory (present-day Oklahoma), the newest, rawest, and most isolated military post in the country.[24]

Following graduation Samuel returned to Ohio. He visited family and friends and made wedding plans with Belinda. He then traveled 1,400 miles by steamboat on the Ohio, Mississippi, and Arkansas Rivers to the Indian Territory. Along the way he stopped in St. Louis, Helena, Little Rock, and Fort Smith, western river towns that would figure prominently in his engineering and military careers.

Samuel reached Fort Gibson in August and officially became part of the Seventh Infantry. The 382 officers and men who comprised the understrength regiment occupied a dozen buildings inside a compact, rectangular palisade. Everything was made of squared logs and rough-hewn planks. Vegetable gardens, woodpiles, corrals, and workshops surrounded the palisade. The post was neat and tidy but the quality of life was austere.[25]

Samuel had only just settled into his new role when he learned that his mother, Phally, had died at the age of sixty-nine. He obtained a leave of absence and returned to Ohio. He arrived far too late for his mother's funeral but just in time for his own wedding, which took place in Mansfield on November 3, 1831. Samuel was twenty-six; Belinda was twenty. He obtained an extension of his leave and remained in Ohio until the end of the year. Samuel and Belinda journeyed to Fort Gibson in January 1832 to complete what remained of his obligatory year of military service.[26]

President Andrew Jackson's controversial Indian removal program was underway; thousands of Native people were streaming into the Indian Territory from their former homelands in the East and Midwest. The Seventh Infantry helped these "civilized" Indians reestablish themselves in an unfamiliar land and protected them from the "wild" Indians of the Great Plains. In addition to dealing with construction and housekeeping duties at Fort Gibson, Samuel surveyed tribal boundaries, built roads, distributed government stores, and mediated squabbles between the locals (mostly Osages) and the new arrivals (mostly Cherokees, Creeks, and Seminoles). Five years earlier, when he had first expressed an interest in West Point, Henry had warned that "in time of peace there is little glory or honor to be won in the army." Samuel confirmed the accuracy of that statement through personal experience. In June 1832, after barely six months of active duty at Fort Gibson, he resigned his commission and returned to civilian life in Ohio. His military career appeared to be over.[27]

• • •

West Point graduates in the antebellum period often left the army to pursue more lucrative careers in scientific or engineering fields. Many maintained an interest in military affairs and served in state militias or volunteer companies. Samuel did all of these things. But his first order of business back in Ohio, after establishing suitable domestic arrangements with Belinda in Mansfield, was to decide what to do with his life. Hosmer and Henry reversed course and invited Samuel to follow them into the law, a career path they had previously discouraged. Now it was Samuel who dug in his heels. Determined to put his hard-earned knowledge of engineering to good use and demonstrate that he was his own man, he chose instead to try his hand at "internal improvements."[28]

The National Road was the largest public works project under-taken by the federal government in the first half of the nineteenth century. The road began in Maryland, wound its way across the Appalachian Mountains, and ran westward across Ohio, Indi-ana, and Illinois toward the Mississippi River. Samuel was hired to oversee construction of a difficult section of the road between Zanesville and Columbus, about sixty miles south of Mansfield. He was not long on the job before the federal government washed its hands of the National Road and handed it over to the states. A general reshuffling followed; in 1833 the Ohio Board of Public Works appointed Samuel chief surveyor for the state, a position he held for the next four years. His surveying experience in the Indian Territory served him well in his new job, but his profes-sional judgment was not always respected. He later recalled that "I carried forward many lines for turnpikes, rail roads, and canals, some of which are now being constructed, though I reported against all of them in 1836."[29]

Samuel enjoyed his work but was frustrated at having to spend so much time away from Belinda. Their first child, Amanda, was born in Mansfield on September 16, 1832. Sadly, she lived only twenty months. Samuel saw little of Amanda during her short life for he was almost constantly in the field, but years later he remembered her as "our first and fairest" and a "most wonder-ful exhibition of beauty and unusually precocious." The cause of death likely was cholera. The previously unknown disease reached the United States in 1832 and killed tens of thousands of people, mostly children, over the next two years. The advances in trans-portation that were transforming the country allowed the disease to spread with unprecedented speed. Blessed, or in this instance cursed, by its many roads and waterways, Ohio was especially hard hit. In addition to little Amanda, Hosmer's wife, Eleanor, and three of Henry's children—Clementine, Adela, and Caroline—died during a six-month span at the height of the pandemic.[30]

Belinda became pregnant again two years later. Samuel was away on yet another surveying assignment as the due date approached. "I am very uneasy and unhappy and will do all in my power to get home [as] soon as possible," he assured Belinda. "The painful anxiety about you unfits me for duty. I am determined to remain near you on my return, till the cause of my anxiety is removed." Unable to offer any assistance save advice, Samuel urged his wife to maintain a "prudent resignation" to God's will. "Be cool, be patient, be resigned," he wrote. "And may Heaven protect and spare you till we meet again." Henry Zarah made his appearance in Mansfield on October 14, 1836. The dark-haired boy was the spitting image of his father.[31]

Samuel's letters reveal his affection for Belinda and his frustration with the requirements of his job: "I am determined to try and get a situation next season nearer home. Or where I can have you nearer to me. My rambling life is worse than a situation in the Army. I am away all the time." Samuel enjoyed working outdoors—his letters often included descriptions of the flora and fauna he encountered—but he desired a position that required less travel. "There is not one in the Engineer Corps of Ohio who has had so much rambling to do as I," he complained. Nevertheless, Samuel was determined to carry on. He explained his thinking to Belinda in words that might have come from Hosmer or Henry: "My character and my fortune both depend on my exertions. Every moment of my time is therefore valuable."[32]

During his years as a surveyor Samuel became interested in "navigation engineering," the creation of artificial waterways. Following the success of the Erie Canal and the explosive growth of steamboat traffic on the western rivers, the United States experienced a "navigation boom" in the 1830s and 1840s. Even the usually somber Hosmer sounded excited when he told Samuel of the changes wrought by the Ohio & Erie Canal, completed in 1832 between the Ohio River and Lake Erie. "Our canal combined with some other causes has given a considerable impetus to business in Ohio," he wrote. "There is obviously more money in circulation with us than formerly. Our towns and country are improving and increasing in population. A vast quantity of produce such as wheat flour pork etc. is pressing in from all quarters and filling the warehouses along the canal to overflowing destined for the eastern market. You would be surprised to see the large canal boats loading and unloading constantly at the warehouses and basins at Newark."[33]

A well-planned artificial waterway could generate spectacular economic growth, but success was not guaranteed. State and local governments and private corporations often announced plans and issued bonds without fully understanding the limitations of early industrial technology. Nonetheless, every community dreamt of boundless prosperity if only the local stream could be dammed, deepened, widened, straightened, cleared, and made passable for commercial traffic.

Samuel plunged into this brave new world in April 1837, when the Ohio Board of Public Works named him resident engineer of the Muskingum River Improvement in southeastern Ohio, one of four public works projects authorized by the state following the success of the Ohio & Erie Canal. The additional canals were intended to generate prosperity in every corner of the state. Samuel received this plum assignment despite having no experience with waterways, but after four years as chief surveyor he had established himself as an engineer of considerable promise. He was also a "decided Whig" at a time when the state government, including the Board of Public Works, was largely dominated by Whigs. The position came with an annual salary of $1,000 plus a monthly allowance of $36, sums that allowed Samuel and Belinda to establish themselves comfortably in the middle class.[34]

Samuel spent the latter part of 1837 in Columbus, preparing skeleton maps of the proposed waterway. Responding to a letter from Belinda, who remained in Mansfield with little Henry, he complimented her on the "plain freedom in the style of composition and style of writing" that made her letter "ten times more interesting and valuable than it would have been if you had laboured three times as long at it." The fate of Belinda's correspondence with her husband is a mystery. Samuel carefully preserved her letters for four decades, but following his death someone—most likely Belinda herself—removed nearly all of them from the family archives. The handful of surviving letters reveals that Belinda avoided the convoluted literary conventions of the day and expressed herself in a clear, straightforward manner. Her neat, legible script is far easier to decipher than her husband's atrocious scrawl.[35]

Early in 1838 the Curtis family moved to McConnelsville, a small town on the Muskingum River midway between Zanesville and Marietta. Belinda was pregnant again and the move allowed Samuel to spend more time at home. The family was still settling in when their third child, Samuel Stephen, arrived on March 7. McConnelsville was some distance from family and friends in Mansfield and Mount Vernon, but Samuel and Belinda were together at last. "I am constantly forming acquaintances and would be glad to have you associated with me in all things," Samuel had written during one of their frequent separations. "I want my friends to be yours, and yours to be mine." Now that was possible.[36]

The oddly named Muskingum River Improvement was an ambitious attempt to "canalize" the Muskingum by converting it into a series of stair-step, slack water lakes. Instead of digging a canal alongside the river, as was common practice, the river itself was turned into a canal. Samuel described the hybrid waterway as a "most difficult and extraordinary *experiment* in civil engineering." On another occasion he called it "quite a new thing in the science of Engineering, and more perplexing for its having been put under contract in hot haste without any determination of plans or locations." The audacious project demanded an understanding of hydraulics and a level of engineering competence that few, if any, possessed in 1837.[37]

In addition to inadequate planning, the Muskingum River Improvement was plagued by political meddling and faulty construction. Work was well underway when the Board of Public

Works ordered the locks enlarged from 34 x 150 feet to 36 x 180 feet. This alteration eventually allowed larger boats and barges to navigate the Muskingum, but it caused delays and generated additional expense. The Muskingum River Improvement ultimately cost $1,662,000, four times the original estimate. It opened for business on a limited basis in 1841 but reconstruction of some locks and dams and reinforcement of caving banks eventually added another $450,000 to the bill.[38]

When finally completed in 1849 the navigation channel (the canalized portion of the river) extended ninety-one miles from Dresden in the north to Marietta in the south, where the Muskingum flows into the Ohio. There were ten dams and eleven locks (the dam at Zanesville had a double lock) along a fall of 154 feet. A short "sidecut" at Dresden connected the Muskingum to the bustling Ohio & Erie Canal. The project provided farmers and merchants in southeastern Ohio with access to the Great Lakes and the Atlantic Coast by way of the Erie Canal, and to the Gulf of Mexico by way of the Ohio and Mississippi Rivers. It also offered traffic on the Ohio & Erie Canal an alternate route to the Ohio River. Navigation was open to steamboats, flatboats, and barges, as well as canal boats.[39]

The age of railroads had arrived by the time the Muskingum River Improvement opened for business, but the project was a success despite the delays, cost overruns, and unexpected competition. Commerce flowed along the Muskingum for seven decades. Farmers, tradesmen, merchants, bankers, and even attorneys prospered as the economy steadily expanded. The waterway ceased commercial operation in the early twentieth century. Today the dams, locks, bridges, and canalized river are preserved by the state of Ohio as the Muskingum River Parkway, a popular historic and recreational area. The American Society of Civil Engineers designated the Muskingum River Improvement a National Historic Civil Engineering Landmark in 2000. It is now part of a select company that includes the Erie Canal, Brooklyn Bridge, Empire State Building, and Hoover Dam.[40]

Alas, Samuel did not see the Muskingum River Improvement

through to completion. He was forced out in May 1839 after two years on the job. "I was informed," he later wrote, "that a revolution in the Board of Public Works rendered it necessary to change the Resident Engineer, and in *nautical* parlance I had to 'walk the plank.'" In short, he was let go for political reasons. He was a Whig and the new majority of the board was Democrat. It would not be the last time he was hired and fired because of his political coloration. All of his assistants were dismissed as well, including a youthful surveyor named John Sherman, a future U.S. senator and brother of William T. Sherman.[41]

It is difficult to determine how much blame Samuel deserves for the problems that dogged the project, or how much credit he is due for his pioneering achievement in canalizing the river. The resident engineers who succeeded him made no significant changes to his original plans. When the waterway finally filled with traffic in 1849, it solidified Samuel's reputation as an innovative and successful navigation engineer. Ironically, the controversial project became his signature accomplishment.

For the next three years Samuel was an engineer for hire. He found employment building, or at least planning, toll roads of varying degrees of difficulty and practicality. All of these projects ground to a halt in the aftermath of the Panic of 1837, an early stock market crash that triggered a sharp economic downturn. Banks and businesses failed and bonds went unsold. "Times changed and the companies languished," Samuel wrote, "until in 1842 I considered Engineering no longer reliable and I betook myself to the practice of the Law." He also betook himself into the political arena, running unsuccessfully for a seat in the Ohio legislature. The family remained in McConnelsville during this uncertain period; another child, Sarah Belinda, soon known as Sadie, entered the world on January 8, 1842.[42]

Samuel had been quietly studying law under Hosmer's guidance for some time—exactly when he began is not known—and shortly after Sadie's birth he finally joined his brothers in the legal profession. Ohio's newest attorney moved his growing family to Wooster, forty-five miles east of Mansfield and the same distance northeast of Mount Vernon, and hung out his shingle. He rented a frame house "finished in the best manner" and set about becoming a respectable citizen. He joined the Masonic Order and the Episcopal Church and was elected to the town council. On Christmas Eve, 1844, an especially welcome present arrived in the person of Goodsell Buckingham Hosmer. The grandly named baby was called Bucky.[43]

Despite the demands of a booming family and a developing legal practice, Samuel worked as a consulting engineer on several projects, one of which involved redesigning the "architectural works" of the Mansfield and New Haven Railroad. This was Samuel's first experience with the most advanced technology of the day and he was never the same afterwards. He became an enthusiastic proponent of railroads and even envisioned tracks stretching across the continent to the Pacific Ocean. Samuel later described his time laboring on the National Road, Muskingum River, and other early projects as "years of toil and anxiety," but despite setbacks and disappointments he continued to think of himself as an engineer. He regarded his legal work as "something to fall back upon after the failure of positions that were somewhat precarious."[44]

Samuel also found time to dabble in paramilitary affairs. Following the War of 1812, state militias across the country atrophied to the point where they were little more than lists of names on paper, and sometimes not even that. Ohio was no exception. An early resident recalled that "militia service was considered a nuisance, and its musters and parades were subjects of ridicule." Here and there, however, citizens with an interest in military affairs—or at least an interest in parading around in colorful uniforms—formed volunteer militia companies of every description. These private organizations participated in civic events and patriotic celebrations.[45]

Barely a year after returning from Fort Gibson, Samuel raised a "splendid volunteer company" called the "Mansfield Blues." He later served as lieutenant colonel of a volunteer battalion and colonel of a volunteer regiment. He was the unanimous choice to oversee Ohio's "great encampment" at Zanesville in 1840, where a dozen volunteer companies took part in a week of amateur soldiering. "Colonel Curtis was the commander," recalled a veteran of that experience, "and most splendidly did he perform his duties." Two years later he participated in a military parade celebrating George Washington's birthday at the Whig Party convention in Columbus.[46]

Samuel's West Point background, his knowledge of military drill and protocol, and his tales of duty in the Indian Territory (doubtless embellished as occasion required) made him a popular and respected militia officer. He enjoyed playing at being a soldier but seems not to have expressed any interest in resuming a military career. That changed when the United States went to war with Mexico.

2

MEXICO

THE UNITED STATES WAS WOEFULLY UNPREPARED FOR AN armed conflict with Mexico or any other nation. When Congress declared war on May 13, 1846, the army was 40 percent under-strength and consisted of only 5,300 officers and men scattered in small detachments across the country. President James K. Polk immediately called for up to fifty thousand twelve-month volunteers to augment the tiny regular force. Ohioans responded with enthusiasm. Governor Mordecai Bartley offered Curtis the position of adjutant general, the highest military office in the state, "for the special purpose of mustering Ohio Volunteers for the Mexican War." Curtis accepted and departed for Columbus.[1]

Curtis was surprised when Belinda urged him to resign his new office and return home: "Why then my dear wife discourage me in this exercise I am making to discharge the most import-ant and most *public* post that I was ever called on to fill." Cur-tis was forty-one years old and had always lived in the shadow of his older brothers. The position of adjutant general put him at the center of things in Ohio, a degree of prominence neither Hosmer nor Henry had achieved. He reveled in his new status and did not want to give it up, though he assured Belinda that "I want to see you and our dear children above all things on earth."[2]

Curtis realized that an extended absence on his part meant more work and responsibility for Belinda. "No doubt this sud-den change in my affairs will place matters in a strange predica-ment about my house and office," he wrote carefully. "I rely very much on your good sense and judgement to regulate the matters about home." In addition to cooking, cleaning, and caring for the children, Belinda would have to manage household finances, deal with merchants and tradesmen, and handle emergencies on her own. The one thing she could not do was look after her husband's legal practice, so Curtis asked Lucas Flattery, a fellow attorney, to take care of his "Court business" for a few weeks. He clearly expected to be back in Wooster before the end of summer.[3]

The first order of business for the new adjutant general was the selection of a suitable assembly point for the "Army of Ohio." Curtis chose a level expanse of ground near Cincinnati and named it Camp Washington. Within a week the site was packed with enthusiastic amateur warriors. "Such a gathering of awkward boys, you never saw," Curtis wrote to Belinda. "You have seen little Henry perform under my command. Well he is a veteran soldier compared to some of these." To complicate matters, every gaggle of volunteers included a full slate of officers, both elected and self-appointed. "I could almost form a regiment of majors, colonels, and generals," Curtis noted wryly. The next task was turning the rabble into soldiers. Curtis gradually imposed order on the formless horde. It was no small accomplishment.[4]

The War Department wanted Ohio to provide three thousand volunteers, organized into three twelve-month regiments, but nearly four thousand men showed up. Consequently, more than eight hundred latecomers "with much clamor and dissatisfaction were turned homeward." Many were German immigrants who believed themselves to be victims of nativist prejudice. A political flap erupted; Curtis was criticized in several newspapers for his supposed bigotry. "I expect before I get through with the matter to be the most unpopular man in the state," he lamented. The office of adjutant general was more of a hot seat than Curtis had expected, so when Governor Bartley suggested that he resign and assume command of the Third Ohio Volunteer Regiment, Curtis jumped at the chance to exchange a suit for a uniform. Bartley insisted that Curtis remain in charge of Camp Washington, so for the next few weeks the newly minted colonel wore two hats.[5]

Command of a regiment in the field meant that Curtis would

be away from home for an indeterminate period, possibly a year or more. Worse, it also meant he would be exposed to the rigors and dangers of a military campaign in a foreign land. Belinda continued to express her unhappiness. Curtis declared, "I cannot bear the idea of your displeasure it would make me always miserable," but he did not offer to give up his new command. Belinda soon realized that her husband was determined to have his way, so she packed up the children and joined him at Camp Washington in mid-June. She obviously believed the family should be together as much as possible before Curtis marched off to war.[6]

Curtis wanted the three Ohio regiments to be the best volunteer units in the service, so he instituted a rigorous program of drill and instruction. The men grumbled every step of the way but made remarkable progress. One day Brigadier General John E. Wool, the third-ranking officer in the regular army, arrived on an inspection tour. Wool reviewed the troops and mustered them into federal service. He declared himself "well satisfied" with everything he saw at Camp Washington and congratulated Curtis on a job well done. He added a few special words of praise for the Third Ohio. Curtis could not have been more pleased.[7]

The Third Ohio broke camp on July 3, 1846, and marched to the Cincinnati waterfront, where the men crowded aboard two steamboats, the *Tuskaloosa* and *New Era*. "The parting scene at the landing in Cincinnati when I commanded 'three cheers for Ohio' was of all things most trying to me," Curtis confessed to brother Henry. "I had suppressed my feelings on seperating from my dear Wife in order to support her in the painful adieu, but then I raised my kerchief at the landing and saw you and . . . my two dear boys standing on the bank waving your adieu." It was a difficult moment. Curtis tried to catch a final glimpse of Belinda and the other children, but they were lost in the crowd. Thirteen months would pass before he saw them again.[8]

Why did Curtis inflict such misery on himself and Belinda? John Teesdale was a family friend and editor of the *Ohio State Journal*. He stated in his newspaper that Curtis's "family and friends dreaded the influences of a Southern campaign on his health" and urged him not to accept command of the Third Ohio, but to no avail. His "nearest kindred" (surely Hosmer and Henry) then lobbied Governor Bartley to keep him in Ohio, but again without success. According to Teesdale, Curtis stated that he had been "educated at West Point and that he owed a debt to the country for that education, which he would pay at all hazards." Curtis later confirmed the accuracy of Teesdale's account but his journals and letters also revealed that he yearned for adventure and reputation. A lawyer's life in a small Ohio town lacked something that he craved.[9]

The primary arena of conflict between the United States and Mexico in the first year of the war was the disputed border along the lower Rio Grande. The opening battles of Palo Alto and Resaca de la Palma took place in the extreme south of Texas, but the victorious American army led by Major General Zachary Taylor soon forced its way across the Rio Grande and occupied Matamoros. Taylor then paused to await direction and reinforcements from the United States. With so few regular troops available, the newly raised volunteer regiments were rushed to Mexico as fast as they could be armed and equipped. Regiments from the Midwest, including those from Ohio, proceeded down the Mississippi River to New Orleans by steamboat, then sailed across the Gulf of Mexico to the Rio Grande.[10]

The *Tuskaloosa* and *New Era* made rapid progress down the Ohio. Curtis recorded in his new journal (his "blank book") that July 5 was "dreadful hot and we have all been longing to get into the river for a bath." When the boats tied up along the bank to cut down trees for fuel, he seized the moment. "I threw off my coat and hat and jumped into the river. I was followed by some three hundred who all enjoyed a fine bath some half clad and some quite naked." After an hour of splashing in the shallows, the troops resumed their passage. That night the little convoy churned past Cairo and entered the Mississippi River.[11]

Aided by the powerful current, the boats fairly raced down the Father of Waters. They put in at Memphis for a few hours, but the volunteers were not permitted to sample the dubious delights of the city. "Great anxiety prevailed among the men to get on shore and they appeared riotous and rather disorderly after we came away from the landing," noted Curtis. The next day the boats again nosed into the bank to gather wood. Officers and men poured ashore to visit a small Mississippi farm. For nearly everyone in the Third Ohio this was their first experience with the peculiar way of life in the South. "Our men were very much amused and disgusted with the Negro quarters," Curtis observed. "The cotton was in bloom and for the first time a great many of our men saw it growing." That evening a thunderstorm swept over the boats and drenched everyone. The cooling rain was a welcome relief from the heat and humidity.[12]

The Ohioans passed Natchez the following day and glimpsed the stately buildings atop the bluffs. A short time later the boats again stopped for fuel and the troops again stampeded ashore into Mississippi. Curtis walked to a nearby farm, much larger than the first. He observed that the "buildings were very neat and the Negro quarters were fit for any one to live in." He watched a gang of "ignorant and stupid" slaves, mostly women and children, picking cotton under the direction of a "very black fine looking Negro." The overseer brandished a whip, a "most villainous weapon." There is nothing in Curtis's Mexican War journals and letters to suggest that only a few years later he would initiate a radical program of military emancipation, liberating thousands of men, women, and children from bondage.[13]

On July 10 the Third Ohio reached New Orleans, assembly point for the men, animals, weapons, stores, and ships gathering for operations in Mexico. Like every summer visitor to the Crescent City, Curtis was nearly prostrated by the sultry, subtropical climate. "Oh it is hot I tell you!" he gasped to Belinda. The boats continued five miles downriver to the Chalmette battleground, where Andrew Jackson's makeshift army had repulsed a British invasion in January 1815. "I hurried off and had my tents pitched on the very ground where the Battle of New Orleans had been fought," he wrote. A breeze from the Gulf of Mexico helped make life bearable, but it also carried in clouds of mosquitoes from coastal marshes. The Ohioans were glad to be back on solid ground, but they had no desire to tarry long in Louisiana's oppressive environment.[14]

Curtis spent the next day in New Orleans making arrangements to transport his regiment to Mexico. He dined at a "fine eating house such as you see no where else in these United States" and stayed the night in the St. Charles Hotel, which he described to Belinda as the "best public hotel in the world and one of the most magnificent buildings you ever saw." The following morning he visited the fabled French Quarter, but the exotic colonial-era buildings with their ornate balconies and shaded courtyards failed to impress him. "I can see nothing American about the city," he huffed to brother Henry.[15]

• • •

The Third Ohio boarded the sailing ships *Gen Vera*, *Charlotte*, and *Orleans* on July 12 and slipped down the Mississippi River to the Gulf of Mexico. Curtis succumbed to seasickness as soon as the vessels entered open water. "I was sick as death, and would have given a months pay for a moments rest on dry land," he moaned. The low profile of the southern Texas coast came into view on July 18. There was no protected anchorage at the mouth of the Rio Grande, and the river was too shallow to admit oceangoing ships, so the Ohioans remained aboard their wallowing transports for two more days until lighters finally came out and ferried them ashore. "The men on the vessel look languid and rather sallow in their complexion," Curtis observed. "I can see that the climate and exposure have made their impression on all of us."[16]

The Third Ohio landed on Brazos Island, southernmost of the sandy, low-lying barrier islands that parallel the Texas coast. Curtis informed brother Henry that a "more poor desolate barren spot could not, I think, be found on the Coast of North America." A recent storm had inundated hundreds of tents pitched along the beach, so he tramped inland and found a relatively water-proof campsite for his regiment amid the grass-covered dunes.[17]

Brazos Island was the base of operations for American military activities in northeastern Mexico. The chaotic conditions there illustrated the institutional weaknesses of the antebellum army. The war with Mexico was primarily an overseas, not overland, conflict. The army had not anticipated such a possibility, and there were no procedures in place—and no specialized units and equipment in existence—to deal with the complexities of what was essentially a sustained amphibious operation.

Curtis decried the confusion he witnessed as the "most intricate labyrinth that ignorance and negligence could create." If he learned anything from his Mexican War experience, it was that raising and drilling troops and leading them into battle were only part of a successful military operation. Transporting, supplying, and supporting those troops—the emerging science of logistics—was every bit as important. It was a lesson that would serve him well in the Civil War.[18]

The Third Ohio was marooned on Brazos Island for nearly two weeks. Curtis made the most of the situation. "I have just been down taking the finest sea bath on a delightful sand beach," he told Belinda. He visited nearby encampments and ran into several West Point schoolmates. "I am surprised to find that seventeen years made so little impression on them," he wrote, and wondered how he appeared to them. The sunburned and sandblasted soldiers of the Third Ohio finally received orders to move forward at the end of July. They marched to the southern tip of the island and waited for shallow-draft steamboats to carry them up the Rio Grande. Curtis and another officer could not wait. They commandeered a small boat and rowed across the river to the Mexican side. "A jump brought me on the hard clean sandy landing," Curtis jotted in his journal. "Walk up the slope and find ourselves on the unquestionable soil of Mexico. Look around here and you see Mexican houses, Mexican men and Mexican women." It was his first experience in a foreign land.[19]

By this time General Taylor had advanced to Camargo, about 120 miles inland from the Gulf of Mexico. Curtis expected to join Taylor, but to his great disappointment the Third Ohio was ordered to occupy Matamoros, a town of twelve thousand people about thirty miles inland. Curtis was intensely disappointed at being assigned to occupation duty. His mission, he informed his journal, was "to defend the place and sustain the laws of the country." His lack of enthusiasm was obvious.[20]

Curtis hitched a ride up the Rio Grande on a passing steamboat and visited Matamoros ahead of his regiment. He found it hard to believe that the sprawl of nondescript buildings was the capital of the state of Tamaulipas: "These homes are generally brick one story high with slate or brick roof all resembling a system of old forts. Every house seems to possess bars and bolts and the windows of the lower storeys are in some instances 14 feet high with iron bars on the inside. The streets are rather hollow in the center and very narrow." He was even less impressed by the people he encountered: "About the principle corners loiter groups of men of all colours and all countries are collected cursing swearing fighting gambling and presenting a most barbarous sight. Volunteers especially are conspicuous in these groups. I hope in conscience the Ohio volunteers will avoid these scenes. Murder rapine and vice of all manner of form prevails and predominates here." The town appeared to be on the verge of anarchy.[21]

The "volunteers" Curtis saw loitering on corners were the remnants of an earlier, ill-advised effort to reinforce Taylor. In response to his call for additional troops in April, the governors of several southern states had raised a mass of untrained and undisciplined six-month volunteers and rushed them to the Rio Grande. Taylor was appalled by this noisome rabble and kept them in the rear, where they terrorized the inhabitants of Matamoros and other towns. This was a serious problem: the American invasion of Mexico could not succeed without the tacit support of the local population, which was not particularly loyal to the distant central government in Mexico City. To encourage that support, Taylor purchased supplies from Mexican farmers and merchants (often at inflated prices) and treated Mexican officials with respect. The chaotic state of affairs in Matamoros threatened to upset everything. Taylor therefore assigned one of the newly arrived regiments the unenviable task of liberating the town from an occupying army of thugs. That regiment was the Third Ohio.[22]

Reestablishing the rule of law in Matamoros was a challenge. "Among other duties expected of my Regiment is that of reducing this bedlam to a state of order and decency," scribbled Curtis in his journal. "I rank these services as honourable but extremely disagreeable. If I can do anything towards reducing this scene of confusion I shall regard it as worthy of all toil." After only a few hours walking the streets, he was convinced that Matamoros was the "receptacle of all the dregs of the United States. As it now stands, it is a disgrace to our country; for our own citizens are much worse than the Mexicans who are mixed up with them." He passed his first night on Mexican soil in the aptly named American Hotel. Two murders were committed while he tossed and turned on his narrow bed.[23]

The Third Ohio reached Matamoros in mid-August and set up camp. Curtis put on his best uniform and met with the alcade and other local authorities. He pledged to respect Mexican laws and to work within the existing administrative and judicial systems whenever possible. The officials promised their cooperation. Military patrols began rounding up murderers, thieves, gamblers, drunks, rowdies, and suspicious characters. Mexicans were turned over to the appropriate authorities. Americans were hustled down the river to Brazos Island and eventually returned to New Orleans. Conditions improved as the number of troublemakers declined. "Our daily duty grows rather monotonous," Curtis informed his journal. "I sit here all day in my tent and sign passes for men, receive reports, and give orders." He had traded an office job in Columbus for one in Matamoros. Meanwhile, regiment after regiment passed upriver and reinforced Taylor, who was approaching Monterrey, the principal city in northeastern Mexico.[24]

Curtis soon contracted malaria, just as his family had feared. The first symptoms—fever, chills, and headaches—appeared in early September and laid him low for several days. At the urging of the regimental surgeon, he moved out of his tent and into a "pleasant one story framed house with trees all around it and a porch in the rear." He assured brother Henry that his bedroom was "well ventilated and every way agreeable" and that he was receiving the best possible attention. He even joked that "I did not have a very hard attack and I was able with the power of seven medics to soon get the better of it." Curtis weighed 190 pounds when he left Ohio in July, but stress, seasickness, heat, diarrhea, and malaria reduced his once robust frame to only 150 pounds. Nevertheless, he soon was back at work in his tent signing passes and reading reports.[25]

Not everyone in the Third Ohio was as fortunate. Malaria, measles, dysentery, diarrhea, and other diseases filled the regimental hospital and the regimental graveyard with victims. "Death makes fearful inroads in the ranks of my regiment," wrote Curtis. "We have been here but a few days; but we have already erected several little mounds over the bodies of our companions." Mexico's coastal lowlands were "sickly"; antebellum medical care could not stem the microbial onslaught. American soldiers in Mexico were seven times more likely to die from "malignant diseases" than wounds or accidents. One September day Samuel noted that only a third of the regiment turned out for dress parade: "Camp looks like a hospital so many pale and sickly faces." In the privacy of his journal he revealed his fears: "I am really terrified at this aspect of my regiment. There can hardly be found a well man in camp." Ten months of noncombat duty in Mexico eventually cost the Third Ohio the lives of sixty-four men.[26]

On a more positive note, Curtis marveled at the variety of exotic plants in Matamoros, especially papayas, pomegranates, peppers, and other colorful fruits. He informed his journal that the "red pepper *kayenne* is also common running up on bushes as high as I can reach and full of peppers as hot as burning coals of fire. It is used by the Mexicans when green and red in cooking. Almost every dish is seasoned with it. They have a kind of *hash* made by cutting up meat and pepper together. It is very nice." He had discovered chili. Less desirable aspects of life in Matamoros made him an authority on entomology. "The musqueetos and fleas are tormenting me to death," he told brother Henry. "You never saw such a country for fleas. They are various sizes, too, from the smallest mites to the size of lobsters!!"[27]

While the Third Ohio imposed order on Matamoros, dramatic events unfolded two hundred miles to the west. Taylor captured Monterrey, the capital of the state of Nuevo León, after a costly battle on September 20–23, 1846. The Americans raised the Stars and Stripes over the city while the Mexicans withdrew to San Luis Potosí, well to the south. Taylor then crossed the Sierra Madre Oriental and occupied Saltillo, the capital of Coahuila. It was his final forward movement. Taylor and his Mexican counterpart agreed to an eight-week armistice that brought major military operations in northeastern Mexico to a standstill.[28]

Curtis and his officers made occasional forays into the countryside during the armistice. "We were all mounted on good Mexican mustang horses and armed with pistols," he assured Belinda. On one occasion the Ohioans chanced upon an isolated ranchero and dined on tortillas, beans, onions, and chili without benefit of utensils. "The Mexicans seemed much amused, and gathered around, as the crowd does at a caravan, to see the animals fed," he informed Belinda. "You ought to have seen us using our tortilla for a spoon! Oh! There was a dinner that would make a soldiers mouth water." On another occasion they splashed across the Rio Grande and explored the Palo Alto and Resaca de la Palma battlegrounds in Texas. "The sights must have been beautiful and terrible," mused Curtis at the former place. "The Mexican line can just be traced by the skeletons that lie bleaching on the field. We followed it for a long time." It was a sobering experience.[29]

Curtis completed his first journal in October and sent it home in a box containing seeds, seashells, and a "horned frog." The reptile was a big hit with the children. He and Belinda corresponded regularly, usually on a weekly basis. He expressed his delight with the "great number of excellent letters you write to me. Even a second and third reading is always a rich treat." Belinda never stopped encouraging her husband to resign his commission and return home. Curtis continued to insist that he would do no such thing: "You could not respect me for an act so unbecoming [to] my life and character." One might imagine Belinda's response to that bit of pomposity.[30]

A colonel of volunteers earned more than the average small-town attorney. Curtis sent home up to $100 each month. The payments allowed Belinda and the children to live comfortably. Curtis retained a portion of his salary to cover expenses in Mexico, but he watched his expenditures so closely that he returned to Wooster with $1,600 in his pocket. In addition to money, Curtis dispatched a stream of advice, encouragement, and, occasionally, odd requests. One day, out of the blue, he informed Belinda that "I want a strong high fence made on the south and all sides of our lot. So high and substantive that things cannot break through. The plank should run perpendicular so they cannot be climbed over. The barn also should be new planked on the outside and the old plank perhaps would do for fencing." He reminded Belinda to save the bill so their neighbors could be assessed a share of the cost, but he never explained what "things" the fence was intended to deter.[31]

Winter arrived in late October with a "roaring rushing mighty wind" that took everyone in the Third Ohio by surprise. "Last night was cold," Curtis noted in his new journal, "so cold I pulled my cloak and blanket both around me. My tent is large and does not come down to the ground close. The front curtains do not come together well, so that I get too much air for cold weather." Other members of the regiment had similar complaints, so the Ohioans struck their defective tents and moved into an abandoned Mexican army barracks in central Matamoros. Curtis took up residence in a stone building on the Plaza Grande. His "snug tenement" on the second floor featured tall windows and an iron balcony.[32]

Christmas brought another dramatic shift in the weather. "A bright sunshine, and warm summer day," Curtis observed. He spent the morning on his balcony watching a spectacle in the plaza below. "Seniors and Senioras dressed in their gayest attire" were streaming into the Catedral de Nuestra Señora del Refugio on the opposite side of the plaza. Curtis decided to join them: "I repaired to the church and took a seat quite solitary though hundreds of every complexion were sitting, kneeling, and standing around me." He tried to focus on the meaning of Christmas but admitted that "my mind was constantly drawn off by the novelty of the service and the changes of the picture that surrounded me." Curtis was fascinated by the murals, statuary, and candles that covered the walls and filled every nook and cranny. The blend of Spanish baroque and indigenous Native traditions was typical of a Catholic church in Mexico, but it must have seemed extraordinary—idolatrous, really—to someone raised in a Calvinist household. "The performance was in every way shocking to my nerves," he wrote. "I was immediately repelled, and left the scene mortified and disgusted."[33]

The next evening, accompanied only by an interpreter, Curtis attended a "regular Mexican *'fandango'*" in a distant quarter of Matamoros. Like his expeditions into the countryside, this nocturnal adventure included an element of risk: "It was rather a remote corner of the city, and I took care to examine the caps on my pistol before entering on the excursion." Curtis was admitted to a small, well-lit house crowded with thirty to forty colorfully dressed partygoers. "The deportment of all exhibited the utmost ease and politeness," he noted with approval (and relief). "I was treated constantly with distinguished attention." He described the ladies as "generally dark and none of them pretty." He attempted a few waltzes but could not master the local steps. After an hour he bid his hosts good night and returned to his residence without shooting anyone.[34]

The influx of Americans and American money transformed Matamoros while the Third Ohio was there. As soon as it became safe to walk the streets again, French restaurants, French cafés, French bakeries, and other Gallic establishments popped up on every block. Curtis observed with a hint of disapproval that the "town is becoming a fragment of New Orleans," but that did not stop him from patronizing the new businesses. Among his favorites was a coffee house near the Plaza Grande run by a French woman. "It seems to me strange that a good looking female should have wandered from Paris to this place and have set up an establishment solitary and alone," he mused in the privacy of his journal. "Women are strange beings capable of any thing and no doubt this woman has borne fatigues and privation with more fortitude than some of our soldiers."[35]

Major General Winfield Scott, general in chief of the army, arrived in late December. Scott stopped in Matamoros while on his way up the Rio Grande to confer with Taylor. Curtis was delighted to meet such an illustrious figure. "The General is very frank and free, showing all my officers the utmost kindness and respect," he noted with approval. "His presence gives new life to our little army." Curtis seized the opportunity to lobby for a combat role for the Third Ohio. Scott was sympathetic but noncommittal.[36]

Scott returned to Matamoros a week later and informed Curtis that the invasion of northeastern Mexico had run its course. With President Polk's approval, Scott had developed a daring plan he believed would end the war. He intended to sail down the coast and seize the port of Veracruz, then march inland across the Sierra Madre Oriental and fall upon Mexico City, just as Hernán Cortés had done in 1519. Taylor would assume a defensive posture around Monterrey and Saltillo and hold the ground he had gained. Scott withdrew four thousand regulars and over three thousand volunteers from Taylor's command and assembled them on Brazos Island. One of the regulars making his way back to the coast was Brigadier General William J. Worth, the officer who had promoted Curtis to first corporal two decades earlier. Curtis observed that Worth "has changed very considerably since I last saw him at West Point."[37]

Curtis received orders to prepare the Third Ohio "for action and dangerous service and be ready to march at any time within ten days or two weeks." He was jubilant. After months of dreary occupation duty, he was going to participate in the decisive American operation of the war. "I am certain to go with the main army," he informed Henry. "If my life is spared I may see the City of Mexico yet before my term of service expires."[38]

Crushing news arrived shortly after Curtis penned those words. In response to Taylor's protests over losing so many troops, Scott decided to leave the Third Ohio in northeastern Mexico. Curtis was devastated: "My disappointment and indignation I cannot express." He started for Brazos Island on horseback to appeal to Scott in person, but after only a few miles he felt a "kind of stitch in my back near my right shoulder which was so painful that I could hardly sit on my horse." He returned to Matamoros and took to his bed. The next day he wrote an intemperate letter practically demanding that Scott change his mind, but the commanding general was unmoved. The Third Ohio would remain on the Rio Grande, only not in Matamoros.[39]

• • •

Scott reduced Taylor's army to roughly six thousand men, mostly untried volunteers, just as the Mexicans launched their largest counteroffensive of the war. The force at San Luis de Potosí, now led by General Antonio López de Santa Anna (of Texas infamy), was reinforced to well over fifteen thousand men. It advanced directly on Taylor's army while a secondary force of 6,700 cavalry and irregulars under General José de Urrea swung around to the east toward Taylor's line of communications, which was secured by fewer than 1,300 Americans scattered in small detachments along the Rio Grande. In response to Urrea's threat, Taylor ordered Curtis to move upriver to Camargo, halfway between Matamoros and Monterrey. The Third Ohio reached Camargo on February 13 after an arduous ninety-mile trek. Curtis reported that "we found water scarce and dust plenty all the way."[40]

Camargo was a letdown after the bright lights of Matamoros. "I could hardly conceive of a more miserable or wretched place than this," wrote Curtis. The town of about two thousand people was laid out "in a confused and disordered condition" along the Rio San Juan, three miles above its confluence with the Rio Grande. Camargo had been inundated the previous spring and the adobe buildings had "crumbled down and left the poor inhabitants in a wretched condition." Winter winds made things worse.

"The dust is terrible," Curtis complained. Despite its dilapidated condition, Camargo was the principal American depot in northeastern Mexico, the base of supplies for Taylor's army.[41]

The Third Ohio set up camp near the Rio San Juan. Curtis moved into a two-story building on Camargo's central plaza: "I have one large room on the first floor, and after having a glass window placed in the front wall (the second luxury of the kind known in the city) I feel quite comfortably located." He was only a few steps from the church, Parroquia de Nuestra Señora de Santa Ana, but he seems not to have attended services there.[42]

Curtis informed Belinda that his freshly whitewashed room was "very much improved by sweeping, brushing and arranging." Furnishings consisted of a cot, table, chair, trunk, candlestick, inkstand, and looking glass. The room was cooled by a "fresh and pleasant current of air, a very comfortable matter on a sultry day. For mind you it is sultry." He remarked that he no longer expected to receive a combat assignment and that upon the expiration of his enlistment, "I shall have cancelled any obligation I may be under to my country for a military education." Belinda must have been pleased to hear it.[43]

Curtis replicated the occupation policy he had employed so successfully in Matamoros: "The Alcadas have their old laws and customs to go by; and I should not meddle much when the matter lies between the Mexicans." He was pleased with the outcome and boasted to Belinda that "rogues stand no chance here under my administration, and honest men are returning to pursue their avocations." He was even more pleased to learn that the alcade in Matamoros had urged his counterpart in Camargo to cooperate with the "Senor Coronel."[44]

Maintaining order in Camargo was relatively easy. Providing security outside the town was another matter. Mexican irregulars emboldened by the prospect of Urrea's support attacked American patrols and trains with renewed vigor. They even sniped at passing steamboats on the Rio Grande. Curtis had complained for months about the dull routine of occupation duty in backwater towns. Scott's departure and Santa Anna's approach changed everything. Curtis was now the ranking American officer between Brazos Island and Monterrey and the person most responsible for keeping Taylor's army in the field.[45]

Taylor halted all traffic on the road between Camargo and Monterrey as Santa Anna and Urrea drew closer. He ordered Curtis to wait for the First Virginia, a newly arrived regiment slowly making its way inland from the coast, then advance to Monterrey with every available man, mule, and wagon. "Every thing indicates a fearful contest above," Curtis wrote. He increased patrols, strengthened fortifications, and cleared fields of fire around the town. Four companies of the First Virginia tramped into Camargo on March 1, much to his relief, but the rest of the regiment was nowhere in sight. Curtis was in a quandary: "Shall I disobey my orders and march before a whole regiment arrives?" He decided to sit tight and hold the depot.[46]

Curtis felt the loneliness of command as never before: "Terrible silence! Not a word from the west." He was so unsettled he wrote directly to President Polk on March 3 and asked for a force of fifty thousand six-month volunteers, "to extricate General Taylor and give a new impetus to our Arms." Curtis knew, of course, that weeks would pass before his plea for reinforcements reached Washington, so he called on Scott (now en route to Veracruz by sea) and the governors of Texas and Louisiana (the nearest states) for more immediate assistance. Curtis realized he was violating military protocol by going outside the chain of command and writing directly to the president, the general in chief, and state officials, but he felt certain he was doing the right thing. "No doubt many will think me crazy," he told Belinda, but someone had "to speak for the army." He added a revealing personal comment in his new journal: "All the responsibility assumed by me is enough to kill any man."[47]

The decision to call for help, made in a moment of anxiety and uncertainty, was a mistake. Polk already knew from New Orleans newspapers that Taylor's army was in a "very critical situation," and on March 22 he had ordered all available regular and volunteer forces to hurry to the Rio Grande. Curtis's ill-advised letter reached the White House the next day and served only to annoy Polk, who believed the author must have been "greatly and unnecessarily alarmed" to call for such a ridiculously large number of reinforcements. After speaking with officers recently returned from Mexico, Polk concluded that the "rumours of the perilous condition of the army on the line of the Rio Grande were greatly exaggerated." After the crisis had passed, Polk released Curtis's letter to the press. It appeared in hundreds of newspapers and was roundly lampooned for its hysterical tone.[48]

Polk's confidence in Taylor was confirmed when Santa Anna struck at Buena Vista, five miles south of Saltillo, on February 22–23, 1847. The outnumbered Americans repulsed attack after attack and won a stunning victory. The battle took place eight days before Curtis called the council of war in Camargo, but he did not learn of it until March 7, four days after his letters to Polk, Scott, and the governors disappeared downriver. Why it took two weeks for such momentous news to reach Camargo is not known for certain, but the disruption caused by Urrea's wide-ranging cavalry was the likely reason.[49]

"Victory! Victory! Victory!" were the first words Curtis penned in an exuberant letter to Belinda. "It was a great battle," he burbled to brother Henry, "the greatest of our day and General Taylor is now the great man of his age." In accordance with his earlier instructions, Curtis set out for Monterrey at the head of a force of 1,260 soldiers (including the 630 men of the Third Ohio) and a train of wagons and pack mules two miles in length. Taylor's order to halt traffic on the road between Camargo and Monterrey had come too late for one train that had been overrun by Mexican cavalry. Curtis stopped to bury the victims and recognized one dead teamster as a former member of his Ohio militia battalion.[50]

Taylor, meanwhile, feared the worst for his vulnerable line of communications and set out for Camargo with a relief force. A few miles east of Monterrey he met the Camargo column coming in his direction. "It was a mutual surprise!" wrote Curtis. Taylor was pleased to learn that all was well along the Rio Grande, and sent Curtis on to Monterrey. The approach to the city provided stunning views of the Sierra Madre Oriental. "I never saw mountains before," Samuel wrote Belinda. "They rise up almost perpendicular from a level plain till their peaks pierce the clouds." The Third Ohio entered Monterrey on March 18. Taylor asked Curtis "to take command of the city" and oversee civil affairs as he had done in Matamoros and Camargo. The local authorities required little supervision, so Curtis spent much of his time in the city strolling along the neatly paved streets and admiring the buildings handsomely finished in dressed stone.[51]

• • •

Taylor and Curtis got along well. "He is a plain frank man easily understood," wrote Curtis. "He speaks very freely and feelingly on the subject of his command." Taylor's headquarters was located outside Monterrey in a large grove of hardwood trees watered by a sparkling mountain stream. From time to time Curtis and members of his staff rode out to enjoy lunch with the army commander and explore the grove. The hardwoods reminded him of Ohio. Despite his volunteer status Curtis was treated by everyone, including regular officers at the highest levels of the service, as a capable and reliable colleague, a brother in arms.[52]

Shortly after reaching Monterrey, the Third Ohio escorted a train to Buena Vista, a three-day march to the south. "The country is the most barren on earth," Curtis remarked as he crossed the Sierra Madre Oriental. "Mountains on each side and rocks between the mountains." When the train stopped in Saltillo to allow men and animals a well-earned rest, he again played tourist. "I have been strolling about as far as prudence would permit viewing the curiosities of this place," he informed Belinda. "I find every place has something in it worth looking at." The principal attraction in Saltillo was the ornate Catedral de Santiago, which Curtis described as "Moorish architecture very well executed." The cathedral was older, larger, and grander by far than the churches in Matamoros and Camargo. "You are overwhelmed with the magnificence, loftiness, extent and beauty of the great hall," he told Belinda. "The number of images, paintings, pictures, altars, and strange constructions would require a book to describe even briefly. I have seen nothing equal to this church any where." Curtis also explored a market and marveled at the variety of foods. "Chockolate every where, as thick as soap," he exclaimed.[53]

Curtis was welcomed to the Buena Vista battleground by none other than Major General Wool, the officer he had met in Cincinnati the previous summer. Wool was happy to see a fresh yet familiar face and provided a "long and very interesting account of the battle." A few days later Wool held a review. While the enlisted ranks polished their buttons and boots, the officers discussed the finer points of military etiquette. They concluded that Curtis, despite his volunteer status, was the senior regimental commander present and therefore entitled to lead the entire force during the review. Curtis was delighted. The seven infantry regiments, two batteries, and two cavalry companies assembled at Buena Vista comprised the "largest force I ever saw, and decidedly the most splendid." He was especially happy that the Third Ohio, clad in regular-style uniforms issued only a few weeks earlier, made a fine impression.[54]

The next day Curtis was brought low by another onslaught of malaria: "Sick! Sick! A slight chill very early in the morning and then a burning fever." He returned to Saltillo and moved into the American House, a hotel run by a woman from the United States. The following Sunday he felt well enough to attend mass in the Catedral de Santiago. Samuel described the "mechanical motions" of the priest in satirical detail, but he also noted that the service was "conducted with the utmost propriety and the men and women show the most perfect devotion." Within a week he was back in his tent at Buena Vista. Life under canvas was decidedly spartan, as he explained to brother Henry. "I left my trunk, cot, table, and all my *business* at Camargo, so that I have to write sitting on the ground and holding my blank book on my knee. My bed is two blankets spread on a goat skin and my dining table an ammunition box."[55]

Taylor's army continued to shrink as the enlistments of the twelve-month volunteer regiments expired. "This point cannot be sustained and the General [Wool] thinks this army will be compelled to fall back onto the Rio Grande," Curtis recorded. Santa Anna thought so, too. Recognizing the threat posed by Scott's relentless advance from Veracruz, he withdrew from Buena Vista and concentrated every available man in front of Mexico City. The war in northeastern Mexico entered a prolonged lull. Like other American officers, Curtis strove to keep busy. He served on a court of inquiry, explored the battleground, and observed the local people at work and play.[56]

Taylor released the Third Ohio in mid-May. Curtis was philosophical about the end of his military adventure: "I feel much regret at the prospect of our returning without being [in] battle but such is our fate." He was packed and ready to go when Wool asked him to stay on as acting inspector general for another four weeks. Curtis agreed. Explaining his decision to his family and friends back in Ohio was difficult. "It is hard, very hard to stay so long from those so very dear to us," he confessed to his journal.[57]

So why did Curtis stay? First, he enjoyed hobnobbing with senior army officers, some of whom were national figures. He confessed to brother Henry that "my pride and vanity were not proof against this temptation." Second, the offer to serve as inspector general helped shield him from the embarrassment he had brought down on his own head by writing the ill-considered letters to Polk and others. It demonstrated that Taylor and Wool, heroes of Buena Vista, had confidence in him despite an occasional slip. As he explained to brother Henry, his appointment as inspector general "will I hope disarm my malignant foes."[58]

Wool also appointed Curtis military governor of Saltillo. At one time or another during his eleven months in Mexico, Curtis governed, administered, and defended Matamoros, Camargo, Monterrey, and Saltillo, "all the important points on this line of operation." His final assignment included a degree of luxury previously unknown. At the end of May he moved into the Hacienda de las Hermanas, the palatial estate of Jacobo Sánchez, the "richest proprietor in all of Mexico." The house and garden came with five servants, marble-topped mahogany furniture, and an enormous gilded bed draped with a silk canopy. It was a big step up from drafty canvas tents and whitewashed adobe rooms. Curtis had the house "fitted up to my own liking" and settled in for the next four weeks.[59]

One of Curtis's final duties in Mexico was the disinterment of his military academy classmate, Henry Clay Jr., killed at Buena Vista. The two had enjoyed a brief reunion at Brazos Island ten months earlier. Clay was a widower who left two orphaned children. Curtis saw that his old friend's body was returned to Kentucky for a public funeral. The experience left him depressed.[60]

Curtis departed when his enlistment expired on June 25. His experience in Mexico had not been all that he had hoped, but he comforted himself with the thought that "I have acquitted myself as well as the fortune of war would permit." He accompanied a train back to Camargo. The wagons were harassed by Mexican irregulars and he experienced "considerable sport" skirmishing in the chaparral alongside a company of Texas Rangers, the only time in the war he was in action. His first sight of the Rio Grande at Camargo caused mixed emotions: "I was glad to find myself again on this noble river. I have spent so much time on its sickly shore that I have a kind of grave yard attachment for it." Curtis stopped at Matamoros to say goodbye to old acquaintances, American and Mexican. A visit to the site of his former camp was a melancholy experience: "No tent or tenant except the little grave yard that still remains though the living have long since deserted the place." He left Mexico on June 17.[61]

The three-day voyage across the Gulf of Mexico was a miserable experience. Seasickness returned with a vengeance, as did malaria, and Curtis did not venture far from his cabin. "I have a tremendous chill and fever," he scribbled in his journal. He stumbled ashore in New Orleans looking, in his own words, like a "poor skeleton half dressed person." He spent a night resting in a Crescent City hotel, then boarded a steamboat and churned slowly up the Mississippi. "Every thing is so very different from

Mexico I feel as though I had awoke from a tedious dream," he wrote in his final letter home.[62]

Curtis reached Wooster on August 1, 1847, thirteen months after his departure: "I arrived safe at home where I found my family and friends all well and rejoiced to see me. All express astonishment at my slender appearance. I was myself surprised to see their astonishment. Well I am 40 pounds lighter than when I started." He closed his third journal with a short prayer of thanks for having come through a "long perilous and tedious campaign."[63]

The citizens of Wooster fired a cannon on the town square to celebrate Curtis's return and held a "great meeting" to hear about his adventures in Mexico. The prospect of a public address caused him much anxiety. He confessed that a "speech *on hand* always spoils me for business or for conversation." Nevertheless, he completed this public service with the same dogged devotion to duty he had exhibited in Mexico. Then he returned to civilian life.[64]

3

ENGINEERING

THE TRANSITION FROM MILITARY TO CIVILIAN LIFE DID NOT go as smoothly as Curtis expected. He had discovered, or rediscovered, that there was a whole world beyond Wooster. After ten months in Mexico, meeting and mingling with people of different habits, hobnobbing with important public figures, and living with the constant threat of military action, life in a small Ohio town was dull. Moreover, his business affairs were a mess and his legal practice was moribund.

Curtis seriously considered returning to the army. "I still think I ought to go back to Mexico," he told brother Henry. "There may be a *permanent* increase of our army, and a *Colonels* office as a permanent one you know is exceedingly valuable and honourable. My standing among the army officers is such as few can boast of, and I therefore still have a hankering after military fame." Curtis's belief that he could obtain a colonelcy in the regular army was wishful thinking, to put it mildly. Scott captured Mexico City in September 1847; American and Mexican diplomats began negotiating a cessation of hostilities. With military operations winding down, the army faced a surfeit, not a shortage, of officers.[1]

Fortunately for Curtis, peace with Mexico coincided with an upsurge in demand for engineers. The "improvement fever" that had transformed the Midwest was now infecting the new states and territories west of the Mississippi River. When Iowa achieved statehood in 1846, one of its first official acts was the establishment of a Board of Public Works to oversee the Des Moines River Improvement Project. As the name suggests, the project was modeled on the Muskingum River Improvement, which was finally nearing completion and generating a good deal of publicity. Iowa wanted to "canalize" the Des Moines from its mouth on the Mississippi River up to its confluence with Raccoon Fork, the site of present-day Des Moines, in order to open the central part of the state to development. The undertaking was not for the faint of heart. The distance and elevation to be overcome was twice that of the Muskingum.[2]

The obvious choice to head the Des Moines project was the man who had tamed the Muskingum. Hugh W. Sample, president of the Iowa Board of Public Works, journeyed to Wooster to speak with Curtis. The two men, both Whigs and similar in temperament, hit it off and quickly came to terms. Sample offered $1,500 plus expenses for the first six months, and $2,500 plus expenses for the following twelve months and for every twelve months thereafter. Curtis accepted.[3]

The Board of Public Works was pleased at having acquired the services of a "gentleman of undoubted qualifications." Curtis was pleased as well. He informed brother Henry that the proffered salary was "infinitely better" than anything he might expect to earn as a small-town attorney. He added that Belinda was also pleased because "she thinks this will keep me out of the way and improve our wealth a little." Curtis meant the wry observation as humor, but Belinda had grown accustomed to running the household during her husband's absence and did not want him underemployed and underfoot.[4]

Curtis set out for Iowa in November 1847, four months after his return from Mexico. "I again leave Ohio and again bid you farewell," he wrote to Belinda from Cincinnati. "I see no present probability of a call [for additional troops] and therefore consider myself doing well to see the far west and upper Mississippi," a hint that his wanderlust had not abated. The voyage down the Ohio River was uneventful; a stopover in St. Louis allowed him to explore that booming city. The second stage of the trip was a difficult passage up the ice-choked Mississippi River in the teeth of a frigid north wind. The "tedious and rather perilous journey" ended in early December when Curtis stepped ashore at Keokuk, Iowa.[5]

Keokuk in 1847 was a raw but rapidly growing town of about two thousand people on the western bank of the Great River. It was located just below the Des Moines Rapids, a barrier that prevented larger steamboats from proceeding up the river except in times of high water. Later in the century a lock and dam would submerge the rapids and open the Upper Mississippi to year-round commercial traffic, but until that happened Keokuk remained the effective head of navigation on the river during the summer and fall months, when the water was low. The mouth of the Des Moines River, the potential highway into the interior of Iowa, was only a mile below the town. Local boosters proclaimed Keokuk to be the "Gateway" or "Gate City." Curtis wholeheartedly agreed with that assessment. "It is the great *natural* point for a city in Iowa," he informed Belinda. Shortly after his arrival, warming temperatures showed the town in a less appealing light. "The place does not present a pleasant picture," he acknowledged. "Mud and rain and rough and tumble is the condition of every thing."[6]

Over the next few weeks Curtis explored southeastern Iowa. The bottomlands along the Mississippi and Des Moines Rivers were very rich; he noted that the "old fashioned Ohio forrest is found here in its native beauty." A mile or two back from the rivers, imposing bluffs marked the eastern boundary of a tallgrass prairie that extended westward to the horizon. Curtis described the rolling terrain as "far superior to any idea I had formed of prairie lands," and noted that it was undergoing a dramatic transformation. "You suppose the country new and wild," he wrote Belinda, "but I must advise you that it is only in spots I find the native wilderness. Settlers are getting in at all points. The prairie only requires fencing and ploughing, and a farmer can thus secure a crop the first year after he settles on his lands."[7]

Curtis was amazed at everything he saw: "Large fields and large quantities of wheat and corn are found every where." He marveled at the "very heavy crops" springing out of the dark prairie soil "with less culture [i.e., cultivation] than required on the best lands in Ohio." He recognized at once that major investments in waterways and railroads would have to be made in order to ship such immense yields to markets in North America and Europe. Iowa and engineers seemed made for each other.[8]

Less than a week after setting foot in the Hawkeye state, Curtis advised Belinda that "I am tempted to make some investment of capital here or hereabouts, and you must not be surprised therefore if I become the owner of a log cabin in the far west." A week later he purchased a prairie farm of five hundred acres about eight miles north of Keokuk. "I got it at four dollars per acre, amounting to two thousand dollars. It is one of the prettiest farms and one of the best locations," he added proudly. "The soil is all of a good quality, and generally level or gently undulating." The bluff-top property was surrounded by "fine farms well improved" and enjoyed a commanding view of the Mississippi River, two miles to the east. Visible on the Illinois side of the river was the "renowned city of Nauvoo," once the center of Joseph Smith's Mormon enterprise but recently abandoned and already falling into ruin.[9]

Curtis seemed determined to convince Belinda (and perhaps himself) that he had made a wise investment. "The more I consider my purchase of lands, the better I am pleased with it," he wrote. "I have one of the best locations and a tract of the very best of land." He admitted that he had only seen the property from the road, and had not yet inspected it closely, but he was confident it was a worthwhile acquisition. He already was thinking about "other valuable purchases which I may desire to make." Curtis urged Belinda to visit: "I am anxious to have you see the country." He suggested she join him the following summer, preferably without the children: "Will they stay at home and keep house, and let Pa and Ma engineer in Iowa?"[10]

Curtis appeared ready to put down roots in Iowa, but he hesitated when Belinda asked about the housing situation. "You desire me to select a home that we may all be satisfied with," he replied. "I am delighted with our home in Wooster, and do not yet see any place where you would be half so well fixed." Economic opportunities abounded west of the Mississippi River, but social amenities and cultural institutions were lacking. "Every thing is so new and so unsettled," he fretted. "I feel that you would be entirely out of your element." He also pointed out that schools in Keokuk "are not yet such as we would want our children to learn at," an awkward sentence that reflected the limits of his own frontier education. "Every thing is uncertain and unsettled here," he concluded, "and our home is comfortable and all arranged in Wooster." All of that was true but Curtis enjoyed exploring new places on his own and it seems he was not yet ready to forgo his rambles around Iowa in favor of domestic bliss. Belinda and the children remained in Ohio a little while longer.[11]

• • •

The Des Moines River Improvement Project got underway in mid-December 1847. The initial task was the most difficult: a detailed survey of the river and its floodplain from the Mississippi River to Raccoon Fork, a distance of roughly two hundred miles. This formidable undertaking required Curtis, three assistant engineers, and a dozen other staffers to live and work outdoors for days at a time, a "very disagreeable" experience in the harsh winter weather.[12]

Mishaps were a constant danger. One day, while crossing the Des Moines on a primitive ferry, Curtis and his horse tumbled into the frigid water. "I can hardly see how I got off without being badly hurt but good fortune saved me," he informed Belinda. The thick underbrush rapidly wore out his wardrobe. "I need new clothes and really begin to look rough and ragged," he observed. Curtis had done the same type of work in Ohio fifteen years earlier, but he was now forty-three years old and no longer enjoyed the resilience of youth. Moreover, he still suffered from the lingering effects of his bout with malaria. After two months he confided to his wife, "I am exhausted with toil." Nevertheless, he carried on, his resolve strengthened by his swelling bank account. "The pay is so much better than law practice I suppose I had best receive it as long as I can."[13]

In March 1848, four months into the job, Curtis informed the Board of Public Works that the survey had reached Ottumwa, ninety miles above the Mississippi River, and that the first contracts for dams, locks, dikes, side canals, and other features on the lower river would be let soon. Impressed by the rapid progress, the board declared the members of the survey party to be "worthy of all praise." When spring arrived the Des Moines overflowed its banks, as expected, and brought surveying activity to a halt for several weeks.[14]

Curtis returned to Keokuk and explored various business opportunities. His legal practice in Ohio had not been a smashing success, but he decided to try again in Iowa. He opened a law office in partnership with John W. Rankin and, later, Charles Mason. Curtis knew Rankin from Wooster and Mason from West Point. Mason had graduated in 1829, two years ahead of Curtis, and been assigned to duty at the school as a professor of engineering, an extraordinary honor. He is remembered today as the highest-ranking cadet in United States Military Academy history, outscoring both Robert E. Lee (a classmate) and Douglas MacArthur. A long-running notice on the front page of the *Keokuk Dispatch* advised readers that the firm of "Mason, Curtis & Rankin: Attorneys at Law" could be found on the second floor of Graham's brick office block in the center of town.[15]

Real estate and other forms of investment beckoned as well. Curtis was no stranger to land speculation. He had purchased town lots and rural tracts in Ohio; now he put his money to work in Iowa. He and Sample pooled their resources and bought four residential lots in a promising part of Keokuk. "We are not determined [i.e., decided] as to what we will do with these but thought we had better buy if we want to sell again," he explained to Belinda. The two men also established a firm to construct a canal around the Des Moines Rapids. The Navigation and Hydraulic Company of the Mississippi Rapids existed only on paper, but Curtis believed it would attract investors as demand for waterborne commerce increased. He thought the company had a "pretty fair prospect of success." He finally got around to visiting his farm

north of town and discovered it was occupied by a family of squatters. Unable to look after the land himself, he allowed the family
to remain "so long as they take care of the fields and fences."[16]

Work on the Des Moines River resumed in June 1848. A short
time later Curtis advised the Board of Public Works that the
survey above Ottumwa was going well, and that construction
of dams and other features below the town was "progressing
with great vigor." He lambasted "local interests" for attempting
to influence the placement of dams, and assured the board that
railroads did not pose a serious threat to the project. Waterways,
he declared, "will always be much cheaper than railroads." To
prove his point, he calculated that the expense of "canalizing"
the first ninety miles of the Des Moines at $5,245 per mile, less
than half the cost of building a railroad line over the same distance. The figure proved unrealistically low.[17]

Belinda and the children arrived in Keokuk that fall. The
reunited family stayed in a boardinghouse while Curtis designed
and supervised the construction of their new home. The L-shaped,
two-story structure was built of dressed limestone blocks two feet
thick. The front porch and side gables were adorned with clas-
sic revival detailing but otherwise the exterior was plain, almost
severe. The house was light gray in color and occupied a large corner lot on a bluff overlooking the Mississippi River. Construction
went slowly, partly because masonry work could not be rushed
and partly because of the disruption caused by the 1849 cholera
epidemic, of which more will be said later. The Wooster house
remained unsold until February 1851, when family friend Lucas
Flattery telegraphed that a potential buyer had been found. Curtis responded with a notable economy of words: "Sell."[18]

The final cost of the Keokuk house was more than Curtis had
anticipated. "I reproach myself for having undertaken so expensive a house," he confessed to brother Henry, "but I had to have a
home out here, and when one gets at a house it always becomes
more expensive than we anticipated." The lament is familiar to
generations of homeowners, but the money proved to be well
spent. The house remained in the Curtis family for half a cen-

tury. It still stands today at 206 High Street in remarkably good condition, a tribute to its simple design and sturdy construction. It has been altered over the years by the addition of two back rooms, a larger front porch, and a hipped roof with dormer windows, but the original occupants would find it quite familiar. It is listed on the National Register of Historic Places as the home of Iowa's most distinguished military figure.[19]

• • •

Curtis wrote little about the conclusion of the Mexican War or the election of Zachary Taylor, his former commander and fellow Whig, to the presidency in 1848, though he was pleased with both developments. Nor did he have much to say about the discovery of gold in California and the rush to the Pacific Coast the following year, events that transformed the nation and triggered a political crisis over the status of slavery in the newly acquired territories. Personal and professional matters garnered most of his attention during this period. Zarah Curtis, soldier, pioneer, and family patriarch, died in Ohio in 1849 at the remarkable old age of eighty-eight. "I could hardly realize that he is gone forever," Curtis wrote to brother Henry. "That we can never again hear him recount his weary life and urge us to avoid dangers and difficulties."[20]

The news of Zarah's death reached Keokuk in the middle of a terrifying cholera epidemic. The dreadful disease had faded away after its first outbreak in North America fifteen years earlier, but it returned with a vengeance in the summer of 1849. The congested cities and towns along the Mississippi River and other busy waterways suffered appalling losses. Thousands died and thousands more fled into the countryside to escape the contagion. Among the latter was the Curtis family, which abandoned Keokuk and sought refuge in Ottumwa. Writing from his isolated retreat, Curtis informed brother Henry that "my family has continued to enjoy almost uninterrupted good health ever since we came to the west." That happy state of affairs would not last.[21]

Work on the Des Moines River ground to a halt as mechanics

and laborers fell ill or ran away. Perhaps it did not matter. The state government had grossly mismanaged the sale of public lands, the sole source of funding, and the project was in financial difficulty. The legislature attempted to fix the problem by appointing a new Board of Public Works composed entirely of Democrats, who cut costs by eliminating superfluous Whigs. Belinda informed her husband of the impending change in their fortunes: "There is not much doubt I suppose but that a new board will make new engineers and then I hope you can be at home more and not expose yourself so much." Curtis had been aware of the shifting political sands for some time and took his termination notice in stride. He told brother Henry, "I am not in the least surprised and shall not be very much grieved as my private business will give me ample employment, if it does not bring in with it quite so great an income."[22]

Curtis remained on the payroll through November 1849. Conscientious to the end, he submitted a final report in which he stated that the completed project would be 204 miles in length with a fall of 308 feet, and include twenty-eight dams, thirty locks, and assorted other features. He projected a final cost of $9,344 per mile, nearly double his earlier estimate. He stated that the project had "prospered with great energy and success" during its first year, but the winter of 1848–49 inaugurated a "succession of reverses which have been as incessant as they have been calamitous." Winter storms and spring floods destroyed months of work. The summer of 1849 brought cholera and a second round of "extraordinary floods." Curtis urged perseverance and published the report in pamphlet form to make certain his views reached the public. He feared the Democrat-controlled board would fudge the numbers and blame everything on the Whigs.[23]

It was all for naught. The Des Moines River Improvement Project was doomed without a more reliable source of income. Construction stopped in the mid-1850s but legal wrangling went on for decades. The fiasco ultimately cost Iowa taxpayers more than $1,500,000 and produced nothing in return. A half dozen features were completed but the crumbling stone walls of two locks at Bonaparte and Keosauqua, designed by Curtis but completed after his departure, are all that remain today. Both are listed on the National Register of Historic Places.[24]

The family returned to Keokuk despite the lingering presence of cholera. They finally moved into their new home and announced that they were "comfortably prepared for receiving our friends who find their way out to Iowa." Curtis was eager to impress his brothers. He urged them to visit Iowa and "see the West." Such a trip, he suggested, would "give you a better knowledge of the future destiny of this Country." With time on his hands and money in his pocket, Curtis threw himself into business, especially land speculation. It was a buyer's market because of the economic downturn caused by the epidemic, and he made the most of it. He purchased more lots in Keokuk, acquired two additional farms outside town, and made a "considerable investment" in a tract of land at the future site of Des Moines. Within a few months he "secured an interest at all the important points on the Desmoines river." He expected to make a killing when the demand for land revived.[25]

In the spring of 1850, Curtis, Belinda, Sadie, and Bucky (now eight and five years old respectively) set out on a month-long journey to New York, Philadelphia, and Washington, with stops in Wooster, Mansfield, and Mount Vernon. Henry and Sam (now thirteen and twelve respectively) remained in Keokuk to attend school. A cook and maid prepared meals and looked after the house, but the boys were responsible for everything else. Curtis provided the teenagers with advice on landscaping and gardening. He also reminded them to build a corral for Filly, the family mare who was in a family way. Belinda's instructions were more general: "I want you to take good care of every thing out doors and watch the gates and take good care of the cows and keep every thing looking nice and in good order." She added, "I hope never to leave you so long again."[26]

The travelers visited dozens of aunts, uncles, brothers, sisters, nieces, nephews, and cousins in the rapidly growing Curtis and Buckingham clans, who by now were scattered across six states from the Atlantic Coast to the Mississippi Valley. The highlight of the trip was a two-week stay in New York. Curtis had not been to the city since graduating from the military academy but he seemed perfectly at home in the teeming metropolis. He opened an account with a Manhattan bank and thereafter the Curtis family purchased clothes, furnishings, and household goods from New York merchants by mail order.[27]

Curtis was a successful man by the standards of his time and place, but he was vaguely dissatisfied with the course his life had taken. He attempted to explain his feelings to brother Henry, who replied that Curtis should be happy with what he had achieved. "I am not sure that mere *happiness* is the object of my exertions," Curtis responded. "A mark in the sand of life that may be traced by those I leave behind, is far more congenial to my feelings. It is a foolish ambition that I feel and I suppose it is common to all of us. I desire that my humble name may be cherished, at least by those I love." But how could he achieve that ambition? He was well into middle age and it appeared his chance of achieving even a modest level of fame had passed.[28]

• • •

A letter arrived in Keokuk shortly after the Curtis family returned from the East Coast. Luther M. Kennett, newly elected Whig mayor of St. Louis, wanted to know if Curtis would be interested in the position of city engineer. Kennett explained that St. Louis was facing two critical problems. The first was natural. The city is located on the inside of a bend in the Mississippi River. The current was cutting away the outside or eastern bank of the bend and depositing silt and sand on the inside or western bank. As a result, the river was moving away from Missouri and toward Illinois (or, more accurately, *into* Illinois). If the Mississippi's eastward movement was not arrested and reversed, St. Louis would find itself high and dry. The second problem was man-made. The 77,860 people in St. Louis lacked an effective drainage system. Rainwater mingled with human waste and produced miasmatic cesspits around the city that looked awful, smelled worse, and bred diseases. Deadly microorganisms seeped through the saturated ground and contaminated springs, streams, and wells, infecting all who depended on them. St. Louis was the sickliest city on the Great River and the situation was growing worse by the day.[29]

The complex engineering challenges intrigued Curtis, but he insisted that he would leave Keokuk only if the price was right: "I have provided myself with a humble station which I will not forsake without adequate inducement." Kennett offered $2,000 per year plus expenses. Curtis accepted. Belinda resigned herself to another extended separation, this time without the comfort of having relatives and in-laws near at hand.[30]

Curtis set out for St. Louis in July 1850, eight months after leaving the Des Moines River Improvement Project. He was surprised to discover the extent of his responsibilities as city engineer. In addition to changing the course of the Mississippi River and constructing a citywide drainage system, he was expected to supervise the municipal waterworks, oversee the street commission (which straightened, leveled, surfaced, curbed, illuminated, and maintained streets and public spaces), and carry out related duties as determined by the city council. With responsibility came power, and Curtis found himself one of the most important officials in the most important city in the West. It was a heady experience but one tempered by daunting challenges and high expectations.

Robert E. Lee had attempted to deal with the wandering Mississippi River a decade earlier. Beginning in 1837, Lee, then an officer in the army's famed Corps of Engineers, constructed dikes that connected the Illinois bank with the head of Bloody Island, a large mudflat in the river opposite St. Louis. The dikes closed the channel between the island and the eastern bank and forced the river back toward the western bank, where the current scoured away the silt blocking access to the St. Louis waterfront. At the same time, backflow deposited silt in the blocked channel between the island and the eastern bank, a process that eventually made the island part of Illinois. Lee had things well in hand but the economic downturn in the late 1830s led Congress to cut off funding before the project was completed, and the Mississippi resumed its eastward creep. Lee prepared extensive notes and maps before he departed in 1840; this material helped his successor get off to a fast start. Curtis incorporated much of Lee's work into his own plans, though he believed Lee seriously underestimated the erosive power of the Great River. Curtis reinforced existing dikes where possible and built massive new ones where necessary.[31]

The task required excavating, transporting, and depositing enormous amounts of dirt, rock, and timber in a physical environment dominated by an immense and unpredictable stream. Hundreds of men, dozens of boats and barges, and all manner of specialized equipment (such as dredges and pile drivers) were active on any given day, save in the most inclement weather. Curtis was a hands-on supervisor who regularly visited construction sites. One December day in 1850 he crossed the river to check on an older dike that was being strengthened. He was "much vexed" to discover that his directions to increase the height of the dike had been misunderstood. Tons of fill had been dumped in the wrong place. A few days later he returned to insure that the contractor had corrected the error and noted that the work "is going on bravely now." All through the winter of 1850–51 construction proceeded at a frantic pace. The system of dikes was still a work in progress and Curtis feared it might not withstand the Great River at spring flood.[32]

In 1851 residents of St. Louis, including the city engineer, watched anxiously as the Mississippi River rose higher and higher, swollen by snowmelt and spring rains. The crisis approached near the end of May. Curtis braved the churning river every day for a week to see for himself what was happening along the threatened eastern bank. "The water looks rather fearful," Curtis noted on May 28. "River still rising," he observed three days later. "Things look bad for the dike but there is not so much of the embankment washed away as we anticipated." The next entry was tense and terse: "Water rising. Dike much damaged." For the next four days the river raged against the barriers, but Curtis recorded that the "works still stand the water very well." The river crested on June 11 and began to recede.[33]

A greatly relieved Curtis informed the city council that the flood had happened at an "unfortunate period in the progress of our works, and rose to extraordinary height," but the "damages are not so great as I apprehended, and the success in effecting the designs are greater than I anticipated." Curtis thought he would have the better part of a year to advance the project before the next spring flood, but he did not take into account the vagaries of the weather. The winter of 1851–52 was exceedingly cold, and the river froze to a greater depth than normal. The current caused the unusually thick ice to buckle and accumulate, forming immense ice dams that caused unpredictable changes in water level. In late January 1852 such a dam developed downstream from the city and the river rose nine feet overnight. Icy slush inundated the St. Louis waterfront and the dikes on the opposite bank. Curtis grumbled that Mother Nature was "making a singular effort to thwart our purpose," before realizing that the absence of a strong current behind the dam minimized the damage. The ice eventually gave way and the dikes emerged from the frigid water, soggy but intact.[34]

The 1852 spring flood arrived earlier than expected. Curtis reported that water "rose over and destroyed" a section of the dike between Bloody Island and Illinois, but working parties repaired the damage. After attempting to force its way over, under, and around the unnatural barriers, the Mississippi gradually withdrew to its old channel close to the western bank. Curtis closely monitored the situation. In August he declared victory, telling the city council that the "success of our former work is clearly indicated by the removal of the river channel towards the Missouri shore, and the heavy deposits and bars that are now seen on the Illinois side of the river." It was an impressive achievement and it proved to be permanent. Today, the Mississippi still flows majestically along the St. Louis waterfront, just as Lee and Curtis intended it should.[35]

···

Solving the drainage problem in St. Louis was a more complex and vexing undertaking. Henry B. Kayser, Lee's principal assistant, had been appointed the first city engineer in 1839. A decade later, in the midst of the second cholera epidemic, the city council directed him to create a citywide sewer system in the hope that this might somehow reduce the death toll. Kayser was a first-rate engineer who quickly got the project up and running. He was also a Democrat who lost his job to Curtis the following year when the Whigs gained control of the city government. Curtis was an old hand at building locks and dams but the St. Louis sewer system was his first experience with urban infrastructure. He studied Kayser's plans and strove to understand the task he had inherited. Some time passed before he felt confident enough to make the project truly his own.[36]

Excavation of trenches and construction of brick tubes (the actual sewers) was well underway in several places when Curtis arrived. He was impressed by the scale of the undertaking and by Kayser's organizational skills. On one of his first inspection trips, just a ten-minute walk from his office, he watched a "very large force" of three hundred laborers, eighty-eight carts, and ten wagons "pressing the excavation" of a secondary sewer line down the middle of Seventh Street. Dozens of bricklayers were hard at work in the trench constructing the sewer proper, in this instance an immense brick tube twelve feet in diameter with an exterior wall one foot thick. Curtis climbed down into the muddy trench to see the details for himself and to talk with the bricklayers and laborers.[37]

The immensity of the project was hard to grasp because it was spread out over so much of the city. A single sewer line required the removal of thousands of cubic yards of dirt, which was then hauled away and used to fill in the noisome ponds and depressions around the city. Sewers of varying size, shape (profile), and purpose (runoff or waste) were under construction in a dozen locations across the city. It was an unending struggle to maintain gradients and establish connections among sewers built by different contractors. Piles of dirt and debris blocked streets and snarled traffic. Cave-ins severed freshwater pipes and caused buildings to settle or even collapse into the streets.

Between 1850 and 1853 Curtis supervised the construction of dikes, sewers, water pipes, wharves, and related features in and around St. Louis. He also prepared reports, calculated expenses (sometimes down to the individual brick), let contracts, inspected work, corrected bad practices, listened to suggestions and complaints, and attended endless meetings. He endured attacks in the newspapers, principally from Kayser, who made what Curtis termed "false and villainous charges" about corruption and incompetence in the city engineer's office. Curtis shrugged off the accusations as a "silly affair full of gasconade and froth." He somehow found time to transform barren Washington Square into a genteel public space with a fountain, curving sidewalks, flowering shrubs, and shade trees, the whole illuminated by gaslights and surrounded by an elegant wrought-iron fence. Curtis was on the move nearly every day. He might spend a morning examining an eroding dike in Illinois and the afternoon overseeing the repair of a leaky sewer on Biddle Street.[38]

Life in St. Louis also had a pleasant side. "My evenings are devoted to my own pleasure," Curtis informed Belinda. "Indeed I could hardly ask for a better situation." He had never lived in a large city before and he made the most of it. He attended dinners, parties, and concerts with the "best men of the city." On Thanksgiving Day 1850 he enjoyed an evening of genteel entertainment among the upper crust. "Very gay," he noted. "Playing cards dancing eating and drinking made up the sum of the amusements." Yuletide celebrations were less inhibited. "Christmas is a merry day in St. Louis," he observed. "The old and young rich and poor all seem to rejoice on a day of festivity." He visited a riverfront warehouse "quite full of people walking, eating, talking, flirting, and keeping up a merry Christmas party." It was, he thought, the "most sociable crowd I have met in the city and their amusements appeared quite natural and agreeable." Curtis embraced the St. Louis social scene, but he continued to profess his love for Belinda and his distress at their separation. "I am very lonely and sometimes almost feel like deserting and going to you," he wrote. "My heart is at home with you on the hill." The rest of him, however, remained in St. Louis.[39]

Curtis lived in a boardinghouse during his first year in St. Louis. The city had experienced a terrible conflagration in 1849 that destroyed hundreds of buildings. The resulting housing shortage was one of the reasons Belinda and the children remained in Keokuk. Following that traumatic experience, fire bells rang so frequently that many residents—including Curtis—paid them little heed. "I am used to it and never move till it feels hot, when I stick my head out of the window," he joked to brother Henry. "My wife berates me for my stupidity and really I must be more careful for my room is in the fourth story, and I might be caught napping." His boardinghouse survived but his workplace did not. Shortly after his arrival a fire "burned out" the city engineer's office in City Hall. Passersby rushed into the building and helped the staff carry irreplaceable documents to safety, but Curtis was annoyed to discover that one Good Samaritan had absconded with a "fine box of drawing instruments."[40]

Belinda was pregnant again, and Curtis returned to Keokuk as often as he could. He was present for Yale's birth on March 10, 1851, and made it back to St. Louis just in time to witness the arrival of Jenny Lind. The celebrated singer was in the midst of a wildly successful tour of the United States. Curtis reported "considerable excitement" over the presence of "so distinguished a personage" in the city. He paid the astronomical sum of $5 to attend one of Lind's concerts. "I was very much pleased with her singing," he told Belinda and the children. "She was very pretty and very graceful on the stage. She had a most splendid voice soaring up about as high as the flute could play."[41]

Two weeks later Curtis was back in Keokuk, "watching and nursing over the sick bed of my wife." Belinda gradually recovered from her illness and Curtis returned to St. Louis, where the Mississippi River was threatening to destroy the dikes, as described earlier. While he was away a disaster of another sort overwhelmed the Curtis household. All five children were stricken with cholera. Yale, the youngest and most vulnerable, became desperately ill. Curtis described the situation in his journal: "Received two dispatches from my family. Youngest child, my little boy Yale, is very sick. 'Can't live long' says the dispatch. They want me to go up. I cannot. My duty is so oppressive." By the time the spring flood receded and Kennett finally allowed Curtis to depart, there was nothing he could do except comfort Belinda, who was "still very feeble." Yale died on June 17 after only three months of life. "Lost my babe Yale, which I followed to the grave in Iowa," Curtis noted stoically. An even heavier blow fell on July 2 when six-year-old Bucky succumbed to the same dread disease: "Sad news of the death of my dear boy Buckingham and sickness of other children." Curtis was again unable to get home before the child died. The three older children—Henry, Sam, and Sadie—recovered.[42]

After two funerals in as many weeks, the grieving Curtis family closed up the house in Keokuk and traveled to St. Louis. Curtis resumed his duties as city engineer while Belinda and the three surviving children departed on an extended visit to see family and friends in Ohio. A few weeks later Belinda suggested to Curtis that they give up on Keokuk and return to Wooster. Curtis gently but firmly resisted. "I do not feel like cutting loose from that place," he replied. "I am attached to my home there, and continue to be. My hopes too are strongly fixed on Iowa and I shall rejoice at a day of return to our home on the hill that overlooks the Great Mississippi."[43]

Belinda and the children returned to St. Louis in December 1851. "I astonished my wife by showing her a house all comfortably furnished instead of boarding," Curtis informed his journal. "My house is a snug small one of seven rooms very well arranged and nicely but not expensively furnished and equipped." The house was located in a pleasant neighborhood on Olive Street and rented for $300 per year. The family was reunited just ahead of the coldest winter yet recorded in St. Louis. Curtis noticed that ice formed in his bedroom "even when a fire was burning." The

Mississippi River froze over, as noted earlier, and navigation shuddered to a halt. The ground froze as well and stopped excavation work on the sewers. The enforced lull allowed Curtis to spend time with Belinda and the children, who were "quite lost and really sometimes homesick and discontented." Christmas 1851 was not very merry for the Curtis family.[44]

Life went on. Cara Eliza, seventh and last of the Curtis children, made her appearance a year later on December 8, 1852. Sadie attended an academy for young ladies and took piano lessons at home. Henry and Sam enrolled at St. Louis University, a prestigious Jesuit institution, but neither showed much interest in academic pursuits. Belinda continued to be dissatisfied with the peripatetic nature of her life. "My wife says she has quite given up the idea of a settled home," Curtis told brother Henry, but in fact the opposite was true. After several months of fitting up the new house, settling the children in schools, exploring the city, and sampling the social whirl, Belinda decided St. Louis was too much for her. She wanted to return to Keokuk, though she was content to stay in St. Louis as long as her husband was city engineer.[45]

Talk of returning to Keokuk must have caused some tension within the family, because Curtis liked St. Louis. "I have never lived so quietly and comfortably in my life," he told brother Henry. He was on good terms with prominent people and had recently purchased a lot near Washington Square and two small farms across the river in Illinois. But his hilltop home, his closest friends, and his heart were in Iowa—as was most of his money. "I have so connected my destiny with Iowa," he informed brother Henry, "that my fortunes must advance with her prosperity."[46]

The immediate destiny of the Curtis family was determined by local politics. Curtis was a Whig political appointee; he knew what would happen when the Democrats regained control of the city government, which they were bound to do, probably sooner than later. He told brother Henry that "there is no certainty as you know in any station of a public character in this Democratic age." If the worse happened, "I shall try to walk the plank with grace and dignity." It was the same metaphor he had used to describe his termination from the Muskingum River project. The Democrats swept the March 1853 municipal elections; Curtis was released after three years on the job. To no one's surprise, the new city engineer was the old city engineer, Henry Kayser.[47]

A substantial portion of the St. Louis sewer system designed and built by Kayser and Curtis between 1849 and 1856 remains in use today under the historic downtown neighborhood known as Laclede's Landing. It is the oldest urban drainage system west of the Mississippi River.

· · ·

Curtis was not unemployed for long. Within two months he was hired as chief engineer of the Philadelphia, Fort Wayne, and Platte River Airline Railroad. The position paid top dollar. "I am getting double the sallary that [the] City Engineer [job] paid," he crowed to brother Henry, "and the business is much more interesting." The goal of the Airline Railroad was to construct a continuous, single-gauge track across the northern states, from the East Coast to the Great Plains—and beyond. This was a novel idea at a time when most railroad lines were short, used different gauges, and did not connect with one another.[48]

The projected terminus of the first phase of this ambitious project was Council Bluffs in southwestern Iowa. The town was located on the eastern bank of the Missouri River opposite the mouth of the Platte River. The well-traveled Overland Trail began on the western bank and followed the Platte to the Rocky Mountains, and thence to Oregon and California on the Pacific Coast. The trail tenuously connected the eastern and western parts of the United States. The Platte Valley's gentle gradient was well suited to railroads as well as wagons and was the obvious route across the Great Plains for a transcontinental railroad. The Airline promoted itself as an essential first step in the creation of a coast-to-coast rail system. Much remained to be done. The line was complete from Philadelphia to Fort Wayne, Indiana, but the nearly six-hundred-mile stretch from there to Council Bluffs existed mostly on paper.[49]

The Airline, like other privately financed projects in the antebellum era, was acutely vulnerable to financial upheavals. The emerging industrial economy was subject to unpredictable booms and busts that caused the money supply to fluctuate wildly. Almost from the beginning of his tenure as chief engineer, Curtis harbored doubts about the company's long-term prospects. "I fear a failure," he confided to brother Henry. Nevertheless, this was his first opportunity to work on a major railroad project, something he had wanted to do for years, and he threw himself into the endeavor.[50]

Curtis desired to learn about railroading from the ground up, so he assigned himself the task of surveying a suitable route across Iowa. "I have been on the Prairies for the last two months, sleeping sometimes under canvas and sometimes without any cover but a blanket," he wrote. "I find that I can bear hard service yet; but do not expect to have much of the field work on my hands." Curtis became a confidant of company president Erasmus Gest and spent more and more of his time meeting and greeting the public. He was the Airline's public face in Indiana, Illinois, and Iowa, as he made dozens of speeches promoting the vision of a transcontinental railroad. When the immense cost of the project became clear, he became the railroad's chief lobbyist in Washington. Curtis spent the first half of 1854 promoting a bill in the House of Representatives that would provide the Airline with grants of public land to offset expenses. Unfortunately, the bill failed. "I confess it is awful tiresome," sighed a disappointed Curtis. "Some days I am quite discouraged and feel like abandoning all efforts."[51]

While a frustrated Curtis bashed his head against a wall in Washington, Belinda developed a lingering respiratory illness during another extended stay in Ohio. Curtis worried about his wife's "feeble health," remarking that "I have been only half myself for the past four months of her illness." Fearing the worst, he took a leave of absence in March to be by her side. Fortunately, Belinda recovered and she and the girls returned to the "snug" house in St. Louis.[52]

Henry and Sam wrote regularly to their father during this period. Curtis critiqued their letters much as Hosmer and Henry had done with his own missives three decades earlier. "I am anxious that each of you should have a fluency of speech and capacity to write correctly," he explained. His academic struggles at West Point had convinced him that a command of Latin was "exceedingly important" for a professional man: "I know that Latin is dry and tedious, but it is a kind of measure of literary knowledge, and you must master it." He assured the boys that once they acquired a "fluent use of our language," they would be able to express themselves "by speaking or writing in a manner creditable to yourselves and interesting to others." He was especially anxious about Sam, whom he thought was "not sufficiently educated and must go to school next winter." Curtis tried to get the boys to understand his motives: "I look forward with the hope that you may grow up with such habits of study, stability, and industry as to assist or succeed me. Good morals and *untiring energy* will bring you forward in this world." He need not have worried. Henry and Sam turned out to be bright, talented, industrious, and successful.[53]

Curtis left Washington in the summer of 1854 and resumed his responsibilities as chief engineer of the Airline, but his railroading days were coming to an end. During an inspection tour across Illinois and Iowa, he noticed that a "feeling of doubt and a desire to escape from a sinking ship prevails along the line." Curtis resigned at the end of the year and joined Belinda and the girls in St. Louis. He got out before the company folded but never received severance pay or reimbursement for his travels and living expenses in Washington. "Not a dime has been paid me," he complained. Curtis later told son Henry that the failing railroad owed him nearly $9,000 but that it was "impossible to collect a dollar from them."[54]

The two years Curtis spent with the Airline was an invaluable learning experience. He mastered the nuts and bolts of planning, financing, building, and operating the most complex industrial enterprise then in existence. He learned that the Platte Valley in

Nebraska was the proper route for a transcontinental railroad. He also learned that such an enormous project could not succeed without financial support from the federal government, and that support would be forthcoming only with a determined advocate in Congress.

The Airline left an even greater mark on young Henry and Sam. Following their brush with higher education in St. Louis, Curtis found them jobs as general apprentices in the railroad's western office in Lacon, Illinois. He hoped they might pick up some useful skills. To his surprise, both boys demonstrated considerable ability in surveying, cartography, and (in Henry's case) administration. They were promoted and soon earned enough money to support themselves. Henry became his father's right-hand man. Curtis informed Gest on one occasion that Henry was working on a skeleton map of potential railroad routes across Iowa: "I will not see the map [until] after it is finished but he will trace out many of the lines. I rely very much on his taste in preparing the map which he will fully explain to you." Henry also prepared, published, and distributed a polished pamphlet for prospective investors. He was seventeen years old at the time.[55]

During this period Curtis served as a consultant or "advisory engineer" on several smaller projects. The mayor of St. Joseph asked him to determine whether his town could be saved from the encroaching Missouri River. St. Joseph was located on the outside of a sharp bend in the river, the reverse of the situation at St. Louis. The fast-flowing stream was scouring away the sandy bluff where the town was located. Several buildings had already fallen into the river and more were poised to follow. The situation was urgent.[56]

Curtis traveled up the Missouri to St. Joseph and inspected the eroding waterfront: "I regard the danger as serious, and only capable of being arrested by united and powerful exertions." He suggested that a "heavy revetment" of brush and stone be constructed across the waterfront at once. He explained how the stone could be quarried from Rattlesnake Bluff in Nebraska, floated down the Missouri on barges, and placed along the eroding bank in large timber cribs. The cost, he estimated, would be between $75,000 and $150,000. He regretted that his railroad duties prevented his "immediate supervision" of the project, but he expressed confidence that if his instructions were followed by a competent contractor the chance of success was high. Like a true Whig, he urged the mayor to seek financial assistance from the federal government.[57]

Engineering challenges fascinated Curtis. In 1851 he spent many hours calculating the cost of a bridge across the Mississippi River at Keokuk. He told a group of local businessmen who had inquired about the matter that the Gate City was "decidedly the best location" for a bridge because of the solid river bottom, relatively shallow water, and firm banks. He estimated the cost of a lightweight suspension bridge at half a million dollars but recommended a heavier truss structure resting on stone piers. The latter bridge cost four times as much but would support the weight of a railroad. Nothing came of the inquiry but Curtis was certain a physical link between Illinois and Iowa was only a few decades away.[58]

Curtis also tried his hand at boosterism. He wrote an article titled "The Desmoines Valley" for a popular regional magazine. The article described how the "rolling prairie, interspersed with beautiful groves of forest trees, extends in all directions like the great ocean, as far as the eye can trace the circle of the horizon." Lyrical accounts of the "majestic landscape" were mixed with statistics about economic development, all designed to encourage emigration to Iowa and, not so incidentally, increase the value of the author's properties. Curtis, however, was no fraud. He believed every word he wrote. Around this time he told a friend, "The more I see of Iowa the more I admire its future prospects."[59]

It was not surprising that the Curtis family bid farewell to St. Louis at the end of 1854 and boarded a steamboat for the short trip to Keokuk. Iowa beckoned.

4

BUSINESS AND POLITICS

THE RETURN TO KEOKUK IN 1854 MARKED ANOTHER CHANGE in Curtis's life. For most of the previous two decades he had worked as an engineer, but his recent experiences left him disillusioned. He confessed to son Henry, "I begin to feel like quitting this engineer business and devoting myself to my law office as [a] means of living. I [would] rather live on less and enjoy the society of my family." But Curtis had little interest in the law and was, at best, an undistinguished attorney. Though he seemed reluctant to acknowledge it, he had gradually become a man of business. For the rest of the decade he pursued financial opportunities with varying degrees of success and, almost incidentally, embarked on a flourishing career in politics.[1]

Curtis made several trips to the Missouri Valley during his two years with the Airline Railroad. As the chief engineer of a potential transcontinental transportation system, he was welcomed to Omaha and Council Bluffs and offered attractive investment opportunities. Curtis was flush with cash at the time and jumped in. He returned to the Missouri Valley on a regular basis for the rest of his life to look after his interests. His first visit as an independent businessman took place in the spring of 1855. Curtis and Sam traveled across Iowa in a two-horse buggy and had a "very delightful trip." Ever the naturalist, Curtis reported that the "prairies are covered with the richest carpet of grass you ever beheld and every thing is just bursting forth into the vigorous foliage of the summer season." The pair passed through Des Moines, where Curtis owned several lots. He was pleased with the hustle and bustle he observed. "This town is growing finely and strangers are rushing in from all quarters," he noted with approval. After making certain the Curtis properties were free of squatters, father and son pressed on to the Missouri River.[2]

Curtis's largest and most successful investment in the region was a partnership in the Council Bluffs and Nebraska Ferry Company. Operating a steamboat on the Missouri River was a perilous undertaking. The firm's first vessel was crushed by an ice jam. As de facto chief engineer, Curtis traveled to Illinois and purchased a replacement boat. Unfortunately, it struck a snag and sank just before reaching Council Bluffs. "Our company affairs are therefore in straitened circumstances," Curtis admitted. "An empty treasury and an outstanding debt of some three thousand dollars." Again acting on behalf of the firm, Curtis bought another vessel, which he later described as a "fine boat doing a large business, but I fear she is so expensive as to be a poor paying concern." His fears proved groundless. The ferry company made enough money to acquire yet another steamboat and to construct a two-story office block in Omaha. The Nebraska territorial government purchased the building for use as a temporary capitol. Income from the sale put the firm solidly in the black.[3]

In addition to a share of the ferry company, which included steamboats, barges, wharves, repair facilities, warehouses, woodlots, and other assets, Curtis acquired 320 acres ("near 200 of which we have laid out into lots") on the outskirts of Council Bluffs. He also purchased a 160-acre farm, seventy-one lots, and a half dozen buildings in and around Omaha, which he predicted would someday become the "greatest city in the West." He still had three farms in southeastern Iowa (including the "original" farm purchased in 1847) and dozens of lots and buildings in Keokuk, Des Moines, and other communities. Finally, he held title to an eclectic mix of properties in Ohio, Missouri, and Illinois. It was an impressive portfolio, but the downside to being awash in real estate was that taxes and mortgage payments came due on a regular basis.[4]

Curtis even established a bank. In 1854 he traveled to the East Coast. The purpose of the trip seems to have been financial in nature but he managed to squeeze in a fair bit of sightseeing. "You never can imagine the change in New York," he told Belinda. "It is so crowded there is no peace or comfort either in walking or riding and the whole city seems to be a prefect jam." On the way home Curtis stopped in Indiana and opened the Bank of Fort Wayne. What he knew about running a financial institution is a mystery. Why he chose Fort Wayne, which he had previously called the "deadest dullest" city in the Midwest, is even more of a puzzle. The staff consisted of teenaged sons Henry (manager and teller) and Sam (clerk). Curtis was proud of his *first class bank*" but was forced to close its doors after only eight months. Sam told Belinda that the number of customers was "not suffi-cient to keep one man busy," but he did not venture a guess as to why. The bank's failure caused Curtis "considerable vexation." How much he lost in this foray into the world of high finance is not recorded. Young Henry blamed himself for the bank's fail-ure, but his father would have none of that. "Do not be disheart-ened," he thundered to his eldest son. "Stand up to your duty and let the storm rage."[5]

Speculation could be risky in other ways, as Curtis discov-ered when one of his Nebraska business partners, William D. Brown, claimed many of the Omaha lots as his own. Legal wran-gling went on for a decade, cost everyone involved a fortune in legal fees and court costs, and eventually reached the Supreme Court. Judges and justices at every level were baffled by the maze of claims and counterclaims; they repeatedly ordered Curtis and Brown to divide the contested property in a mutually agreeable manner, a predictably fractious process that outlasted the Civil War. This experience led Curtis to grumble that the "trouble on the frontier [is] to get men to act fairly," but it did not dampen his enthusiasm for the West. He continued to urge brother Henry to visit. "You have never been on the very verge of settlement and slept out at night among the wolves, Indians and Rattlesnakes," he joked, knowing full well that Henry preferred the comforts of civilization. "I am confident you would enjoy and profit by the trip," he continued, on a more serious note. "I would like it if brother Hosmer could go with us." The trip never materialized, but Hosmer moved to Keokuk in 1858 and purchased a house on High Street within shouting distance of Samuel's residence. The brothers and a nephew named Robert H. Gillmore set up a legal practice ("Curtis, Gillmore, & Curtis") on Main Street. The firm dissolved when the Civil War erupted, but Hosmer remained in Keokuk until his death in 1874.[6]

Land prices rose during the first half of the 1850s. Curtis sold several properties at a substantial profit, including a lot in downtown Keokuk that generated a gain of $800. "I am determined now to sell enough to clear me from *all* debts," Curtis told brother Henry. That did not happen, but Henry probably appreciated the thought. He provided financial advice and assistance to his younger brother for forty years and eventually joined him in several investment partnerships.[7]

Curtis chose this time to add a new dining room and a fourth bedroom to the family home in Keokuk. The timing seems odd because Henry and Sam were about to move out, leaving only Sadie and Carrie at home. The addition was built of the same gray limestone as the original structure and cost $3,000. Curtis grumbled that the contractor was putting the walls up "rather too fast and there is danger that it may be poorly done," but he later acknowledged that the addition was "very nice and the whole house much improved in appearance." He estimated the market value of his enlarged home at between $8,000 and $9,000, a sizable sum in antebellum Iowa.[8]

Curtis did not have a regular income after leaving the Airline Railroad, but he continued to pour cash into various projects. In 1856 the inevitable happened: he ran out of money. "My expenses and advances out west and my building have cramped me prodigiously," he admitted to brother Henry, "but by shifting, selling, and a little borrowing at ten per cent I keep getting along without knowing hardly how." He and Belinda even took in a boarder to earn a few extra dollars. Curtis was quite anxious about his straitened financial condition. "I am hard up for cash and must sell some property soon," he fretted.[9]

Despite a grounding in business going all the way back to his youth in Mansfield, Curtis lacked certain entrepreneurial skills. He achieved success as an engineer and administrator but was unaccountably careless and disorganized when it came to overseeing his own finances. He acknowledged as much to brother Henry: "The eternal shifting about and unsettled condition of my papers, and a natural aversion for details, keep my accounts of matters too much disarranged. I need a carefully arranged system of books which I have several times attempted to get up and keep up, but which I have not yet accomplished." Curtis never seemed to know how much he owed or when payments were due. He often stated that he wanted to "ascertain how my finances are," but shrank from the task of sorting through the piles of deeds, bills, tax notices, bank statements, and legal documents cluttering up his office. Curtis was slipping into a downward spiral largely of his own making when his life took an unexpected turn.[10]

• • •

The proposed admission of California to the Union as a "free state" infuriated proslavery southern Democrats, some of whom threatened to leave the United States and form an independent confederacy if they did not get their way. "The idea of disunion is exceedingly obnoxious to me," Curtis wrote. "The consequences that must follow are deplorable at best." He predicted that within a year or two "civil war will begin [and] insurrections and anarchy will follow until military despotism will rule in this country." After prolonged negotiations, Congress finally approved the so-called Compromise of 1850, which admitted California in return for various concessions to the South. The agreement led to a temporary cessation of overheated rhetoric about secession and civil war, but the uproar left Curtis deeply disturbed.[11]

Curtis was a Whig for most of his life. He supported government aid for economic development and opposed the expansion of slavery into the western territories, though he feared that efforts to restrict that expansion might lead to serious trouble. In the early 1850s the Whig Party dissolved, undone by its inability to offer creative solutions to the pressing issues of the day. The brief calm generated by the Compromise of 1850 soon passed, and angry voices again overwhelmed civil discourse. In 1854 the Democratic-controlled Congress passed the Kansas-Nebraska Act, which opened the Kansas Territory, and by extension all western territories, to slavery. The North erupted in outrage. A new political organization, the Republican Party, emerged amidst the turmoil. Curtis, like many former Whigs, Free Soilers, Know Nothings, and northern Democrats, found the new party congenial. He declared himself a Republican and jumped into local politics.[12]

Curtis was elected mayor of Keokuk in April 1856 with a comfortable majority of 249 votes. The town was a Democratic stronghold and he had not expected to win, which probably explains why he was in Council Bluffs tending to "ferry business" on election day. He barely got back to Keokuk in time for his own inauguration. The Democratic editor of the *Keokuk Daily Post* offered Curtis a lukewarm endorsement: "He will make a good officer, we think, and if he carries out the pledges he made before his nomination, which we believe he will, he will close his term with credit to himself." Those pledges included building a drainage system, improving streets and sidewalks, establishing better railroad connections, and seeking federal support for his longtime pet project, a canal around the Des Moines Rapids. In addition to his mayoral duties, Curtis raised money for the Keokuk Female Academy and, with old friend Hugh Sample, helped found the Young America Fire Company and equip it with pumps, hoses, and axes. His support for infrastructure, improved navigation, female education, and fire protection reflected his experiences in St. Louis and his belief that Keokuk was destined for great things.[13]

Iowa Republicans were impressed and urged Curtis to run for the House of Representatives in the First Congressional District, essentially the southern half of the state. He agreed, largely because of his recent experience with the Airline's ill-fated Pacific railroad bill. If elected to Congress, Curtis would be in a position to promote a future railroad bill. The election was only weeks away. Curtis threw himself into the campaign with more vigor than might have been expected from a man his age. He traveled hundreds of miles and made forty-two speeches—some more than four hours long—walloping audiences with what he described as a "full showing of Republican principles." He condemned the Kansas-Nebraska Act, denounced talk of disunion, and demanded government support for railroads. Democrats had dominated southern Iowa since statehood. Curtis believed they were too entrenched there and elsewhere to be easily overcome. "I have great fear that all our efforts to check the progress of slave power will fail," he confessed to Belinda. "If we are defeated at this election disunion and civil war will *proceed* as it has now *commenced*," a reference to the recent eruption of violence between proslavery and antislavery settlers in nearby Kansas. "This government of ours is likely to be fearfully tested in any event."[14]

A man who saw Curtis at a political rally in Ottumwa described him as "tall, finely though heavily formed, with high forehead, large hazel eyes, decidedly grave face adorned by side whiskers; in demeanor, serious, deliberate, in speech and action, undemonstrative." He added that, while Curtis was "not an imaginative or eloquent man, he was a solid and substantial one." Apparently that was sufficient. On election day in August 1856, Curtis upset the Democratic incumbent, Augustus Hall, 18,065 votes to 17,110 votes, a margin of just under 3 percent. He was the first Republican congressman elected from Iowa.[15]

During the campaign Curtis met the Republican Party presidential candidate, John C. Fremont, nicknamed the "Pathfinder" for his well-publicized expeditions in the West. Fremont was a man of many flaws, but few were evident in 1856. Curtis told brother Henry that Fremont "made a very favourable impression on my mind. I like him better than I expected I would. He is a modest intelligent gentlemanly man even when surrounded with flatterers and enthusiasts." Curtis would encounter Fremont in St. Louis five years later and come away with a very different impression.[16]

Democrat James Buchanan defeated Fremont for the presidency but the Republicans made a respectable showing in Congress, winning 20 of 66 seats in the Senate and 90 of 237 seats in the House of Representatives. Curtis traveled to Washington in January 1857, two months before the beginning of the congressional session, to meet with Republican leaders. He stayed at Willard's Hotel on Pennsylvania Avenue, reputedly the best hostelry in the city. That evening he wrote to sons Henry and Sam, who were back in Keokuk: "I have what they consider a choice room but it is nothing to brag of. This won't suit ma [i.e., Belinda] I know and I must try to do better when she comes on in." Curtis expressed the hope that the entire family would join him in Washington and take advantage of the schools, just as they had done in St. Louis.[17]

At this point in the letter Curtis commenced another lecture on the value of education. His tone and even his words echoed those of his elder brothers decades earlier. "Recollect it is by your own efforts *alone* [that] you can hereafter expect to succeed in scientific and other pursuits," he advised his sons. "Dilligence is necessary to gain the position you must try to occupy among your peers." Curtis urged Henry to avoid frivolity and asked how his studies were progressing, evidence that Henry was taking lessons of some sort. "Your evenings must be devoted to study at home," he intoned. Curtis reminded both boys that they did not want to be mistaken for illiterate bumpkins when they encountered "eastern society." Perhaps for that reason Henry and Sam elected to remain in Iowa. Curtis disliked the idea of his sons, now twenty and nineteen years old respectively, idling away their time in Keokuk, so he sent them to Council Bluffs to look after the family's interests and get a feel for business. The decision changed all their lives.[18]

Belinda and the girls joined Curtis in Washington in March 1857. The family rented rooms at the Washington House, a popular hostelry for married members of Congress. Curtis described the place as a "very good clean cheap hotel." Sadie, now fifteen, attended a boarding school in Georgetown while Belinda watched over Carrie, age two. As a freshman member of the House, Curtis received about four thousand dollars per year: three thousand in salary and another thousand or so in "mileage" to cover travel expenses. This was more than he had earned in St. Louis but less than he had received from the Airline Railroad. Fortunately, antebellum Washington was an inexpensive place to live in. Curtis estimated that room, board, tuition (for Sadie), and incidentals came to roughly $1,500 per year. "I am glad I have a certain income for the next two years," he told brother Henry. To sons Henry and Sam he announced, "I am saving a good share of my pay which is helping to pay taxes, pay off your little debts, and [pay back] some of the money I had to borrow as means to get away from Keokuk." The Curtis business empire was extensive but seems not to have generated a significant cash flow.[19]

The Thirty-Fifth Congress began in March 1857. "I am gradually acquiring a knowledge of men and things, and in due time expect to make some headway," Curtis wrote. He requested and received a seat on the Committee on Military Affairs. The spring session was unproductive. Curtis spent much of his time in the House chamber chatting with fellow members, reading newspapers, and keeping up with his correspondence. On weekends, when Sadie was home from school, the family explored the city and its environs. Curtis and Carrie particularly enjoyed the botanical garden at the foot of Capitol Hill. They also visited Mount Vernon and the Great Falls of the Potomac.[20]

Curtis and family escaped from Washington's heat and humidity during the 1857 summer recess. After a brief stop in Keokuk they continued to Council Bluffs by steamboat to see how Henry and Sam were getting along. Curtis was surprised to discover that the boys had established storefront offices in both Council Bluffs and Omaha, each adorned with a large sign that proclaimed "Office of Curtis Brothers: Surveyors and Land Agents." The harsh weather had not been kind to the real estate business. "The cold winter has driven everybody to Kansas," Sam stated, "and there has been, as yet, but very little emigration in this direction." Curtis observed that business was down throughout the region. Even the ferry company was staying afloat only by hauling bulk freight up and down the wide Missouri. He had no way of knowing that the situation was about to get much worse.[21]

Omaha boasted several respectable hotels, but Curtis thought an Iowa congressman ought to patronize Iowa businesses, so the family stayed in a suite of rooms at the Pacific House in nearby Council Bluffs. One fine day he and Belinda rented a carriage and drove along the rolling bluffs west of the Missouri River. The weather was perfect and the sweeping vistas of the Great Plains were stunning. Curtis described the trip as "one of the most charming of the many charming drives that may be found around this city." He began to think seriously about moving to the Missouri Valley.[22]

The bottom dropped out of the faltering economy in August, when several major banks failed and triggered a brutal downturn. The Panic of 1857, the name given to the crash and ensuing depression, lasted for years. Businesses closed their doors, westward migration slowed to a trickle, thousands were thrown out of work, and ready money all but disappeared. When Curtis, Belinda, and the girls got back to Keokuk, they found letters from Henry and Sam reporting that commerce in Omaha and Council Bluffs had come to a standstill. They could not sell property because people could not obtain loans from banks with empty vaults. "Hard times are becoming awful hard and I will have to let taxes and many other matters hang over," Curtis informed his sons. "At present we can hardly expect to make cash sales and we will have to defer payments that ought to be met." Curtis told brother Henry that the boys "are in tribulation, but I hope to help them a little in the way of paying some of their expenses." He asked Henry to provide moral support: "In your letters be careful to give them encouragement against the fears they naturally entertain."[23]

Curtis bombarded Henry and Sam with all the practical advice he could muster: "You must both learn in the school of adversity I suppose, and we have it now all of us in awful perfection." He urged them to keep expenses down and maintain a positive outlook: "Do not spend a *dime* foolishly. Do not for a moment despond. Keep your offices up and open. Attend to small matters." Once again, echoes of long-ago admonitions from Hosmer, Henry, and even Robert McComb, the Mansfield merchant, are discernible. The only thing missing was a reminder to dust the shelves.[24]

While Henry looked after the moribund real estate business and the struggling ferry company, Sam put his surveying skills to good use. He was hired to lay out a new town on the Overland Trail about 180 miles west of Omaha. The place was named Kearney, after a nearby military post. Sam, not yet twenty years old, had the time of his life. He mingled with soldiers and westbound travelers, talked with survivors of a Cheyenne ambush, endured a grasshopper swarm, and hunted bison on the Great Plains. He returned to Omaha in mid-September "looking as near like a Pawnee Indian as a white man very well could," according to his brother. Sam's experience establishing a new town in the middle of nowhere would have unexpected consequences.[25]

Back in Keokuk, Curtis, Belinda, and the girls prepared to return to Washington. "It is hard to leave our pleasant house where we are so nicely fixed," Curtis told Henry and Sam, "but home is not the only place for us." Before Curtis could get away, however, Republican leaders in Iowa prevailed upon him to "stump the state" on behalf of candidates for local and state offices. Political tensions and economic fears were running high; Curtis was surprised at the size of the rallies he addressed. "People turn out in crowds to hear me," he reported to brother Henry. He was becoming a person of consequence in Iowa politics.[26]

Curtis resumed his duties in the House of Representatives in November 1857. He met with Secretary of War John B. Floyd and proposed that Council Bluffs, not Fort Leavenworth in Kansas, be made the principal supply depot for army posts along the Overland Trail. Curtis thought he made a strong case, but Floyd was unmoved. A short time later, Curtis and his colleagues in the House rejected the Lecompton Constitution, a fraudulent document supported by southern Democrats that would have established slavery in the proposed state of Kansas. Not long afterward, Curtis denounced efforts by those same southern Democrats to seize potential railroad routes across Central America. He argued that building railroads over impassable terrain in foreign countries, even if eventually completed at prohibitive cost, would benefit only southern seaports such as New Orleans and Mobile. He insisted it would be far better to construct a railroad to the Pacific alongside the Overland Trail, a "central route" that lay entirely within the boundaries of the United States and was already secured by the army. Such a railroad would benefit the entire country, not just one section. Curtis also vigorously supported a bill granting pensions to veterans of the War of 1812. He was proud of his remarks on railroads and pensions and had them extracted from the *Congressional Record* and published in pamphlet form.[27]

Life in Washington had its moments, even for a financially strapped freshman member of the House. One evening in February 1858 Curtis and Belinda braved the weather to attend a fancy dress ball. "Your ma was dressed in her rich crimson velvet dress, with low neck, plumes in her hair and short sleeves," Curtis informed Henry and Sam. "She looked very pretty for a woman of her years and seemed to delight Carrie who [stayed] up to see her dress." Another happy moment came when Curtis learned that his eldest son was studying law. With the economy in the doldrums, Henry had plenty of time to talk with lawyers, attend court sessions, and study law books. Curtis was also pleased to learn that brother Henry, upon hearing the news, wrote his namesake nephew an encouraging letter.[28]

Belinda and the girls left Washington in May to escape the heat. Curtis remained until the official recess began in June then hurried back to Iowa. The 1858 congressional elections were only weeks away and he wanted to win a second term in Congress. "I am exceedingly anxious to be returned [to the House] as it will help me in pecuniary matters very sensibly," he informed brother Henry. "The compensation of a member is a great consideration [in] these hard times." A regular income of $4,000 a year was nothing to sniff at.[29]

• • •

The contest in Iowa's First Congressional District was another close-run affair. As before, Curtis canvassed the southern half of the state with all the energy he could muster. He benefited from being an incumbent, but the Democrats campaigned furiously on behalf of their candidate, Henry H. Trimble. The moribund economy was the principal issue. Curtis tirelessly called for the federal government to promote economic development. He emphasized his engineering background, his lifelong involvement in internal improvements, and his vision of a railroad running from Iowa to the Pacific coast. The Republican-controlled legislature helped by gerrymandering the First District in his favor. Curtis prevailed 23,529 to 22,929 votes, a margin of slightly more than 1 percent.[30]

The Republican Party made major gains in both the Senate and the House and dominated the Thirty-Sixth Congress. Encouraged by this development, Curtis sought support for a transcontinental railroad when the new Congress opened for business in March 1859. He lobbied his colleagues on and off the House floor and began the tedious process of drafting an acceptable proposal. Sectional tension was a constant distraction, but Curtis persevered. It would be nearly a year, however, before he felt the time was right to submit an actual bill.[31]

Curtis and family returned to the Washington House. Sadie enrolled in a different school as a day student but there were no other significant changes in their domestic arrangements. The year passed uneventfully and, when the 1859 summer recess arrived, the family again headed west to the Pacific House in Council Bluffs. The local economy was experiencing a modest revival. Curtis told brother Henry that "Omaha is a gay place and Henry and Sadie are delighted with the society there." Belinda was unwell and spent much of her time resting at the hotel. Curtis wrote that "her health is delicate and I fear she will continue feeble," but after a few weeks Belinda felt well enough to request another carriage trip out on the Great Plains.[32]

Sam was absent. The previous fall he had set out to seek his fortune in the Rocky Mountains, lured by news of a gold strike in the Colorado Territory. Sam informed his father that the "gold is there in paying quantities, but the work is so hard few are willing to engage in the toil of digging." He somehow talked his way onto the board of directors of the Denver City Town Company and put his surveying skills to work. He laid out the original 320-acre plat of the future metropolis and built one of the first houses (a log hut) on the site. Within a few months Sam became company treasurer, opened a clothing store, and acquired a gold mine. The following year Curtis informed Belinda, "Sam wants the Post Office at Denver and I am going to try to get it for him." In 1861 Sam was named Denver's first postmaster.[33]

Back in Nebraska, trouble erupted between settlers and Pawnee Indians midway through the 1859 Curtis family vacation. The so-called Pawnee War lasted only a month and cost few lives, but it caused considerable excitement. When settlers complained of Indian depredations, John M. Thayer, commander of the Nebraska Territorial Militia, led a force of 194 men to chastise the Natives and recover stolen property, mostly cattle. Curtis offered to accompany the "Pawnee Expedition" and assist in any way he could. Thayer was happy to gain the services of an experienced officer. "I was very glad to receive him," Thayer said later, "because I knew he had a military education, was really a military man." Thayer appointed Curtis acting inspector general with the temporary rank of lieutenant colonel. The Nebraskans (and one Iowan) tracked down the Pawnees and compelled them to surrender seven miscreants, only one of whom survived the journey back to Omaha. Curtis was fascinated by his first encounter with "wild" Indians. He returned to Council Bluffs dirty, scruffy, sunburned, and happy. Curtis may have been the only sitting member of Congress to participate in a military operation against "hostile" Indians on the Great Plains.[34]

Curtis and Sadie returned to Washington that fall. Father and daughter took up residence at Mrs. Joy's Boarding House on Pennsylvania Avenue and Eighth Street. "We have new rooms and better fare than we had at the Washington House and for about the same rates," Curtis explained. Sadie enrolled as a boarder at the Washington Female Institute near the White House, her third school in three years. "I regret my inability to have my boys also at school, but it is impossible," Curtis confessed. "My affairs are so extended, I almost fear an entire failure," that is, bankruptcy. Curtis put such gloomy thoughts aside when Belinda and Carrie arrived after Thanksgiving. They had remained in Keokuk to allow Belinda to recover her health. Both seemed "fair and fresh" after the long trip, but there was something different about Belinda. "My wife being forty-eight years of age is just learning to wear glasses," Curtis informed his journal.[35]

The journal was a recent acquisition. Curtis purchased the volume at the beginning of December and penned a brief statement on the first page: "Being now in public positions when stirring events are daily occuring, I have at some expense procured this very substantial volume in which I desire to transmit to my friends and posterity some of the passing events of the hour." For the remainder of his time in Congress and part of his military service in the Civil War, Curtis maintained a detailed record of his experiences. He asked his wife to keep his letters in a safe place because he thought they, like the journal, might be of interest to future generations. He seems not to have known that Belinda and brother Henry had preserved his correspondence since his West Point days and continued to do so until his death.[36]

John Brown's seizure of the United States Armory and Arsenal at Harpers Ferry, Virginia, in October 1859 was a tremendous shock. Brown hoped to incite a servile insurrection and to use the weapons in the arsenal to arm the slaves. The half-baked plan failed; most of the conspirators were killed or captured and later executed. The entire country condemned Brown in the immediate aftermath of the raid, but as time passed some in the North came to view him as a martyr to the cause of human freedom. Southerners were incensed by this shift in attitude. Curtis noticed that slave-state congressmen began to view "every body and every thing coming from the North as incendiary" and to speak openly of secession. "Some talk freely and frankly of disunion," he told brother Henry. "I fear the secession movement will give us much trouble."[37]

Debate in the House was notably acrimonious in the months following Harpers Ferry. Curtis rarely made speeches, but he responded sharply to remarks he considered offensive or inaccurate, and southern Democrats provided him with plenty of material. "I entered with considerable zeal in the debate," was how he described his behavior on one occasion. Curtis was pleased to see his name mentioned favorably in Horace Greeley's *New York Tribune*, the most influential newspaper in the country. The paper reported that Curtis "especially distinguished himself by his brief and pointed replies" to the rants of southern demagogues. Winter became spring and spring became summer, but little was accomplished in the halls of Congress. "We did no good, and made no progress," was how Curtis summed up the session.[38]

On February 3, 1860, Curtis paused to consider his life. It was his fifty-fifth birthday, but he pretended not to remember his exact age "because I do not care to keep a note of approaching dissolution. Old age is dreaded, because I do not feel ready for it." Recalling his father's long, slow decline, he added, "I dread the days of decrepitude." He could not know that he would be spared that indignity.[39]

• • •

In 1860 Curtis ran for a third term against a Democratic candidate named Chester C. Cole. Public opinion in Iowa had shifted toward the Republicans and Curtis felt confident of success. "I think I shall beat him," he told brother Henry, "but the matter is a little doubtful." The campaign was another grueling test of endurance. Curtis and Cole agreed to campaign together, as Abraham Lincoln and Stephen Douglas had done in Illinois two years earlier. The candidates visited all thirty-nine counties in the First Congressional District and gave sixty to eighty speeches apiece. "We canvassed from three to six hours a day and made many side speeches to Wide Awakes and other visitations by day and night," wrote Curtis. Political interest in Iowa was at an all-time high: "Audiences are large and excited, and it seems to one travelling as I do, that the people have nothing else to do but attend to political matters." In person and in a widely distributed sixteen-page pamphlet, Curtis presented himself as a defender of the Union, an opponent of slavery in the territories, and a supporter of agricultural and mechanical colleges, a homestead program, and a transcontinental railroad. He won by 3,696 votes, a margin of nearly 6 percent. "I have evidently a stronger hold of the affections of the people than I ever hoped to secure," he observed.[40]

The 1860 election elevated Abraham Lincoln to the presidency and gave the Republicans an effective majority in the Thirty-Seventh Congress. It also gave southern Democrats the excuse they needed to dissolve the union of the states. Sitting in the House chamber near the end of 1860, Curtis scribbled letters to Belinda describing the "exciting scenes and gloomy prospects" of a national government in the process of disintegrating. "The flag of the *Union* still floats over the Capitol and the House is apparently tranquil," he wrote, "but South Carolina and Mississippi members assure me that the work of Secession must and will be carried out. All do not perceive as I do that in going out they will drag other states with them. I look upon it as the greatest calamity that could befall the world to destroy the best government ever devised by man. Still I am perfectly calm as I cannot avert the crisis." To brother Henry he was less philosophical. "I have talked calmly with the fire eaters," he wrote. "They consider the matter *is done*."[41]

South Carolina declared its independence on December 20, 1860, and demanded the surrender of Fort Moultrie, one of several federal fortifications protecting Charleston Harbor and the only one occupied by the army. With outgoing President Buchanan paralyzed by indecision, Major Robert Anderson took matters into his own hands. He relocated his small garrison to Fort Sumter, a more defensible bastion in the middle of the harbor. Curtis was impressed by the bold move. "The only ray of light I have seen is the *coup de main* of Major Anderson," he informed Belinda. "That has animated a spark of loyalty and I hope it may kindle to a flame." As the stalemate in Charleston Harbor dragged on, six more slave states seceded and, with South Carolina, formed the Confederate States of America. Eight other slave states remained in the Union—for the moment.[42]

In the midst of this unfolding crisis, Curtis learned that son Henry had been admitted to the Nebraska bar and won his first case. He was "much delighted and surprised" at the news and offered to find enough money to provide Henry with an office. "We must encourage him now as much as we can to favor the law as a regular profession," Curtis told Belinda. The financial turmoil Curtis experienced in the 1850s had convinced him that "lawyering" was a more dependable line of work than engineering or business.[43]

Curtis had little time to celebrate Henry's achievement. In December the House established the Committee of Thirty-Three (one representative from each state) to discuss the "present condition of national affairs" and propose a solution. Curtis, the Iowa representative, thought the committee was a waste of time but dutifully sat through hours of alternatively boring and inflammatory speeches. The arrogance and intransigence of the southern representatives left him more determined than ever to resist secession. When brother Henry opined that any attempt to preserve the Union by force was doomed to failure, Curtis disagreed. "I would try force," he replied. "The Union should be maintained, at the hazard of much sacrifice." In the privacy of his journal he wrote, "I still believe force is the only remedy. It is a desperate prescription . . . but the disease is desperate, and nothing but desperate remedies will avail."[44]

Nine months earlier, in March 1860, Curtis had introduced his bill for the construction of a transcontinental railroad along the "central route," the well-traveled Overland Trail corridor. The House created a Select Committee on the Pacific Railroad to consider the matter and appointed Curtis chairman. As expected, southern Democrats raised objections and amended the bill to include a needless "southern route." After much debate, the committee voted 10 to 6 in favor of the amended bill. Curtis was less than thrilled by the change but in the spirit of compromise he made a speech to the full House, "under the disagreeable effects of hoarseness," urging passage of the amended bill. "I illustrated my argument by using a large map which was no doubt the strongest part of the argument," he remarked. After a lengthy hiatus caused by the summer recess and the presidential and congressional elections, the House voted 95 to 74 in favor of the bill in December 1860. Curtis complained that the railroad bill "cost me a great deal of toil," but he noted proudly that it was the "first ever" passed by the House. The Airline bill had not even made it out of committee.[45]

The Pacific railroad bill then went to the Senate, where forty-five amendments were added, including one that provided for a "northern route," even though no suitable route near the border with Canada had yet been found. The Senate finally passed the bloated bill 37–14 at the end of January 1861 and returned it to the House for reconciliation. Curtis wondered whether he should continue to promote a bill "so loaded down with useless amendments," but the decision was taken out of his hands. The bill was sidetracked by more urgent legislation dealing with military appropriations, and by a growing feeling among Republicans that "we had better not at this time embark in such a measure." Curtis consoled himself with the thought that recent events "have been enough to kill any bill." He had nearly succeeded on his first attempt; he vowed to try again at the next opportunity. A modified version of his railroad bill would, in fact, pass both houses of Congress the very next year, but he would not be there to enjoy the moment.[46]

Meanwhile, events proceeded apace. The embryonic Confederate government in Montgomery, Alabama, assumed control of the military forces at Charleston and fired upon an unarmed commercial vessel, the *Star of the West*, when it attempted to enter the harbor and deliver stores to Fort Sumter. The incident led Curtis to remark that the "future is about as dark as it can be." He attended Lincoln's inauguration and listened carefully to the new president's address, which he pronounced "excellent." He shared Lincoln's hope that the northern tier of slave states could be kept in the Union, and "we may afterwards come down on secession and destroy the monster." The only constant during these turbulent events was Curtis's pinched financial situation. "My creditors are after me with a sharp stick," he told brother Henry. "If they pursue me much longer I think of going out to Pikes Peak."[47]

Not long after the inauguration, Curtis and Brigadier General John Wool, his old friend from the Mexican War, called on Lincoln in the White House to discuss military matters. They found the president "overwhelmed with visitors and oppressed with care," so they left without adding to his burden. Curtis then made a quick trip to Iowa to see Belinda and Carrie and to deal with business matters. Sadie remained with friends in Washington in order to continue at school. Curtis was still in Keokuk when Confederate artillery bombarded Fort Sumter on April 12, 1861. The garrison surrendered the following day. Lincoln called on the loyal states for seventy-five thousand troops to suppress a rebellion. Civil war had come at last.[48]

5

GENERAL

CURTIS HURRIED BACK TO WASHINGTON. AT EVERY STOP he heard rumors that secessionists were gathering to capture the national capital. He was not alarmed, because he knew from experience that an organized military force could not be conjured into existence overnight. He also had "great confidence" that Major General Winfield Scott, still general in chief of the army at the age of seventy-five, would "provide against any pending danger." So when Curtis reached Philadelphia on April 20, he was surprised to learn that the train could go no farther. Secessionists had torn up the track in Maryland and temporarily severed rail connections between Washington and the northern states.[1]

While Curtis was standing on the station platform contemplating his next move, a train arrived, carrying the Seventh New York Militia. The "silk stocking regiment," so called because of the social standing of its members, was en route to Washington to help defend the city. Curtis introduced himself to Colonel Marshall Lefferts and offered his services. Lefferts accepted, glad to have an experienced officer at his side as his command prepared to enter hostile territory. After a brief council of war, which included Curtis, Lefferts decided not to march directly south to Washington but to sail down Chesapeake Bay to Annapolis and approach the capital from the opposite direction. The regiment proceeded to the Philadelphia waterfront, boarded the steamer *Boston*, and reached Maryland's quaint colonial capital on April 22. The bay must have been unusually calm, because Curtis did not complain of seasickness. At Annapolis the New Yorkers met another steamer carrying the Eighth Massachusetts Militia, led by Colonel Benjamin F. Butler.[2]

The Federals occupied Annapolis and camped on the grounds of the United States Naval Academy. Curtis stayed at the "eligant home" of the academy superintendent. He wrote to Sadie, who was staying with friends in Washington, that he was only fifty miles away with "about two thousand of the best troops I ever saw," and assured her that "so many troops are coming I think there will be no possibility of a fight in Washington." He encouraged her to ignore alarmist talk: "I hope you are perfectly cool. You are a soldier's daughter and ought to be brave also." He explained, "I am a kind of high private in the New York Seventh doing all sorts of duty and becoming well acquainted with things." He added that he was "in good health but [as] rough as I was when I came home from the Pawnee War." Curtis also wrote to Belinda and brought her up to date. He mentioned that he met several times a day with Lefferts and Butler, "being I suppose you may say on the staff of each."[3]

Butler devoted several pages of his postwar memoirs to his exploits in Annapolis. He exaggerated his own importance and portrayed his opposite number in the Seventh New York Militia as weak, indecisive, and in thrall to a certain shadowy character. "The trouble with Lefferts," Butler wrote three decades later, "appeared to be that he had picked up somewhere a man who had once been at West Point, to accompany and cosset him in his command. Lefferts never called upon me without him, and he at times was somewhat officious, and not always too courteous." Butler continued in that vein for some time without mentioning Curtis by name. Curtis, by contrast, had little to say about Butler and referred to him only in passing.[4]

The relief column entered Washington on April 25, after a tense, two-day march from Annapolis. Curtis bid farewell to the Seventh New York Militia, but not before he was made an honorary member of the regiment. He reunited with Sadie, then hurried to see the secretary of war, the secretary of the navy, and the heads of various military bureaus. When Curtis informed the assistant commissary general that as many as fifty thousand volunteers and militiamen were en route to the capital, that elderly bureaucrat exclaimed: "Great God, Curtis! What are you going to do with such an army here?" Curtis then visited Scott. Despite the passage of fourteen years, the general in chief remembered the former colonel of the Third Ohio and welcomed him warmly. Curtis told Scott of his adventures with the Seventh New York Militia and assured him that thousands of additional troops were on their way to Washington by land and sea. Unlike the assistant commissary general, Scott was relieved at the news and impressed with Curtis's energy and initiative. He urged him to obtain an officer's commission from Iowa as soon as possible and, in the meantime, to use his position on the House military affairs committee to support several pending army reform bills.[5]

All the while, the United States continued to unravel. Four additional slave states—Virginia, North Carolina, Tennessee, and Arkansas—responded to Lincoln's call for volunteers by seceding and joining the Confederacy, bringing the number of rebellious states to eleven. The Confederate government relocated its capital to Richmond, one hundred miles south of Washington. The four remaining slave states—Delaware, Maryland, Kentucky, and Missouri—waffled but remained in the Union for the time being. Of the four, Missouri seemed the least steady and the most likely to cause trouble.

Curtis escorted Sadie back to Iowa, where Governor Samuel J. Kirkwood, a fellow Republican, offered him command of the First Iowa Volunteer Infantry, a ninety-day regiment. Curtis declined. He believed it was more important to focus on his duties in the House of Representatives, "where my services are considered of great importance to the army." Then the War Department, at Scott's urging, appointed Curtis mustering officer for Iowa, with authority to enroll, equip, provision, and otherwise prepare volunteers for military service. Curtis accepted the appointment on the condition that he could return to Washington for the special session of Congress scheduled to begin on July 4. When Kirkwood learned of this development, he promptly put Curtis in charge of the assembly point for Iowa volunteers at Keokuk, with the understanding that he could leave when duty called elsewhere. Curtis could not refuse. The two jobs—one federal, one state—were so similar he could do both at the same time.[6]

The War Department initially called on Iowa for three infantry regiments. Curtis began the familiar process of turning civilians into soldiers. It was Ohio all over again, except that he went home to Belinda and the girls every night. On June 2, with Kirkwood's encouragement, the officers of the Second Iowa Volunteer Infantry, the state's first three-year regiment, elected Curtis as their commanding officer. After some hesitation he accepted the position, with the familiar caveat that his congressional responsibilities took precedence.[7]

Curtis informed the War Department a few weeks later that Iowa's three regiments were "earnestly and anxiously awaiting complete equipment." He disparaged the antiquated flintlocks he had received and asked for rifled muskets. He noted that his own regiment, the Second Iowa, was "already pretty well advanced in company and battalion drill" and would be ready for service in the near future. The other two regiments were not far behind. He suggested that standard rations be supplemented with local foodstuffs, given the "abundance of wholesome and cheap food found in the Mississippi Valley." He believed this would save money and relieve the overburdened transportation system.[8]

Suddenly the war intruded. Brigadier General Nathaniel Lyon was commanding officer of the sprawling Department of the West, headquartered in St. Louis. Lyon faced a difficult situation. Missouri was a slave state, though only a small percentage of its citizens owned slaves or favored secession. Most Missourians were content to remain in the Union, but a militant secessionist minority led by Governor Claiborne Jackson was determined to have its way. Jackson enrolled his followers in a new secessionist militia, the Missouri State Guard, and prepared to seize control of the state. Lyon held St. Louis with a small force of regular soldiers and the support of the German immigrant population, but he needed help if he was to prevent Jackson from dragging Missouri into the Confederacy.[9]

Curtis advised Lyon that the three regiments at Keokuk, especially the Second Iowa, were coming along nicely: "I am drilling my regiment very hard, and will soon have it in excellent condition as the material cannot be beat." He invited Lyon to visit: "Come up and review us. You will find a hearty welcome, and it will give encouragement to my efforts in advancing organization discipline and drill." In a more serious tone Curtis assured Lyon, "I am keeping myself advised of [secessionist] movements" in northern Missouri; "In case of emergency command me and I will respond promptly."[10]

Lyon did just that. On June 12 he telegraphed Curtis that a "terrible" insurgency was underway in Missouri. Negotiations between Lyon and Jackson had broken down and both sides were preparing for immediate hostilities. Lyon intended to go on the offensive, but he did not have enough manpower to secure the northern part of the state, where bands of secessionists reportedly were up in arms. "I want you to come at once," Lyon told Curtis, "with all the force you can command, to Hannibal, Missouri, and move over the [rail]road from there to St. Joseph and put down the traitors everywhere on both sides of the road."[11]

Curtis responded with alacrity. Lyon's telegram reached Keokuk around one o'clock on the morning of June 13. Four hours later the First and Second Iowa were on their way "Dixieward." The Iowans crowded aboard a pair of steamboats and sped down the Mississippi River to Hannibal, fifty-five miles to the south, where they joined forces with a battalion of the Sixteenth Illinois. The Federals commandeered the rolling stock of the Hannibal and St. Joseph Railroad and rattled west. Detachments of the First Iowa and Sixteenth Illinois occupied towns and other important points along the line, but the Second Iowa stayed aboard and reached St. Joseph early on June 15. "We have taken all sorts of arms flags and many prisoners," Curtis told Belinda. The Federals also killed three rebels in arms and prevented a party of arsonists from burning a railroad trestle. Curtis selected a campsite for his regiment near the Missouri River, "very much as I was first located on the Rio Grande near Mattamoras in the summer of 1846." That night he wrote to Belinda and asked her to fill out the life insurance form on his desk and to request additional coverage to include death from acts of war. He felt the 5 percent surcharge would be money well spent: "If that be arranged for your benefit I shall feel a little easier."[12]

The next day Curtis informed the citizens of St. Joseph that he had come to suppress rebels engaged in a "foolish and wicked assault on the Government and laws that protect them." He had no desire to disturb "peaceable law abiding citizens." Indeed, he wanted only to protect them from "insult, anarchy and oppression." He urged everyone to remain calm and return to their everyday pursuits. When it became clear that the Federals were not going to unleash a reign of terror, life in the town returned to normal.[13]

The dash to St. Joseph was an unusually bold undertaking at this early stage of the Civil War. The combined use of the telegraph, steamboats, and the railroad to rush thousands of men and their equipment hundreds of miles in little more than two days, and to do it in a part of the country only one generation removed from the frontier, demonstrated the impact of the Industrial Revolution on warfare. It also revealed Curtis to be an active and enterprising officer who was not averse to taking risks. In less than fifty-six hours he established control over a swath of northern Missouri with the only railroad between the Mississippi and Missouri Rivers. His success allowed Lyon to concentrate on the rebels in the central and southern parts of the state.

Curtis returned to Keokuk a few days later. He wrote to Lieutenant Colonel James M. Tuttle, commanding the Second Iowa in his absence, to say that he was about to depart for Washington. Curtis remembered the hazards of occupation duty in Mexico and urged Tuttle to keep the regiment well in hand. "Above all things try to keep up the discipline of the men," he wrote. "There is great danger discipline will be relaxed and our men become demoralized. Do all you can to counteract this." He wrapped up military matters in Keokuk as best he could, said goodbye to his family, and set out for the national capital. He never resumed command of the Second Iowa.[14]

Upon returning to Washington in early July, Curtis took his familiar seat in the House of Representatives. "I am doing double duty playing Congressman and Soldier," he told brother Henry. He worked long hours pushing Scott's reform bills through the military affairs committee. Two weeks after his arrival the hodge-podge of Union forces in Washington, the future Army of the Potomac, advanced into northern Virginia and attacked a large body of Confederates near a stream called Bull Run. The Battle of First Manassas, fought on July 21, 1861, was the first large-scale engagement of the Civil War. The Federals gained ground at first but were brought to a halt by Confederate counterattacks and their own disorganization. When they fell back late in the day, discipline broke down and the withdrawal degenerated into a rout.[15]

Curtis followed the army to Manassas. He missed the battle but not the aftermath. "I got there in time to see the foolish flight and try to check it," he told brother Henry. "It was a farce after a tragedy. There was no earthly need of the retreat and I felt it then just as terribly as I do now for I knew the enemy was not able after being sorely pressed all day to pursue us even if we were repulsed." Politicians and newspaper publishers had erred in calling on inexperienced soldiers to make an immediate march on Richmond. "I shall profit by it," Curtis wrote. "I shall never push my command into battle till I am ready according to scientific principles." Always a stickler for discipline and drill, Curtis was more convinced than ever that preparation was the key to military success.[16]

Shortly after the Manassas debacle, President Lincoln acted on the recommendation of the War Department and appointed Curtis a brigadier general of U.S. Volunteers, with his commission dated May 17, 1861. The appointment required Curtis to give up his seat in the House of Representatives, which he did at the end of July. Had he been satisfied with an Iowa colonelcy he could have remained in Congress and drawn two paychecks, $3,000 per year from Iowa and about $4,000 from the United States. A brigadier general's pay was $3,800, which, he pointed out to brother Henry, was "not any better than a Congressman's pay and mileage" and the duty was "much harder and more exciting and perilous." In brief, Curtis's promotion cost him money. "I sacrifice $3000 a year for the rank of Brigadier," he explained. "But to refuse the military appointment would never do." Curtis was ordered to St. Louis, as he hoped and expected: "I am much needed with my friends and comrades in arms in Missouri and I expect very soon to leave Congress for the tented field."[17]

Scott invited Curtis to dinner at his home on July 26 to discuss the military situation in the West. The elderly general could not rise from his chair without assistance, but Curtis noted that "his head seems to be as sound as it was when I saw him in Mexico." The two men would not meet again. Three days after the dinner, Curtis departed for St. Louis. "I am called and must go," he told Belinda.[18]

Curtis allowed himself a moment of introspection before leaving for the West: "So I must follow my destiny, and as in all my eventful life, trust that Providence opens the way for me to follow, and sustains me in the trials and toils that attend me in my journey of life." Then he was off.[19]

• • •

Curtis reached St. Louis on August 4. The next day he called on the new commander of the Department of the West, Major General John C. Fremont, the 1856 Republican presidential candidate. The meeting left Curtis uneasy. Fremont seemed unsure of himself and overwhelmed by responsibilities. "The General said he was glad to see me and told me all his difficulties," Curtis wrote Belinda. "The General seemed excited and perplexed, and I confess things look a little squally." Fremont put Curtis in charge of Jefferson Barracks, an antebellum army post eight miles south of St. Louis. His orders were to "direct the drill and discipline" of volunteer regiments and prepare them for active service. It was a task Curtis was quite familiar with.[20]

Curtis assumed command of Jefferson Barracks on August 12 and inspected his charges. "Jack Falstaff's regiment was a dress parade compared to my command," he moaned. "Some have guns but none have uniforms, and many are destitute of shoes. They lay around loose on the hillsides, without tents or covering." He got to work, whipping the men into shape and finding them uniforms, equipment, tents, and arms. Curtis wanted to have his family "in some convenient place as near me as safety and comfort and economy may allow," but the spartan quarters at the post were not inviting and there was no suitable civilian housing in the vicinity. He advised Belinda to stay in Keokuk for the time being.[21]

Fremont, meanwhile, rushed construction of a much larger training facility north of the city. Benton Barracks was one of his few undisputed successes. The spacious post covered 150 acres. It consisted of a rectangular parade ground enclosed by rows of whitewashed barracks, kitchens, latrines, warehouses, and stables laid out in regular order. Fresh water from nearby springs was piped directly into the buildings. With room for eight thousand troops, all of them "drilling and arming to move forward," Benton Barracks was the largest military base west of the Mississippi River.[22]

Curtis transferred his command to Benton Barracks on September 7. He was pleased with the change, not least because of the marked improvement in his living conditions. "My command here is decidedly conspicuous and elegant," he informed brother Henry. "I have a large showy house with porches all around it situated centrally in a vast parade ground." Curtis expected to be at his new post for some time. He urged Belinda to rent their Keokuk house to a "choise tenant" and join him as soon as possible: "I will want you and Sadie to help me with your taste in keeping the household affairs all snug." Curtis realized he was dumping a great deal of responsibility on his wife's shoulders: "All this will give you much care and trouble I fear but we are in for the war and must suit ourselves to the occasion."[23]

By October most of the Curtis family was living in the "large showy house" in the center of Benton Barracks. Belinda, assisted by Sadie and Carrie, supervised the household staff "in her quiet way" and looked after the "crowds of visitors with great ease to herself and satisfaction to others." Young Henry, now a newly minted captain, served as an assistant quartermaster on his father's staff, where his managerial skills proved invaluable. Curtis thought his eldest son made a "fine looking soldier." The only absentee was Sam, who had gone to Fort Laramie at the request of the Colorado territorial governor to obtain weapons for the Denver militia. He, too, soon wore a uniform as major of a Colorado cavalry regiment.[24]

Fremont loved military display, insisting that even routine activities be "done up on a grand scale." Curtis complied but felt ridiculous, because he was accompanied by a retinue of overdressed aides and bodyguards whenever he stepped out of doors. He complained to brother Henry, "I have more of 'the pomp and circumstance of war' than any other General"—except, of course, Fremont. In all other matters, Fremont allowed his principal subordinate a free hand. Curtis wrote that he had "everything to do with the organization of the parades and drills and school which is now pretty well established." He thought Benton Barracks was the "most elegant Camp of Instruction in this country and under the best state of discipline," and he probably was right.[25]

These events took place against a background of intensifying military activity in Missouri. Despite Fremont's nominal assumption of authority in St. Louis, Lyon retained operational command of most of the Union troops in the field. His ambitious campaign to crush rebellion in a single stroke had gotten off to a promising start. The Army of the West, as Lyon styled his command, streamed out of St. Louis on rivers and rails and overran a good part of the state. The rebels put up only feeble resistance. Within a few weeks every major town in Missouri, including the state capital of Jefferson City, was in Union hands. Lyon's campaign, which began with Curtis's occupation of Hannibal and St. Joseph, was the first strategic offensive of the Civil War. When

Curtis left to attend the special session of Congress in early July, events in Missouri continued to unfold.[26]

Sterling Price, commander of the Missouri State Guard, fled into the southwest corner of the state. Lyon followed and occupied Springfield on July 13, four weeks and 260 miles from his starting point in St. Louis. The Federals were poised on the brink of a remarkable triumph, but everything changed when Price called on Brigadier General Benjamin McCulloch for help. McCulloch commanded a force of 8,700 Confederates in northwest Arkansas. He watched the struggle in Missouri with interest because the State Guard served as a buffer between Union and Confederate forces west of the Mississippi River. So long as the State Guard remained in the field, Lyon posed no immediate threat to Arkansas and the Indian Territory, but when Price fell back toward the Arkansas-Missouri line in late July, McCulloch felt he had to intervene in order to sustain the secessionist cause. He crossed into Missouri and joined forces with Price, who placed the State Guard under McCulloch's command for the duration of the emergency. The combined armies, about twelve thousand strong, advanced to Wilson's Creek, just south of Springfield.[27]

The object of McCulloch's attention, the Army of the West, was in serious difficulty. Lyon had outmarched his supplies and supporting forces in his single-minded pursuit of Price. Hundreds of men, including Lyon, were ill and the enlistments of several three-month regiments were about to expire. Lyon should have fallen back and regrouped, but he refused to budge, even as the rebels reached the outskirts of Springfield. "I feel great anxiety about General Lyon's command," Curtis told brother Henry.[28]

Lyon chose to strike before his command melted away. He knew he could not win a decisive victory with only 5,300 men, but he hoped to rock the rebels back on their heels and buy time. The Federals attacked the combined Confederate and State Guard armies at Wilson's Creek on August 10, 1861. This was the second major battle of the Civil War and the first in the West. After several hours of intense fighting Lyon was killed and his men withdrew, first to Springfield and then to the railheads at Rolla and Sedalia. The outcome shocked Unionists, who had enjoyed an almost unbroken string of successes since the beginning of the offensive. "It is a bad time here in Missouri throughout the length and breadth of the state," Curtis confided to Belinda. "Of course [I] am glad you are not here now and no doubt you are [too]."[29]

Price urged McCulloch to lead the combined armies north to the Missouri River, but McCulloch declined and returned to Arkansas. Price set out alone and captured a Union garrison at Lexington, on the southern bank of the Missouri, then fell back to Springfield and resumed his defiant stance. With Lyon dead, the Union response to Confederate movements was sluggish and ineffective. "We ought to assume the offensive and drive the rebels out of Missouri," Curtis fumed, "and we could do so immediately if we did not have our forces scattered everywhere throughout the state."[30]

Fremont was more of a spectator than a participant in these momentous events, but as pressure mounted to do something about Price, he assembled a sizable force and set out for Springfield in late September. Curtis hoped to be included in the expedition, but Fremont ordered him to remain behind at Benton Barracks and look after affairs in St. Louis.

• • •

Fremont's brief tenure as commander of the Department of the West was marked by military incompetence and political ineptitude. Among his most egregious blunders were declarations imposing martial law and freeing the slaves of all rebels in arms, the latter an inflammatory act that Lincoln quickly nullified. Curtis was disturbed by Fremont's high-handed behavior and tried to avoid enforcing his more outrageous edicts. "I here record my entire disapproval [of martial law], believing the exigencies do not require it," he told Belinda.[31]

The situation in Missouri raised alarms in Washington. On October 11 Secretary of War Simon Cameron and Brigadier General Lorenzo Thomas, adjutant general of the army, arrived at Benton Barracks and handed Curtis a letter from the president.

Lincoln wrote that he was "greatly perplexed about General Fremont" and asked Curtis whether he thought Fremont should be "relieved from, or retained in his present command." Lincoln explained that he urgently needed an "intelligent unprejudiced, and judicious opinion from some professional Military man on the spot," and he believed Curtis to be that man.[32]

Curtis told his distinguished visitors that he was on good personal terms with Fremont and had no complaints about the way Benton Barracks was administered. He did, however, feel anxious about Fremont's obvious lack of qualifications to be at the head of such an important department. Curtis described the Fremont he saw nearly every day as insecure, secretive, imperious, and "no more bound by law then by the winds." He thought the man was a charlatan, a poseur, who had no notions of strategy or tactics and was utterly "unequal to the command of an army." Thomas took careful notes and included many of Curtis's remarks verbatim in a scathing indictment of Fremont that he submitted to the War Department upon his return to Washington.[33]

That evening Curtis took pen in hand and wrote directly to Lincoln. His rambling letter must have tried the president's patience, but eventually he got to the point. "In my judgement," wrote Curtis, "General Fremont lacks the intelligence, the experience, and the sagacity necessary to his command." Curtis recommended that Fremont be relieved as soon as possible. Lincoln now had the considered opinion of a "professional Military man on the spot." His next task was to find a way to remove Fremont without inflicting additional damage on the flailing Union war effort in Missouri.[34]

Curtis, as always, kept brother Henry informed: "I have written [to Lincoln] very fully and frankly. Fremont will not do. He has not the sagacity or capacity for such a command. He is really [a] little imposter so far as talent is concerned and evinces no capacity or experience as a soldier. Extravagance and wrecklessness pervades his administration without regard to law or custom. His appointments, his contracts, his formations of forces are wild and confused and his army is entirely destitute of system and solution." A few weeks later, when the full extent of Fremont's maladministration was revealed, Curtis described him in even darker hues: "Fremont never could have been restrained and never would have been if his career had been carried on two more months with even temporary success." In light of such strong words it is worth repeating that there was no personal animosity between the two men. Curtis maintained what he called a "very cordial" relationship with Fremont right up to the end, even as it became clear that the "little imposter" was a failure as department commander and a threat to Union success in the West.[35]

Lincoln acted quickly but quietly. He again wrote to Curtis and gave the letter to a trusted friend, Leonard Swett, who carried it in his pocket halfway across the continent. Swett reached St. Louis on October 29 and handed Curtis the letter. It began abruptly:

> On receipt of this, with the accompanying enclosures you will take safe, certain, and suitable measures to have the inclosure addressed to Major General Fremont, delivered to him with all reasonable dispatch—subject to these conditions only, that if, when General Fremont shall be reached by the messenger (yourself, or any one sent by you) he shall then have, in personal command, fought and won a battle, or shall then be actually in a battle, or shall then be in the immediate presence of the enemy, in expectation of a battle, it is not to be delivered, but held for further orders.

This was the longest and most complex sentence Lincoln ever wrote.[36]

The enclosure Lincoln mentioned was a War Department order relieving Fremont of command of the Department of the West and appointing Major General David Hunter in his place. Lincoln did not want to remove Fremont if the military situation in Missouri had changed, or was about to change, for the better, but if the strategic stalemate continued as before then Fremont's time was up. Curtis, once again the man on the spot, would decide whether to pull the trigger on his superior.

Swett warned Curtis that a New York newspaper had already

published the removal order. He feared Fremont might learn of his impending dismissal and try to prevent the order from reaching him, most likely by sealing off his lines. Swett and Curtis made copies of the order and selected Captains Thomas J. McKenney and Ezekiel Boyden to carry them to Fremont by different routes. Curtis told the two officers that a "delicate but important duty is devolved on you" and repeated Lincoln's convoluted instructions. He added that the officer who first reached Fremont was to "give me the earliest possible advices of the fact by telegraphing to me that my orders have been obeyed." McKenney and Boyden departed on separate trains.[37]

Since leaving St. Louis six weeks earlier, Fremont had assembled an army and reoccupied Springfield, but he could not decide on his next move. McKenney reached Springfield on November 2 and slipped into the Union camp. He found no signs that the Federals were about to engage the rebels, or even that there were any rebels in the area. When McKenney was certain no battle was imminent, he barged into Fremont's headquarters and presented the removal order. Caught off guard, Fremont blurted, "Sir, how did you get through my lines?" Fortunately for all concerned, Fremont responded to his removal in a soldierly fashion. He transferred command to Hunter, issued a farewell address, and departed.[38]

Curtis learned of McKenney's success on November 6. "Your orders were sent and delivered at General Fremonts Head Quarters," he telegraphed Lincoln. "The General has relinquished the command to General Hunter." He added a bit more detail in a telegram to Scott: "Fremont very indignant at my messenger and at me." Curtis was unaware that Scott had just stepped down as general in chief in favor of Major General George B. McClellan, who directed Curtis to arrest Fremont's provost marshal and paymaster and maintain a firm grip on St. Louis, where most of Fremont's civilian supporters were concentrated. "All quiet here," Curtis assured McClellan. "I have the right men in the right place." Hunter withdrew to Rolla and Sedalia in accordance with Lincoln's wish to avoid any more battles until he could sort out the mess in Missouri. A mystified Price reclaimed Springfield.[39]

What Curtis labeled the "Fremont embroglio" was not quite over. Curtis did not like the way Fremont was parading around St. Louis making speeches to adoring crowds. "He ought to be called away from here, so he cannot do much more harm," he telegraphed McClellan. A short time later Thomas's report leaked, and Curtis's unflattering remarks about Fremont appeared in the newspapers. Curtis sent Lincoln another tiresome letter complaining that his confidential statements had been made public. Lincoln penned a gracious, if slightly barbed, reply. "In all sincerity I thank you for the complete and entirely satisfactory manner in which you executed the tasks I confided to you by letter," the president began. He acknowledged that several persons, Curtis among them, had been wronged by the publication of Thomas's report: "I have no apology only to say it never would have been done, if I had had the least suspicion it was to be done. Being done, I thought the maxim 'least said, soonest mended' applied to the case." Curtis sent a copy of the "exquisite little note" to brother Henry: "I had always perceived a cordial friendship was entertained by the President for me and I take this in the hurry and pressure of the times as a gracious legacy." He felt the note compensated for the "many jibes" he had received from Fremont partisans.[40]

Around this time Curtis also exchanged letters with a future occupant of the White House. In addition to his many other duties in and around St. Louis, Curtis was responsible for "infusing legal elements" into "steamboat commerce" on the Mississippi River and its tributaries. This brought him into conflict with Brigadier General Ulysses S. Grant, the Union commander at Cairo, Illinois, who was engaged in a crackdown on illicit trading on those very waterways. Grant accused Curtis of issuing too many passes to dubious characters who desired to travel downstream into the Confederacy and purchase cotton from the rebels. Grant asserted that he, not Curtis, was the person best qualified to decide who should receive passes: "I shall in future exercise my own judgement, about passing persons through my lines, unless the authority comes from a senior [officer], and one who exercises a command over me." Curtis was taken aback by Grant's belligerent tone. He responded that he had not intended to create difficulties. "In all cases I design to avoid the least intrusion on your command," he wrote. Grant did not bother to reply. This odd episode was the first indication that not all was well between Curtis and Grant.[41]

In November 1861 the Department of the West was divided into the Departments of Kansas and the Missouri. Hunter assumed command of the former, Major General Henry W. Halleck the latter. Halleck was known as "Old Brains" in the antebellum army because of his intellectual pursuits. He was an adequate administrator and strategist, but his fussy manner and peevish personality made him a difficult superior. It did not take Halleck long to recognize that the Missouri State Guard was more than a local threat. St. Louis was the base of operations for projected Union offensives on the Mississippi, Tennessee, and Cumberland Rivers. These operations required an enormous amount of manpower, and Missouri was a manpower sink. Because of Price, the thousands of Union soldiers standing idle in garrisons across the state were unavailable for the upcoming offensives. If they were ordered elsewhere, Price would be free to threaten St. Louis. This was an intolerable situation. Price exercised a veto over Union operations from Kentucky to Kansas.[42]

Halleck's first order of business was to neutralize Price, but he did not intend to take the field himself. "Old Brains" was more comfortable behind a desk than astride a horse. He established his headquarters in the Planters' House, the city's premier hotel, and appointed Curtis commander of the newly created District of St. Louis, essentially formalizing the position Curtis had held for the past six weeks. Halleck and Curtis occupied offices only a few doors apart. They never became friends—far from it—but they got to know one another quite well.[43]

Curtis told Halleck that he wanted to be relieved from the "drudgery" of drilling new regiments. He desired a more active command. Halleck was agreeable. On Christmas Day 1861 he placed Curtis in charge of the brand-new District of Southwest Missouri, with orders to defeat, disperse, or destroy the Missouri State Guard. Halleck never explained why he chose Curtis, but the latter's West Point education, Mexican War experience, engineering background, political connections, and demonstrated ability to bring order out of chaos all counted in his favor. Curtis, once again, was the man on the spot.[44]

6

OZARKIA

ON DECEMBER 26, 1861, CURTIS SAID GOODBYE TO BELINDA
and the girls and set out for Rolla, one hundred miles southwest
of St. Louis. Rolla was the terminus of the Southwest Branch
Pacific Railroad and an important military depot. It was also a
major refugee camp. Thousands of Union troops, mostly veterans of Fremont's abortive campaign, occupied well-ordered
encampments around the town, while thousands of civilian refugees, mostly Arkansas and Missouri Unionists driven from
their homes by secessionists, huddled in makeshift shantytowns
wherever space was available. Curtis arrived late on December
27 and established his headquarters in a tumbledown log building in the center of town. The next morning he assumed command of the District of Southwest Missouri and its military arm,
which he named the Army of the Southwest.[1]

His actions were immediately challenged by Brigadier General Franz Sigel, the ranking Union officer at Rolla, who claimed
the command rightfully belonged to him. Sigel was a graduate of
a German military academy who had immigrated to the United
States a decade earlier. Because of his military background and
his participation in every major operation in Missouri since the
start of the war, and because most of the Union troops at Rolla
were fellow Germans, Sigel believed he should be in charge.[2]

Sigel asked Curtis for the date of his commission. Curtis
checked the army register and found that he and Sigel had been
appointed brigadier generals on the same day, but his name was
nineteenth on the list and Sigel's was twenty-fifth. Curtis was the
superior officer. He sent the register to Sigel with a brief note:

"You will therefore see there is no question about our relative rank." Sigel resigned in a huff.[3]

Sigel had made himself into a symbol of German-American patriotism. His resignation caused a nationwide furor. Halleck recognized Sigel's importance to the Union cause and urged him to put his feelings aside and do what was best for his adopted country. After a few days Sigel withdrew his resignation and agreed to serve in a subordinate position, but his petulance and posturing irritated Curtis to no end. In a letter to brother Henry, Curtis sarcastically referred to the "fuss in the papers" over the "very great wrong done to *all* Germany because *somebody* else is in command."[4]

While the Sigel affair played out, Curtis turned his attention to the challenges involved in conducting a military operation two hundred miles west of the Mississippi River in what was essentially a frontier region. Once the Army of the Southwest marched away from the railhead at Rolla, it would have to rely on teams and wagons making their way along primitive roads in one of the least developed parts of the country. The tenuous line of communications would be vulnerable to weather, terrain, enemy action, and the inevitable breakdown of animals and equipment. The Federals would have to travel light and live off the land as much as possible.

Curtis ordered "immediate and vigorous preparations for a winter campaign in a rough and rather desolate country." He limited the amount of clothing, bedding, camp equipment, and personal items permitted on the wagons, and issued detailed lists of what officers and men could carry in their packs, right down to the number of pairs of socks (two). "The order to reduce baggage is again renewed," complained an Illinois infantryman. "We have cut down our baggage three or four times, and the officers still seem to think there is a surplus." Halleck was impressed. "I have just seen your orders," he telegraphed Curtis. "I like them very much—they have the true ring of *work*." Halleck demonstrated his support by appointing one of his favorites, Captain Philip H. Sheridan, a hard-driving regular officer, chief quartermaster and commissary officer of the army.[5]

Meteorology compounded logistical concerns. Winter weather in a mid-latitude continental climate is wildly unpredictable. Blasts of snow, sleet, hail, and freezing rain alternate with thaws and downpours on a weekly and sometimes daily basis. Crude dirt tracks were sheets of ice one day and rivers of mud the next. "Did you ever see such changeable weather," Curtis exclaimed after one temperature swing. Terrain made matters even more challenging. Rolla was located atop the Ozark Plateau, a massive limestone uplift that makes up the southern half of Missouri and the northern third of Arkansas. The immense formation extends from the Mississippi River to the Great Plains; its physiography varies from rolling highlands in the west to rocky bluffs and winding valleys everywhere else. It was the most difficult place in the trans-Mississippi to fight a war.[6]

In the midst of these preparations Curtis was laid low by a painful malady, probably the same nervous condition that had afflicted him in Mexico: "I am troubled with inflammatory rheumatism so I can hardly walk. I suppose it comes of sleeping in a tent [in] this cold weather." A day later he added, "I had a pretty hard night with my side, but by hard rubbing with oily linament made out to get up and come to the office to do business." Several days passed before Curtis was able to resume his regular activities. The malady disappeared once the campaign was underway.[7]

Duty, not illness, prevented Curtis from attending the wedding of son Henry and Julia Dudley in Keokuk on January 22, 1862. Curtis and Belinda heartily approved of the match. "She is a very sweet girl and every way worthy of him," Curtis told brother Henry. "She is poor like the rest of us, but these times of rebellion make me quite indifferent to matters of prosperity." Henry was supposed to serve as his father's adjutant, but soon after arriving in Rolla he fell seriously ill and missed the first two months of the campaign. Julia and Sadie traveled to Rolla to look after him and keep each other company. Belinda remained in St. Louis with Carrie.[8]

Following the Fremont fiasco, Lincoln had decreed that no new offensive in southwest Missouri could go forward without authorization from the War Department. Halleck dutifully requested permission for Curtis to proceed. "Winter is already upon us," he telegraphed McClellan, "and I fear much longer delay will render it exceedingly difficult to operate, and yet a winter campaign seems absolutely necessary." There was no response. Annoyed at being ignored, Halleck adapted a sterner tone. He warned McClellan that unless Curtis advanced at once, Price would "unquestionably return to the Missouri River" and wreak havoc among the isolated Union garrisons there. McClellan remained silent.[9]

While telegrams hummed along the wires from St. Louis to Washington, Curtis edged forward on his own. He sent Colonel Eugene A. Carr and 1,500 cavalrymen to Lebanon, a town halfway between Rolla and Springfield, to find out what Price was up to. The troops displayed what Curtis called the "usual lack of discipline" as they clattered out of Rolla, which did nothing to ease his concerns about sending a small mounted force into enemy territory. He told Halleck, "I earnestly desire to move infantry and artillery forward to support the cavalry," but was instructed to wait. Carr found small bands of rebels "scouting about the country and stealing and robbing," but he detected no signs of large-scale enemy activity. He pushed to within eight miles of Springfield and reported that the State Guard appeared to be in winter quarters. Then Carr carelessly repeated a baseless rumor that five thousand rebels were heading in his direction.[10]

Alarmed, Curtis rushed additional cavalry to Lebanon and authorized Carr "to fight or run as occasion may demand." He then forwarded Carr's message to Halleck, who interpreted it to mean that Price was attempting to gobble up another Union garrison, as he had done at Lexington. Halleck's repeated messages to McClellan had failed to elicit any response, so on January 13 he directed Curtis to begin the offensive. The news from Lebanon, he wrote, "has determined me to order an advance without waiting any longer for advices from Washington." Halleck offered no guidance except to remind Curtis of the stakes involved: "We must have no failure in this movement against Price. It must be the last." Halleck learned a few days later that the five thousand rebels were a mirage, but he did not rescind the order to march. The campaign was on.[11]

Halleck's directive coincided with a slight improvement in the abysmal weather that had gripped Missouri for weeks. Curtis noted that it was "still very cold, but clear and moderating." Assuming the worst of winter was over, he set his army in motion only hours before a ferocious storm buried the Ozark Plateau in snow and ice. Alternately freezing and thawing, the roads degenerated into sloughs. Wagons sank up to their axles in mud during the day, froze in place overnight, and had to be chopped free with axes and shovels the next morning. An Illinois soldier wrote that "our pantaloons, when we drew them on at reveille, were stiff with ice, so also were shirts, coats, boots, everything. Yet there was no remedy, so we shivered till our animal heat thawed the ice, and wore wet clothes till they dried upon us." Halleck offered encouragement from his well-heated office in the Planters' House. "I am well satisfied that Price will not stand if you press on," he advised Curtis. "Push on as rapidly as possible and end the matter with Price."[12]

Curtis tried his best, but his troops and trains required nearly three weeks to slip and slog the fifty miles to Lebanon. Curtis admired the fortitude and perseverance displayed by the men in the ranks, but he was less than impressed by the performance of some of his officers. Sigel was the worst offender. He was slow getting his troops in motion and, if some reports can be believed, he even attempted to return to Rolla in violation of orders. Curtis made sure Halleck knew that Sigel's "hesitation and delay" was the reason the operation was behind schedule.[13]

Thousands of weary Federals straggled into Lebanon during the first week of February. They cleaned and repaired clothing and equipment as best they could and gradually recovered from their ordeal. Curtis occupied the only habitable room in a ramshackle frame house on the edge of town. His staff camped in the yard. Curtis was pleased (and not a little surprised) to discover that his army had come through its first test with flying colors. "Our stock have not broken down and we have lost nothing," he reported. Officers and men were in good health except for a mild outbreak of dysentery: "I was right sick yesterday myself, but I am well today." He added that the storm had passed and the weather was improving.[14]

Curtis told brother Henry that the "cold and wet and mud and toil do not dampen the zeal of my forces. They stand or lay by camp fires consoling themselves with the argument which I have tried to impress upon them that the rebels are worse off than we are." The campaign was behind schedule but unfolding according to plan: "I have many trials and constant apprehension some of these operations may fail but so far they are moving quite as well as I could expect." Curtis worried that Price "may yet escape us before we can reach him. Still he must also contend with bad roads and he cannot be so well supplied with iron, tools, and artisans to supply broken shafts and wheels, a very common occurrence on such roads at such a cold season." In the midst of all this Curtis somehow found the time to wonder about his place in the history books: "If I drive Price out of Missouri in dead of winter after three or four campaigns have failed unfortunately to do so, I trust I shall have the credit due to the occasion."[15]

While in Lebanon Curtis organized his army into four small divisions of roughly equal size. Brigadier General Peter J. Osterhaus's First Division was composed of five infantry regiments and two batteries. Brigadier General Alexander S. Asboth's Second Division consisted of three infantry and two cavalry regiments and two batteries, and was the smallest of the lot. Colonel Jefferson C. Davis's Third Division, which had come from Sedalia by a different route, was made up of five infantry regiments, one cavalry regiment, and two batteries. Colonel Carr's Fourth Division had four infantry regiments, one cavalry regiment, and two batteries. Curtis kept one infantry battalion, two cavalry regiments, and two cavalry battalions under his direct command. At this stage of the campaign the army had a strength of 12,100 men (9,600 infantry and artillery and 2,500 cavalry) and fifty guns. The all-volunteer force was small by Civil War standards but larger than the armies Scott and Taylor had led to victory in Mexico. Curtis was satisfied. "I have a splendid command," he told brother Henry.[16]

More than one-third of the regiments and batteries were wholly or largely made up of recently arrived immigrants, overwhelmingly Germans but also Scandinavians and Central Europeans. Curtis placed these units in the First and Second Divisions, commanded by a German (Osterhaus) and a Hungarian (Asboth), respectively. He assigned units composed wholly or largely of native-born soldiers to the Third and Fourth Divisions. The creation of ethnically homogenized divisions was an attempt to reduce friction in the ranks by minimizing contact between "Germans" and "Americans." (Diversity was something to be avoided, not embraced, in nineteenth-century America.) For the same reason, Curtis named Sigel second-in-command of the army and commander of the First and Second Divisions, impressive-sounding but essentially meaningless titles. The recognition was intended to salve Sigel's wounded feelings, though it seems only to have heightened his sense of self-importance.[17]

In February 1862 the offensives on the Mississippi, Tennessee, and Cumberland Rivers got underway, more or less simultaneously. Union resources in the West were stretched to the limit. Halleck advised Curtis not to request reinforcements: "Don't ask for any more if you can possibly help it, as everything else I can rake and scrape together is wanted in another direction." Halleck had his hands full overseeing the new offensives and told Curtis he was free to run his campaign as he saw fit: "I leave Price to you." Curtis realized Missouri was his to win or lose. "General Halleck seems to have great confidence in my judgement," he told brother Henry.[18]

The Federals struck their tents around Lebanon on February 10 and set out for Springfield with bands playing and flags flying. Curtis and Sigel rode together near the head of the column. The weather cooperated for once and the army made rapid progress. Price had neither fortified Springfield nor planned for an orderly withdrawal because he believed it was impossible to carry out a winter campaign atop the Ozark Plateau. When he learned to his astonishment that a large Union force was fast approaching, he panicked and ordered an immediate evacuation. Chaos ensued as the rebels abandoned the town on February 13 and fled south on Telegraph Road, the principal thoroughfare linking southwest Missouri and northwest Arkansas.[19]

The Army of the Southwest entered Springfield a few hours later. The town was a shambles after months of occupation by Price's ill-disciplined men. Stores and houses were ransacked and vandalized; streets were littered with carcasses and offal. In their haste to depart, the rebels left behind four hundred invalids, half as many stragglers, and storehouses filled with forage and foodstuffs, including, improbably, gingerbread and beer. Curtis had the Stars and Stripes raised over the Greene County courthouse amidst "great rejoicing." The Federals had gained and lost Springfield twice before but this time they came to stay. The town remained in Union hands for the rest of the war.[20]

• • •

Curtis was pleased with his bloodless conquest of Springfield but disappointed that Price had escaped. He informed Halleck that the rebels were in "precipitate flight" and announced his intention to follow: "Shall pursue as fast as the strength of the men will allow." To facilitate his pursuit, Curtis ordered another reduction in baggage. "The army had already dispensed with superfluities," wrote a staff officer, "now everything not absolutely necessary was left behind."[21]

Sigel proposed that Curtis and the Third and Fourth Divisions pursue Price on Telegraph Road, while he and the First and Second Divisions hurried along a meandering country lane a few miles to the west. Sigel claimed the lane would bring him back to Telegraph Road ahead of Price at a place called McDowell. Trapped between converging Union forces, Price would have no choice but to surrender. Curtis was dubious but he approved

Sigel's proposal. The chance, however slight, to bag Price and bring the campaign to a close probably influenced his thinking. He may also have wanted to give Sigel something important to do.[22]

About this time Halleck learned of Sigel's behavior at Wilson's Creek. Sigel had convinced Lyon to divide his already outnumbered command and strike the combined Confederate and State Guard armies from two directions. On the day of battle, while Lyon and the main body made a head-on attack, Sigel led a smaller force into the rebel rear. His attack fell apart and he fled, leaving Lyon to his fate. Halleck rushed a warning to Curtis: "Be careful in your pursuit of Price. Don't separate or divide your forces. Keep them together and well in hand. Sigel's detour lost the battle of Wilson's Creek. Don't let him lead you into the same error." There was as yet no telegraph line between Rolla and Springfield; the message reached Curtis too late to prevent Sigel from setting out on another "detour."[23]

The Federals marched out of Springfield just as another storm arrived. Freezing rain glazed everything with a sheet of ice and made movement extremely difficult. Sigel dawdled and failed to spring the trap on Price. By the time he reached McDowell, both Price and Curtis had passed through the junction. Mortified by his failure to cut off the rebels, Sigel turned onto Telegraph Road and hurried after the rest of the army. He offered no more suggestions.[24]

Confederates and Federals trudged across the frozen Ozark landscape, stopping only to fight or sleep. Curtis kept up the pressure, determined not to let Price's "fleeing frightened column" get away. Evidence mounted that the State Guard was unraveling. "We continually take cattle, prisoners, wagons, and arms, which they leave in their flight," he told Halleck on the third day out of Springfield. "More straggling prisoners are being taken than I know what to do with." The Federals also experienced their share of hardships. They foraged vigorously, but the hardscrabble highland farms offered little sustenance and most of that was gobbled up by the rebels, whose logistical situation was desperate.[25]

On February 17 the Federals crossed into Arkansas and the

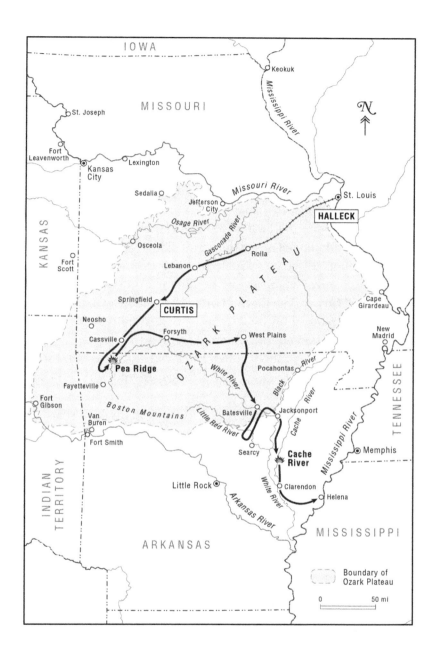

MAP 1. The Pea Ridge campaign, January–July 1862. Route of the
Army of the Southwest. Created by Erin Greb.

Confederacy. Officers made speeches and bands played patriotic airs. Curtis thanked his troops for their heroic efforts, then informed Halleck that the "flag of our Union again floats in Arkansas." Halleck passed that information on to McClellan, adding that the Army of the Southwest "is doing its duty nobly." Three miles south of the state line, the Union column emerged from a deep ravine, tramped past a two-story residence known locally as Elkhorn Tavern, and crossed a rolling tableland called Pea Ridge. In three weeks the bucolic landscape would be the scene of a desperate battle.[26]

That afternoon the Federals encountered a force of infantry and artillery deployed along the south side of Little Sugar Creek. Curtis thought Price was finally making a stand, but the rebels in his front were Arkansas and Louisiana Confederates, part of McCulloch's army. The Confederates allowed the exhausted Missourians to pass, then established a line of battle across Telegraph Road. The Federals formed their own line and a sharp fight erupted. When the Confederates were satisfied that Price had made good his escape, they disengaged and withdrew into the gathering dusk.[27]

The clash at Little Sugar Creek was the first Civil War battle in Arkansas. It cost the Federals thirteen dead and twenty wounded. The Confederates lost at least twenty-six killed. During the fight Curtis learned that he was engaged with Confederate, not State Guard, troops. This meant, of course, that he now faced the two largest rebel armies west of the Mississippi River, armies that had not cooperated for months until he had literally driven them together. Lyon had come to grief at the hands of these combined armies at Wilson's Creek. Curtis knew he had to be careful. Instead of haring after the rebels, he decided to stay the night at Little Sugar Creek and concentrate his forces.[28]

McCulloch and Price spent the night twelve miles farther south at Cross Hollows, a large Confederate cantonment composed of huts, storehouses, and mills. Curtis believed, incorrectly, that Cross Hollows was heavily fortified. Convinced that a direct assault by way of Telegraph Road would be too costly, he initiated a wide turning movement around the west side of Cross Hollows. It was the right move for the wrong reason.[29]

McCulloch knew Cross Hollows was no place to make a stand, so he fell back deeper into Arkansas. Confederate and State Guard forces resumed their retreat just as another storm dumped yet more snow, sleet, and freezing rain on the long-suffering men and animals. As the last of the rebels trudged away, McCulloch ordered Cross Hollows set ablaze. The next day, for reasons never explained, the rebels also burned most of Fayetteville, the principal town in northwest Arkansas. Two days later McCulloch finally called a halt in the Boston Mountains, the rugged southwest rim of the Ozark Plateau. Price's Missourians were despondent. After eight days on the run they found themselves exiled in a barren mountain fastness more than one hundred miles south of Springfield.[30]

When Curtis learned that McCulloch had abandoned Cross Hollows, he canceled the turning movement and hurried south on Telegraph Road. Most of the cantonment was a smoking ruin by the time he arrived, but he was surprised to see that the surviving buildings "were better than ours at Benton Barracks," and even more surprised to discover how much food, clothing, and equipment the rebels had left behind. It was Springfield all over again. Later in the campaign Curtis estimated that "most of our provisions for the last ten days have been taken from the enemy."[31]

Curtis declined to follow the rebels beyond Cross Hollows. He was over two hundred miles from his starting point in Rolla; even Sheridan found it difficult to keep supplies moving over such a distance in the dead of winter. Not only had the Union army reached the end of its logistical tether, it had shrunk alarmingly. After dropping off garrisons in Springfield and other towns along the way, Curtis was down to about 10,500 men. He considered falling back to Springfield to relieve the pressure on his line of communications, but he decided he could best shield Missouri by remaining in Arkansas.[32]

The key to his thinking was Little Sugar Creek. The steep-sided valley, carved by the stream, is an enormous, rockbound moat over twenty miles in length. It runs east-west, directly athwart Telegraph Road, about six miles south of the state line. The line of steep bluffs along the north side of the valley was a perfect location for rifle pits and artillery emplacements. Curtis examined the ground with an engineer's eye and came to a decision. If the rebels counterattacked he would concentrate his command on the bluffs and fight a defensive battle. The position offered another advantage. The bluffs form the southern rim of the Pea Ridge tableland, which would provide a secure place for the army's trains. Curtis later told brother Henry that Little Sugar Creek was the place "where I knew I could make the best fight."[33]

The Federals spread out to facilitate foraging but did not stray far from Little Sugar Creek. Osterhaus's First Division and Asboth's Second Division, both under Sigel's control, moved six miles west to McKissick's Creek and established the Union right. Davis's Third Division and Carr's Fourth Division occupied Cross Hollows on Telegraph Road and formed the Union left. Quartermaster, commissary, medical, and other noncombatant units accompanied the trains back to Pea Ridge. Detachments operated mills or manned advanced pickets between Little Sugar Creek and the Boston Mountains. Curtis established his headquarters at Cross Hollows.[34]

While at Cross Hollows Curtis received a letter from a group of Fayetteville citizens who had formed a home guard to maintain order in the chaotic aftermath of McCulloch's flight to the Boston Mountains. The citizens asked the Union commander for advice. Curtis responded with a carefully worded proclamation in which he urged Arkansans to reject secession and return to their proper relationship with the United States, but he tried not to promise more than he could deliver. He was in the uncomfortable position of encouraging Unionism by his presence, without having the authority or, given the small size of his army, the ability to support any Unionists who actually stepped forward. Instead, the proclamation rather lamely expressed the hope that, if people put down their arms and went about their business, "much of the havoc of war will be avoided, and many poor families can be protected from distress and misery."[35]

Families, poor and otherwise, were already suffering. "The ravages of war, in spite of all I can do to prevent havoc, is a sickening sight," Curtis confessed to brother Henry. "The poor ignorant people of this country are to be pitied. The monstrous lies that have been told of us have frightened everybody to death, and the men have run away leaving their wives and little ones poorly provided [for] and subject to the demands of my hungry troops many of whom had been four days without bread." The Union incursion triggered a humanitarian crisis that Curtis felt compelled to ameliorate, even though the effort exacerbated his already critical logistical problems: "I am obliged not only to improvise a system of supplies for my army but also for the families and sick of the enemy."[36]

As the days passed Curtis detected an increase in Confederate activity. He reported that rebel cavalry was "crowding my flanks and attacking my foraging parties." Attacks on wide-ranging Union foragers were worrying, because food for the army's horses and mules was exhausted in the vicinity of Cross Hollows, which had been occupied by the rebels for months. Without adequate food the animals would soon be too weak to haul the guns and wagons. Curtis feared that if he did not move soon he might not be able to move at all.[37]

On March 3 Curtis sent Davis's Third Division back to Little Sugar Creek to begin constructing fortifications. That same day he advised Sigel to prepare the First and Second Divisions for a similar move. Following the flap over seniority, Curtis avoided giving Sigel direct orders. On this occasion he couched his instructions in the form of a wish: "I hope I meet you soon, say in two or three days, in position on [Little] Sugar Creek where we must entrench ourselves." Curtis remained at Cross Hollows with Carr's Fourth Division for the time being. He informed Halleck of the latest developments and closed on an upbeat note: "Shall be on the alert, holding as securely as possible."[38]

Major General Earl Van Dorn, the new Confederate commander in the trans-Mississippi, reached the Boston Mountains on March 2. He united McCulloch's and Price's troops into a new force that he named the Army of the West, and announced his intention to defeat Curtis and liberate Missouri. His plan was simplicity itself. He would rush north to Bentonville, midway between the two wings of the Union army, turn west and overwhelm Sigel at McKissick's Creek, then turn back east and do the same to Curtis at Cross Hollows. For that to happen the Federals would have to cooperate in their own destruction by remaining deaf, blind, and inert, but Van Dorn ignored such inconvenient facts. To maximize speed and surprise he decided to march without a train. His troops stuffed their packs and pockets with three days' rations. Whatever else they needed (such as tents, bedding, cooking equipment, and additional food) would be taken from the vanquished Federals.[39]

The Army of the West set out from the Boston Mountains on March 4 with 16,500 men and sixty-five guns, the largest military force yet assembled west of the Mississippi River. Van Dorn had reason to feel confident. He had a three-to-two advantage in manpower and a four-to-three advantage in artillery over Curtis. No other Confederate army ever marched off to battle with greater numerical superiority.[40]

As the Confederates emerged from the Boston Mountains they were struck by the last—and by some accounts the worst—of the season's storms. They trudged north into the howling wind, heads down, struggling against sheets of snow and sleet while trying to keep their footing on the icy road. That night they huddled in the snow near Fayetteville without tents or extra blankets. The next day they resumed their advance through drifts of snow and shivered through another sleepless night at Elm Spring. The following day, March 6, they continued on to Bentonville and consumed the last of their meager rations.[41]

Curtis was at Cross Hollows on March 5 when a Unionist resident of Fayetteville rode into camp with startling news: a Confederate column was moving north toward Bentonville. Curtis immediately concentrated his forces. "This may be only a feint," he wrote to Sigel, "but we had better unite our forces at [Little] Sugar Creek, and be ready for any occasion." To make certain the dilatory German general grasped the urgency of the situation, Curtis added a postscript: "Our stand must be at [Little] Sugar Creek, where I hope to join you tomorrow."[42]

Later that day a Union spy reached Cross Hollows and confirmed everything the loyal Arkansan had said. Curtis rushed a second message to Sigel. He summarized the spy's report and, for the first time, issued a direct order: "They are coming sure, he says. Make a night march, if need be, so as to join me at [Little] Sugar Creek early tomorrow." Curtis then informed Halleck that the rebels were on their way. He promised to "give them the best reception possible."[43]

Curtis and the Fourth Division left Cross Hollows that night. The withdrawal took place in total darkness and was extremely difficult. "It was snowing and most intensely cold," recalled one officer. "I never suffered so much in my life." Curtis endured the same trials as his men. He reached Little Sugar Creek early the next morning, March 6, and discovered that Davis had done little to fortify the position. Despite having no sleep, Curtis personally laid out a line of earthworks along the bluffs. The Federals then attacked the rocky soil with picks and shovels. Curtis reported that "breastworks of considerable strength were erected by the troops on the headlands of [Little] Sugar Creek as if by magic." Traces of those rifle pits and artillery emplacements are still visible today. They are among the earliest surviving examples of Civil War fieldworks.[44]

By midday Sigel's First and Second Divisions had passed through Bentonville and were nearing Little Sugar Creek. Sigel, however, was not with them. He formed a small rear guard and stayed behind to await Van Dorn, probably in a misguided attempt to demonstrate his mettle. Sigel predictably misjudged the situation and became entangled in a running fight with a superior force of Confederate cavalry. Curtis dispatched a relief force that arrived in the nick of time and drove off the rebels. Curtis was confounded by Sigel's erratic behavior but wisely declined to get into a tiff with his principal subordinate on the eve of battle.[45]

Curtis spent the remaining hours of daylight overseeing the disposition of his forces along Little Sugar Creek. By sunset the Army of the Southwest was in place and ready for a fight. Satisfied that there was nothing more he could do, Curtis rode two miles up Telegraph Road to his new headquarters at Pratt's Store on Pea Ridge. When an anxious staff officer asked what would happen next, Curtis replied in oracular fashion: "I will either fight them tomorrow or they me."[46]

As darkness fell on March 6, Van Dorn recognized that his plan had failed. His men and animals were in pitiful condition after three days and nights in the open, and he did not intend to see them slaughtered in a hopeless assault against the Union earthworks looming over Little Sugar Creek. As he cast about for some other way to come to grips with Curtis, Van Dorn learned of an obscure road that meandered around the right of the Union position and intersected Telegraph Road five miles north of Little Sugar Creek. McCulloch and Price wanted to let their exhausted men and animals rest before setting out on another march, but Van Dorn insisted that the army move at once. For the rest of the night the weak and weary Confederates trudged slowly along the oddly named Bentonville Detour. Curtis had issued orders to interdict all roads passing around the Little Sugar Creek position, including the Detour, but the chaotic arrival of Sigel's First and Second Divisions and the need to rescue Sigel himself caused confusion on the Union right. Whoever was assigned to block the Detour failed to do so. When Curtis finally learned of the oversight, he authorized a last-minute effort to fell trees across the road. The timber barricade slowed but did not stop the rebels.[47]

The head of the Confederate column reached Telegraph Road in the Union rear at seven o'clock the next morning, March 7. Van Dorn was exultant, but his army was so strung out on the Detour it would take all day for the tail to arrive. Assuming Curtis was still awaiting an attack at Little Sugar Creek, Van Dorn decided it was safe to divide his force. Price's division, in the lead, turned south on Telegraph Road, while McCulloch's division, well back down the column, turned south on Ford Road, a few miles to the west. It was a risky maneuver, because the two wings of the army were marching on parallel roads separated by an impassable feature called Big Mountain. Van Dorn, however, was confident he could reunite his entire force on the broad expanse of Pea Ridge before Curtis realized what was happening. As the sun rose in the sky the Confederate commander appeared to have victory within his grasp.[48]

7

PEA RIDGE

MARCH 7 DAWNED COLD AND CLEAR. CURTIS WAS EATING A spartan breakfast in his tent when he looked up and saw Major Eli Weston standing in the entrance. Weston, the provost marshal, was responsible for guarding prisoners and securing the army's rear. He reported that his pickets on the Bentonville Detour, several miles north of Pratt's Store, were being driven in by a large body of Confederates. Weston was so alarmed he decided to tell Curtis in person rather than send a courier.[1]

Curtis was puzzled by Weston's report. After a hurried conference with his staff he tentatively concluded that the Confederate force on the Detour was either a diversion or a turning movement designed to pry him out of the Little Sugar Creek position without a fight. As yet he gave little credence to the unlikely possibility that it was an envelopment, and that the *entire* rebel army was moving around his right flank and into his rear. After all, if Van Dorn marched into the Union rear, he placed Curtis in the Confederate rear, effectively isolating *both* armies. Surely no professional military man would do such a thing. So, for the next few hours Curtis acted on the reasonable but erroneous assumption that he was confronting *two* enemy forces, one in his front and one in his rear.[2]

Curtis called a meeting of his senior officers at Pratt's Store. The impromptu council of war began at nine o'clock and lasted forty-five minutes. Curtis brought everyone up to date and asked for opinions. Some officers declared that the army should hold its ground and fend off the rebels, others argued for an immediate withdrawal to avoid being cut off, and still others were noncommittal. Curtis listened to everyone without comment, then announced his decision to stand and fight.[3]

Subsequent reports from Weston indicated that the Confederates had turned off the Bentonville Detour and were moving south in parallel columns on either side of Big Mountain. The news spurred Curtis into action. He decided to hit the rebels before they hit him. He ordered Osterhaus and Carr to pull their troops out of the Little Sugar Creek fortifications and march north as rapidly as possible. They were to intercept and engage the enemy columns regardless of the odds. Curtis hoped these spoiling attacks would stop the rebels in their tracks, or at least slow them down, and allow him additional time to assess the situation. By eleven o'clock nearly half of the Army of the Southwest was in motion over the snow-covered ground, Osterhaus's First Division heading northwest toward the hamlet of Leetown, and Carr's Fourth Division heading northeast toward Elkhorn Tavern. Still uncertain what Van Dorn was up to, Curtis kept the rest of his force at Little Sugar Creek.[4]

The spoiling attacks worked perfectly. Shortly before noon Osterhaus collided with McCulloch's division on an expanse of level ground southwest of Big Mountain. The Confederates were startled by the appearance of a Union force so far north of Little Sugar Creek and stumbled to a halt under a hail of artillery fire. Attacks and counterattacks followed. McCulloch and his second-in-command were killed early in the fighting and thereafter the leaderless rebels failed to make effective use of their superior numbers. They also failed to resume their forward movement and were unable to rendezvous with Van Dorn as planned. Osterhaus knew nothing of the disarray on the Confederate side of the field and feared his command was about to be swept away by superior numbers. He called for help.[5]

A mile or so to the east, Carr ran headlong into Van Dorn and Price's division on Telegraph Road, east of Big Mountain and north of Elkhorn Tavern. The Federals occupied a maze of ridges and ravines called Cross Timber Hollow and brought the Confederate advance to a halt. Van Dorn was surprised by this unexpected development. He assumed a defensive posture and awaited the arrival of McCulloch's division, but as the hours passed and there was no sign of the other half of his army, he finally ordered Price to advance and drive the Federals away. Outnumbered and under mounting pressure, Carr also dashed off a plea for support.[6]

Carr's message reached Pratt's Store first. Curtis rode up Telegraph Road to see what was happening. He stopped in front of Elkhorn Tavern to study the terrain, which favored the Federals, then descended into Cross Timber Hollow "as cool and unconcerned as if on dress parade." When a shell screeched overhead and caused some of his staff to duck, he called out, "Boys you dodged too late." Curtis found Carr "under a brisk fire of shot and shell, coolly locating and directing the deployment" of his forces. Exactly what the two men shouted to one another over the din was not recorded, though Carr surely said he was hard pressed and Curtis surely urged him to hang on.[7]

Curtis had never experienced the sights and sounds of a major battle. After concluding his interview with Carr, he lingered in the hollow, fascinated by the chaotic scene. The scale and intensity of the fighting caused him some uneasiness. The Confederate force in Cross Timber Hollow seemed far too large to be a diversion or turning movement. He rode back to Pratt's Store, mulling things over in his methodical fashion. Shortly after noon he ordered Davis to move his Third Division from Little Sugar Creek to Carr's support. Curtis thought two divisions would be sufficient to drive the rebels away from Telegraph Road and restore his line of communications (and potential line of retreat, if it came to that). Then a courier arrived with Osterhaus's call for help. Curtis had not realized Osterhaus was engaged because the racket at Elkhorn Tavern masked the more distant sound of battle at Leetown. He correctly judged the Confederate force on Telegraph Road to be the greater threat, but Carr held the high ground and was putting up a stiff fight. He felt the Fourth Division could hold on a little longer. The Confederate force at Leetown, however, seemed to have Osterhaus on the ropes. Curtis reversed himself and instructed Davis to reinforce Osterhaus instead of Carr.[8]

In the days after the battle, Carr and other officers in the Fourth Division privately criticized Curtis for failing to support them in a timely fashion. Curtis learned of this faultfinding but chose not to engage in an unseemly squabble with his subordinates. "I did not err" in sending Davis to support Osterhaus, he told Halleck, though he acknowledged that Carr "also needed re-enforcements." With the benefit of hindsight it appears Curtis made the correct decision, but at the time it seemed to many, especially the embattled Union soldiers in Cross Timber Hollow, that he was guilty of an error in judgment.[9]

Curtis ignored Sigel and dealt directly with his division commanders during the first day of the battle. This left the army's second-in-command with nothing to do, which was exactly what Curtis intended. Sigel prowled around the field and tried to make himself useful. Around two o'clock he informed Curtis that Asboth at Little Sugar Creek had not seen a single rebel since early morning. Curtis rode to Little Sugar Creek to assess the situation for himself. To his relief he found everything just as Sigel had described it: "All was quiet, and the men, not having been under fire [were] fresh and anxious to participate in the fight." This was the moment Curtis realized the Confederates were behind him in full force. He ordered Asboth to take part of the Second Division and hurry to Carr's support at Elkhorn Tavern. His faith in Sigel partially restored, he instructed the German general to lead the rest of the Second Division to Leetown and help Osterhaus and Davis drive off McCulloch. If any daylight remained, Sigel was to march cross-country and assist Carr. By late afternoon the imposing Little Sugar Creek fortifications were empty, save for a single regiment of infantry.[10]

This marked the conclusion of an extraordinary, daylong reorientation of the Army of the Southwest that has never received the attention it deserves. When the battle began the Union army faced south, but after learning of the Confederate presence on the Bentonville Detour, Curtis incrementally shifted his cavalry, infantry, and artillery northward from Little Sugar Creek to Pea Ridge. At the same time, and on the same narrow country roads, he moved reserves, prisoners, stores, trains, remounts, cattle, and civilian refugees to safety in the opposite direction. By the close of fighting on March 7 the Union army faced north instead of south. The remarkable 180-degree change of front was a unique event in the history of the Civil War.[11]

Curtis accompanied Asboth up Telegraph Road, setting a brisk pace and "moving forward some straggling commands" he found along the way. The relief column reached Carr just as the sun was setting. By this time Price's division had fought its way out of Cross Timber Hollow and forced Carr back half a mile. The embattled Federals made a stand midway between Elkhorn Tavern and Pratt's Store and repulsed a final Confederate attack. Curtis witnessed the twilight encounter. When the rebels fell back, he ordered a counterattack, supposing that "with my reinforcements I could easily recover our lost ground." Curtis underestimated the difficulty of the task at hand. He also demonstrated more courage than sense by riding close behind the line of advancing infantry. He escaped injury, but a member of his escort was decapitated by an artillery round, an aide riding by his side was struck by a bullet, and Asboth was severely wounded in the arm by a canister ball. Confederate resistance stiffened; the advance faltered. Curtis recognized he could do no more and led the Union troops back to their starting point. Darkness ended the fighting.[12]

Curtis returned to Pratt's Store, now only a short distance behind the Union line, where he learned that Osterhaus and Davis had driven off McCulloch without Sigel's help. This news convinced Curtis that the battle had turned in his favor. As he saw it, the Army of the Southwest had routed the rebels on one field (Leetown) and fought an effective delaying action on another (Elkhorn Tavern). Curtis believed the commander who delivered the first blow in the morning would emerge the victor, and he intended to strike Van Dorn with everything he had. The first order of business was to concentrate the army on Telegraph Road. Curtis ordered Sigel, Osterhaus, and Davis to join forces with Asboth and Carr. He then directed the quartermaster, commissary, ordnance, and medical departments to distribute food, water, and ammunition and recover as many of the wounded as could be found in the dark. When daylight returned, Curtis wanted his soldiers rested and ready to resume the fight.[13]

Not everyone in Union blue was confident of victory. Colonel Grenville M. Dodge, a brash Iowa railroad engineer who had known Curtis before the war, was alarmed by the defeatist talk he heard around the campfires of the battered Fourth Division. He went to Pratt's Store to find out what Curtis planned to do on the morrow. Dodge arrived around midnight and found the Union commander fully dressed and lying on his cot under several blankets. Curtis was annoyed at being awakened and brusquely told Dodge that, rather than surrender or retreat, he intended to "fight it out right where they were." Unaware of the troop movements from Leetown to Telegraph Road then underway, Dodge urged Curtis to concentrate every available man and gun against the foe in the morning. "That is just what I am going to do," snapped Curtis. Reassured, Dodge departed and Curtis went back to sleep.[14]

• • •

March 8 was another cold, clear day. Curtis awoke and rode back to the Union position on Telegraph Road to see whether Van Dorn would continue to press the attack. The sun rose into the sky, but the Confederates remained quiet. Curtis must have felt an enormous sense of relief. The rebels had shot their bolt; the initiative had passed into his hands. By now the troops from Leetown had arrived and Curtis formed his entire command into a single, continuous formation nearly a mile in length. The imposing array stretched across the snow-covered fields on either side of Telegraph Road, "German" divisions to the left and "American" to the right. It was the only time in the Civil War a Union army was visible in line of battle from flank to flank.[15]

At eight o'clock Curtis directed his artillery to open fire. The ensuing cannonade lasted over two hours and was the largest, most intense artillery barrage ever to take place on the North American continent up to that time. The roar of the guns, the shriek of projectiles, the clatter of shrapnel and canister, and the billows of smoke swirling across the landscape overpowered the senses. "It was a continual thunder and a fellow might have believed that the day of judgement had come," wrote an Iowa infantryman. Sigel had been trained as an artillerist in Germany, and he directed the fire of the Union batteries west of the road. He methodically advanced the guns and supporting infantry and hammered the Confederates at ever closer range. Under his direction, the left wing of the line of battle swung forward until the overall Union formation assumed the shape of a shallow V.[16]

Curtis and his staff sat on their horses on Telegraph Road and watched these developments with interest. Midway through the bombardment Curtis decided to pay Sigel a visit. He found the German general on the far left of the line personally sighting an artillery piece. The gaggle of horsemen must have attracted the attention of Confederate gunners, because in the space of a few seconds a shell shrieked close overhead and another plunged into the ground beneath Curtis's horse. The Union commander was engaged with Sigel and ignored or failed to notice the near miss, but everyone else watched anxiously as a plume of smoke rose from the small crater, the telltale sign of a burning fuse. The shell failed to explode.[17]

After a little while Curtis concluded that the artillery had done its job. He shouted to Sigel, "General, I think the infantry might advance now," and returned to Telegraph Road. The ride to the left, like the trip to Little Sugar Creek the previous afternoon, reflected Curtis's doubts about Sigel. Once again reassured that all was well, he issued orders for a full-scale assault. He stated in his official report that, from this moment forward, he believed victory was "inevitable."[18]

The Union guns ceased firing around ten o'clock. The infantry dressed ranks and fixed bayonets. Officers shouted commands. The long blue line started forward with flags flying, drums beating, bands playing, and men cheering. It was one of the most picture-perfect assaults of the Civil War, visible to nearly every-one on the field, Union and Confederate alike. Curtis rode up Telegraph Road behind the advancing line, enthralled by the seductive grandeur of battle. "A charge of infantry like that last closing scene has never been made on this continent," he informed brother Henry. "It was the most terribly magnificent sight that can be imagined."[19]

The remaining Confederates—exhausted, famished, demor-alized, and low on ammunition—watched as the seemingly irre-sistible Union formation swept toward them. Some fought, others fled. Van Dorn and Price realized the day was lost and slipped away, leaving thousands of their men still engaged on the field. The Federals crashed through the open woods skirting the base of Big Mountain and poured into the clearing around Elkhorn Tavern. Curtis and Sigel met and shook hands, surrounded by wildly yelling soldiers. Curtis was not given to displays of exu-berance, but on this occasion he let himself go, cheering and waving his hat as he greeted each regiment. Curtis confessed to brother Henry that "I rode along our line shouting Victory! Victory!" The raucous affair at the tavern was the high point of his military experience; he savored the memory for the rest of his life.[20]

While the Federals celebrated their implausible triumph, the Confederates vanished into the drifting smoke. "The rebel army seemed to have sunk into the earth," Curtis told Belinda. Many enemy troops fled north and west, retracing their steps through Cross Timber Hollow to the Bentonville Detour, but most, includ-ing Van Dorn and Price, escaped to the southeast on Huntsville Road and made a complete loop around the Army of the South-west. Curtis did not have this information for several hours and was perplexed by the Confederate disappearing act. He rode north into Cross Timber Hollow accompanied only by Sigel, staff officers, and a small escort. The road was littered with cast-off equipment of every description. Curtis concluded, incorrectly, that Van Dorn and his entire force had departed the way they had come. Sigel volunteered to assemble a cavalry force and pursue the rebels. The German general's performance that morning had been unimpeachable and Curtis gave his permission.[21]

Curtis made his way back to Pratt's Store, unaware that Sigel intended to run from the rebels, not after them. As soon as Curtis was out of sight, Sigel ordered the First and Second Divisions to follow him north on Telegraph Road. Later that day Sigel informed Curtis that he was on his way back to Missouri with "his" half of the army. He urged Curtis to follow with the rest of the troops. Curtis was flabbergasted. "I am going forward, not backward," he raged. Struggling to control his temper, Curtis ordered Sigel to return to Pea Ridge at once. He then instructed the remaining Federals to stay on the battlefield for the next few days, because with Sigel in flight, the "least backward movement now would ruin the moral effect of a complete victory." Sigel's inexplicable behavior did not affect the outcome of the battle— the rebels were gone—but it caused anger and anxiety at headquarters and put him in the doghouse for good.[22]

A courier carried an account of the battle to Springfield the next morning; by nightfall the news was humming over the telegraph wire to St. Louis. Halleck had been on pins and needles for days and it is easy to imagine his relief as he scanned the message that closed with these words: "Indiana, Illinois, Iowa, Ohio, and Missouri very proudly share the honor of victory which their gallant heroes won over the combined forces of Van Dorn, Price, and McCulloch at Pea Ridge, in the Ozark Mountains of Arkansas."[23]

• • •

Pea Ridge was a hard-fought affair. The Federals lost 1,384 killed, wounded, and missing, roughly 13 percent of the 10,250 troops engaged. The Confederates suffered upwards of two thousand killed, wounded, and missing, a casualty rate of at least 15 percent. No one knows how many thousands of civilians were injured, displaced, or otherwise impacted by the marching and fighting.[24]

Curtis deserved the credit for the Union victory. He concentrated his army at Little Sugar Creek as planned, checked Van Dorn's bold opening move with an equally bold countermove, and realigned his forces while closely engaged with the enemy. He grasped the altered tactical situation at the close of the first day and organized a massive and decisive blow on the second day. Few Civil War commanders, and even fewer volunteer officers, exhibited such a sure touch in their first engagement.

At some point during the fighting, Curtis asked his staff to come up with a suitable name for the battle. Several suggestions were made and rejected. Then a local Arkansas Unionist, a civilian guide, spoke up: "Whatever you call it, the people here will call it the battle of Pea Ridge, for that is the name by which the ridge is known all through this country." After a moment's reflection, Curtis made up his mind: "Better call it Pea Ridge then." Aides groaned, but Curtis approved of the homely appellation. "I like it," he said. "It is something new."[25]

A Union officer observed that, throughout the battle, Curtis behaved "as calmly and with as much composure as if overseeing a farm." Other Federals used similar language to describe their undemonstrative leader. A journalist traveling with the army noted that, even when things looked bad, Curtis maintained a confident demeanor "as if he felt an assurance of victory." Curtis may not have been as calm and confident as he appeared. He revealed to brother Henry that the battle was "intensely interesting and anxious—I watched the minute hand of my watch a thousand times."[26]

Soon after the guns fell silent Curtis penned a note to Belinda to let her know he was safe. Two days later he wrote at greater length, describing (without benefit of punctuation) the "anxieties responsibilities the thrilling excitement and magnificence of a great battle." Curtis stated that the "responsibilities resting on me caused me great anxiety, but at no time any emotion of terror or fright, and I felt conscious that I would be sustained by my friends under the circumstances if I did my best without any exhibition of cowardice." He acknowledged that the "terrible consequences" of a defeat were "constantly before me and augmented the burden of my cares more perhaps than at any other period of an eventful life," but added that the pressure did not "effect my health or spirits to any great degree." In other words, it had been an intense few days, but he had come out of it in good shape.[27]

Curtis described the battle to Belinda as a "most signal victory," in which a "kind Heavenly Father preserved my brave army from disaster and myself from injury although many fell, some near to my person and dear to my affections." He wrote little about the fighting but provided a candid description of the aftermath: "Shells and balls have been scattered in profusion over the battlefield, and the dead friends and foes in all the horrors of mutilated forms lay thick over broad areas of our field of carnage. Burying of the dead is still going on but go where I may I still find straggling bodies in the thickets and ravines." A few days later he penned a gloomy letter to brother Henry, in which he described the sprawling battleground as a vast grave: "The scene is silent and sad. The vulture and the wolf have now the dominion and the dead friends and foes sleep in the same lonely graves. Many a kind friend and bold spirit is there interred."[28]

Spring arrived with a rush immediately after the battle, but the rapidly warming temperatures proved to be a mixed blessing. The stench of decaying bodies, human and animal, became so great Curtis was forced to move the army south to Little Sugar Creek, then north to Cross Timbers, a defile on Telegraph Road straddling the state line. Meanwhile, the search for dead and wounded led to a grim discovery near Leetown. The bodies of eight Union soldiers were found to have been scalped and mutilated by members of two Cherokee regiments attached to McCulloch's division. Curtis complained to Van Dorn about this lapse from "civilized warfare" and condemned the use of Indians. Van Dorn tried to change the subject by accusing Union soldiers of murdering Confederate prisoners, a baseless charge Curtis properly dismissed. The commander of the Confederate Indians, Brigadier General Albert Pike, was more forthright. He expressed his "horror" at the incident and promised Curtis it would never happen again. Curtis did not pursue the matter.[29]

For some time Curtis had been annoyed by newspaper stories giving Sigel the credit for driving Price out of Missouri; he feared the same thing would happen regarding Pea Ridge. He was right to be concerned. As soon as the shooting stopped, Sigel's flacks churned out letters to newspapers across the North, touting the German general as the victor and belittling or ignoring Curtis. One widely reprinted account claimed that a cowardly Curtis turned over command of the army to Sigel, then hid in his tent. Supporters urged Curtis to counter the "infamous slander" with his own version of events, but he declined to engage in such petty behavior. "I can survive it," he responded. (He did, however, denounce the press as a "medium of false puffing and quack heroes to the disgust of honorable men.") Curtis believed his official report would set the record straight; to a large extent, it did. His anger faded as congratulations poured in from family, friends, and colleagues. In response to one complimentary letter, he stated that the "glory of the battle is due to soldiers and officers who knew no such words as retreat or fail."[30]

Curtis complained to Halleck about Sigel's behavior in a letter marked "*Private*": "I may sometime hereafter verbally explain to you my trials in regards to detachments and detours which have periled at various times the very existence of this army." Curtis wanted to be rid of his erratic and untrustworthy second-in-command: "If General Sigel be indeed a good leader of an Army, I hope he may have a separate command where he may be satisfied. I cannot understand him and do not wish to have the honor of commanding him." Halleck commiserated with Curtis. "I am glad that you prevented his projects and saved your army," Halleck replied. "I cannot describe to you how much uneasiness I felt for you. You saved your army and won a glorious victory by refusing to take his advice." While Halleck sought a way to remove Sigel without causing another uproar, fate took a hand. Sigel became ill and requested medical leave. He soon departed, never to return.[31]

Curtis labored for weeks to restore the Army of the Southwest to fighting trim. He needed replacements, but manpower was at a premium, with so many military operations underway at the same time. Grant's Army of the Tennessee required a substantial infusion of fresh troops after the fighting at Fort Donelson on February 14–15. Halleck rushed every available man to Grant, which put him in a bind three weeks later when he learned of Pea Ridge. He authorized Curtis to bring forward a regiment that had been left behind to defend Rolla, and he promised to send more replacements as soon as they became available.[32]

The shortage of horses and mules, especially the former, was even more critical. "I *must have* horses or I cannot haul my cannon forward or back," Curtis argued. "I must also have my cavalry kept up or I cannot forage." Before the battle, Curtis had urged Sheridan to use every available means, legal and extralegal, to obtain horses. Sheridan fired back an intemperate reply. He declared that "no authority can compel me to Jayhawk or steal," implying that Curtis had ordered him to do just that. This ill-advised missive reached Curtis shortly after the battle, when he was fuming over Sigel's insubordinate behavior. Unable to arrest Sigel, he arrested Sheridan instead. Curtis explained his decision to Halleck in a letter that seems to contain more gossip than fact. "Sheridan my quartermaster has about fizzled out," he wrote. "He does not seem to have judgement or energy enough. Besides he has got mixed up with secession lady friends till his sympathies seem almost against us and he frets about the irregularities of our troops which are mainly owing to a want of supplies which he ought to provide." Sacking Sheridan in a fit of pique was the only serious mistake Curtis made during the campaign. Halleck thought well of Sheridan and reassigned him to Grant's army, where he soon found his true calling as a combat leader. Sheridan never blamed Curtis for his temporary fall from grace, but his departure did nothing to resolve the equine shortage.[33]

Munitions were another source of friction. Curtis needed nearly five thousand rounds of artillery ammunition and three hundred thousand rounds of small arms ammunition to replace the ordnance expended in two days of furious fighting at Pea Ridge. Two weeks after the battle he had received only eleven rounds per man. "Of course this is not a 'drop in the bucket!'" he exclaimed. Growing more frustrated by the day, Curtis unleashed a stream of demands, complaints, and irate outbursts. He reminded deskbound bureaucrats in Rolla and St. Louis of his precarious situation deep in hostile territory: "I cannot rest easy till my arms are fully replenished and my artillery horses and harness are properly fitted out." Halleck urged patience. "We are doing everything in our power to supply you," he insisted. Nevertheless, the Army of the Southwest remained short of men, animals, and ammunition for weeks.[34]

The mild weather and the absence of any immediate threat provided a welcome interlude for the survivors of so much hard marching and fighting. Curtis tried to spend at least an hour every day strolling through Ozark meadows, "looking at the spring buds and leaves with the same interest I used to watch my seeds in the garden." On March 19 young Henry arrived and took up his duties as adjutant and unofficial private secretary. "Henry is very well and taking a great deal of labor off my shoulders," Curtis wrote. Another welcome arrival was the journal Curtis had left behind at the outset of the campaign. "I regret exceedingly that this book has not been with me for the past month," he noted in his first entry since January. "But so it is when I should write most I have neither time nor convenience." His next entry revealed the private burden he was carrying: "I have been daily receiving dispatches concerning the illness of my dear daughter Sadie who has been very low for days and weeks." Sadie, now twenty, had contracted typhoid in Rolla while looking after her brother. She returned to St. Louis in the care of her mother, sister, and sister-in-law. Curtis became increasingly alarmed as her illness dragged on. "The news unnerves me and gives me great anxiety," he confessed.[35]

On March 21 Curtis was promoted to major general of U.S. Volunteers, in recognition of his victory at Pea Ridge. The former West Point first corporal was immensely gratified by his elevation to the highest grade in the army. His new salary was nearly $5,500 per annum, an increase of more than $1,600, no small matter for someone still burdened with debt. On the morning of March 27 the officers of the First and Second Divisions called on Curtis to congratulate him on his promotion. Asboth led the delegation and made a complimentary speech. Curtis responded in kind, attributing his success to the "endurance and valor displayed by my officers and men." Curtis enjoyed the little ceremony and thought the scene "would have been a good picture for an artist."[36]

That afternoon Curtis learned that Sadie had died in St. Louis the previous day. "I was probably writing to her when her spirit was passing away from Earth," he confided to his journal. "Oh how sad! How terrible. In full life full bloom of womanhood; how suddenly she has left us!" He composed a melancholy letter to Belinda: "I may as well write as weep and I can do a little of both. My tent is closed and Henry is the only one who intrudes on our hour of sorrow and he dear boy feels with me how much we had occasion to love and how much we now have reason to mourn." Midway through the letter he burst out, "Oh God, it is a deep affliction. How strange the ways of Providence." Young Henry was close to Sadie and described her death as the "deepest affliction we have ever known."[37]

A month later Curtis learned, to his great surprise, that a short time before her final illness Sadie had quietly become engaged to Major Chapman S. Charlot, a Union officer stationed in St. Louis. After some hesitation, Charlot wrote Curtis an anguished letter explaining the circumstances of the engagement and expressing his deep sense of loss. He requested and received permission to place a "lofty marble monument" over Sadie's grave. Curtis later assigned Charlot to his staff, where he proved to be a highly capable officer.[38]

Belinda and Carrie took Sadie back to Keokuk for burial in the family plot. Curtis remained with the army in northwest Arkansas. "My duty is unquestionably here," he explained to his wife. Curtis moped around Cross Timbers in a fog of grief. Four of his seven children—Amanda, Yale, Bucky, and now Sadie—had died "when bright and blooming"; three of those deaths had occurred while he was away from home, leaving Belinda to bear the burden alone. The impact of Sadie's death was "almost overpowering," he confessed to brother Henry. "Yet I have borne up and now my heart begins to resume its functions." Two weeks after the terrible news arrived he informed Halleck that he was ready to get back to work: "Much care and private grief bear heavy on me, but I can still do my duty."[39]

1. Curtis at the beginning of his second term in the House of
Representatives, spring 1859. This is the earliest known photograph
of him. Library of Congress, LC-DIG-ppmsca-26830.

2. Brigadier General Curtis at Matthew Brady's Washington studio, July 1861. Note the sash, sword, epaulets, and plumed hat. Author's collection.

3. Sarah Belinda "Sadie" Curtis in early 1862, shortly before her death at age twenty. State Historical Society of Iowa, Des Moines.

4. Major General Curtis in St. Louis, October 1862. He grew the beard during the Pea Ridge campaign. Missouri State Historical Society.

5. The commander of the Department of the Missouri and his staff in St. Louis, spring 1863. Curtis is flanked by Norton P. Chipman (*left*) and Clinton B. Fisk (*right*). Ferdinand S. Winslow stands in the back (*far left*). Wilson's Creek National Battlefield.

6. Major Henry Zarah Curtis, summer 1863, a few months before his murder at Baxter Springs. Wilson's Creek National Battlefield.

7. Curtis at Fort Leavenworth, February 1864.
Wilson's Creek National Battlefield.

S. R. Curtis

MAJ. GEN. SAMUEL R. CURTIS.

8. This fine engraving based on the Leavenworth photograph was widely circulated and served as the frontispiece of Hinton's *Rebel Invasion of Missouri and Kansas*. Author's collection.

8

MARCH TO THE MISSISSIPPI

NEAR THE END OF MARCH 1862 CURTIS LEARNED THAT VAN
Dorn was making his way down the Arkansas Valley toward the
Mississippi River. He decided to move in the same direction in
order to stay between the Confederates and Missouri. "I have
about concluded to move eastward," he told his division commanders, "Get your troops ready to march at a moment's warning." On April 5 the Army of the Southwest broke camp and left
Cross Timbers. The second phase of the Pea Ridge campaign
was underway.[1]

Marching an army across the deeply eroded central part of the
Ozark Plateau proved to be more difficult than Curtis had anticipated. Roads were mere tracks through a sparsely inhabited wilderness. Streams were swollen with snowmelt; men, animals,
and wagons were sometimes swept away by the raging waters.
Trains and foraging parties lost their way in the maze of winding
valleys and food ran short. "The utmost effort must now be made
to procure flour," Curtis informed Halleck. "I can get along without much other baggage but the men insist on bread." The hungry Federals spread out and gobbled up everything within reach.
"I leave nothing for man or brute in the country passed over by
my army," Curtis recorded. The damage inflicted on civilians in
a nominally Union state caused him grief, but he saw no alternative. It was steal or starve. On April 27, after three weeks of toil
and hardship, the Federals reached West Plains, 135 miles east
of Cross Timbers. "The mountains have been overcome," Curtis exulted. The army paused for several days to rest and refit.[2]

Curtis had been living in a tent since leaving Springfield in mid-February. A nomadic existence did not offer much in the way of creature comforts, even for generals. His furnishings were spartan: a camp bed, table, chair, lantern, and trunk. The lack of privacy was a constant annoyance: "I try to get my tent a little isolated, but [the soldiers] will crowd in on me, and it is hard to get a moment's relief from the presence of a crowd of troops that camp close around me." Now and then something happened that brightened or darkened his day. One morning, for instance, Curtis noted in his journal that "George my orderly has set a tumbler of flowers on my table giving my tent quite a cozy appearance." On another morning he learned that a young Iowa officer had been shot by locals and buried where he fell. "A pine board marked W.A.H. will tell his place of rest," Curtis wrote after passing the lonely grave. "Let him sleep in peace. He fell as many have to maintain the Government of our Fathers the best Government in the world."[3]

While Curtis inched eastward across southern Missouri, Halleck learned that Van Dorn had crossed the Mississippi River and joined forces with the Army of Tennessee in Corinth. In remarkably cavalier fashion, without consulting or even informing his superiors in Richmond, Van Dorn abandoned Arkansas, Missouri, and the Indian Territory and moved his entire command (including Price and the Missouri State Guard) to another state and another department. He did not arrive in time to participate in the bloodbath at Shiloh, fought April 6–7, but his troops replaced many of the rebels who fell in that horrific slaughter. With the Army of the West out of the picture, the Army of the Southwest was now the only military force of any size in the entire trans-Mississippi.[4]

Halleck digested all of this and concluded, incorrectly, that the trans-Mississippi was no longer of any strategic value. He left St. Louis in mid-April and assumed command of Grant's army on the Tennessee River. Up to this point Halleck and Curtis had maintained regular, almost daily, communications. That was no longer the case after Halleck took the field. Curtis continued to report to department headquarters in St. Louis, but few of his telegrams and letters reached Halleck in their original form, if they reached him at all. For reasons never explained, the staff at the Planters' House forwarded only some of Curtis's messages to Halleck, and only after editing them to the point where much valuable information was lost or garbled. Halleck's messages to Curtis seem to have passed through St. Louis unscathed. This one-sided lapse in communications went undetected for months and caused misunderstandings that seriously hampered the Union war effort in the trans-Mississippi.[5]

With Missouri safe for the first time since the beginning of the war, Halleck wanted the Army of the Southwest to add its strength to Union efforts to secure the Mississippi Valley. He directed Curtis to cross the Mississippi River and capture Memphis, on the eastern bank. When Halleck asked Curtis what he required in the way of supplies to carry out this maneuver, the latter replied testily: "You ask me to tell you what I want? I want shoes for men horses and mules. I want horses, harness, mules and wagons. I want boats to cross rivers or tools to make them. Requisitions have over and over again been sent for all these things except boats." Following this outburst, Curtis assumed a reasonable tone, like a parent explaining matters to a child: "I know you have many demands but I would like to have one man near you, required to devote his time to this army. My long inland marches wear out marching machinery and no other command has so much need of constant repairs." This message, like so many others, was nearly edited out of existence in St. Louis. The condensed version that reached Halleck reported only that Curtis still needed horses.[6]

In the privacy of his journal, Curtis expressed his frustration at Halleck's perplexing inability to understand his logistical situation: "I have reported by telegraph or otherwise daily and General Halleck now telegraphs that he is quite ignorant of my wants and my movements. It is enough to try the patience of Job."[7]

The Army of the Southwest marched out of West Plains on April 28 and reentered Arkansas the following day. Curtis shook off the lethargy that had dogged him since Sadie's death and dashed ahead with several cavalry regiments in the hope of surprising a large guerrilla band reported to be in Batesville, the principal town in the northeastern part of the state. The Federal horsemen stormed into Batesville on May 3, but the guerrillas had fled. The town fell into Union hands without a shot being fired.[8]

Curtis described Batesville as a "pretty town quite covered with shade trees" and its eight hundred inhabitants as "refined and very respectable." He noted that the townspeople "are generally secesh but the country people are generally for the Union." Curtis moved into a pleasant, two-story brick house with a "very pretty yard" and enjoyed having a roof over his head and a proper bed to sleep in for the first time in months. The Federals remained in Batesville for nearly two months. During that time Curtis worked tirelessly to encourage good relations between soldiers and civilians. He established a pro-Union newspaper (the only one in the state at the time) and enrolled hundreds of volunteers into what became the First Arkansas Infantry (Union), the first of several white regiments drawn from the state's northern counties. "Union men in Arkansas are beginning to show their faces," Curtis observed. He also noted that many people in the region seemed ready "to abandon the scheme of secession. They say it is played out." Meanwhile, Brigadier General Frederick Steele and three thousand promised replacements arrived from southeastern Missouri and occupied nearby Jacksonport. Curtis and Steele would become the bitterest of enemies, but for a time they got along well enough.[9]

Batesville is located where the White River emerges from the Ozark Plateau and enters the alluvial valley of the Mississippi River. The broad floodplain, known locally as the Delta, makes up the eastern third of Arkansas and a good part of Louisiana and Mississippi. At the time of the Civil War it was a mix of farms, gallery forests, canebrakes, and swamps. Each spring the Mississippi overflowed its banks and submerged the Delta with a sheet of muddy water, as Curtis discovered when he attempted to plot his approach to Memphis. Scouts reported that eastern Arkansas was an "endless lake" and that it would be weeks before the water receded and the land dried. When Halleck was advised of this development, he told Flag Officer Charles H. Davis, Union naval commander on the Upper Mississippi, that the navy would have to capture Memphis on its own, which it did on June 6. Halleck then informed Curtis that the Army of the Southwest had accomplished its mission in the trans-Mississippi, and that he should send half of his infantry to reinforce Grant, who was confronting a large Confederate force at Corinth. Breaking up the victorious Army of the Southwest was a bad idea. Had Halleck simply sent Steele back to southeastern Missouri, and from there to Corinth, much trouble would have been avoided.[10]

Curtis did not like being forced to give up so many of his veteran troops "while I am so far in advance of other armies," a not-so-subtle reminder to Halleck that he had penetrated deeper into the Confederacy than any other Union general, including Grant. Grumbling all the while, Curtis selected ten regiments and formed them into two temporary divisions under Asboth and Davis. On May 10 the chosen officers and men bid farewell to their comrades and set out for the war on the other side of the Great River. Curtis reorganized his nine thousand remaining soldiers into three new divisions, carefully arranging regiments and batteries along familiar ethnic lines. Steele's First Division and Carr's Second Division were composed largely of midwestern soldiers from Illinois, Indiana, and Iowa. Osterhaus's Third Division consisted of the remaining German-speaking Missouri troops.[11]

Halleck now reversed course and ordered the reorganized and much-reduced Army of the Southwest to turn south and capture Little Rock. Once Curtis was in possession of the Arkansas capital, he was to rule by martial law until a Unionist state government could be installed. Halleck's directive was influenced by political as well as military considerations. U.S. forces had recently captured two rebel state capitals, Nashville and Baton Rouge; the Lincoln administration was anxious to keep up the momentum and add a third.[12]

Halleck seems to have expected a walkover with Van Dorn out of the way, but Curtis did not think his overland supply line would stretch another eighty miles to Little Rock. "I have a long, rough road before me," he warned. Halleck brushed these and other concerns aside. He blithely assured Curtis that he would have the navy establish a supply line to Batesville via the Mississippi and White Rivers in short order, but he failed to follow through on his promise.[13]

The first of several Union attempts to capture Little Rock began in early May. Osterhaus got his Third Division across the White River at Batesville on a rickety rope ferry despite almost constant rain. Four days and forty-five soggy miles later, he reached the Little Red River, only thirty-five miles from his objective. Curtis was pleased to learn from Arkansas newspapers that his approach was causing a "great commotion" in Little Rock. The Army of the Southwest appeared to be on the verge of another triumph. Then things began to go wrong. Despite its diminutive name, the Little Red proved to be a formidable obstacle. Osterhaus was forced to stop and construct two dirt causeways and a lengthy timber bridge across the swollen stream. Progress was slow because Halleck had ordered away Curtis's only engineering officer a few weeks earlier. Then the ferry across the White at Batesville capsized, with the loss of eleven lives. The fatal accident stranded Osterhaus on one side of the stream and Steele and Carr on the other, with no effective way to move troops back and forth in case of emergency. "My arrangements for crossing the White are so precarious I do not like to rely on them," Curtis told Osterhaus. "It will not do to have our forces separated by so many rivers." He suspended the offensive.[14]

Curtis had reason to be anxious: the rebels were stirring. Major General Thomas C. Hindman had recently arrived in Arkansas with orders to restore Confederate fortunes in the trans-Mississippi. Hindman instituted a draconian conscription policy to raise troops and authorized the creation of independent guerrilla bands to harass Union trains and foraging parties. When reports of Hindman's activities reached Batesville, Curtis realized that subjugating the state was going to be a more formidable task than previously imagined. He predicted that the new Confederate commander was "likely to give me trouble in Arkansas." Nevertheless, Curtis was cautiously upbeat in a letter to brother Henry: "At present I am arranging for taking Little Rock and crushing rebellion in Arkansas. No trifling job of course."[15]

Not only were the Confederates becoming more active, they were raising the level of violence. Hindman's rebels usually fought from ambush and rarely took prisoners. Osterhaus described them as "outlaws" who "do not deserve the name of soldiers." Curtis agreed, ordering that such "villains" were "not to be taken as prisoners." A particularly brutal engagement on May 19 near Searcy cost the Federals fifty men killed, wounded, and missing. Curtis was outraged to learn that Union soldiers had been murdered while they lay wounded. He reiterated his earlier instructions to "take no more prisoners of armed banditts."[16]

Meanwhile, Osterhaus bridged the Little Red and Carr ferried his Second Division across the White on a flotilla of hastily built boats and rafts. Curtis ordered the advance on Little Rock to resume on May 21, but before anything could be done he received a letter from Captain Ferdinand S. Winslow, Sheridan's successor as quartermaster and commissary. Winslow informed Curtis that the Army of the Southwest had reached the end of its logistical tether. The Union line of communications extended an astounding 320 overland miles from Rolla to the Little Red, but it could stretch no farther. In addition to the difficulties caused by distance, terrain, weather, guerrillas, and the seemingly insoluble shortage of draft animals, wagons and harnesses were falling to pieces after five months of constant wear and tear. Winslow stated in the strongest terms that the army could not be sustained where it was much longer, and most certainly could not be supported if it advanced any farther.[17]

Curtis reviewed the details and concluded to his own satisfaction that Winslow was correct: "Going forward *in force* seems *absolutely impossible* at present even if rivers and mud were not in the way." Nothing more could be done until Halleck's promised waterborne supply line was up and running. It was now clear to Curtis that the Mississippi, Arkansas, White, and other waterways "must be made available for transportation before Arkansas can be properly held and the rebels subdued." On May 24 Curtis went forward to confer with Carr and Osterhaus on the Little Red. They agreed that the best way to cover the army's withdrawal was to knock the rebels off balance. On May 27 Union cavalry, closely followed by foraging teams, surged across the new bridge and put the surprised Confederates to flight. The Federals collected enough food, much of it from enemy camps, to supply their needs for a week. The successful operation raised Curtis's spirits. He informed a colleague in Rolla that "I am crowded a little bit but I am troubling Rebeldom in Arkansas considerably."[18]

The brave words could not hide the fact that the Army of the Southwest and its commander were wearing down after five active and difficult months in the field. "I have led a *forlorn hope* long enough," Curtis confided to brother Henry. "My position in this war has been very different from that which I had in Mexico. Here I am almost daily in actual conflict with the foe; there I hardly got in sight of him. Here I have been so long in the van guard and seen so much fighting service I would be very willing to have a little chance in the reserve corps in order to allow rest to my weary soldiers." Letters from Belinda, who remained in Keokuk following Sadie's burial, provided Curtis with some relief from the endless grind of the campaign. In one missive Belinda proudly announced that she had rented the Keokuk house to a "nice family," with the proviso that she and Carrie could occupy one bedroom and share the kitchen. Curtis praised Belinda's business acumen and rejoiced at her "extremely economical" living arrangements.[19]

At the end of May Curtis confessed, "I feel exceedingly averse to a backward movement but my forage and food supplies are indeed growing desperate." He ordered Carr and Osterhaus to destroy the bridge over the Little Red and fall back to Batesville, thereby bringing to a close the first attempt to capture Little Rock. Steele moved up from Jacksonport. By mid-June the Army of the Southwest was concentrated around Batesville. Curtis brought Halleck up to date and pointedly asked when he could expect the navy to arrive with the promised supplies and reinforcements. This message seems to have passed through department headquarters without being edited to death. Halleck was shocked to learn that the Little Rock offensive had been canceled and demanded an explanation.[20]

Curtis exploded. "I have telegraphed you daily through your proper adjutant-general and inspector-general for the last two months," he declared. "I have told you that my troops were unable to hold position. I have asked for re-enforcements, which have not been received. Troops promised have been stopped. My troops have had to fall back; my stock almost starving, and the enemy has been animated, learning I had sent to you a large portion of my force." Curtis closed his tirade by pledging "to keep [in] communication with you, as [I] supposed I had been doing during the past sixty days." This message also reached Halleck more or less intact.[21]

Only now did Halleck realize how badly his communications with Curtis had broken down. He immediately organized a rescue effort. "Rely on it I will reinforce you as soon as possible," he messaged Curtis. He told Flag Officer Davis that it was a matter of "pressing importance" to reach Curtis, who was effectively marooned in northeastern Arkansas. "It is the earnest wish of the War Department that this be done without delay," Halleck declared. Davis promptly dispatched a force of gunboats and transports loaded with rations, hay, ammunition, and a brigade of infantry. The Union vessels churned down the Mississippi River then turned into the looping White River. On June 17 the gunboats engaged a Confederate fort at St. Charles. The ironclad *Mound City* was disabled with a heavy loss of life, but the infantry went ashore and captured the earthworks. The Union vessels pressed on to Clarendon, where they were stopped by, of all things, low water. Curtis learned of this latest setback and announced that, since the transports could not come to him, "I must go to them." He decided to sever his fraying supply line with Rolla and live off the land. He assured his anxious officers and men that an "army like this will not fail for want of supplies as long as anything remains in the country."[22]

•••

The Army of the Southwest left Batesville near the end of June and proceeded down the eastern bank of the White River toward Clarendon and the Union flotilla. Sick and wounded soldiers floated downstream on rafts and barges alongside the marching column. For the next two and a half weeks Curtis operated independently of a base of supplies in hostile territory, the first time in the Civil War any army commander attempted such a daring maneuver. It would not be repeated until eleven months later, when Grant adopted a similar course of action during the Vicksburg campaign. Curtis never made much of his break with military convention, but he knew he had done something remarkable. "My command has no doubt been more intensely and constantly laborious than any in the army," he told brother Henry. "I have marched further over worse roads than any other General and subsisted my force in the country. *Nobody else has done this*."[23]

The Federals had struggled over the Ozark Plateau in the dead of winter; now they trudged across the Delta at the height of a southern summer. The spring flood had finally receded but heat, humidity, dust, and swarms of insects made everyone miserable. Curtis did not envisage his march across eastern Arkansas as a form of economic warfare, but that is exactly what it was. Despite orders to respect private property and take only what was needed, the Federals foraged and pillaged on an unprecedented scale and committed "great irregularities along the line of march." Homes were spared, but mills, warehouses, sheds, wharves, woodpiles, and fences were destroyed. Crops were trampled or burned and orchards were cut down. Smokehouses were plundered. Horses, mules, cattle, wagons, and tools were confiscated. "Desolation, horrid to contemplate, marks every section of the country through which the army has passed," wrote an appalled Illinois soldier. An Arkansas civilian agreed: "No country ever was, or ever can be, worse devastated and laid waste than that which has been occupied, and marched over, by the Federal army. Every thing which could be eaten by hungry horses or men has been devoured, and not content with foraging upon the country, almost every thing which could not be eaten was destroyed." The Army of the Southwest was the first Union force to inflict systematic destruction on the Confederacy's civilian population and economy. It would not be the last.[24]

Curtis's march also sounded the death knell for slavery across a wide swath of Arkansas. While at Cross Timbers in March, Curtis had emancipated five slaves "employed in the rebel service and taken as contrabands of war." Acting in accordance with the First Confiscation Act, he meticulously recorded the proceedings and declared the men "forever emancipated from the service of masters who allowed them to aid in efforts to break up the government and laws of our country." Three months later his attitude toward slavery and slave owners had hardened, and his patience with bureaucratic procedures had evaporated. Curtis began to emancipate slaves on an industrial scale, ignoring the fact that, until the passage of the Second Confiscation Act on July 17, he lacked the authority to do any such thing. His troops commandeered printing presses in towns along the line of march and cranked out stacks of official-looking emancipation forms. They then distributed the forms to nearly everyone who asked for them. News spread like wildfire. Within days thousands of men, women, and children, "free papers" clutched in their hands, were trailing the dusty blue column en route to an uncertain future. Few soldiers in the Army of the Southwest had encountered a black person before, but they quickly adjusted to people of African descent "wandering around the camp as thick as blackberries."[25]

No one bothered to keep an accurate count, but Curtis probably freed more human beings from bondage than any other political, military, or religious leader in the first eighteen months of the Civil War. What he did is well documented. Why he did it is not. His public and private comments in the 1840s and 1850s reveal strong opposition to the expansion of slavery into the West but no outrage over the existence of slavery in the South or concern for those enslaved. By the early 1860s, however, Curtis had become an abolitionist of sorts. He blamed slave owners for the war (and for the loss of so many innocents, including his beloved daughter) and was determined to make them pay a heavy price for their hubris. He still seemed to care more about punishing the beneficiaries of slavery than he did about rescuing its victims.

The march across Arkansas offered Curtis an opportunity to chastise slave owners who had plunged the United States into turmoil and misery. "The rebellion must be shaken to its foundation, which is slavery," he told a fellow officer. "The idea of saving rebels from the inevitable consequences of their rebellion is no part of our business." Curtis never offered a public justification of his actions, but a passage in his private journal provides a clue to his thinking: "I give captured slaves their freedom on the ground that they become captured captives and therefore subject to my disposal instead of a former captor or assignee." The legalistic language demonstrates no sense of moral outrage over slavery or sympathy for the plight of the enslaved, but that would change. Curtis the abolitionist was a work in progress.[26]

Reports of economic destruction and social turmoil led Hindman to make an ill-advised attack on Curtis at Cache River on July 7. The Army of the Southwest was fording the sluggish stream when the rebels struck the head of the column. Curtis remained at the ford (which he described as a "thicket of brush and trees very gloomy and uncomfortable") and hurried reinforcements forward to Steele, whose troops bore the brunt of the fighting. Despite being caught in an awkward position, the Federals drove off the attackers and pursued them for miles. Curtis informed Halleck that the battle resulted in a "complete rout of the rebel army of Arkansas. They ran in all directions." The Federals lost six killed and fifty-seven wounded; Confederate casualties amounted to 136 dead and at least as many wounded. Cache River was the only time Hindman directly challenged Curtis. Having no desire to repeat the experience, the rebel commander withdrew to Fort Smith, on the border with the Indian Territory.[27]

Curtis halted for a day to succor the wounded and bury the dead. The delay had important consequences. The Federals reached Clarendon on July 9, only to discover that the gunboats and transports had departed less than twenty-four hours earlier. Curtis fired cannons and sent couriers galloping after the Union vessels, but to no avail. The attempt to establish a waterborne supply line had failed by the slimmest of margins. Curtis acknowledged that the "disappointment is most overwhelming." He had no choice but to turn away from Little Rock and march to Helena, forty-five miles to the east on the western bank of the Mississippi River. Establishing a reliable line of communications was more important than gaining additional territory. Little Rock would have to wait.[28]

On July 12 the Army of the Southwest tramped into Helena. There was no resistance. Curtis described his troops as being "in rough attire, but in fine health and spirits." Thousands of Federals crowded atop the Mississippi River levee and flagged down a passing vessel. The Union gunboat *General Bragg* cautiously approached the throngs of dusty, ragged soldiers, then sped away to spread the welcome news that the "Lost Army" had emerged from the Arkansas wilderness. Curtis salved his disappointment at failing to capture Little Rock by moving into Hindman's elegant Helena mansion and flying a large U.S. flag from its roof. The rest of the army, trailed by hundreds of wagons and thousands of Black refugees, gradually trickled into town. The Pea Ridge campaign was over.[29]

During the first six months of 1862 Curtis and his men marched 750 miles across mountains and swamps, endured ice storms and stultifying heat, won the largest battle fought west of the Mississippi River in the first half of the war, pioneered a novel form of mobile warfare, and emancipated slaves on an unprecedented scale. No other Union operation at this stage of the conflict lasted as long or covered as much territory, and few achieved their objectives so effectively. Curtis could not have foreseen that his campaign, initially limited in scope, would wreak such havoc on the rebellion in the trans-Mississippi. By the time he rode into Helena, Missouri was secured for the Union, much of Arkansas was lost to the Confederacy, and the strategic balance in the Mississippi Valley and beyond was permanently altered.

The Helena waterfront was soon crowded with transports from St. Louis disgorging supplies of every description. With a reliable line of communications finally in place, Curtis expected to resume operations against Little Rock in the near future. "A few days will be required to overhaul my equipment, rest my men, and enjoy once more the luxury of a full army ration," he informed Halleck. The usually irascible Halleck was in an expansive mood after the remarkable success of his campaigns in Missouri, Arkansas, Kentucky, and Tennessee, and he expressed support for whatever Curtis had in mind. He even offered reinforcements: "How many additional troops do you want to take Little Rock and clear out northern Arkansas?"[30]

Halleck and Curtis now enjoyed reliable communications through Memphis instead of St. Louis. They seemed poised to resume their successful, if sometimes prickly, partnership, but barely a week after Curtis marched into Helena, Lincoln summoned Halleck to Washington to replace McClellan as general in chief. "How long I shall be absent I know not," Halleck wrote Curtis. "You therefore must act in Arkansas as your own judgement indicates." As a parting gift Halleck, ever the military bureaucrat, established the District of Eastern Arkansas and placed Curtis in command. He also transferred a division from Memphis to Helena, which enlarged Curtis's force to eighteen thousand men.[31]

Halleck was appointed general in chief because of his success in the West, as measured against McClellan's notable lack of success in the East. The victories at Forts Henry and Donelson, Pea Ridge, Island No. 10, Shiloh, Memphis, and Corinth, combined with the seizure of New Orleans and Baton Rouge by Union warships moving up the Mississippi River from the Gulf of Mexico, dramatically altered the strategic situation west of the Appalachian Mountains. The Confederate government scrambled to fortify Vicksburg and Port Hudson in order to deny the Federals free use of the Mississippi and to maintain a tenuous connection with the trans-Mississippi states and territories. Seizure of those two rebel strongpoints became the primary objective of Union military and naval operations in the Mississippi Valley between July 1862 and July 1863.[32]

Helena was for many months the southernmost Union base on the Upper Mississippi River, so it followed that Curtis was the first Union general to explore the possibilities of a waterborne approach to Vicksburg. Some Federal commanders in the West were already familiar with riverine operations. Grant, for example, made effective use of the Tennessee and Cumberland Rivers in his seizure of Forts Henry and Donelson and his movement to Pittsburgh Landing, but following the Battle of Shiloh he moved inland toward Corinth, away from navigable waterways. Grant attempted an overland approach to Vicksburg in the fall of 1862 based on a railroad line, a novel idea at the time, but it was only after that approach failed that he decided to move his army down the Mississippi. For most of July and August of that year, Curtis had the field—or, rather, the river—to himself.[33]

Lacking strategic guidance from Washington but eager to maintain pressure on the reeling Confederates, Curtis put aside his plans for taking Little Rock and turned his attention to Vicksburg. A movement down the Mississippi River required naval support, so he invited Flag Officer Davis to visit Helena. The two officers hit it off. Davis subsequently informed the Navy Department that he and Curtis shared the "most perfect harmony of purpose and of cooperation."[34]

Curtis and Davis agreed to "scour" the Mississippi River below Helena and prepare the way for a waterborne offensive against Vicksburg. Acting entirely on their own initiative, they assembled a "considerable force" of gunboats and transports at Helena, packed the latter with troops from the Army of the Southwest, and proceeded downstream. The Confederates had slipped a large quantity of arms and ammunition across the Mississippi the previous week at Gaines Landing in southeastern Arkansas; Curtis hoped to seize or destroy the matériel before it reached Hindman. He failed in that but captured two steamboats and destroyed eighty barges, flatboats, and rafts, making another such shipment impossible. A second expedition seized the transport *Fair Play* at Milliken's Bend in northeastern Louisiana. The vessel was loaded with more arms and ammunition for Hindman, including a four-gun battery and thousands of British-made Enfield rifles. The Federals came within sight of Vicksburg and raided towns in Arkansas, Louisiana, and Mississippi. They confiscated food and cotton, burned mills and warehouses, and skirmished with rebel bands. Davis termed the second expedition a "great success." Curtis, to his great regret, missed it because of administrative duties in Helena.[35]

After months spent trudging through the wilds of Missouri and Arkansas, Curtis was amazed at the mobility of riverine operations in the Mississippi Valley. Union soldiers could appear wherever they chose along the western waterways, carrying "death and desolation" into the Confederate countryside. He wanted Halleck to provide him with a fleet of transports capable of carrying ten thousand men and their equipment. "Such boats are easily improvised," he stated, "and the rivers of Mississippi and Arkansas can be cleared and the adjacent country completely overpowered." The two recent expeditions encountered so little opposition that Curtis believed it might be possible to rush down the river with the eighteen thousand troops at Helena (or as many of them as could be crowded aboard the boats at hand) and fall on Vicksburg without warning.[36]

The more Curtis and Davis discussed the idea of a dash on Vicksburg, the more they liked it. They hurried up the Mississippi River to Cairo, to avail themselves of a direct telegraph connection with Washington. Davis later explained that the "general and myself" wanted to discuss "plans of joint operations" against Vicksburg with their respective superiors in the War and Navy Departments. Curtis made the pitch to Halleck. He proposed an offensive composed of troops from both his Army of the Southwest and Grant's Army of the Tennessee: "General Grant and myself should unite with the Navy in a new effort to scatter the batteries" at Vicksburg and "destroy the gunboats and rams of the enemy." Curtis argued that such an operation, if carried out promptly and boldly, would be "disastrous to the enemy." Grant outranked Curtis and would command such an expedition, but Curtis did not seem to mind. He closed with a flourish, reminding Halleck that the "hopes of the West float on the Mississippi." In a more prosaic postscript Curtis requested permission to fortify Helena so that it could be held by a small garrison when the rest of Army of the Southwest pushed off for Vicksburg.[37]

Curtis's proposal to rush downstream and take Vicksburg by storm seems familiar because it is *exactly* what Grant ordered Major General William T. Sherman to do four months later, following the failure of his railroad-based overland offensive in northern Mississippi. By that time, however, the Confederates had ringed Vicksburg with fortifications and poured in reinforcements. Sherman had no chance of success, but he did as ordered. In December he carried off most of the Army of the Southwest from Helena, steamed downriver to Vicksburg, and was repulsed at Chickasaw Bayou with heavy losses. In August, however, when Curtis and Davis telegraphed Washington, the bulk of the Confederate army was in northern Mississippi confronting Grant. Vicksburg was still only lightly defended. Under these circumstances a sudden descent on the "Gibraltar of the Mississippi" might have met with success. We will never know.[38]

Curtis and Davis were victims of bad timing and Halleck's flawed temperament. The Second Manassas and Antietam campaigns were underway in Virginia and Maryland. Halleck, new to his job as general in chief and unnerved by the threat to Washington, did not want to hear about proposals for additional operations in the West. He curtly dismissed Curtis's proposal for a waterborne operation against Vicksburg, insisting that the Army of the Southwest must remain in Helena "to prevent a foray from Arkansas into Missouri." An overland expedition, he said, would be "fitted out against Vicksburg as soon as troops can be spared for that purpose." Halleck brusquely instructed Curtis to confine his activities to the trans-Mississippi and cease meddling in affairs not his own. In other words, stop bothering the busy general in chief.[39]

Halleck's reasons, or excuses, for inaction in the West at this time were nonsense. The tens of thousands of Union soldiers standing idle in the Mississippi Valley, including the Army of the Southwest at Helena, offered no protection whatsoever to Missouri and could easily have been "spared" for an attempt on Vicksburg. The only part of Curtis's proposal Halleck approved was the construction of a substantial fort at Helena. The resulting earthwork, appropriately named Fort Curtis, played a key role in defending the town against a Confederate assault on July 4, 1863.[40]

A disappointed Curtis returned to Helena. "My force is not idle," he stiffly informed the general in chief, "and I will continue to press the enemy to the best of my ability." Instead of rushing down the Mississippi River to Vicksburg, Curtis and Davis decided to make their way up the Arkansas River and seize Little Rock. The state capital was said to be defenseless, but when Union gunboats nosed into the Arkansas they found the way blocked, not by rebels but by sandbars. The western Confederacy experienced a severe drought in the late summer and early fall of 1862; water levels in the Arkansas, always unpredictable, dropped too low for ironclad gunboats and heavily laden transports. "If a fleet goes up [the river] there is no safety," Curtis explained, "it is more than likely to be caught by a fall that leaves the boats high and dry." He described the shallow, winding Arkansas as a "trap." Stymied, Curtis revisited the possibility of an overland operation. He reoccupied Clarendon and constructed a pontoon bridge across the White River, but the parched countryside could not sustain his horses and mules. Two months earlier the Delta had been submerged; now it was dry as dust. On August 6 Curtis concluded that an advance on Little Rock was "not immediately possible." The Federals pulled up the bridge and returned to Helena to wait for rain.[41]

• • •

With operations along the Mississippi and Arkansas Rivers on hold, Curtis turned his attention to administering the Union enclave of Helena. As he had done in Batesville, he imposed martial law, encouraged good relations between soldiers and civilians, attended church services, and even allowed the local newspaper to resume publication, albeit with a change in editorial policy. He spent most of his time, however, grappling with problems caused by the influx of freedmen and the buying and selling of cotton and other commodities.[42]

Helena quickly became a refuge for former slaves from all over eastern Arkansas and western Mississippi. Halleck was a social conservative who disapproved of mass emancipation, so Curtis downplayed the scope of his abolitionist practices. He assured Halleck that he freed only those slaves "who were mustered by their rebel masters to blockade my way to my supplies," a reference to Hindman's use of slave labor to obstruct the Union army's march to Helena. The slaves in question, he added somewhat fancifully, "are now throwing down their axes and rushing in for free papers." In fact, Curtis provided "free papers" to almost anyone who asked; he did not mention that most of the refugees crowding into Helena were women and children. Curtis also told Halleck that sensational newspaper accounts of Africans running amuck were exaggerated. The slaves, he stated, are "mutinous but do not abuse their masters."[43]

Curtis established refugee camps and provided food, clothing, and cooking equipment as such items became available, but the army's needs came first and the freedmen suffered accordingly. Helena was a small town and the local economy offered few opportunities for employment, so Curtis encouraged his officers to hire freedmen as teamsters, laborers, cooks, stewards, servants, seamstresses, and laundresses. He put hundreds to work on Fort Curtis and other construction projects at a minimum wage of $10 per month, plus rations and cast-off uniforms. He even provided free passage up the Mississippi River to those who wanted to start a new life in the North. In addition to establishing welfare and workfare programs, Curtis handed out cash.

He gave $100 to a group of freedmen who came to army head-quarters in search of work. When a colleague expressed surprise at such generosity, Curtis shrugged and said the "poor fellows must be fed, and taken care of." The money came from a headquarters slush fund supported by the sale of confiscated rebel property.[44]

Not everyone in the Army of the Southwest shared Curtis's enlightened attitude. Frederick Steele was one of many ultra-conservative, proslavery Democrats in blue. He complained to Halleck, a kindred spirit, about what he believed were illegal and inappropriate emancipation practices in eastern Arkansas: "General Curtis, in my opinion, violated both law and orders, and instituted a policy entirely different from that indicated by the President in regard to slaves." To Steele's dismay and disgust, the Second Confiscation Act and Lincoln's Emancipation Proclamation subsequently validated everything Curtis did in Arkansas. Curtis hoped there would be "no further attempt to ignore my free papers," but he underestimated Steele, who continued his efforts to turn back the clock and cleanse the army of abolitionist generals.[45]

The buying and selling of cotton was an even more contentious issue. After eighteen months of war, blockade, and embargo, textile mills in the North were shutting down for lack of raw material. Unemployment was rising, as was fear of civil unrest. Curtis understood the economic and political ramifications of the situation. "I consider it important to get the cotton to our factories," he assured Halleck, "and where it belongs to the poor and needy sufferers of Arkansas there is a double reason for disposing of it." Cotton traders (also called agents, buyers, speculators, and less complimentary names) followed close behind advancing Union forces, eager to acquire as much of the precious crop as possible. The banks of the Mississippi River between Memphis and Helena were said to be "lined with cotton speculators."[46]

Cotton traders had a well-deserved reputation as sharps, crooks, and even spies, because they sometimes provided military information to the Confederates in exchange for access to cotton. Grant famously denounced cotton traders, especially Jews, and tried to expel them from his department. Sherman, then commanding in Memphis a short distance upstream from Helena, was appalled at the influx of cotton traders, whom he regarded as little better than criminals and traitors. He informed Curtis that Memphis was overrun by "speculators and Jews who would sell our lives for ten percent profit on a barrel of salt," and he warned that the scoundrels were heading downriver to Helena in droves. Sherman advised Curtis to be vigilant and firm. (Derogatory remarks about Jews made by Grant, Sherman, and Curtis reflect the casual anti-Semitism that pervaded American culture in the nineteenth century.)[47]

Curtis initially adopted a hands-off policy, allowing buyers and sellers to make their own arrangements. This approach resulted in widespread fraud and theft, just as Sherman had predicted, so Curtis quickly altered course and adopted policies similar to those Grant and Sherman had established. At the end of July he announced that "confusions and corruptions" in the cotton trade had reached a point where the army had to step in. Henceforth, he allowed only licensed traders to operate in Helena, and he issued licenses only to those who met his standards. "I at first let everybody trade in cotton," Curtis reported to Halleck, "but soon found my camp infested with Jews, secessionists, and spies, and had to issue an order confining the business to a few, whom I restrain as sutlers under military law." He described the favored few as "persons of undoubted loyalty," though he never explained how he made that determination.[48]

The new rules generated furious resentment. Cotton traders who were denied a license claimed, without evidence, that Curtis issued licenses in return for bribes and kickbacks. Curtis ruefully informed Halleck that the "cotton lords are down on me." He told brother Henry that the "mean criticism" came from "Jews and sharpes [who] I would not allow to trade in my lines as they were ready to sell my army for a few bales of cotton." He described his critics as men "whose interests were affected and whose patriotism was absorbed by love of gold or affection for slavery." Curtis expected the clamor to fade away, like the uproar over Sigel's resignation eight months earlier. Instead, allegations of corruption triggered an inquiry that tarnished his reputation and nearly drove him out of the army. But in August 1862 all of that was still in the future.[49]

9

MISSOURI

ON JULY 1, 1862, PRESIDENT LINCOLN SIGNED THE PACIFIC Railroad Act into law. The act was a modified version of the bill Curtis wrote and shepherded through the House of Representatives the previous year. It called for a board of commissioners to meet in Chicago and lay the groundwork for the mammoth undertaking. When Curtis learned that he was one of the commissioners named in the act, he requested a leave of absence to attend the meeting. Halleck wanted Curtis to remain on the job in Arkansas and grumbled, "Your presence with the army in the field is deemed very important." Nevertheless, he passed Curtis's request on to Secretary of War Edwin M. Stanton, who approved a generous sixty-day leave.[1]

Curtis left Helena on August 27. He proceeded up the Mississippi River to Keokuk, where he stopped briefly to see his family, then pressed on to Chicago. On September 2 he attended the opening session of the Pacific Railroad Convention in Bryan Hall, then the largest public building in the city. The assembled commissioners elected Curtis president of the convention. He acknowledged the honor and made a brief speech emphasizing the "importance of the enterprise they were about to inaugurate." He then presided over the nomination and election of officers for the aptly named Union Pacific Railroad Company. Curtis declined any role for himself, explaining that his military duties "called him elsewhere and would engross all his energies until the rebellion is put down." The convention established the framework of the new company, though the financial arrangements proved inadequate and required major changes. On September 5 Curtis closed the meeting and congratulated his fellow commissioners on providing the country with a "highway to the Pacific." The long hoped-for transcontinental railroad was finally becoming reality.[2]

Acquaintances were struck by Curtis's gaunt appearance and unsteady manner. "My friends all speak of my emaciated form and I find my muscular efforts feeble," he told brother Henry. A few weeks earlier, while still in Helena, Curtis had confided to Belinda that he felt "very much debilitated," but provided no details. He was even less forthcoming to Halleck, stating only that he was "not exactly well." Curtis was doubtless worn down by months of toil, worry, and exposure to the elements. He may also have been afflicted with one or more of the subtropical diseases endemic to Helena. At age fifty-seven he was the oldest Union general commanding an army in the field, and he had just completed the longest and most grueling campaign of the war. Whatever the exact nature of his ailments, Curtis found the Windy City to be a welcome change from sultry Helena. Belinda joined her husband after the convention. The couple spent several days at her brother's house near Lake Michigan, where they enjoyed the "cool refreshing breeze of the lake and the kind hospitalities of dear friends."[3]

Curtis and Belinda returned to Keokuk on September 9. Throngs of well-wishers gathered to see Iowa's most celebrated soldier. Curtis enjoyed the cheers and accolades but declined the honor of a "public ovation." He wanted to rest, recover his strength, and look after his business affairs, which were in even more disarray than usual. While at home Curtis discussed aspects of the Pea Ridge campaign with brother Henry by mail. He was especially proud of the fact that he had been "constantly in advance of all other forces" during the spring and summer, and that, even after two months of inactivity in Helena, the Army of the Southwest was still the "farthest South" of all Union armies.[4]

On September 22 Curtis was relaxing at home when he received a telegram from the War Department. "Your leave of absence is revoked," wrote Halleck, "and you will immediately assume command of the Department of the Missouri, headquartered at St. Louis." Curtis was pleased with his elevation to the top of a major military command. Nevertheless there was a downside. The demands of running a busy, high-profile department made it unlikely that he would play a significant role in opening the Mississippi River.[5]

Hindman was indirectly responsible for Curtis's elevation to department command. Following his unsuccessful attempt to stop the Army of the Southwest at Cache River the previous July, the Confederate commander had withdrawn to Fort Smith in western Arkansas. There he prepared his force, now styled the Trans-Mississippi Army, to march north and recover the territory Van Dorn and Price had lost to Curtis earlier in the year. In August the Confederates crossed the Boston Mountains and reoccupied northwestern Arkansas, including the old Pea Ridge battleground. Then they halted to see how the Federals would react. Hindman's gambit was more bluff than invasion, but it rattled Brigadier General John M. Schofield, the senior Union officer in Missouri. Schofield claimed that thirty thousand Confederates were marching north in two columns. "Unless something be done soon," he wailed, "I shall lose a large part of Missouri." Hindman's modest force in northwestern Arkansas, about six thousand strong, was real enough, but a second force in northeastern Arkansas existed only in Schofield's feverish imagination.[6]

Halleck was disturbed by Schofield's hysterical outbursts and asked Curtis for his take on the situation. Curtis dismissed the figure of thirty thousand Confederates as absurd and described the youthful, mercurial Schofield as "over-anxious." He stated emphatically that there was only one rebel army in the trans-Mississippi, not two, and that Union forces in Missouri, if properly managed by a competent officer, were sufficient to defend the state. Curtis also pointed out, not very tactfully, that Halleck had erred in writing off the trans-Mississippi a few months earlier. The Confederates obviously considered the region to be an active theater of war; against all expectations, they had raised a new and potentially troublesome army on the frontier.[7]

Halleck believed Missouri's ills could best be resolved by rearranging lines on a map. In April 1862 the Department of the Missouri had been enlarged to form a huge new Department of the Mississippi. When Halleck left for Washington in July to become general in chief he never got around to naming a successor. As a result, the Department of the Mississippi was headless and directionless for two months, which helps to explain why Curtis and Flag Officer Davis were able to operate so freely in the Mississippi Valley. In September Halleck dissolved the unwieldy Department of the Mississippi and resurrected the more manageable Department of the Missouri. Then he ordered Curtis to cut short his leave of absence and hurry to St. Louis.[8]

Curtis bid farewell to his wife and daughter in Keokuk and boarded a steamboat for the short trip to St. Louis. He assumed command of the Department of the Missouri at the Planters' House on September 24. Curtis had established an office in the hotel the previous fall when Fremont put him in charge of St. Louis, but he lost it when Halleck arrived and appropriated the spacious corner room for his own use. Curtis was bumped several doors down the hall. He now reclaimed his former territory. "My office is where I was before General Halleck took it," he noted, with a hint of satisfaction.[9]

The second incarnation of the Department of the Missouri consisted of Missouri, Kansas, Arkansas, a sliver of Illinois, the Indian Territory, and the distant Colorado and Nebraska territories. (Arkansas and the Indian Territory were added to the department because of Curtis's success in sweeping the rebels out of those regions.) The department extended from the Mississippi River to the Rocky Mountains, and included the well-worn routes of the Santa Fe and Overland Trails and the projected route of the Union Pacific Railroad. It was the largest and most diverse of the nation's military departments and, as Curtis would soon discover, the most volatile and least governable.[10]

Headquarters was not exactly a beehive of activity when Curtis arrived. Dozens of staff officers, aides, and clerks, along with files, office supplies, and even furniture, had followed Halleck to Tennessee and thence to Washington. "General Halleck took away everything, and I have to begin de novo," Curtis grumbled to a colleague. He focused on larger issues when he reported his arrival to the War Department the next day. "As yet I know but little of strength and position of [my] forces," Curtis telegraphed. "They seem to be too much scattered." He added cryptically that he desired "some older or wiser generals for remote commands." Curtis never identified the officers he wanted to replace, but Schofield's name likely headed the list.[11]

Curtis had driven the rebels out of Missouri and he was not about to let them return. This time around, however, he decided to remain in St. Louis and allow his subordinates to handle matters in the field. Curtis's health was likely a factor in that decision. He did not venture far from the Planters' House during his eight months as department commander, a change from his usual practice in Arkansas and (later) Kansas, where he seized every opportunity to take the field and command in person. Curtis, like Halleck before him, managed military operations by telegraph. He provided subordinates with guidance and encouragement but tried not to become involved in matters best left to commanders on the scene.

While Curtis settled into his new job, a disgruntled Schofield headed for Springfield to assemble an army capable of fending off Hindman. Schofield believed he should have been named department commander, complaining to Halleck about the injustice of it all. Halleck shot back, "General Curtis as the ranking officer is given the command," which put an end to Schofield's whining. Curtis and Schofield never got along, but they established an effective working relationship for a few months. The next officer in line after Schofield was Brigadier General James G. Blunt, commanding next door in Kansas. Curtis asked Blunt to join forces with Schofield and serve under his command until Hindman was defeated. Curtis emphasized that the arrangement was temporary: "It is not my purpose to merge the Kansas District with any other, but we must at present unite forces to meet emergencies." Unlike Schofield, yet another socially conservative regular officer, Blunt was a volunteer and a radical Republican who wholeheartedly approved of Curtis's abolitionist activities in Arkansas. Blunt assured Curtis of his willingness to cooperate and promptly set out for Springfield. It was the beginning of a successful partnership.[12]

Near the end of September elements of Hindman's army edged into southwestern Missouri and occupied Newtonia. For several weeks Schofield had been loudly proclaiming his inability to defend the state against a Confederate invasion. Now, with Blunt and reinforcements fast approaching, he changed his tune and announced his intention of driving the rebels back into Arkansas. Curtis was pleasantly surprised by Schofield's newfound aggressiveness and promised to provide him with whatever logistical support he needed.[13]

While Schofield and Blunt converged on Newtonia, Curtis turned his attention to domestic and administrative matters. He invited Belinda to join him in the Planters' House, but she chose to remain in Keokuk. Perhaps St. Louis held too many sad memories. Belinda kept her husband informed of daily developments in the Gate City, including Cara Eliza's academic progress. "I am glad to hear my dear little daughter is becoming so good a student," Curtis replied to one letter. When the nine-year-old announced that she wanted to be called Caddie instead of Carrie, Curtis accepted the change without comment.[14]

Around this time Curtis visited John A. Scholten's photographic studio, a short walk from the Planters' House, to record his appearance. He wore a brand-new major general's uniform, complete with presentation sword, and sported a neatly trimmed white beard he had grown during the Pea Ridge campaign. The photographer produced a pair of full-length images. Curtis sent copies to Belinda and to all of his siblings, with the quip that "every body says my beard improves the picture and the appearance of the soldier and 'every body' ought to know." Praise for his stylishly hirsute appearance was not quite as universal as Curtis suggested. Belinda thought the beard made him look older.[15]

Running the Department of the Missouri was a labor-intensive job, and the shortage of headquarters staff was a problem. Several of Curtis's most experienced staff officers, including son Henry, were suffering from lingering diseases picked up in Helena, another was bedridden after his horse fell on him, and two more had taken to drink during their dreary sojourn in Arkansas. Curtis complained to Halleck that he was forced to put in long hours despite his impaired health, and he asked for additional qualified officers. "I am over-worked," he informed a friend. "Still business goes on."[16]

· · ·

Schofield and Blunt struck the Confederates at Newtonia on October 4. Hindman had gone to Little Rock a few days earlier to confer with the new department commander, Lieutenant General Theophilus H. Holmes. His timing could not have been worse. While Hindman was away, his troops, outnumbered and outgeneraled, put up only a brief fight before giving way. Schofield's anxieties evaporated as he watched the enemy flee southward in disorder. He informed Curtis of the victory—his first—and declared that he was going to pursue the rebels "as far and as fast as prudence will justify." Curtis applauded Schofield's success. "Your progress so far is highly commendable," he wrote on October 7, "and I trust you will soon clear Missouri of the last of the invaders." The "invaders" were in full flight. Schofield advanced so rapidly Curtis had to warn him not to outrun his supplies.[17]

On October 12 Curtis created the Army of the Frontier and placed Schofield in overall command. Blunt headed the First Division, essentially his Kansas contingent, while Brigadier General James Totten led the Second Division and Brigadier General Francis J. Herron the Third. The army was unusually diverse by Civil War standards. It included three Indian regiments, two Black regiments, and a white regiment recruited largely in the highlands of northern Arkansas (the "Mountain Feds"). Curtis wondered about the Indians, but Blunt assured him they were good soldiers. The Federal force consisted of roughly fourteen thousand men, about the same size as Hindman's Trans-Mississippi Army.[18]

Lincoln was a western man and closely followed events in the trans-Mississippi. In October he asked Curtis whether Blunt's Indian troops could occupy the Cherokee Nation in the northeastern corner of the Indian Territory. The Cherokees were divided into warring camps over secession and other issues; Lincoln reasoned that the presence of several thousand blue-clad Indian soldiers would tip the balance in favor of the Unionist faction. Curtis did not want Schofield to become bogged down in a sideshow, but he was reluctant to refuse a presidential request, so he finessed the answer. "I doubt the expediency of occupying ground so remote from supplies," Curtis replied, "but I expect to make rebels very scarce in that quarter pretty soon." He informed Schofield and Blunt of the president's concerns and suggested they pass through the Cherokee Nation and show the flag. Lincoln was satisfied.[19]

On October 17 the Army of the Frontier entered Arkansas and stopped on the old Pea Ridge battleground to rest and allow the trains to catch up. Schofield enjoyed the rustic comforts of Elkhorn Tavern while his men explored the shattered landscape and collected souvenirs, mostly bullets and bones. The Federals unrolled a telegraph wire as they advanced, establishing a line connecting the tavern with department headquarters in St. Louis. This arrangement allowed Curtis to stay abreast of developments at the front and to provide Schofield with timely advice.[20]

Hindman returned from his meeting with Holmes in Little Rock and quickly righted the ship. Over the next few weeks he and Schofield maneuvered back and forth across northwestern Arkansas, neither commander able to land a decisive blow. Then, on October 22, Blunt, operating independently, routed a Confederate cavalry force at Old Fort Wayne in the Indian Territory. Four days later, Schofield clashed with Hindman's main body along the White River near Fayetteville. The engagement was inconclusive, but the rebels withdrew across the Boston Mountains to Fort Smith, their base of supplies on the Arkansas River.[21]

An exuberant Schofield rushed back to the telegraph station at Elkhorn Tavern and informed Curtis that the "whole Rebel

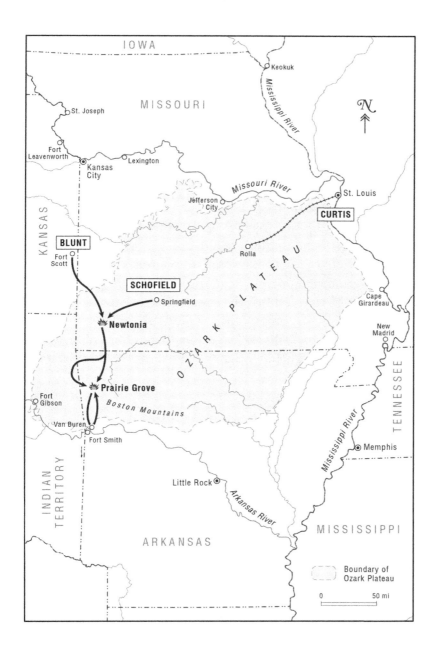

MAP 2. The Prairie Grove campaign, September–December 1862. Route of the Army of the Frontier. Schofield's retrograde movement into Missouri is not shown. Created by Erin Greb.

force has fled into the Arkansas Valley very much scattered and demoralized." He claimed that the "country south and west of here is substantially in our possession as far as the Arkansas River." The latter part of the message was an exaggeration, but it accurately reflected the heady mood at Schofield's headquarters. Curtis informed Halleck that the Army of the Frontier had "gallantly and successfully accomplished its mission." All of the principal Union actors believed the campaign was over, but they underestimated Hindman's resiliency. The Confederate general was down but not out.[22]

Schofield proposed that the Army of the Frontier remain in place to protect the Unionist population in northwestern Arkansas and the adjacent Cherokee Nation, but Curtis rejected the proposal. "Your expedition has been successful," Curtis telegraphed Schofield. "If, as you think, the enemy has gone beyond the Boston Mountains, your main force should immediately fall back" to Missouri. Schofield was baffled by this cryptic message but returned to Springfield with the Second and Third Divisions as ordered.[23]

Halleck, not Curtis, was responsible for the abrupt change in plans. The long anticipated campaign against Vicksburg was finally getting underway and the general in chief was scouring the West for every available regiment and battery. When he learned of Schofield's success in driving Hindman back to the Arkansas River, he leapt to the conclusion that it was safe to withdraw troops from Curtis and send them to Grant. Halleck went about this in his typical abrasive manner. Instead of congratulating Curtis on his success in securing Missouri, Halleck played the scold. "Are you not employing more troops in Missouri than are really necessary?" he snapped. "No troops not absolutely necessary will be kept in Missouri."[24]

Curtis held his temper in check. He informed Halleck that as soon as Schofield returned to southwestern Missouri, he would "draw troops from that region to aid the downriver movement, for I shall be glad to share the glory" of capturing Vicksburg. Schofield reached Springfield a few days later. Curtis ordered him to proceed to Cape Girardeau on the Mississippi River, where a flotilla of transports would take him to join Grant. Schofield thought this was a grand idea, but he became seriously ill and sought medical care in St. Louis. Schofield tried to direct the movements of the Second and Third Divisions from his sickbed, but Curtis would have none of it. "Do not bother your brains about the troops until you are quite well," he wrote in an almost fatherly fashion. Herron assumed command of the Second and Third Divisions and resumed the march, but he got only as far as Ozark before Curtis ordered him back to Springfield. Something was happening in Arkansas.[25]

Blunt and the First Division remained in Arkansas when Schofield fell back to Missouri. On November 28 Blunt handed the Confederate cavalry another defeat at Cane Hill in the Boston Mountains. (Curtis called the affair a "handsome victory.") Blunt was now more than one hundred miles south of Schofield's Second and Third Divisions at Springfield but only thirty-five miles north of Hindman's Trans-Mississippi Army at Fort Smith. Blunt advised Curtis that the rebels were "badly whipped and will probably not venture north of the Boston Mountains again this winter," but he knew his advanced position was dangerously exposed, so he kept a close watch on the enemy. Hindman, despite his recent string of defeats, could not pass up the opportunity to strike an isolated Union division. In early December he marched toward Cane Hill.[26]

Blunt detected Hindman's approach and alerted Curtis, who promptly issued the order that sent Herron back to Springfield. Curtis informed Halleck that he was holding on to Herron's troops, because of ominous developments in the Boston Mountains. He explained that he intended to keep Herron within supporting distance of Blunt until further notice. Halleck reluctantly concurred. Grant would have to do without reinforcements from the Army of the Frontier for the time being.[27]

Curtis wanted Blunt to retire toward Herron, who had edged forward to the old Wilson's Creek battleground south of Springfield. "You are too far in advance of support and supplies," he wired. "Had better fall back to meet Herron's re-enforcements." Blunt rejected the suggestion and announced his intention to stand and fight at Cane Hill. Curtis must have ground his teeth at Blunt's intransigence, but he did not issue an order to withdraw because he did not want to overrule the commander on the scene. Instead, he directed Herron to hurry to Blunt's support: "Have advised Blunt to fall back so as to join your advance. Push forward." Herron did just that. During the next three days the Second and Third Divisions marched an astounding 110 miles across rugged Ozark terrain in frigid conditions. It was the most remarkable march of the Civil War and it made the difference between victory and defeat.[28]

Curtis expected Herron to reach Cane Hill on Sunday, December 7. He awoke early that morning and paced the floor of his office for hours, awaiting word from northwestern Arkansas, but the telegraph remained silent. Around midday he sent a terse message to Blunt that revealed his state of mind: "Have been very anxious. Hope you have been re-enforced. Herron is a true man. Success to you." By the time his words reached the telegraph station at Elkhorn Tavern, the battle was joined and a column of smoke was rising over the Boston Mountains.[29]

• • •

Herron's arrival in northwestern Arkansas came as a complete surprise to the Confederates. Hindman's Trans-Mississippi Army was moving around Blunt's position at Cane Hill when it collided violently with Herron's troops, rushing south from Wilson's Creek. Fighting erupted at Prairie Grove, ten miles southwest of Fayetteville. Blunt heard the roar of battle to his rear and joined forces with Herron. The Army of the Frontier had barely eight thousand men on the field because of straggling in Herron's ranks, but while the Federals were few in number they were well equipped with artillery. The eleven thousand soldiers of the Trans-Mississippi Army were not so fortunate, thanks in part to Curtis's earlier efforts to "scour" the Mississippi River and interdict Confederate shipments of arms and ammunition.

The lines of battle swayed back and forth all afternoon, neither side able to gain an advantage. When darkness fell the rebels, out of food and low on ammunition, slipped away and returned to Fort Smith. The Federals remained on the field to claim the victory and look after the dead and wounded.[30]

Both sides experienced heavy losses. The Army of the Frontier suffered 1,251 men killed, wounded, and missing, a casualty rate of about 16 percent. The Trans-Mississippi Army lost 1,483 soldiers, a 13 percent casualty rate, but the numbers do not include hundreds of Confederate deserters, mostly Arkansas conscripts, who ran away or changed sides. A Kansas soldier wrote that "for the forces engaged, there was no more stubborn fight and no greater casualties in any battle of the war than at Prairie Grove, Arkansas." Sadly, he was correct.[31]

Curtis was immensely relieved to learn that the Army of the Frontier had triumphed. The battle was a tactical draw but a resounding strategic victory for the Union. Hindman's attempt to reclaim a large part of the trans-Mississippi for the Confederacy had been beaten back. Curtis congratulated Blunt and Herron on a victory "that will carry despair into the hearts of our foes and gladness to the friends of liberty throughout our country." He passed the good news on to Halleck with a recommendation that Blunt and Herron "deserve special commendation for their gallantry." Curtis had received a major general's star after Pea Ridge; he believed the victors of Prairie Grove deserved no less. He maintained an upbeat tone in his official correspondence but privately commiserated with Herron, a fellow Iowan, over the severe losses in his two divisions, which bore the brunt of the fighting: "Due credit is given to you and Blunt both, although you had the long, hard day's work."[32]

Blunt and Herron closed out the campaign with a spectacular raid. On December 27–31 the Army of the Frontier surged over the Boston Mountains and seized Van Buren, a town on the northern bank of the Arkansas River. The Federals burned warehouses and steamboats packed with provisions, nearly incinerating downtown Van Buren in the process. Panicked rebels in nearby Fort Smith destroyed more stores and boats. Now destitute as well as demoralized, Hindman and his men departed for Little Rock with only the food they had in their packs. The Federals returned to Prairie Grove in high spirits, accompanied by as many as a thousand liberated slaves. Curtis praised the "daring dash" and congratulated both generals for "another gallant achievement which deserves the gratitude of your country." The Van Buren operation was the first army-sized raid of the Civil War.[33]

The Prairie Grove campaign was the last in a series of Confederate counteroffensives in Maryland, Kentucky, Mississippi, and Arkansas in the latter half of 1862. Each began with impressive gains but ultimately failed. Prairie Grove did not receive much attention at the time, because reports from the distant trans-Mississippi were crowded off the pages of northern papers by news of larger battles at Fredericksburg, Virginia, and Stone's River, Tennessee. "I wonder if they know in New York or Boston that there is an 'Army of the Frontier,'" wrote a disgusted Missouri soldier. Nevertheless, the Federals who took part in the campaign understood what they had done. An Iowan aptly described Prairie Grove as a "powerfully stunning blow from which the western portion of the so-called Southern Confederacy never recovered."[34]

Curtis believed Schofield was "deeply mortified at not being in the fight," but he was wrong. Schofield was seething with frustration and resentment at having been denied his moment of glory. Prairie Grove meant fame and promotions for Blunt and Herron, but not for him. He sent Curtis a vicious, nearly deranged letter in which he asserted that the "operations of the army, since I left it, have been a series of blunders, from which it narrowly escaped disaster where it should have met with complete success." Schofield claimed that Blunt and Herron had been "badly beaten in detail" at Prairie Grove and "owed their escape to a false report of my arrival with re-enforcements." Curtis chose to ignore the letter. This episode marked the beginning of a malicious, lifelong campaign by Schofield—an obsession, really—to blacken the reputations of Curtis, Blunt, and Herron and down-play their achievements.[35]

Unlike Schofield, Curtis was pleased with the way things had turned out. "My success in my Department has been so far extraordinary," he exulted to brother Henry, a week after Prairie Grove. Curtis played only a supervisory role during the campaign, but he intervened on two critical occasions: he halted Herron's eastward march toward Cape Girardeau and, a few days later, rushed Herron south to Blunt's relief. These decisions delivered Blunt from disaster. Curtis never left St. Louis, but he helped save the day at Prairie Grove.[36]

• • •

While the Prairie Grove campaign played out in northwestern Arkansas, Confederates in southeastern Missouri went on the attack. With so many Union troops engaged with Hindman or on their way out of the state, rebel cavalry and guerrillas had a field day. Curtis needed more men to mount an effective defense, but where to find them? The only untapped source of manpower in the department was the Army of the Southwest, earmarked for Vicksburg but still sitting idle in Helena in the fall of 1862. Curtis reasoned that, if no one was using his Pea Ridge veterans, he would borrow them. "I could not draw from any other source but Helena," he later explained. Curtis ordered Steele, now in command, to take half of the army up the Mississippi River to Ste. Genevieve, then proceed inland about fifty miles to Ironton. Halleck feared for the safety of Helena, which he aptly described as "too important a place to risk," but he allowed Curtis to proceed: "You know your own condition better than I do, and must decide about this. At so great a distance I can only advise."[37]

Steele was looking forward to participating in the Vicksburg operation and was not happy at being sent in the opposite direction. He complained to Halleck (again) and accused Curtis of siphoning off soldiers from Helena to make another overland invasion of Arkansas. What Curtis actually had in mind was an aggressive push south from Ironton that he hoped would compel the Confederates to abandon their mischief in Missouri and look to the defense of Arkansas. Halleck, already edgy about weakening the Helena garrison, seized on Steele's misleading letter as an excuse to apply the brakes. "It is reported that you have ordered an expedition from Pilot Knob to Batesville," he telegraphed Curtis on November 15. "If so, it will be immediately countermanded." Halleck reminded Curtis that the Army of the Southwest would soon be needed at Vicksburg. Then he laid down the law: "You will not operate on any new lines without first reporting to this headquarters. Unless this is done the plans of the Government are continually disarranged." Curtis denied planning to invade Arkansas, but he could not argue with Halleck's larger point about Union forces operating at cross purposes. He sent Steele and his men back to Helena and promised to dispatch additional troops to Vicksburg as soon as they became available.[38]

Despite Halleck's rebuke, Curtis went ahead with a scaled-down version of his original plan, using only the troops at hand. He established the Army of Southeastern Missouri in early November 1862, placing Brigadier General John W. Davidson in command, with orders to harry the rebels out of Missouri. Unfortunately, the operation was plagued by delays. By the time Davidson marched out of Ironton, the fall campaigning season had given way to winter. The Federals were immobilized by snow, ice, and rain. Curtis eventually canceled the operation.[39]

Curtis made no secret of his desire to participate in opening the Mississippi River. He was disappointed when Halleck relegated him to a distant supporting role in St. Louis. The disappointment deepened when most of the Army of the Southwest—*his* army—departed for Vicksburg with Sherman in December 1862. Two months later Curtis wrote to a colleague in that army: "I am very sorry that I cannot be with [Grant] to help him and all of you in this important crisis, and only console myself for my absence in knowing that I have enough to do to regulate a department that somebody must take care of, and I am always ready to do my share of drudgery." If he was destined to play a supporting role, then he would play it to the best of his ability: "I have desired that [Grant] should have all needful power to secure the earliest possible success."[40]

During his eight months in St. Louis Curtis sent thousands of troops to Vicksburg: most of the Army of the Southwest, the Army of the Frontier, and the Army of Southeastern Missouri, and nearly all of the new regiments emerging from Benton Barracks. Annoyed, then angered, by Halleck's baseless accusations that he was hoarding troops, Curtis stated that all military activities in his department were "secondary to the move on Vicksburg, where I have tendered nearly all my force." Curtis also wrote to Grant, wished him well, and expressed his hope that the regular infusions of manpower from the Department of the Missouri would help him "close out Vicksburg" in short order. Grant never acknowledged the letters or the aid.[41]

Despite all this, Halleck continued to berate Curtis for failing to forward even more men to Grant. In March 1863 he accused Curtis of maintaining an "unnecessarily large force" in Missouri based on "exaggerated accounts of impending dangers." Halleck added outrageously that "most of such accounts are mere pretenses." Curtis erupted in fury and frustration: "Every order or request requiring troops from my command has been filled with all the promptness possible, and to the full extent of your meaning," and whoever reported otherwise "gives you false and pernicious representations." As usual when challenged, Halleck backed off and Curtis enjoyed a few weeks of relative peace. The litany of complaints was a manifestation of Halleck's well-developed tendency to blame anyone but himself when things did not go as planned. It may have helped the general in chief feel better, but it was a powerful irritant in his eroding professional relationship with Curtis.[42]

Missouri's dual militia system was a particular source of friction between the feuding generals. The Missouri State Militia was a force of ten thousand mounted troops armed, equipped, trained, and paid by the army. Regiments operated independently or in conjunction with volunteer forces as circumstances dictated.

In fact, Missouri State Militia regiments were almost indistinguishable from volunteer regiments, except that they could not be ordered out of the state. The Enrolled Missouri Militia, by contrast, was an old-fashioned local defense force. It was larger but less effective than the Missouri State Militia, and because it included nearly every man in a given locality, secessionists and Unionists alike, it was not always reliable. Halleck added the total number of men in the two militias and concluded that Curtis had tens of thousands of armed Missourians to draw upon, deliberately overlooking the fact that only a portion of the combined militia was dependable and effective. In December 1862 Curtis wrote to Lincoln, accurately described the militia situation, and explained why he needed a "considerable military force [of soldiers] to keep things quiet in Missouri." Statistics did not tell the whole story, Curtis argued, but Halleck pretended not to understand and continued to censure Curtis for failing to send more men to Vicksburg.[43]

Confederate activity in Missouri died down during the winter of 1862–63 but resumed in the spring. Halleck could not resist the temptation to meddle. He advised Curtis to concentrate his troops in the larger towns and cities and let the rebels have the run of the countryside. Halleck must have forgotten that Missouri was a Union state, not occupied rebel territory, and that its citizens were entitled to protection from marauding insurgents. He also scolded Curtis for failing to anticipate the exact time and place of enemy attacks. An exasperated Curtis complained to Belinda that Halleck seemed to think "I ought to know just when and where the rebels were coming."[44]

Despite many disadvantages, Union forces in Missouri, usually a mix of soldiers and militiamen, scored some significant victories. On April 26, 1863, Curtis was pleased to inform his crotchety superior that the garrison at Cape Girardeau had "handsomely repulsed" a Confederate cavalry force operating out of northeastern Arkansas. The success produced a "general quiet throughout the state," but within a few weeks rebel raiders and irregulars were back in business. In Missouri, as in Arkansas,

Curtis insisted that guerrillas and brigands receive "no quarter, no terms of civilized warfare." He ordered his subordinates to "pursue, strike, and destroy the reptiles" without mercy.[45]

Curtis commanded the Department of the Missouri from September 1862 to May 1863. The Prairie Grove campaign was the high point of his tenure, but battlefield successes had little effect on the guerrilla conflict, which intensified as the number of Union soldiers dwindled, or on the political struggle, which followed its own peculiar arc.

10

INQUISITION AND INTERLUDE

MISSOURI GOVERNOR HAMILTON R. GAMBLE WAS A CONSER-
vative Unionist who opposed with equal fervor secession, emancipation, and federal authority. He feared for the worst when
he learned that Curtis was to command in Missouri. "How on
earth did he come to be appointed to this department?" Gamble
exclaimed. He called on Postmaster General Montgomery Blair,
a Missourian in Lincoln's cabinet, to "help us to get clear of Curtis." Blair promised to "do what I can to get rid of him," but it was
too late. Gamble's reaction to news of Curtis's appointment pre-
saged a difficult partnership.[1]

Despite his obvious dissatisfaction, Gamble gamely attempted
to establish good relations with the new military commander. On
October 12, 1862, two weeks after Curtis arrived, Gamble had a
division of the Enrolled Missouri Militia, the larger but less effective of the state's two paramilitary organizations, put on a public
display of military might in St. Louis. Thirteen thousand militiamen paraded through the heart of the city in a column two
miles long. Flags and bunting adorned buildings, bands played
patriotic tunes, and cannons boomed salutes. Everyone agreed
it was a "most imposing scene." The "splendid cavalcade" was
entirely a state affair, but Gamble invited Curtis to join him at
the head of the column. The two men rode side by side and con-
versed in an amiable fashion.[2]

The parade was as much a political statement as a show of
force. Gamble controlled the Enrolled Missouri Militia. He wanted
to reduce (or remove altogether) the federal military presence
in Missouri, which he regarded as a check on his authority and

a threat to slavery, which was legal in Missouri. He used the parade to demonstrate the supposed power and prowess of the Enrolled Missouri Militia, the message being that the federal military establishment in the state could be dispensed with because Missourians under Gamble's leadership could take care of themselves. Curtis soon realized what the governor was up to. When Lincoln asked what would happen if federal forces were withdrawn as Gamble wished, Curtis had a ready answer. He predicted that the rebels would overwhelm the militia in short order and bring Missouri under Confederate control. "The peace of this State rests on military power," Curtis told Lincoln, by which he meant the army, the Missouri State Militia, and the Enrolled Missouri Militia operating together in a mutually supportive fashion under his, not Gamble's, command. "To relinquish this power would be dangerous." Lincoln, of course, also wanted to whittle down the number of Union troops in Missouri, if only to placate Halleck, but he declined to overrule Curtis. Gamble did not get his way, but he never stopped trying.[3]

The military tug-of-war was one of several contentious issues that divided Curtis and Gamble. Curtis had served in the Department of the West and the Department of the Missouri since June 1861, but he had spent much of that time in camp or in the field. Having to deal with Missouri's fractious and often duplicitous politicians, business leaders, and editorial writers on a daily basis proved more difficult than he had anticipated. And then there was the state's large and troublesome pro-Confederate minority. Missouri was home to more secessionists than any other Union state. Some had enlisted in the Missouri State Guard and marched off to war in the heady days of 1861. Others became guerrillas or brigands. The vast majority, however, stayed home and awaited liberation. Many in this last group engaged in disloyal (or at least provocative) acts that ranged from seditious speech to providing guerrillas with food, shelter, and information.

Curtis's predecessors had placed Missouri under martial law and established a statewide network of army provost marshals, a quasi-military police force charged with enforcing martial law and keeping secessionists in check. Curtis expanded and strengthened this system. Under the aggressive leadership of Provost Marshal General Franklin A. Dick, the marshals punished those believed guilty of encouraging, supporting, or committing disloyal acts. Secessionists were banished, jailed, fined, or had their property confiscated, depending on the severity of their actions. The funds and goods acquired by such "assessments" went to support the thousands of destitute Arkansas and Missouri Unionists who had been driven from their homes by rebels. The program was open to abuse, but at first neither Gamble nor Curtis saw any alternative. In time, however, both realized just how arbitrary the assessments were and agreed to suspend the program. It was a rare moment of agreement.[4]

Enforcement of martial law frequently clashed with civil rights. It was generally acknowledged, for example, that an editor who called for the overthrow of the government could be jailed, fined, or have his paper shut down or his press confiscated. But what about other means of expression? In Missouri in the fall of 1862 it was sermons, not editorials, that became a flash point. The McPheeters brothers of St. Louis were a troublesome pair. William M. McPheeters, a respected physician, challenged federal and state authorities at every turn and loudly expressed his Confederate sympathies. Harried by provost marshals, McPheeters decamped for Arkansas, where he became a surgeon in the Confederate army and a confidant of Sterling Price. His younger brother, an equally well-respected Presbyterian minister named Samuel B. McPheeters, displayed less brazen rebel sympathies while pastor of the Pine Street Church, but Unionist members of the congregation demanded that he be removed from the pulpit.[5]

Curtis declared that religious services at the Pine Street Church had been perverted "from divine to disloyal purposes" and banished McPheeters from the state. That was a mistake. Gamble, a devout Presbyterian, defended the minister's right to shepherd his flock without government interference. McPheeters traveled to Washington and, through the good offices of Attorney General Edward Bates, Gamble's brother-in-law and former law partner, he gained an interview with the president. Lincoln suspended the banishment order. He was reluctant to punish a minister upon "suspicion of his secret sympathies," but he did not want to force his views on Curtis. The president hearkened back to the language he had used in the Fremont case two years earlier: "I agree that this must be left to you, who are on the spot; and if, after all, you think the public good requires his removal, my suspension of the order is withdrawn." After a stern warning that the federal government must not "undertake to run the churches," Lincoln encouraged Curtis to use his best judgment, "with a sole view to the public interest, and I will not interfere without hearing you." Curtis acknowledged that he had overreacted and rescinded the banishment order, though he did not permit McPheeters to resume his ministry. Curtis's ill-considered actions generated a storm of controversy and frayed his relations with both the president and the governor. This round went to Gamble.[6]

Lincoln knew from experience that Gamble was difficult, but he urged Curtis to try and find some common ground with the governor. In December 1862 the president addressed another note to Curtis: "I am having a good deal of trouble with Missouri matters, and I now set down to write you particularly about it. One class of friends believe in greater severity and another in greater leniency in regard to arrests, banishments, and assessments." Lincoln was vexed because neither side seemed willing to accommodate the other. "Now, my belief," he continued, "is that Governor Gamble is an honest and true man, not less so than yourself." Lincoln thought Curtis should get together with Gamble, talk over their differences, then act on "whatever you and he agree upon." There was, he emphasized, "absolutely no reason why you should not agree."[7]

The following month, January 1863, Curtis and Gamble met and reviewed a number of contentious issues. They did not come to blows, but neither did they reach any substantive agreements. The two men remained at odds over just about everything. Curtis reported the disappointing outcome to the White House. He assured the president that "I have so far great reason to rejoice in the success of our arms and the progress of our principles," but the letter made it clear that, after months of squabbling, he and the governor were at an impasse. Gamble must have felt the same way, because after the meeting he asked his conservative allies in Washington, cabinet secretaries Bates and Blair and Missouri senator John B. Henderson, to put all their energy into convincing Lincoln to remove Curtis. For his part, Curtis turned his back on Gamble and publicly allied himself with the radical wing of the Republican Party, a collection of factions that made up the principal opposition group in Missouri. He had been drifting in that direction for months.[8]

The Emancipation Proclamation took effect on the first day of 1863, but it affected only states in rebellion against the United States. Slavery existed in Missouri until late in the war, but there was little Curtis could do about it because Lincoln refused to approve any action that might antagonize Unionist slave owners. The practical side of emancipation—how to treat former slaves—surfaced in March 1863, when a steamboat packed with five hundred men, women, and children arrived in St. Louis. The leader of this exodus, Chaplain Samuel W. Sawyer, had been directed by Major General Benjamin M. Prentiss, now commanding in Helena after Steele's departure for Vicksburg, to relieve overcrowding in the town's refugee camps by shipping some of the freedmen to St. Louis. Curtis did not learn of the impending influx until the first boat arrived. "Five hundred contrabands!" he exclaimed to Sawyer. "What in the world shall I do with them!" Curtis rebuked Prentiss for exporting his problems to Missouri, and even threatened to send the freedmen back to Arkansas, but after he calmed down he realized he had an opportunity to make a statement of his own.[9]

Gamble wanted the newcomers gone for obvious reasons, but Curtis sought to demonstrate that "contrabands" could function in society if given a chance. He commandeered a vacant hotel to house the freedmen and assigned Sawyer the task of finding them suitable employment. Labor was in short supply in wartime St. Louis; the Arkansas refugees were soon loading and unloading steamboats along the bustling waterfront and strengthening the earthworks that ringed the city. When some freedmen expressed a desire to get as far away from Dixie as possible, Curtis provided them with free passage up the Mississippi and Ohio Rivers on empty transports returning from Vicksburg. Curtis also arranged for relief organizations such as the American Missionary Association, the Western Sanitary Commission, and the St. Louis Ladies' Contraband Relief Society to establish a school and a hospital and to provide clothing and bedding. Sawyer supervised the transfer of more than one thousand people from Helena to St. Louis and beyond. He worked closely with Curtis and came to regard him as a "humane commander of large intellect and heart, loving his country and sincerely hating oppression and treason." Curtis would have liked that description. It was how he saw himself.[10]

In addition to directing military operations, suppressing secessionists, looking after freedmen, butting heads with Gamble, and trying to remain in Lincoln's good graces, Curtis spent a good part of every day reading and writing letters and reports and meeting with visitors. He saw a dozen or more citizens, soldiers, and officials in a typical day, each of whom had a problem to solve, a complaint to lodge, a favor to beg, or an ax to grind. Curtis's suspect managerial skills sometimes made his life more complicated, in ways large and small. "I am glad to get letters," he confided to a friend in early 1863, "but you know I have no time to respond." He then proceeded to respond for two closely written pages.[11]

Much of Curtis's correspondence was routine, but now and then something unusual turned up. He occasionally communicated with his Confederate counterparts on subjects such as prisoner exchanges, incidents of military misbehavior, and the fate of civilians. In October 1862 Curtis asked Hindman to return a cotton trader who had strayed into Confederate lines near Helena and been spirited away. Curtis had no love for traders, but this particular individual was the only means of support for his widowed mother. Curtis and Hindman had served together in the House of Representatives and were acquainted, so Curtis gave his personal assurance to the rebel commander that the errant trader was "in no way in my employ." In other words, he was not a Union spy. How this matter turned out is not known.[12]

Curtis maintained a civil tone in his correspondence with Hindman, but the same could not be said of his exchanges with Halleck. In November 1862 Curtis blasted the "scolding style" of Halleck's dispatches: "Halleck seems as cross as a Grizzly bear for no reason that I can imagine except it may be some false notions [my enemies] may have whispered into his ear," a reference to Steele, Schofield, and others. Military protocol required Curtis to exhibit a degree of deference when dealing with the general in chief, which irked him all the more. "Of course I want no war with Halleck in his position," he told brother Henry. "I know Halleck well enough to know he can play the tyrant terribly if he gets a disposition to do so. It would astonish you to see how like a cross schoolmaster he snaps out in his telegraphic responses to the most reasonable questions." After more, much more, in that vein Curtis concluded that Halleck's behavior "indicates petulance and I fear hatred."[13]

Near the close of 1862 Curtis made an effort to repair his relations with Halleck. It did not go well. "I desire only to carry out your plans and put down rebels in my department," Curtis assured the general in chief. "Rogues and rebels are trying to embarrass me by false representations at headquarters." Halleck retorted that he was not in the habit of consorting with rogues and rebels, which led Curtis to declare that he did not intend to allow himself "to be a victim to false or frivolous friends to you and traitors to our country." On that testy note the exchange ended and the tendered olive branch withered.[14]

Curtis displayed noticeably less deference toward his superior as the months went by. By the beginning of 1863 he snapped at Halleck almost as often as Halleck snapped at him. Curtis described the general in chief as a "bull headed fault finder" who "insults all his generals, and then by some means pushes them from places to put some toady like Steele or Schofield in position. Men who have not brains or influence enough to murmur at his repeated blunders." He could not understand why Lincoln kept "Old Brains" at the head of the army.[15]

Gamble doubtless felt the same way about Lincoln and Curtis. The Missouri governor's ceaseless efforts to replace Curtis finally bore fruit in March 1863, when the War Department, at Lincoln's direction, ordered Major General Edwin V. Sumner to proceed to St. Louis. Elderly, infirm, and possessed of no discernible political skill, Sumner was an odd choice to head the Department of the Missouri. He seems to have been selected because he was a conservative regular officer who lacked political baggage. In the end it did not matter, because the old soldier died before he could take up his new assignment. This put Curtis in an "unpleasant and inexpedient" position. He remained in nominal command of the department for two more months while politicians in Washington, St. Louis, and Jefferson City tried to find a suitable senior officer willing to serve in Missouri. "It is evidently hard to get a substitute," Curtis observed drily.[16]

Curtis described the Department of the Missouri to brother Henry as the "hardest place I have ever found," confessing that "I would rejoice to be honorably relieved." He finally got his wish on May 24, 1863, when Lincoln appointed Schofield as his replacement. Curtis privately scoffed at the choice of the "Democratic Pro Slavery Schofield" to follow the "Republican Anti Slavery Curtis." He had permanently fallen out with Schofield after Prairie Grove and now regarded him as a "kind of pet" of Governor Gamble, which was not far from the truth.[17]

In an oft-quoted letter to Schofield, Lincoln explained why he had removed Curtis. "I did not relieve General Curtis because of any full conviction that he had done wrong by commission or omission," Lincoln wrote. Rather, Missouri Unionists had fallen into what he described as a "pestilent factional quarrel," in which the elected governor was the head of one faction and the appointed military commander was the head of the other. That being the case, Lincoln's options were limited: "As I could not remove Governor Gamble, I had to remove General Curtis."

Lincoln then provided Schofield with a few words of wisdom: "If both factions, or neither, shall abuse you, you will, probably, be about right. Beware of being assailed by one and praised by the other." While Schofield pondered the president's words, Curtis issued a gracious farewell message to his troops and departed. He had expected to feel "vexed and mortified" at being shown the door, but to his surprise he experienced only a profound sense of relief. He was glad to put Missouri behind him.[18]

• • •

During most of his tenure in St. Louis, and for some time afterward, Curtis was plagued by a War Department investigation ostensibly aimed at the buying and selling of cotton in Helena. He knew as early as August 1862 that certain cotton traders, politicians, and army officers were circulating lies about his activities, but he did not address the outlandish fabrications because he did not think anyone would take them seriously. Curtis was surprised to receive a private note from Lincoln in November 1862 warning of trouble ahead: "I feel it my duty to you, as a friend, to tell you, that . . . charges have been preferred against you, something about speculating in cotton, as I understand, which cannot be overlooked. I am sorry to write on so unpleasant a subject." Lincoln promised to take no action until Curtis had an opportunity to tell his side of the story.[19]

As Curtis knew nothing of any charges, he could only reply to "rumors and imputations which I have heard on the subject." He told Lincoln that Helena had been "infested with spies, secessionists, and traitors dealing in cotton," and that he had limited the buying and selling of cotton to individuals he believed were loyal and honest, or at least not obviously disloyal or corrupt: "This excluded a great number, who were exasperated, and threatened vengeance." These scurrilous characters "immediately proclaimed that I only licensed those with whom I was in partnership." Curtis stated emphatically that he was "*in partnership with no one directly or indirectly.*" He added that in the absence of any guidance from the War Department—the root of the problem—he had aligned his policies with those formulated by Grant and Sherman on the eastern side of the Mississippi River. He wondered why he was being singled out.[20]

Curtis concluded his letter with a strong assertion of his innocence: "I have lived too long and filled too many private and public places, without reproach, to be afraid of lies invented by rebel sympathizers and exasperated knaves generally. I do not shrink from any and all fair scrutiny. I can explain any special act of mine to the satisfaction of any honest man." He asked for the names of his accusers and a copy of the charges and expressed his willingness to defend his actions in writing or in person at a court of inquiry or court martial. He thanked Lincoln for his "kind letter" and for affording him the opportunity of "maintaining my honor unsullied."[21]

Curtis informed brother Henry that the "cotton dealers and slave worshippers have made great efforts to ruin me." He believed at first that his anonymous accusers were "scoundrels whose negroes I set free because they had been employed in blockading the roads and making rebel forts" and "Jews and knaves that I arrested for stealing, and would not allow to stay and trade in my lines." They were "terribly infuriated and swore vengeance." He also thought some "drunken officers that I could not trust" might have "joined in the clammer." He mentioned only one officer by name, an obscure lieutenant, because he did not yet realize the scope of the conspiracy against him, a conspiracy that included at least two generals. "This is all I know of my accusers and their charges," he told Henry. "It is something about cotton buying or cotton speculation." Curtis added rather plaintively, "I do not know that it is dishonorable for an officer to buy and sell cotton, but I did not."[22]

During the first weeks of the Union occupation, nearly everyone in Helena, or so it seemed, had sought Curtis's advice about trading in cotton, which quickly became a form of local currency. "I especially directed negroes when they asked me, to go to those who would not cheat them, but rather treat them kindly," he explained to Henry. "[I] acted as I thought right, disregarding what knaves and rebels might say. . . . If I had stood still, and let every body steal the cotton from the negroes, they would have starved." He never wavered from his conviction that he had done the right thing and violated no regulations or laws.[23]

The War Department showed no particular interest in Helena, because conditions in Memphis and other occupied towns in the Mississippi Valley were just as chaotic. Then a clique of politicians and army officers got involved. John S. Phelps, a one-time Missouri congressman, began a sustained assault against Curtis. Lincoln had appointed Phelps provisional military governor of Arkansas a few months earlier, but Phelps could not assume the powers of his new office until Union forces captured Little Rock, which, for reasons discussed in a previous chapter, was temporarily impossible. The Arkansas state capital would not fall into Union hands until September 1863, a year in the future.[24]

Frustrated at being a governor without a state, Phelps blamed Curtis. He told Halleck that Union officers did not want to leave Helena because they were engaging in illegal practices there, and that the "late commander of this Army of the Southwest is not exempt from such charges." Phelps was careful to add that he had no evidence and was merely passing on hearsay, then he abruptly changed the subject. He accused Curtis of exceeding his authority to free slaves and assist freedmen. This was the crux of his antagonism toward Curtis. Phelps wanted Curtis gone more than he wanted to reach Little Rock. He was an ultra-conservative, proslavery Democrat whose racial attitudes were indistinguishable from those of Steele. Phelps and Steele were connected through the latter's brother, New York congressman John B. Steele, yet another proslavery Democrat. The three men decided they could best preserve the social order in Arkansas (and, by extension, everywhere else) by accusing Curtis of illegal practices and pressing for his removal. Phelps and the Steeles bombarded Halleck and other officials with letters so similar in tone and content they might have been written by the same person. Curtis soon learned of this insidious epistolary effort:

"They whine about [my anti-slavery views] to Halleck who seems to sympathize with them." He was right on both counts.[25]

Phelps then wrote to Stanton and repeated the outrageous charge that Curtis was keeping the Army of the Southwest immobilized in Helena so that he and his officers could "enrich themselves by buying cotton from loyal and disloyal men and from negroes who did not own it." He added that, "if reports are true, [Curtis] made 'a good thing of it.'" Phelps claimed melodramatically that Curtis and his clique were "making fortunes with the blood of our brave men," though he again stated that he had not personally witnessed any wrongdoing. Phelps assured Stanton that he did not make these accusations because of personal animosity toward Curtis but because "duty compels me to say it." Phelps traveled to St. Louis and Washington and repeated his accusations to anyone who would listen. Eager to tar Curtis with the brush of corruption and hasten his removal, Governor Gamble and Attorney General Bates jumped on the anti-Curtis bandwagon and spread fictional accounts of the general's "notorious" activities. One of their stories had Curtis depositing $100,000 in a Chicago bank while attending the Pacific Railroad Convention.[26]

A clique of disaffected army officers also had Curtis in their sights, and for the same reasons. During the fall and winter of 1862–63 loyal officers in the Army of the Southwest warned their former commander that evil doings were afoot in that organization. One such letter came from Captain Richard R. Ballinger, Third Illinois Cavalry. Writing in December, Ballinger told his friend Henry Z. Curtis that General Carr and a cabal of conservative officers from the old Fourth Division objected strongly to his father's enlightened attitude toward slaves and freedmen. "They are proslavery and General Curtis emancipated too many negroes to suit their feelings," declared Ballinger. About the same time, Lieutenant Colonel James M. Ruggles of the same regiment warned Curtis that he had made "bitter enemies" of Carr and other "rank proslavery men" in the division. Like Phelps and the Steeles, Carr and his fellow plotters seized on the cotton trading uproar as a means of damaging Curtis's reputation and compelling his removal. Curtis thought well of Carr as a soldier and was disappointed to learn of his underhanded behavior.[27]

In February 1863, three months after Lincoln warned Curtis that something was afoot, the War Department established a court of inquiry to investigate whether the officers and men of the Army of the Southwest had violated any of the confusing rules, regulations, directives, and laws issued by military and civil authorities regarding trading with the Confederacy. The scope of the investigation was limited to the brief period in late July and August 1862, when Curtis was in Helena, strong evidence that he was the target from the beginning. (If that were not proof enough, many of the court's internal documents are labeled "Curtis court of inquiry" or "Curtis inquiry.") The court was in session, mostly in St. Louis, for three and a half months from March 18 to July 2, 1863. The board consisted of Major General Irvin McDowell, Brigadier General Philip S. Cooke, and two junior officers. None of these regular officers had served in the West or operated on their own deep inside the Confederacy. None had administered liberated territory or dealt with throngs of hostile whites and hopeful Blacks. None had experienced the free-for-all that was cotton trading in the Mississippi Valley. In short, none were likely to understand the situation in Helena.[28]

In addition to its dubious charge, the court of inquiry went about its business in a most peculiar fashion. McDowell literally threw open the doors and invited anyone who claimed to know anything about affairs in Helena to walk in and make a statement. The dozens of people who testified relied heavily, and in many cases exclusively, on rumor, hearsay, and innuendo to make their points. The proceedings were supposed to be confidential, but the court leaked like a sieve. St. Louis newspapers had a field day publishing lurid tales of shady dealings, though a close reading reveals that the leaked testimony was larded with phrases such as "I heard" and "it was said" and "everybody knew." Had the court of inquiry been a court of law, much of the testimony would have been excluded.[29]

Curtis submitted a statement and answered questions before

the court in March 1863. He stated emphatically that he had not committed, permitted, or encouraged illegal activities during his five weeks in eastern Arkansas. He made no effort to hide his belief that the inquiry was a travesty of justice—a kangaroo court. "I think it is time this self constituted star chamber rascality should be checked," he complained to brother Henry. "I do not like this secret accumulation of infamous matter held for villainous use when no refutation could be provided." Lincoln had not responded to his request for the names of his accusers and a list of charges, so he asked Henry to travel to Washington and obtain that information directly from the War Department. Curtis warned his brother that Halleck "has sympathized with my accusers and has never given any intimation as to who they are or what they have said and sworn to." Henry tried his best to pry that information—or any relevant information—out of Halleck but without success. The general in chief was well practiced in evading responsibility—it was the foundation of his management style.[30]

· · ·

Upon being relieved from command of the Department of the Missouri in May 1863, Curtis returned to Keokuk to await orders, in accordance with the military protocol of the day. "I am glad to get out of the snarl even if it does seem to reflect on my official capacity," he confessed to brother Henry. "I think posterity will give me credit for having shaped the destiny of the Country west of the Mississippi River whatever partisans may do to keep me out of their way." Curtis took some comfort in the knowledge that Lincoln had removed him "solely on political grounds," and not for any military failure. He expected to receive a new assignment in due time. Until then he thought it best to maintain a low profile and "very quietly bide my time."[31]

Curtis put away his uniform and established a daily routine indistinguishable from that of any small-town businessman. He set out from High Street every morning, weather permitting, and made the rounds of the town. He found business to be rather "dull," by which he meant that the local economy remained depressed because of the closure of the Mississippi River at Vicksburg. He hoped Grant's campaign, now approaching its climax, would soon put things right. At home he scrutinized the newspapers (he subscribed to several), expanded the flower and vegetable gardens, constructed a stable in the backyard, and looked after his nearby farms, which had "improved considerably" since his last visit. He wrote to his siblings and expressed a desire to visit the "old simple scenes and sunny places that we once enjoyed in Ohio." While Curtis puttered around and waxed nostalgic, Belinda participated in sanitary fairs to benefit Keokuk's three military hospitals.[32]

The rigors of the past two years had not permanently affected Curtis's soldierly bearing. He had regained the weight and muscle tone he had lost in Arkansas and seemed restored to good health. "He has a tall, fine form, and, though nearly sixty years of age, is erect and vigorous," noted an acquaintance. "His large, hazel eyes give his countenance an expression of gravity and thoughtfulness which comports well with the dignity of his movements and manners." There was only one obvious change in his appearance. Sometime during the summer of 1863 he bowed to Belinda's wishes and converted his bushy beard into the familiar muttonchop side whiskers evident in all his later photographs.[33]

Curtis may have been "resting on the shelf," but military matters, specifically his place in history, were never far from his mind. He told brother Henry, "I have done as much as any one man for freedom and the Federal Union west of the Mississippi and posterity will give me some credit for it." Curtis decided to make it easier for posterity to appreciate his achievements. Several of his former staff officers were idling in St. Louis awaiting reassignment, so Curtis asked them to organize his papers and paste them in scrapbooks: "As I have served in all the campaigns west of the Mississippi my current papers will comprise a very interesting volume of the war and it is hard to see how the future settlement of this great section of the continent can fail to bear some marks of my engineering. Slavery has received some of its most fatal blows at my hands and the rebellion has also felt the force of my untiring labors." He now regarded his military and abolitionist achievements as equally important. Curtis had the bulky scrapbooks, eight in number, shipped to Keokuk for safe-keeping. In August he made a quick trip to St. Louis for the wedding of a former staff officer. He wore his dress uniform and gave the bride away. He did not make a courtesy call on Schofield.[34]

Having drifted—or been driven—toward the radical wing of the Republican Party, Curtis followed with interest the intro-duction of men of color, the vast majority of them former slaves, into the Union army. Helena became the primary enrollment and training center for U.S. Colored Troops in the Mississippi Val-ley; some of the earliest recruits were men Curtis had emanci-pated during his sweep through Arkansas. "The success of the negro enrollment is a triumph for me," he told a colleague. "I hope they will be made good soldiers."[35]

For a few weeks Curtis was content to rest and reconnect with the social and commercial life of Keokuk: "I enjoy the shade of my home and the society of my neighbors who are extremely friendly and cordial." Then he began to fidget. Grant captured Vicksburg in July, Union forces achieved a hard-won victory at Gettysburg that same month, and the war seemed to be enter-ing a new and decisive phase. Curtis felt left out: "I am tired of being idle and hope the President will give me some sort of employment soon."[36]

Having nothing else to do, Curtis went on the offensive against the War Department or, more precisely, the Helena court of inquiry. He asked Colonel Norton P. Chipman, a friend and for-mer chief of staff, to serve as his emissary in Washington. Chip-man journeyed to the national capital and met with Lincoln in the White House. According to Chipman, Lincoln insisted that there was no reason why his friendship with Curtis "should be weakened in the least, that he was your friend, [and] that your removal was not ordered because he doubted your ability, your patriotism or honesty, but as a necessity demanded by a condi-tion of things wholly beyond your control." Lincoln went on to describe Curtis as "one of the ablest and best men in the country." Chipman came away convinced that the president was genuinely solicitous of Curtis's feelings and earnest in his praise. "I felt like embracing the honest old man," he wrote. Chipman advised Curtis that Lincoln did not intend "to shelve you permanently or place you on exhibition among his collection of fossilized Generals." The problem was a shortage of suitable positions for major generals: "There really is no place for you now and it don't seem to me politic to urge the matter of a command till there is." Chipman considered paying Halleck a visit but decided against it: "I am afraid he would bite my head off or give me provocation to decapitate him." Curtis knew that feeling.[37]

After his chat with Chipman, Lincoln sent a note to Curtis belatedly explaining why he had been removed from command of the Department of the Missouri. "It became almost a matter of personal self-defense to somehow break up the state of things in Missouri," Lincoln wrote. "I did not mean to cast any censure upon you, nor to endorse any of the charges made against you by others. With me the presumption is still in your favor; that you are honest, capable, faithful, and patriotic." Curtis was pleased with the note and had it published in the *Keokuk Gate City*, but the president's carefully chosen words did not alter the fact that Curtis remained idle while the war raged. He never understood why Lincoln kept him sidelined for so long, and he never quite forgave him for it.[38]

Encouraged by Chipman's success, Curtis redoubled his efforts to denounce the "inquisitorial" and "secret and illegal" proceedings of the court of inquiry. He called on family, friends, fellow Republicans, and comrades in arms to document what had happened in Helena. He provided guidelines, reminded everyone to have copies of documents notarized, and offered to pay expenses ("which I hope will be light"). Curtis's supporters bombarded the White House and War Department with affidavits and depositions affirming his innocence and copies of orders, reports, letters, telegrams, and receipts. "I have sent on quite a volume of evidence," Curtis informed brother Henry, "all corroborating what I had [testified] before, or rebutting what my enemies had put in." He joked that the cost of paper, postage, and notary fees was going to put him in the poorhouse. The documentary deluge, some of which found its way into the newspapers, shifted opinion in his favor.[39]

Throughout this ordeal Curtis maintained a calm and confident demeanor in public, but in private he raged against the unfairness of it all. He dismissed the court's proceedings ("vast volumes of trashy testimony" provided by "unscrupulous malicious enemies") and expressed his innocence ("*I did not* speculate, or wrong my country out of a farthing"). The proceedings dragged on so slowly he commented that it would be nice "to have the matter concluded sometime during my life."[40]

The court of inquiry finally issued its report in June 1863. It concluded that Curtis had not committed any crimes or violated any military regulations. He was guilty of nothing more serious than questionable judgment, inadequate oversight, and careless bookkeeping. Curtis was stung to see himself portrayed as an inept and inattentive administrator, but on the whole he was satisfied. The report "vindicated his character against all the malicious efforts of enemies in the rear." Curtis finally had a chance to see the so-called evidence brought against him. He found it laughable and detestable in equal measure. "It is dangerous to be a General," Curtis once wrote. "We make many very violent and desperate enemies. I have made many." First among them was Frederick Steele, whose "malicious and silly" testimony was a mass of distortions, contradictions, and outright lies. Steele "tried all he could to destroy me," snarled Curtis. "He is [a] pro slavery drunken rascal."[41]

Curtis was not quite out of the woods. The court of inquiry's findings were reviewed by Colonel Joseph Holt, the army's judge advocate general, who came to the confounding conclusion that a court martial was in order. Fortunately, Holt sabotaged his own case by arranging the testimony against Curtis into four categories, which he helpfully labeled "rumors," "opinion," "alleged admissions," and "general appearances at his office and place of business, as described by General Steele." And there the matter rested while the president decided what to do next.[42]

Curtis and Chipman seized the moment and resumed their offensive. In early November each wrote to Lincoln refuting Holt's case point by point. Their arguments must have had the desired effect, because Lincoln declined to act on Holt's recommendation and allowed the proceedings to lapse. Curtis's long ordeal came to an end as the court of inquiry quietly faded away. Having never been formally charged, Curtis was never formally exonerated.[43]

The Helena court of inquiry was an attempt by a group of disaffected conservative politicians and regular army officers to reverse the progress of military emancipation in the Mississippi Valley by using an elaborate form of character assassination to remove the principal architect and prime mover of that progress. The attempt curbed emancipation only briefly, but it distracted, then benched, one of the Union army's most successful generals for the better part of a year.

• • •

While Curtis fought to save his reputation and career, son Henry was reassigned to Blunt's staff in Kansas. Henry and Julia set up housekeeping at Fort Scott in the eastern part of the state and all seemed well. Then disaster struck. On October 6 Blunt led a column out of Fort Scott on a routine mission to the Indian Territory. The Union force consisted of Blunt, several of his staff officers, the headquarters band, and a strong cavalry escort. Near Baxter Springs, about sixty miles south of the fort, the column was overwhelmed by a large band of Confederate guerrillas. Blunt and a handful of others escaped, but everyone else, including Henry, was killed. Curtis was informed by telegraph that, after a "gallant resistance," his son had been taken prisoner and "afterwards murdered by his captors." The guerrillas carried away Henry's coat, boots, and arms but overlooked his watch, which was later recovered.[44]

The family was devastated. "We are all overwhelmed with sorrow," Curtis told brother Henry. "Poor Julia is heart broken." He found it hard to believe that an officer serving as chief of staff to a major general should fall victim to a guerrilla ambush. "The world seems like a burden to me," he continued. "There is very little left to live and fight for." In a series of emotional letters, Curtis struggled to express what his son had meant to him: "He was so good so dutiful so affectionate so manly. His life was beautiful and his death glorious; but oh it is hard to part with him forever." Henry died a few days short of his twenty-seventh birthday. His passing meant that only two of the seven Curtis children still lived.[45]

Julia, six months pregnant, accompanied her husband's body back to Keokuk for burial. Blunt provided a military escort for the melancholy journey. Henry's funeral on October 15 was "one of the most impressive ever conducted" in the Gate City, reported a local newspaper. Businesses were closed, buildings were draped in black bunting, and U.S. flags flew at half-staff. The service was held in the local Episcopal church. Afterward the grieving family, military units, city officials, and civic organizations followed the coffin to Oakland Cemetery. The route was lined with hundreds of people, many in uniform. Curtis reckoned it was the "most melancholy parade ever seen here." Henry was interred in the family plot next to Yale, Bucky, and Sadie.[46]

Curtis penned a sad, disjointed letter to Sam, who had not been able to attend the funeral because of his military duties in Missouri. Curtis wrote that he and Belinda were "reconciled to our sorrows" and that it was a "great consolation" that Henry had "died gallantly for his country." He reminded Sam that "you are now our only son" and encouraged him to follow in Henry's footsteps and study law. He urged Sam to be careful but not to shirk his duty.[47]

Near the end of 1863 a grieving Curtis learned that Lincoln had at last decided to return him to active duty. The news lightened his mood. "I am breathing easier now," he confided to brother Henry. "I think they will keep me in the West and I am holding myself ready for any post." Early in the new year the long-awaited telegram arrived from the War Department. Curtis glanced at the contents and announced: "I am ordered to Kansas." He was back in the war.[48]

11

FORT LEAVENWORTH

ON JANUARY 1, 1864, THE WAR DEPARTMENT, AT LINCOLN'S direction, reconstituted the old Department of Kansas and placed Curtis in command. Not everyone was thrilled with the arrangement. Sherman believed it was a mistake to fashion special positions for people like Curtis. He wanted Lincoln to retire aging officers and make room for promising younger men. "By manufacturing commands for old Generals as in the Curtis case, he ties up the army," Sherman complained to Grant. Curtis neither knew nor cared what Sherman thought. He was satisfied just to be back in the war.[1]

Curtis officially learned of his new assignment on January 3. He wanted to leave for Kansas at once, but a severe winter storm kept him housebound for a week. The temperature in Keokuk dropped to twenty degrees below zero; the Mississippi and Missouri Rivers froze over as far south as St. Louis. "It is awful cold," Curtis noted. By January 11 the worst of the storm had passed and Curtis bid his family farewell. The rivers were still impassable, so he traveled overland in fits and starts. The arduous journey took five days.[2]

Fort Leavenworth, still in service today, sits atop a bluff overlooking the Missouri River in northeastern Kansas. In 1864 it was the administrative and logistical hub for military installations on the Great Plains and beyond. Curtis informed Henry that it was "quite a village of excellent government buildings used as barracks and storehouses." Post headquarters was a handsome, two-story brick structure "about the size or larger than your residence and [in] everyway a very comfortable building." The commanding officer's residence was equally impressive. Curtis wanted his family to join him in the spring, but he was worried about the expense of "furnishing such an establishment during these precarious war times."[3]

Curtis assumed command on January 16 in a low-key ceremony. He observed that the soldiers "seem very glad to see me, and the press and people express great gratification at my arrival." That was no exaggeration. The citizens of the nearby town of Leavenworth organized a spectacular welcome for the "warrior hero" of Pea Ridge. The celebration included a reception, parade, illumination, and all the fireworks Kansas could muster. Curtis wrote that the "great event of the day and an epoch in my life was the magnificent ovation or illumination in honor of my arrival." He thanked the crowd (the "largest I ever addressed") for coming out on a winter night and made a few "simple and earnest" remarks about preserving the Union and establishing liberty for all. He noted, "I was listened to attentively and the response was hearty." His tenure was off to a rousing start.[4]

Letters and telegrams poured in as family, friends, colleagues, and complete strangers congratulated Curtis on being restored to his rightful place in the military hierarchy. Many correspondents stressed that his appointment to a "respectable command" like Kansas was a "complete vindication" of his policies and practices in Arkansas and Missouri. Henry was relieved beyond measure, informing his younger brother that "your friends all rejoice . . . at you having at last obtained justice."[5]

Belinda viewed events somewhat differently. "We have been very lonely since you left," she informed her husband. "The house seems so deserted that I almost dread coming into the parlor where I am now writing at your table." Belinda's letters manifested a more religious tone after the deaths of their two oldest children; her missive to Curtis reflected that change. She expressed her hope that God would make her husband a "blessing" to the "long oppressed and suffering people" of Kansas. Sadie and Henry were never far from Curtis's mind as well. On January 26 he noted that it was two years since he had marched out of Rolla: "Alas it was the last I ever saw of my dear dark eyed and darling daughter."[6]

Kansas was a Republican stronghold, which explains Curtis's warm welcome, but state and local officials were mired in bitter disputes that had little to do with ideology or policy and everything to do with power and place. After his recent experience in Missouri, Curtis understandably feared that these "desperate political scrambles will make my administration very difficult. I can only do my best to keep out of them." He vowed to avoid saying or doing anything that smacked of politics. Curtis was right to be concerned. Despite his determination to steer clear of all things political, factional squabbling would undermine his efforts to defend Kansas in its hour of greatest danger.[7]

The new Department of Kansas was essentially the old Department of the Missouri, only without Missouri. It consisted of Kansas, the Indian Territory, the Nebraska and Colorado territories, and, oddly, a few acres of western Arkansas. Curtis was responsible for securing the department against rebel incursions, guerrilla raids, and Indian attacks. Manning isolated outposts on the Great Plains was not the sort of activity that generated headlines in the eastern newspapers, but it was important work and Curtis recognized it as such. He may even have welcomed his assignment to a relatively quiet command, for he was quick to point out that "in the forepart of the war I did my full share of arduous active service."[8]

By the time Curtis reached Fort Leavenworth, the Civil War in the West was being transformed in ways that made his job far more difficult than it would have been a year or even six months earlier. Following the Union victory at Chattanooga in November 1863, the focus of the conflict shifted eastward. Lincoln appointed Grant general in chief and demoted Halleck to chief of staff, though his administrative duties remained much the same. Grant directed the War Department to draw men, animals, and equipment out of the western states and territories and send them eastward to support the mammoth operations taking shape in Virginia and Georgia. As part of this general reallocation of resources, Grant moved to Virginia to personally oversee operations in that theater. Regular military activity beyond the Mississippi River declined, though the brutal guerrilla struggle showed no signs of abating. The trans-Mississippi, once a vital part of the larger conflict, was becoming a backwater.

The effect of the Union drawdown was readily apparent at Fort Leavenworth. Curtis discovered that the "new and excellent store-houses" that had so impressed him from a distance were, upon closer examination, nearly empty. He complained to Stanton that the "supply formerly held at this place has been entirely exhausted" and requested that the secretary rectify the situation at once: "I hope you will favor my efforts to get this depot properly supplied, for the few troops I have need arms, and new difficulties connected with great excitement in the gold mines [in the Rocky Mountains] may require prompt use of light artillery and cavalry." Curtis asked for carbines, pistols, mountain howitzers, and ammunition for his poorly equipped cavalry regiments. He had so few soldiers that he also asked for ten thousand muskets to arm the Kansas, Colorado, and Nebraska militias in case of a rebel invasion or Indian uprising. Curtis's prodding had the desired effect for once, doubtless because of his reference to the western gold mines, a vital source of funding for the war. The War Department dispatched several shipments of arms, ammunition, accoutrements, and camp equipment to Kansas that proved invaluable in the months ahead. Curtis was satisfied. "Matters seem quiet," he reported, "and I shall do all in my power to keep them so."[9]

Curtis marked his return to active duty by having his picture taken at the A. C. Nichols photographic studio in nearby Leavenworth. The seated image is one of his best. He appears fit, rested, and every inch a major general. While in town Curtis picked up another journal. In the past he had always used a common ledger, but on this occasion he acquired an expensive lawyer's notebook with decorated endpapers and a lock. He wrote on the flyleaf that he intended to keep an accurate account of events for "future review by myself or family," and that he did not want his observations to see the light of day: "What I write is *private* views of public and private events." He composed informative entries for three months, then stopped.[10]

The eastern edge of the Department of Kansas included four antebellum military posts: Forts Leavenworth and Scott in Kansas, Fort Gibson in the Indian Territory, and Fort Smith in Arkansas. Blunt had wrested the latter two from the Confederates the previous summer in a follow-up to the Prairie Grove campaign, but the isolated posts were a constant source of concern. Curtis decided to judge for himself whether they could or should be held, and if so, how best to go about it. Two weeks after assuming command, he set out on a monthlong fact-finding tour, the first of several lengthy journeys he made during his tenure in Kansas. Curtis was the only department commander in the trans-Mississippi who actually visited most of the people and places he was pledged to defend.

Curtis left Fort Leavenworth on February 1 with an escort of two hundred "well armed and well mounted soldiers" and a small train. The weather had moderated and the party made good progress. Curtis described eastern Kansas as the "richest and finest natural country of land water wood stone and gentle rolling topography I ever saw." He was also impressed by Fort Scott, the only true defensive bastion in the department. After a formal welcome ceremony and a tour of the post's artillery redoubts and other outworks, he concluded it was a "pretty strong place." Curtis stayed at the fort for several days, time enough to explore the place where young Henry and Julia had spent their final months together. The party then continued south. The countryside between Fort Scott and Fort Gibson, a distance of nearly two hundred miles, was completely depopulated after three years of guerrilla depredations. "I did not see a living soul," wrote Curtis. Nevertheless, he continued to be impressed with the land's potential. "What a country this will be when all these broad acres are under cultivation," he mused.[11]

Two days out of Fort Scott Curtis passed by Baxter Springs, the place where young Henry had been murdered by Quantrill's "fiends" four months earlier. "It was the saddest spot in the world to me," Curtis confessed to his brother. "A cold bleak rolling prairie scenery where General Blunts escort was surprised, broken, scattered and inhumanly slaughtered except himself and some dozen men who escaped by flight to the hills." There was little to see and nothing to be done, so a somber Curtis resumed his southward progress. Belinda later wrote that it must have been "sad and sorrowful" to visit the place where "our beloved Henry poured out his life blood in the holiest of causes." She added, "It is hard yet to realize our loss, and the truth when it does flash over me seems more than I can bear."[12]

The next day Curtis entered the Indian Territory. He observed that the "whole country belongs to eight or ten thousand miserable Indians" and wondered whether their claims to the land would be recognized after the war. Upon arriving at Fort Gibson, Curtis discovered that the two thousand Union soldiers stationed at the post belonged to the Indian Brigade, a force of Indian Home Guard regiments led by Colonel William A. Phillips. The Indians were "bad off for supplies"; their families, huddled in makeshift shelters outside the walls of the fort, were in "still more destitute circumstances." Curtis was no stranger to the post or the people. Fort Gibson had been his only duty assignment during his brief stint in the regular army after West Point. He told Henry, "I saw the building where I lodged thirty-three years ago when I was a Brevet Second Lieutenant of the Seventh Infantry and my wife accompanied me to this far off post. It has changed but not so much as I have."[13]

Curtis wrote to Lincoln about the strategic importance of the Indian Territory and the crucial role played by the Indian Brigade in the defense of southern Kansas. He urgently requested that the War Department send arms, ammunition, supplies, and horses so that the Indians could better maintain themselves in the field. Curtis assured Phillips that help was on the way but cautioned that it might take a while for things to improve: "I only promise to do all I can." When Curtis learned that some white officers had mistreated Indian soldiers, he ordered Phillips to discipline or remove the guilty parties. Indians, he insisted, "must be treated with kindness, care, and diligence on the part of all my officers."[14]

Lincoln passed Curtis's letter on to Secretary of the Interior John P. Usher, who asked Curtis for his thoughts on the military situation in the Indian Territory. Curtis replied that without a "vast deal more of force in this department I cannot promise security to whites or Indians, but I do promise you that with such force as I have I will use my best efforts to protect both." The Arkansas River was the only natural line of defense in the Indian Territory. Curtis stressed that it "must be well guarded," but he did not see how the threadbare Indian regiments could accomplish this task unless they were better armed and equipped. Curtis did not think his pleas on behalf of the Indians would do much good. He was right.[15]

Curtis left Fort Gibson and proceeded down the Arkansas Valley to Fort Smith, located just inside the state of Arkansas. The Departments of Arkansas and Kansas were established at roughly the same time, but for some unfathomable reason Fort Smith was included in the latter, not the former. The post was a small antebellum depot. It consisted of several brick buildings, one of them a storehouse, enclosed by a wall designed to prevent pilferage, not resist an attack. "It is no fort and no place for troops," Curtis observed. He urged Stanton to relocate the garrison and stores to Van Buren, an "unquestionably" better site four miles away. Curtis also suggested that the departmental boundary be adjusted to conform to the political border between Arkansas and the Indian Territory. That would bring all of the state of Arkansas, including Fort Smith, into the new Department of Arkansas and greatly simplify administrative and logistical arrangements. After weeks of dithering, the War Department finally came around to Curtis's sensible point of view and transferred Fort Smith to the Department of Arkansas.[16]

While at Fort Smith, Curtis received a message from Belinda telling of the birth and death of their first grandchild three weeks earlier. Henry Zarah Curtis Jr. arrived on February 3, Curtis's fifty-ninth birthday, but lived only two days. Curtis passed the sad news to his brother. He wrote that the infant "now sleeps by our dear Henry at Keokuk. Just born to see and receive parental smiles and kisses and then away to the world his father knows and we must soon inhabit."[17]

Sunk in gloom, Curtis returned to Kansas by way of northwestern Arkansas and southwestern Missouri. In the Boston Mountains he trotted ahead of his escort and stumbled into an ambush: "I was fired upon by guerrillas from the bushes by the roadside, but escaped uninjured." Curtis did not mention this incident to Belinda or Henry. The weather turned sharply colder and the party was buffeted by blizzard-like conditions. Curtis took shelter in the ambulance, where he "suffered with cold in spite of robes and blankets." The Federals passed through Fayetteville and Neosho and eventually returned to Fort Scott, where they stopped for several days to recover from their ordeal. Curtis took advantage of the stopover to provide Stanton with an account of his travels. "I have seen the troops, the people, and country," he concluded. "Although I am weary, I am much better prepared and qualified to administer the affairs and protect the interests of my department." He also was much better armed. Colonel Charles W. Blair, Fort Scott's commanding officer, presented Curtis with a "very nice" pair of revolvers and holsters.[18]

Still feeling low, Curtis extended his tour into the interior of Kansas rather than return to his empty quarters at Fort Leavenworth. Now riding in a "rather sorry looking buggy," he traveled west to Humboldt, then north and east to Topeka and Lawrence. Everywhere he went he found people in a "great state of anxious fear." He ordered blockhouses constructed in every town and, standing amid the charred ruins of Lawrence, pledged to protect Kansas from the "merciless bushmen of Missouri." He informed Stanton that Kansans felt "cruelly neglected" by the government, with good reason. "The outrages which have been committed against the towns and peoples of Kansas by our common foe exceed any atrocities committed by Sepoy or savage warfare," he wrote. "I have passed over ruined towns, and the ravaged and ruined country, heard the story of Kansas suffering, and witnessed the sighs and tears of the people. It is sickening and painful."[19]

Curtis got back to Fort Leavenworth on February 26 after four weeks on the road. He sent a summary of what he had seen and heard to the White House. "I have returned to headquarters after eight hundred miles of travel a wiser but sadder soldier," he told Lincoln.[20]

• • •

The military drawdown forced hard-pressed Union department commanders west of the Mississippi River to cooperate. Curtis appears to have initiated this process. While on his way back to Fort Leavenworth, he learned that Major General William S. Rosecrans had replaced Schofield as commander of the much-reduced Department of the Missouri. Curtis welcomed Rosecrans to the trans-Mississippi. He described his recent "reconnaissance" to the Indian Territory and confessed that he had "intruded a little on your dominion" on the way home from Fort Smith. Curtis pledged his cooperation on matters of mutual concern: "I shall therefore constantly try to keep you advised of whatever I may learn of interest to your command, and hope you will as far as convenient reciprocate my advances." He asked Rosecrans to carry out preemptive strikes against guerrilla lairs in "bushwhacker country," the lawless Missouri counties adjacent to Kansas. He declared melodramatically that the "eggs should be crushed before the vipers come forth in the spring."[21]

By April Curtis was satisfied that Rosecrans was "cooperating cordially on his side of the Missouri line" and directed his subordinates to reciprocate. He encouraged Brigadier General Thomas J. McKean, commanding in southeastern Kansas, to work closely with Brigadier General Egbert E. Brown, his counterpart across the state line in southwestern Missouri: "I have written General Brown, urging him to a cordial cooperation with you, and giving him assurance of your cordial cooperation with him, in efforts to preserve the peace of the border." Curtis cautioned McKean not to do anything that might seem "discourteous" to "our comrades of another department." Similar directives went to all district commanders in Kansas.[22]

Curtis followed his own advice about not stepping on toes. In June soldiers from Fort Leavenworth pursued a band of guerrillas across the Missouri River. Curtis informed Rosecrans that his troops were temporarily operating in northwestern Missouri. "Hope I don't intrude," he added. Rosecrans expressed his wholehearted approval of interdepartmental cooperation, which prompted Curtis to exclaim: "Who cares who kills bushwhackers?" Following up on the earlier reference to vipers, Rosecrans assured Curtis that he was taking "vigorous measures" that he believed would "kill the snake before it has grown too large." Rosecrans ultimately proved to be mostly talk and little or no action, but at least his words were encouraging.[23]

Major General John Pope, commanding the Department of the Northwest, asked Curtis for the loan of a battalion of cavalry to deal with Indian unrest on the northern plains. Pope was headquartered in Milwaukee, several hundred miles to the north, and mistakenly believed that the Department of Kansas, as a frontline command, must be awash in troops. Curtis disabused Pope of that notion and expressed his regrets at being unable to spare a company, much less a battalion. "I have nothing like adequate force to resist rebel raids," he wrote. "I am sorry, general, but I can't do better." Curtis and Pope stayed on good terms, though neither had enough manpower to cooperate in any meaningful way.[24]

While Curtis established new relationships with Rosecrans and Pope, his old relationship with Halleck continued to deteriorate. In his new role as chief of staff, Halleck handled routine communications (orders, reports, requests, and general correspondence) with department commanders, thereby freeing Grant to focus on operations in Virginia. Curtis noted in his journal that, although Halleck's authority was diminished, he continued to exhibit an "indifference or hostility to my Department which gives me much anxiety." His anxiety soon turned to anger. He accused

Halleck of abandoning the Indian Territory to the Confederates and demanded that the Department of Kansas receive a "fair and favorable allotment of forces." During one heated exchange, Halleck claimed not to understand what Curtis was getting at. Curtis replied that he had expressed himself "in my plain vernacular" and was not going to change just to suit Halleck. He repeated his original point in much the same language and asked, "If I have not plainly presented the matter before have I done it now?" On another occasion, Curtis accused Halleck of deliberately distorting facts. He fended off a potential rebuke by issuing a preemptive denial: "I do not desire the command of an inch of territory or a corporal's guard beyond my proper limits and [what] the common safety seem[s] to require." While trading barbs with Halleck, Curtis was careful to stay on good terms with Stanton.[25]

With "guerrilla season" fast approaching, Curtis made a major effort to convince the War Department of his precarious situation. Stores were beginning to arrive, but manpower was still short. He pointed out that he was the only department commander fighting on two fronts against two different enemies. "The Indians and guerrillas keep all my troops on the stretch," he reminded both Stanton and Halleck. "In consequence of past disasters I am obliged to place guards at many important towns to prevent a general departure of terrified inhabitants; and the little force I have is therefore all employed guarding the [Overland Trail] route, the Santa Fe route, and the posts and stores of my command." With his meager force thus dispersed and immobilized, Curtis could not respond effectively to guerrilla raids. He had only 2,400 soldiers in Kansas and 4,300 in the entire department. "I have no reserve to repel or pursue a raiding force," he warned. Halleck, to his everlasting discredit, again played fast and loose with the facts. He manipulated the numbers on departmental returns to make it appear that Curtis had more troops than he actually did. Uncertain whom to believe, Stanton adopted a middle course. He authorized Curtis to arm and equip the Kansas State Militia should the need arise but did not dispatch additional troops.[26]

The only reinforcement of note to reach the Department of Kansas at this time came in the person of Major General George Sykes, late of the Fifth Corps of the Army of the Potomac. Sykes reported for duty at Fort Leavenworth in April. "I hardly know what disposition to make of him," Curtis admitted. "I am better provided with generals than troops." Sykes exhibited little energy or initiative, so Curtis placed him on medical leave a few months later.[27]

Curtis received another surprise when the War Department transferred the Indian Territory to the Department of Arkansas. The Indian regiments had long served as a buffer between the Confederacy and Kansas, but after the transfer Curtis was no longer in a position to supply their wants or direct their movements. Steele was in charge of the Department of Arkansas, a reward for having finally captured Little Rock in September 1863, and Curtis did not expect much cooperation from his old antagonist. He urged Stanton and Halleck to make certain Steele guarded all the crossing points on the Arkansas River, but Steele proved to be immovably uncooperative. He not only failed to guard the Arkansas, he ignored the Indian Territory and allowed matters there to go from bad to worse. And all the while he continued to denounce Curtis. In March 1864, for example, Steele falsely accused Blunt of hijacking troops from his department and insinuated in his usual manner that "General Curtis is most likely his accomplice in this matter."[28]

Belinda fell seriously ill in April. Curtis hurried back to Keokuk. "I have had so much of sorrow and death this year I cannot remain away," he wrote in his journal. Curtis found his wife afflicted with a case of "severe congestion," probably pneumonia. For the next three weeks Curtis kept Belinda company, chatted with Julia, helped Caddie with her homework, rambled around Keokuk, and visited his farms. He put in vineyards despite a tight wartime labor market. "I am trying to get some farming done but find it very troublesome to raise hands," he complained to Henry. The few available laborers demanded exorbitant wages; Curtis was forced to pay what they asked. He was still grumbling about the "outrageous" expense months later. Belinda recovered her health and agreed to join her husband "out west" as soon as practicable. Reassured, Curtis returned to Kansas.[29]

Belinda, Caddie, and Julia moved to Fort Leavenworth in July. Curtis was happy with his new domestic arrangements. "I now have all but Sam of my family with me keeping house," he wrote to Henry. "We have a beautiful place and building and comfortable arrangements for ourselves and a few friends." Curtis paused a moment to take in his surroundings, then returned pen to paper: "While I conclude this I am entertained by a fine band of music and my wife is looking out at dress parade in front of our quarters on a beautiful shaded lawn." Curtis slipped into a contemplative mood. His described his first six months on the job as "entirely successful," but admitted that he disliked being "so constantly worked and worn with duties relating to my command." He was also unhappy that the War Department had "drawn away" so many soldiers from the trans-Mississippi "to help crush the rebel armies" in Virginia and Georgia. He understood why, but it still irked him: "I have to depend on militia and strategy to keep matters quiet." He wondered what would happen if an emergency arose.[30]

The absent Sam (or "Major Sam," as Curtis called him) was on leave to attend the Republican Party convention in Baltimore, where he and the rest of the Colorado delegation voted to nominate Lincoln for a second term. Curtis remained active in Republican Party politics in Iowa, but his Missouri experience had made him cynical. He told Henry that Lincoln "expresses himself very friendly towards me although I have no reason to thank him for much in the way of favors." In his next letter Curtis described his feelings toward the president more fully: "I suppose Mr. Lincoln is one of the most honest hearted men in the world; but he was induced to remove me for political reasons. . . . I can see therefore his honesty may be diverted into great wrong, as it surely has been in the matter of Missouri. Not wrong to me of great consequence, but to the people of all sections west of the Mississippi." Curtis supported Lincoln's re-election but disagreed with his "soft" approach to rebellion and reconciliation. Curtis favored a harsh war and a punitive peace. Sadie's death and Henry's murder had hardened his resolve to make traitors pay.[31]

Lincoln continued to make small gestures to demonstrate his goodwill toward Curtis. In the summer of 1864 Curtis wrote to Brigadier General Montgomery C. Meigs, quartermaster general of the army, to request that his efficient department quartermaster, Captain Merritt H. Insley, be given authority over the depot at Fort Leavenworth to better facilitate the distribution of supplies. The letter somehow found its way from the War Department to the White House, where it came to the attention of the president, who endorsed Curtis's request: "I shall be personally obliged if General Curtis' wish, expressed within, be gratified. A. Lincoln." Meigs approved the request.[32]

A few weeks earlier Insley had presented Curtis with a framed printed copy of the Emancipation Proclamation. Curtis appreciated the gesture. The proclamation, he wrote in a thank-you note, is "one of the wonderful products of this terrible struggle, and probably the only great good that can flow from the terrible aggregate of sorrow and war." He added a wish: "I trust in God the Proclamation may secure universal Freedom to all mankind." Curtis was among like-minded friends in Kansas and no longer felt the need to downplay his abolitionist beliefs.[33]

Whenever time permitted, Curtis put his official duties aside and tended to his personal interests. Lawsuits and countersuits over ownership of the Omaha properties continued to make their way through the territorial and federal courts. Curtis and brothers Hosmer and Henry established a business partnership in 1863; thereafter Curtis urged Henry, the most accomplished attorney in the family, to become more involved in the ongoing legal struggle. "Our Omaha matter must indeed be arranged if possible but I do wish you could come and help me," Curtis wrote in June. "Public affairs keep me very busy but if you come I will make a great effort to go with you up to Omaha." Curtis wanted to obtain clear title to as many of the disputed properties as possible, because construction of the transcontinental railroad was getting underway and Omaha was beginning to boom. He was also tired of paying taxes on *all* the properties, disputed and otherwise. (The amount due in 1864 was a hefty $213.98.) "All of which makes it necessary to hurry a settlement of the whole matter which could be better done if you were here to press your rights," he wrote to Henry. "I am confident Omaha is well deserving of our best joint business consideration and care."[34]

Curtis's personal finances were much improved by 1864, thanks to the salary and benefits he earned as a major general. At the end of May, for example, the Fort Leavenworth paymaster handed him an envelope containing $574 in cash. "My pay is such as to soon replenish my means," he informed Henry. "I am working off my debts gradually." By this time he owed less than $1,500 and his properties outside Omaha were clear of liens and other claims. He hoped "sales of real estate may some day soon enable me to clean out arrears." The war still raged with all its cruelties and uncertainties, but Curtis was no longer haunted by the specter of financial failure.[35]

• • •

Guerrillas and brigands awaited the springtime emergence of grass and leaves (the former for fuel, the latter for cover) before resuming their murderous attacks. As the snow melted and the roads dried, Curtis made ready to defend thousands of square miles of sparsely settled territory. He prepared his soldiers for action, advised Governor Thomas Carney to place the Kansas State Militia on alert, and firmed up mutual-aid arrangements with Rosecrans. There was little else he could do except watch and wait.

The first signs of trouble appeared in June 1864. Brigadier General Clinton B. Fisk, a former member of Curtis's staff, was in command of Union forces in northwestern Missouri, directly across the Missouri River from Fort Leavenworth. A guerrilla band several hundred strong took over Platte City, a few miles north of Kansas City, raising a Confederate flag over the courthouse. The local Enrolled Missouri Militia regiment defected to the rebels, and Fisk asked Curtis for help. "I determined to strike the enemy at once," Curtis later wrote. He led three companies of cavalry across the Missouri River to Weston, while Fisk assembled all the Federal troops and Missouri State Militia he could find.[36]

Curtis thought it impolitic to be seen leading troops into battle in Rosecrans's department, so he and Fisk agreed to put Colonel James H. Ford in command of the operation. The Federals converged on Platte City from several directions and struck the guerrillas at Camden Point on July 13. The rebels lost fifteen dead and at least as many wounded in the initial exchange of fire, and another twenty to thirty dead in the swirling fight that followed. One Union soldier was killed. Curtis informed the War Department that a "combined force of cavalry belonging to [the] Departments of the Missouri and Kansas" successfully carried out a "gallant dash" on a large guerrilla force, completely "routing and scattering" the enemy. He properly credited Ford with the victory.[37]

Camden Point was a signal victory by the standards of irregular warfare. It also demonstrated that Curtis was right and Gamble was wrong when it came to the most effective means of defending Missouri. Fisk thanked Curtis for his "prompt and cheerful cooperation" and offered to reciprocate: "I shall be glad to march a force into Kansas and aid you whenever a similar misfortune befalls your people." Rosecrans, who remained in St. Louis, was "very much obliged" to Curtis for his help and asked if he would be willing to participate in another joint operation south of Kansas City, where insurgents were plentiful. Curtis likely would have agreed, but just then he learned that the Department of Kansas was under attack from another direction.[38]

• • •

Indian depredations on the Great Plains increased in the spring and summer of 1864. The upsurge in violence was caused by expanding settlement, increasing traffic on the Santa Fe and Overland Trails, and, of course, a shrinking military presence. Cheyennes, Kiowas, Sioux, Comanches, and Arapahoes attacked travelers and settlers across a wide area. They ran off cattle, burned homesteads and stagecoach stations, and even raided undermanned army posts. The murders, rapes, and kidnappings created widespread panic in Kansas, Nebraska, and Colorado. Several hundred Indians, mostly Cheyennes, pushed into central Kansas and interdicted traffic on the Santa Fe Trail near the Great Bend of the Arkansas River. They besieged several westbound trains and herds, including a train hauling ordnance stores to army posts in Colorado and New Mexico. The situation was intolerable. A few hundred Indians had severed commerce and communications between the northern states and the western territories.[39]

These events caused Curtis to step back from the guerrilla conflict along the Kansas-Missouri line. "I am troubled with Indians," he telegraphed Fisk. "I am going to look after the western portion of my command." As a parting gift he sent Fisk five hundred muskets and twenty thousand rounds of ammunition, explaining, "I cannot spare more without robbing myself." Curtis left Fort Leavenworth on July 19 and hurried west to Fort Riley, where he picked up a company of cavalry and a section of light artillery. He continued west toward Great Bend, gathering up about three hundred Kansas State militiamen along the way. "Militia collecting to aid me in attacking the Indians, but they gather slowly," he reported. His command ultimately consisted of nearly four hundred soldiers and militiamen, all mounted, and two light guns. The battalion-sized command was better suited to a major than a major general, but Curtis wanted to see the country and get a feel for fighting Indians.[40]

The relief column reached the besieged trains and herds at Great Bend on July 27, after a march of three hundred miles in eight days. Curtis reminded the militiamen that they were to act in accordance with army regulations, which meant they were not to harm Indian women and children, if any were present. The soldiers and militiamen formed a ragged line of battle and advanced, but the Indians chose not to fight. They hurried away with about 150 head of cattle and as much loot as they could carry.[41]

The next day Curtis wrote to Belinda: "I have raised and marched my little army to this place all entirely safe and sound." He explained that the Indians had killed two teamsters in their initial attack, but the survivors armed themselves with the weapons being transported to New Mexico and thereafter kept the raiders at a distance. Curtis thought additional military force was needed in the Great Bend area, so he authorized the construction of Forts Ellsworth and Zarah in the gap between Forts Riley and Larned. He named Fort Zarah, located where the Santa Fe Trail crosses Walnut Creek, for his son, Henry Zarah.[42]

Curtis created a new military district in western Kansas to provide better protection for settlers and travelers on the Santa Fe Trail, placing Blunt in command. The victor of Prairie Grove, Honey Springs, Cane Hill, and other engagements was available because his former district in the Indian Territory had ceased to exist when that region was detached from the Department of Kansas. Curtis and Blunt had worked well together during the Prairie Grove campaign. When Curtis arrived at Fort Leavenworth one of his first acts was to write to his "Dear Friend," but his attitude changed after he uncovered evidence of Blunt's mismanagement and corruption. "I am out of all patience with Blunt," Curtis confessed to his journal. "I fear he is unfit for any administrative duties." But Curtis did not want to be rid of Blunt altogether. The department was short of experienced combat leaders and Blunt was every inch a fighting man. Curtis therefore ordered Blunt to head west and take the field as soon as possible. He warned that many Plains Indians were in "defiant array" against the United States and authorized Blunt to act accordingly.[43]

Officers were required to submit a report after every military operation. That is what Curtis did, though he did not think his superiors in Washington cared much about conditions on the frontier. He summarized the expedition to Great Bend and stated his intention to escort the trains and herds to Fort Larned, thirty miles farther west on the Santa Fe Trail. Curtis said that he was going to issue "further measures of caution and security for the trains and travel and safety of the settlements on the frontier," but did not elaborate. He described the Indians as "evidently determined to do all the mischief they can." Curtis also wrote to Governor Carney and explained that he had "borrowed" three hundred members of the Kansas State Militia without going through official channels. He added diplomatically that the presence of the militia "greatly expedited and strengthened my exertions."[44]

Curtis reached Fort Larned on July 29. He was tempted to push on to Colorado and see the fabled Rocky Mountains, but the Santa Fe Trail was once again open for business and the Kansas militiamen were anxious to return home. The expedition turned back and fanned out along both sides of the Arkansas River to search for hostile stragglers. None were found, but Curtis noticed that even friendly Indians fled at his approach. He suspected they were wary of the militia, whose members were "not very particular in their discriminations, as they are much enraged at the hostile acts perpetrated." Curtis rode into Fort Leavenworth on August 8, tired and travel-worn after a six-hundred-mile, three-week odyssey.[45]

• • •

Curtis had little time to enjoy the comforts of hearth and home. On August 8 hundreds of Sioux and other Indians launched a coordinated attack along a four-hundred-mile front extending from northeastern Colorado to south-central Nebraska. As before, dozens of men, women, and children—homesteaders, teamsters, westbound emigrants, and commercial travelers— were killed, wounded, or abducted and large numbers of buildings, wagons, stages, and stock were destroyed or stolen. It was the costliest Indian attack since the Sioux Uprising in Minnesota two years earlier.[46]

The Nebraska frontier rolled back dozens of miles as terrified settlers abandoned their homes and workplaces and fled to the relative safety of military posts and larger towns. Traffic on the Overland Trail came to a standstill and connections with Colorado, Utah, and the Pacific Coast were severed. Curtis's advice to the state and territorial governors in his department revealed his lack of resources: "Do all you can with militia. I will do my utmost to keep lines open." Faced with mounting turmoil in Nebraska and, to a lesser extent, in Kansas and Colorado, Curtis decided to take charge in person. "I became convinced that the condition of affairs in Nebraska demanded my presence," he later wrote. Curtis informed Stanton of his plans, such as they were: "Have with me small force, which, with militia, I hope sufficient to scatter [the Indians]." He did not bother asking for reinforcements.[47]

As Curtis was preparing to depart for Nebraska, a dispatch arrived from Fisk in northwestern Missouri. Aware that Curtis was busy dealing with trouble farther west, Fisk wrote to say that he had taken the liberty of sending some of his troops to "see, catch, kill, and otherwise exterminate" a band of guerrillas that had crossed the Missouri River into northeastern Kansas. Curtis heartily approved of Fisk's initiative and encouraged him to continue. "Go ahead and take any bushwhackers that attempt to come to my side of the river," he replied. Then he was off to save Nebraska.[48]

Curtis and a small escort boarded the steamboat *Colorado* and proceeded up the Missouri River to Omaha. Low water caused several delays; the party did not reach the territorial capital until August 16. Curtis met with Governor Alvin Saunders and observed that "much excitement prevails," a polite way of saying Nebraskans were in a panic. "Trifles are magnified into terrible affairs," he noted. Despite the uproar, the wheels of the territorial government turned slowly. While waiting impatiently for the civil authorities to act, Curtis explored the growing town, observed the progress of the Union Pacific, and, inevitably, conferred with his local attorney about the status of the disputed properties.[49]

Saunders wanted to raise twelve companies of mounted volunteers—Nebraska's informal version of a territorial militia—to chastise the Indians, but Nebraskans largely ignored his summons. "Militia very tardy in coming forward," Curtis informed Halleck. He finally decided to act, with or without the assistance of the civilian population. On August 19 Curtis and several companies of cavalry set out for Fort Kearney, 250 miles west on the Overland Trail. The Federals searched for Indians along the way but found only tracks. "As usual," Curtis reported, "the Indians skulked away." The column reached Fort Kearney without incident four days later. Another week passed while additional troops and supplies trickled into the fort. At the end of August sixty-four Nebraska militia volunteers finally made an appearance, as did seventy-six Pawnee Indians, implacable enemies of the Sioux. The situation required Curtis to make a mental adjustment. The last time he had fought Indians in Nebraska, Pawnees had been the enemy. "Am collecting militia and friendly Indians," Curtis told Sam.[50]

Curtis had no illusions about his ability to locate the elusive Sioux and bring them to battle. He informed Stanton that the Indians "operate so wildly and strangely it is exceedingly difficult" to anticipate their movements. Nevertheless, should he encounter the Cheyennes he intended to make full use of the "shrewdness and fleetness" of his Indian allies. He issued regulation blue blouses to the Pawnees to reduce the chances of a friendly fire incident and provided them with all the ammunition they could carry. Curtis advised the War Department that he was determined to drive the hostile Indians away, "be they many or few."[51]

On September 1, three weeks after the initial attacks, Curtis and Brigadier General Robert B. Mitchell, the Nebraska district commander, led over six hundred soldiers, militia volunteers, and Indians and two sections of light artillery out of Fort Kearney. With one major general, one brigadier general, and two colonels along, the column was even more top-heavy than the expedition to Great Bend. The Federals proceeded west up the Platte Valley to Plum Creek, then turned southwest into an expanse of grass-covered hills in southwestern Nebraska and northwestern Kansas. Curtis finally called a halt on Solomon's Fork and divided the column. Mitchell, the blue-clad Pawnees, and most of the cavalry headed west toward Fort Laramie. Curtis, the militia volunteers, and the rest of the cavalry—slightly less than half of the original force—turned east and followed the Kansas River toward the frontier. Curtis thanked the Nebraskans and sent them back to Fort Kearney, then dropped off the cavalry at Fort Riley. He reached Fort Leavenworth on September 16. He had been away for a month and had traveled over one thousand miles, most of it on horseback. Curtis described himself as "well, but weary," but family members recalled that he returned "weak and enfeebled" and was slow to regain his old vigor.[52]

Curtis did not encounter any hostile Natives during his sweep. "Buffalo plenty, but Indians only in small, shy bands," he reported. Disappointed, he described the expedition as a failure, which it was in a narrow military sense, but as a demonstration of the government's determination to secure the frontier in the midst of a titanic civil war it was a success. The presence of so many soldiers, militia volunteers, and allied Indians raised morale. Settlers reclaimed their holdings and merchants restarted their endeavors. By the time Curtis returned to Fort Leavenworth, farmers were back toiling in their fields and wagons and stagecoaches were again rolling across the plains. Sporadic attacks continued into the fall but did relatively little damage. "Indian troubles have abated," Curtis informed Brigadier General James H. Carleton in New Mexico, "the Indians having left lines of travel and gone to parts unknown." The danger continued, but the crisis had passed.[53]

As the summer of 1864 faded into fall, it may have seemed to Curtis that he was destined to end his military career chasing guerrillas and Indians through the brush, but fate had something else in store for him.

12

WESTPORT

CURTIS RETURNED TO FORT LEAVENWORTH ON SEPTEMBER 16, 1864, and found a message from Rosecrans on his desk. It began with the disturbing news that Sterling Price and a large Confederate cavalry force had crossed the Arkansas River above Little Rock ten days earlier, and ended with a bit of neighborly advice: "While it is reported that [Price] is coming into Missouri, and we are preparing for him, I think you should be on your guard. He may go . . . into Kansas."[1]

The 1864 Missouri Expedition (often called Price's Raid) grew out of the mismanaged Red River campaign earlier in the year, when Union forces in Louisiana and Arkansas tried but failed to capture Shreveport. After intense fighting at Mansfield, Pleasant Hill, and Jenkins' Ferry, the Federals withdrew and slumped into a defensive posture throughout the Lower Mississippi Valley. The shift in momentum presented the Confederates with a chance to regain the initiative in the trans-Mississippi, but most rebel leaders, including overall commander General Edmund Kirby Smith, were content to see the enemy withdraw. Price, however, viewed the Union reverse as an opportunity to reestablish himself in Missouri. He requested permission to move north with his newly organized Army of Missouri, a mobile force of about twelve thousand horsemen, and liberate his home state. Kirby Smith did not believe the proposed operation had much chance of success, but he hoped it might create unrest in the North and disrupt the 1864 election. He gave his approval.[2]

Rosecrans assumed Steele would make some effort to block, slow, or at least track Price's progress through Arkansas, but Steele did none of these things. Having barely escaped defeat and capture during the latter stages of the Red River campaign, a badly shaken Steele huddled inside the Little Rock fortifications and allowed the Confederates free passage across his department, coming and going. Curtis was more surprised by Price's choice of an invasion route than by his ability to intimidate and befuddle Steele: "The country is so destitute of everything I do not see how Price can bring a large army through Arkansas." Nevertheless, Curtis heeded Rosecrans's advice and prepared for the possibility that the enemy might turn up on his doorstep. He advised Governor Carney to have the Kansas State Militia ready "to aid in checking rebel approaches."[3]

When Carney and Curtis met earlier in the year, the governor had assured the general that he would "cooperate cordially" in the defense of Kansas. "Says if I want militia forces he will call them out and turn them over to me," Curtis noted in his journal in January. At the time Curtis had no reason to doubt Carney's sincerity. Now, nine months later, when Curtis sounded the alarm, Carney proved less than helpful. He ignored mounting evidence that the Confederates were approaching and attempted to keep the militia at home and under his control. Curtis was perplexed by the governor's behavior but made it clear that in an emergency he expected the army and militia to serve together in the field under his command. This squabble over the Kansas State Militia quickly escalated into a major breach between the two most important officials in Kansas.[4]

Price had gained a great deal of weight since the Pea Ridge campaign and now traveled in a mule-drawn carriage. Consequently, he exercised little direct control over his wide-ranging cavalrymen. He also demonstrated little sense of urgency and dallied for nearly a week in northeastern Arkansas to rest, recruit, and reconnect with Missouri guerrilla leaders. The lull was a godsend to Rosecrans, who used the time to pack the fortifications around St. Louis and Jefferson City with thousands of soldiers and Missouri militiamen. Price resumed his northward movement in late September but erred in needlessly attacking Pilot

Knob, a fortified Union outpost eighty miles south of St. Louis. The rebels were repulsed and the garrison escaped. Jolted by this fiasco, Price veered away from St. Louis and headed toward Jefferson City, only to discover that the state capital was equally well defended. After skirmishing listlessly for several days, Price turned west toward Kansas City, the only other sizable city in Missouri and the gateway to Kansas.[5]

The nature of the Confederate incursion changed after the half-hearted jab at Jefferson City. Price abandoned any pretense that his ill-planned and ill-managed operation had a purpose other than accumulating plunder and gathering recruits (often at the point of a gun). He embraced Kirby Smith's suggestion that if he could not achieve a lodgment in Missouri, he should lay waste to Kansas on the way home by "sweeping that country of its mules, horses, cattle, and military supplies of all kinds." The rebel horde, for such it had become, now consisted of sixteen to eighteen thousand soldiers, volunteers, conscripts, hangers-on, and guerrillas, all accompanied by an unwieldy train. The disorderly mass of men, animals, and vehicles moved slowly, almost leisurely, up the Missouri Valley on a broad front, seizing valuables and edibles and burning everything else.[6]

Lincoln once said of Rosecrans that he acted "like a duck hit on the head." That was in reference to the general's peculiar conduct after his crushing defeat at Chickamauga a year earlier, but it also described his passive behavior during the Missouri Expedition. It was only after much prodding that Rosecrans finally placed his mounted regiments under the command of Major General Alfred Pleasonton, former head of the cavalry corps of the Army of the Potomac, and sent them after Price. Rosecrans himself followed more slowly with a large force of infantry.[7]

The Confederates cut telegraph wires and burned bridges as they rampaged through Missouri, complicating Curtis's efforts to stay in touch with Rosecrans. The Federals established an alternate telegraph line through Iowa, but Rosecrans remained strangely uncommunicative. "Not a word from St. Louis for several days," Curtis grumbled at one point. When Rosecrans did bother to communicate, his messages were not always helpful. "It seems to me we can push the old fellow and make him lose his trains" was a typical Rosecrans missive. Curtis was puzzled by the paucity of information from his Missouri counterpart. Rosecrans claimed he was right behind the rebels, nipping at their heels. How could he not know where they were? And why were the rebels moving so slowly if Rosecrans was in hot pursuit? Curtis grew anxious as the days passed without reliable intelligence about Price's progress. "Are the militia ready?" he asked Carney. "We must take care of our corner of the field." Carney, however, was no more communicative than Rosecrans. He merely repeated his promise to call out the militia when he, not Curtis, felt it was needed.[8]

These developments put Curtis on edge, and he prepared for the worst. He told his staff, "I want to know every move of Price now, from this time on," and issued a stream of orders, inquiries, warnings, and updates to his district commanders. His exchange with Colonel Blair at Fort Scott in southeastern Kansas was typical. "How are matters in your vicinity?" Curtis asked. The post was located close to the Kansas-Missouri line and Curtis warned Blair to keep his guard up: "Keep sending out scouts and keep everything snug and close." He shared what little information he had about Price's movements and stated, possibly with more confidence than he felt, that if the rebels "come an inch farther the whole militia force of Kansas will be called out." Curtis urged Blair to stay in touch with the militiamen in his vicinity and make certain they were prepared, like minutemen of old, to march at a moment's notice. He wanted "every man's haversack and cartridge box ready to sling." Blair pledged that his men would be "ready in all respects when the time of action comes."[9]

Blair may have been confident that Kansans would do their duty, but Curtis had serious doubts about the only Kansan that really mattered. He tried again and again to convince Carney that the state was in danger: "As all the forces moving against Price tend to drive him this way, we better be prepared to give him the warmest attentions we can." Carney seemed indifferent to the approaching threat. Then, on October 5, Rosecrans telegraphed that the Confederates were nearing Sedalia, halfway between Jefferson City and Kansas City. Encouraged by this rare nugget of information from Missouri, Curtis put Carney on notice: "I desire that you will call out the entire militia force, with their best arms and ammunition, for a period of thirty days." Curtis wanted all adult males, "without distinctions of color," to muster at designated assembly points in the eastern part of the state. "I will do all in my power to provide provisions and public transportation," he told the governor, "but hope every man will be as self-sustaining as possible, and ready to join me in privations, hardships, and dangers, to aid our comrades in Missouri in destroying these rebel forces before they again desolate the fair fields of Kansas." A few days later he reminded Carney that time was critical: "Hurry out the militia."[10]

Having begun the mobilization process, or so he thought, Curtis called on Rosecrans to increase the pressure on Price from the rear. "Push forward your forces tonight," he telegraphed. "Delay is disastrous." A few months earlier Curtis had been careful not to step on Rosecrans's toes. Now, faced with an approaching calamity, he cast protocol aside and all but ordered Rosecrans to hurry up. He also reached across department boundaries and state lines and assumed command of "orphaned" Union forces in western Missouri, northwestern Arkansas, and the Indian Territory. No one, not even Halleck, challenged the propriety of these actions until after the crisis had passed.[11]

Curtis was determined to defend Kansas and deal Price and his "fiendish followers" a heavy blow in the process, but he discovered that assembling an effective fighting force from the hodgepodge of available army units was a "most difficult and perplexing duty." During the next two weeks Curtis organized regiments, battalions, batteries, and stray detachments into operational formations. He also selected suitable sites for camps and depots, established lines of supply, searched for the enemy's most likely avenues of approach, and laid out fortifications. "We have but [a] very small force and must try to have it in the best possible position," Curtis reminded everyone. Fortunately, Price's unhurried pace gave the Federals time to prepare.[12]

Carney was responsible for mobilizing the Kansas State Militia. Curtis tried to stay out of his way, yet he could not help but worry about how things were going. The recent militia boondoggle in Nebraska, which Curtis had witnessed during his visit to Omaha two months earlier, was very much on his mind. Twenty-three thousand Kansans were listed on the state's militia rolls, but it was anyone's guess how many would answer the governor's call, particularly with the frontier counties still facing the threat of Indian attacks. When a Kansas newspaper predicted that only ten thousand militiamen would turn out, Curtis reminded the editor that the rebels could read. "Do not give [a] clue to numbers," he cautioned. "If anything be said talk of 25,000 or 30,000. We must depend a good deal on bluster till we get stronger than we are."[13]

On October 9 Curtis discovered to his utter astonishment that Carney had ignored his call to mobilize the militia. He pressed for an explanation, but the governor merely repeated his vague assurance that he would act "whenever action is needed." Curtis countered that action was needed immediately, but Carney was unmoved. The two men were at an impasse. Carney then telegraphed Rosecrans and imperiously demanded to know whether the threat of a Confederate invasion was real, or if Curtis was making the whole thing up: "Are we in danger here from Price? Inform me." An incredulous Rosecrans confirmed that Curtis was telling the truth, warning Carney that "no effort should be spared to secure yourselves from Price." He urged the governor to cooperate with Curtis and take all steps necessary to prevent the rebels from "plundering" Kansas.[14]

Shocked to learn that Price really was bearing down on Kansas, Carney finally lurched into action. He called the entire Kansas State Militia into service and issued a series of appeals and proclamations. "These efforts aroused the whole people," observed Curtis. "The excitement was intense and universal." Some of Carney's political followers, however, failed to come around. They continued to deny the threat was real and did all in their power to undermine the mobilization. They urged fellow citizens to ignore the governor's summons or, if already on the march, to return home. "No time for using the militia could [have been] more unfavorable," Curtis later wrote. "Motives, measures, and men were all distrusted. . . . It required the greatest exertions to draw attention of officers and men from the political to the military necessities of the hour."[15]

The reason for this extraordinary state of affairs was the toxic state of Kansas politics. In the fall of 1864 the two principal factions of the Republican Party were engaged in a no-holds-barred election fight. Carney headed the moderate pro-business faction, Senator James H. Lane the radical abolitionist faction. Carney believed that Curtis, who was friendly with Lane and shared many of his political views, wanted the militia mobilized in order to minimize the number of men available to cast their ballots for Carney's faction in the coming election. Carney convinced himself that Lane and his minions would benefit from such a fantastical (not to mention nonsensical) plot. Curtis denounced these "shocking enunciations" as base lies but to little effect. It was his misfortune to be the only Union general whose military authority was undercut by paranoid state politicians and their even more paranoid supporters, the very people he was trying to protect.[16]

On October 9, the day Carney belatedly mobilized the militia, Rosecrans confirmed that Price had reached Sedalia, only sixty miles from the Kansas-Missouri line. "I shall follow him wherever he goes," Rosecrans promised. Not to be outdone in the platitude department, Curtis pledged to give Price a "warm welcome if he comes this way." By this time Curtis was losing patience with Rosecrans. He began to wonder whether Rosecrans really wanted to engage the Confederates or merely escort them out of Missouri and into Kansas. Curtis decided to keep his doubts to himself, at least for the time being. He informed the War Department that Price was approaching (slowly), Rosecrans was following (also slowly), and Carney was mobilizing the militia (finally). He added that he had declared martial law in the Department of Kansas "to secure prompt organization and unity of action," that is, to limit Carney's ability to meddle in military matters.[17]

Curtis experienced several bouts of fatigue after his return from Nebraska. He feared he might "break down" (his words) at an inopportune moment and decided he needed an experienced general by his side, someone prepared to assume overall command if that proved necessary. He directed Blunt to drop what he was doing on the Great Plains and hurry to Paola, about fifteen miles west of the Kansas-Missouri line. Shortly after reaching Paola and familiarizing himself with the situation, Blunt proposed that the Federals advance and meet the Confederates as far inside Missouri as possible. Such a movement, he argued, would stop Price in his tracks and give Pleasonton an opportunity to catch up and pitch in. Curtis was heartened by Blunt's aggressive proposal, which mirrored his own inclinations, but given the circumstances he chose to adopt a slightly more cautious approach. "Of course Price is to be met," he replied. "When and where will depend on his position and our collection and organization," an oblique reference to the militia. "This latter business should occupy your whole attention now."[18]

Curtis recognized that the Kansas State Militia was going to be his "main dependency" in the coming campaign. He also recognized that the militia, despite a decade of strife with Indians, a long-running border conflict with proslavery Missourians, and three years of murderous encounters with rebel guerrillas, was far from ready to fight a war. Kansans were generally willing to take up arms to defend hearth and home, and many had already done so, but few had ever tramped across a drill field or engaged in a stand-up fight. Blunt reported "considerable difficulty" getting the militiamen at Paola into "fighting trim." He observed that they looked "very much like bushwhackers" in their scruffy civilian garb and worried about distinguishing friend from foe in the confusion of battle. Curtis was concerned about that as well and ordered the militiamen to wear something red in their hats or on their sleeves for identification purposes. It soon became apparent, however, that the most serious shortcoming of the militia was not a lack of uniforms but an unwillingness to serve outside the state.[19]

• • •

On October 12 Curtis left Fort Leavenworth to take charge of preparations along the Kansas-Missouri line. He was tired of depending on Rosecrans for information, so after establishing a temporary headquarters in Olathe he sent patrols fanning out across western Missouri in search of Price. Curtis worried that the Confederates would put on a burst of speed and arrive before his preparations were complete. "Troops turning out rapidly everywhere," he fretted, "but not going forward fast enough."[20]

Curtis tried to maintain an upbeat attitude in public, but in private he experienced at least one moment of doubt. The evening of his arrival in Olathe, October 13, he penned a somber note to Belinda. "If Price determines to move into Kansas I cannot resist his power," he admitted. "I will bluster and bushwhack as best I can but I cannot get more than half his reported force and I will not be half organized." Curtis wanted Belinda to remain at Fort Leavenworth and use her influence to keep the other military families "cool and quiet," but suggested that she put all her valuables in a small bag in case a quick getaway became necessary.[21]

When Curtis awoke the next morning, October 14, after a good night's sleep, he was his usual confident self again. As his first order of business he created the Army of the Border and placed himself in command. He put Blunt in charge of the First Division, a mounted force composed of four brigades of cavalry, both soldiers and militiamen, and five batteries. He selected Brigadier General George W. Dietzler, a veteran of Wilson's Creek and commander of the Kansas State Militia, to head the Second Division. This rather unwieldy formation consisted of all the militia infantry (including a "considerable colored force") and one battery. On the eve of battle Curtis had between sixteen and eighteen thousand men under arms: four thousand soldiers, twelve to fourteen thousand Kansas and Missouri militiamen, and at least thirty guns. In strength and firepower, if not experience or effectiveness, the improvised Army of the Border was a rough match for the Army of Missouri.[22]

Later that day Curtis "reconnoitred entirely around" Kansas City. The terrain east and south of the city is rolling, sometimes hilly, and in 1864 was covered with a patchwork of farms, forests, and prairies. Curtis described the ground as "rough brushy and dangerous for an advancing foe." He was particularly taken with the incised channels carved by the Little Blue and Big Blue Rivers, which flow south to north into the Missouri directly athwart the main road linking Sedalia and Kansas City. He thought the two streams would make excellent defensive positions.[23]

That evening Curtis shifted his headquarters from Olathe to Wyandotte, a few miles northwest of Kansas City and very near the state line. This brought him closer to what he believed would be the scene of action. After settling into a house owned by an old friend from Mansfield, Curtis brought Belinda up to date: "I am very comfortably seated in a little library where I have a nice table two candles and every thing nice as at home. So you see I am in good hands tonight." He appreciated such little comforts because he was feeling his years. "I need rest," he wrote. "I have been on my horse much of the time for the past three days and having a crowd about me night and day [I] could not sleep. I have stolen a march on them tonight. The only trouble is the dispatches that have to be opened and answered at all hours." Curtis went on to say that his soldiers were "crowding into Missouri" and the Kansas militia was congregating along the state line: "A little time is necessary to arm and equip [the militia] but every thing moves with great success so far." Despite his fatigue, he closed with a mild flourish: "The Army of the Border is no longer a myth." The difference in tone between this upbeat letter and the gloomy note penned twenty-four hours earlier is striking.[24]

Curtis also wrote to Blunt and Dietzler that evening, outlining a tentative plan of action. He wanted to advance "quickly and rapidly" into Missouri and establish two defensive positions. Blunt's cavalry division (soldiers and militiamen) would form the first line in front of the Little Blue River near Lexington, forty miles or so inside Missouri. The Federals would aggressively engage the oncoming Confederates, disrupt their approach, and inflict as much damage as possible. Dietzler's infantry division (all militiamen) would form the second line behind the Little Blue and support the cavalry as needed. When enemy pressure proved too great, as surely it would, everyone would withdraw to the Big Blue River, fifteen miles farther west, and carry on the fight.[25]

An advance into Missouri, Curtis believed, would give his troops the "prestige of aggressive movement," while burdening the enemy with the "great apprehension of assault from unknown numbers." In other words, the Federals would enjoy the psychological advantage of taking the fight to the enemy. Curtis did not, however, allow himself to become carried away. He had witnessed the chaotic aftermath of First Manassas three years earlier and had no intention of engaging Price's veterans in a stand-up fight with an army composed largely of untried militiamen. He knew his best chance of success was to hold the rebels at bay—to fight, fall back, and fight again—until Price turned away or Pleasonton arrived. Delay was the order of the day.[26]

Blunt found the plan agreeable because it reflected his earlier proposal for a general advance and because it allowed him considerable freedom of action. Dietzler approved as well, though he warned Curtis that the Kansas militia might not be willing to march forty miles into Missouri. With his two principal subordinates on board, Curtis informed Rosecrans of his intention to meet Price east of the Little Blue and bring him to a halt, or at least slow him down. He again urged Rosecrans to get a move on: "Push matters on the other side, and let me know where your advance is." Getting information out of Rosecrans was like pulling teeth.[27]

• • •

During his stay in Helena Curtis had discovered the advantages of controlling local waterways, so he commandeered every transport, ferry, barge, rowboat, and raft on his part of the Missouri River. He used the vessels to move men and supplies by water and to prevent the Confederates from doing the same. He also dispatched the steamboats *Benton* and *West Wind* down the Missouri to see what could be learned about Price's movements from the water's edge. Both vessels were packed with infantry and artillery and protected with stacks of cordwood. The *Benton* also carried a member of Curtis's staff, his son Sam. The boats proceeded downstream without incident to Glasgow, not far above Jefferson City, where they encountered a large force of rebels preparing to storm the town. The troops and guns hurried ashore to bolster the local garrison and the *Benton* returned upstream, at one point running aground near Lexington and coming under a storm of small-arms fire. The little stern-wheeler was struck by more than three hundred bullets, an experience Sam described as the "most anxious moments of my life," but it pulled free and escaped. Sam went ashore at Wyandotte on October 16 and reported to his father, then continued up the river to Fort Leavenworth on a supply run. The daring operation produced little useful intelligence.[28]

Belinda learned of Sam's presence aboard the *Benton* and began a fiery letter to her husband, insisting that he not send their only surviving son on any more harebrained missions into enemy territory: "A little fame and glory are nothing when compared with life which is even more precious to us then to him." Just as she finished that sentence, the front door opened and Sam stepped into the parlor, safe and sound. Belinda later resumed the letter, still upset over what might have happened: "I cannot bear to have him exposed again to the bullets or the tender mercies of those fiends who are murdering and committing every species of cruelty within the sound of Price's Headquarters."[29]

A few days later Curtis informed Belinda that a notorious guerrilla named George M. Todd, "one of the murderers of our son," had been killed in a skirmish with Blunt's troops. Curtis received the news of Todd's death, and the death soon afterwards of the even more savage guerrilla William T. Anderson, with grim satisfaction. He had authorized the execution of captured guerrillas as far back as the Pea Ridge campaign, and his attitude had hardened as the war progressed and the atrocities mounted. About this time the U.S. attorney in Colorado wrote to Curtis to protest the recent summary execution of "certain brigands calling themselves Confederate soldiers." He argued in legalistic fashion that the five men should have been treated either as prisoners of war or as civilians entitled to constitutional protections. Curtis was unmoved. "I have not the least sympathy for such fiends," he snarled in reply. "We are disposing of them very summarily everywhere."[30]

• • •

Price arrived with the first blast of winter. "Turned awful cold," wrote an unprepared Union officer, "like to froze." Sleet, snow, biting winds, and plunging temperatures made life miserable for men and animals in both armies but did not seriously obstruct operations. On October 18 Curtis set his plan in motion. He sent Blunt and half of the First Division, about two thousand men and eight guns, across the Little Blue to Lexington "to feel for the enemy." Curtis realized Blunt's command was "vastly inferior" in numbers to the Confederates but it was the best he could do. The rebels arrived the next day, October 19, in the form of Brigadier General Joseph O. Shelby's division. Skirmishing erupted, soon punctuated by artillery fire. Shelby gradually pushed the outnumbered Union cavalry through Lexington and back to the Little Blue, where Blunt expected to rendezvous with Dietzler. To his surprise, the militia was nowhere in sight.[31]

Dietzler was a no-show because, as he had feared, most of the Kansas State Militia balked at marching so far into Missouri. Some Kansans still scoffed at the notion that there were any rebels within a hundred miles; a few even packed up and attempted to leave for home. Curtis angrily denounced the "political folly" behind the mutiny and arrested the ringleaders. He forced most of the deserters back to their camps and dispatched every Kansas politician in the vicinity—including the governor and the state's two senators—to rally their fellow citizens. Curtis reported that "some severe measures and much remonstrance" were required to bring the mutiny under control. Order was soon restored, but most of the militiamen remained immovable. They would fight for their homes, they declared, but only in or near Kansas.[32]

Curtis had been active in the Ohio militia for years and felt he understood citizen-soldiers. He decided to take the Kansans at their word. He offered to forgo the movement to the distant Little Blue in favor of a more limited advance to the Big Blue. The Kansans began to discuss the matter, but their deliberations were cut short by the rumble of artillery fire to the east, where Blunt and Shelby were engaged. They quickly voted their approval and began crossing into Missouri. By the end of the day, October 19, the militia was digging in along the rugged west bank of the Big Blue. The emerging Union position was a dozen miles in length from north to south. It consisted of an intermittent line of rifle pits, artillery redoubts, and timber barricades fronted by a tangle of felled trees. The defenses made what Curtis called a "strong natural position" even stronger. A second, inner line of defensive works was constructed around Kansas City.[33]

Curtis congratulated Blunt on holding Shelby in check and making enough noise in the process to convince all but the most intransigent Kansans that the Confederates were near. "The blow you gave the enemy is doing good in the rear," he told Blunt. "It is crushing some of the silly rumors that had well nigh ruined my prospects of a successful defense." Curtis explained his decision to relocate the "main line for battle" to the Big Blue, and asked Blunt to hold his position along the Little Blue a bit longer to allow the militia more time to prepare. Nothing could have pleased Blunt more. He halted his withdrawal and turned to confront the Confederates.[34]

Fighting intensified when Brigadier General John S. Marmaduke's division joined the fray on October 20. Blunt's troops fought tenaciously but the Confederates, now nearly eight thousand strong, were too numerous to resist. Curtis went forward on October 21 to see the deteriorating situation for himself. Major Charlot, Sadie's onetime fiancé, reported that Curtis rode back and forth along Blunt's line and was "exposed to a very hot fire

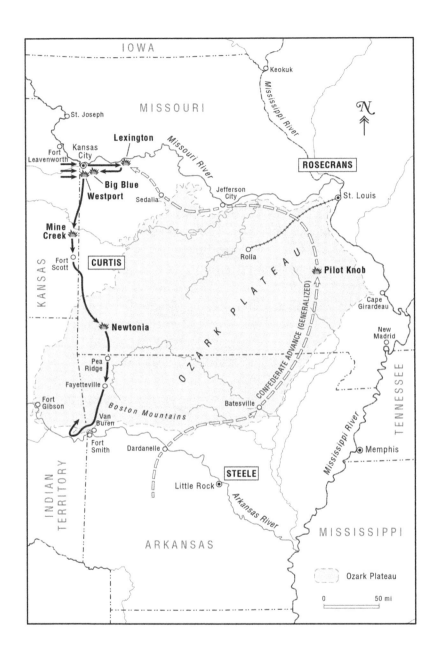

MAP 3. The Missouri Expedition and Westport campaign, September–November 1864. Route of the Army of the Border. Created by Erin Greb.

of artillery and small arms for two hours." Another Union officer described Curtis as "actively engaged" in the fight, waving his hat, shouting encouragement, and repositioning artillery (much to Blunt's annoyance). The rebels gradually forced their way across the Little Blue and reached the outskirts of Independence late in the afternoon. Blunt wanted to fight for the town, but Curtis decided otherwise. "Let Price have Independence," he said to Blunt. "Don't exhaust our troops, but fall back to [the Big Blue] with the least further effort." Blunt did as instructed. He had stalled Price's advance for the better part of three days, time that both Curtis and Pleasonton put to good use. "Our men are doing finely," Curtis told Halleck. "I am fighting and falling back to avoid flank movements, designing to make another strong stand at Big Blue, where the militia, with artillery, are located in strong positions."[35]

The three days of fighting that erupted on October 19 near Lexington marked another shift in the nature of the Missouri Expedition. Up to this point the Confederate incursion had not been seriously contested. Union commanders in Arkansas and Missouri had done their best to stay out of Price's way, but that changed when the Army of Missouri collided with the Army of the Border. Unlike Steele and Rosecrans, Curtis marched out and met the rebels head on at the time and place of his choosing. The emergence of Curtis as the principal Union actor had significant consequences. The opposing armies became locked in a nearly continuous series of battles, skirmishes, and running fights that extended over three hundred miles from the Missouri River to the Arkansas River. This part of the Missouri Expedition was so distinctive it has earned a separate name: the Westport campaign.

• • •

As daylight faded on October 21, Blunt's weary troops rode west on Independence Road and joined Dietzler's militia in the prepared positions behind the Big Blue. The Army of the Border was united for the first time in the campaign. Curtis concentrated most of his force on the Union left, directly in Price's path, where Independence Road crossed the stream. This was known locally as Main Ford. Curtis realized, of course, that Price would have to turn south in order to return to the Confederacy. The only questions were when and where. Price had been moving west on Independence Road for several days. Curtis initially assumed the rebel commander intended to force his way across the Big Blue at Main Ford, sack Kansas City, and sweep through eastern Kansas before turning toward home. As the evening wore on, however, memories of the Confederate movement on the Bentonville Detour at Pea Ridge flooded into his mind. The parallels between the Union positions on Little Sugar Creek and the Big Blue were obvious and disturbing. Curtis began to worry that Price might sidestep to his left and attempt to pass around or break through the Union right, just as he and Van Dorn had done two and a half years earlier. "We have to fear a flank movement tonight," he warned Blunt. Curtis instructed his subordinates to maintain a sharp watch "to see if Price is moving towards my flank," and to send reports to headquarters every thirty minutes whether they had anything substantive to report or not. Some officers did as instructed, but some did not.[36]

Since learning that Price had crossed the Arkansas River five weeks earlier, Curtis had thought almost exclusively in terms of defending Kansas. Now, with the Army of the Border deployed in a strong blocking position across Price's path, and Pleasonton's troops from the Department of the Missouri rapidly approaching from the east, he realized he might be able to do more than simply bar the way to Kansas. He might be able to bottle the Confederates up and prevent their escape. Curtis advised Rosecrans of his position and expressed his newfound conviction that Price was going to turn south, probably sooner rather than later. "I am confident I can stop Price at [the Big Blue] and hope you will come up in his rear and left so he cannot get out" by turning south, he wrote. "If you can get that position we bag Price." Unfortunately, Federal commanders did not have reliable or compatible maps and failed to coordinate their movements. By chance, a Union infantry column was marching southwestward behind the Confederate left, precisely where it needed to be. Had that force continued on it might have reached Curtis's right flank in time to block Price's escape, but Rosecrans and Pleasonton miscommunicated and the infantry turned northwest to support Pleasonton's cavalry. Thereafter, all of Rosecrans's troops followed in Price's footsteps instead of maneuvering to cut him off. Fortunately for Curtis's peace of mind, he knew nothing of this fiasco until after the campaign was over.[37]

Curtis passed the night of October 21 at Main Ford. Despite having to suppress a mutiny and improvise a new defensive scheme on the fly, he was satisfied with the way events were unfolding. Blunt's prolonged delaying action at Lexington filled him with confidence. "It seems to me we can stop Price" on the Big Blue, he told a Missouri officer, echoing his words to Rosecrans. "We have fought him inch by inch, with only a small part of my forces, and in many instances beat him back with heavy damage." He added, prophetically, "I am busy preparing for harder work tomorrow." Just before turning in for the night, Curtis committed his thoughts to paper. "My troops have fought well. I am now with the militia, in a very strong position, which Price cannot attack tonight and cannot take tomorrow. I think not at all." On that optimistic note, he blew out the candle and went to sleep.[38]

• • •

On the morning of October 22, another cold and blustery day, Price showed a flash of his old ability. The Confederate commander knew by now that Curtis was dug in across his front. He also knew he was being overtaken by Pleasonton, who had gained an alarming amount of ground during the past three days while the rebels were stalled at Lexington. Price decided to write off Kansas, turn south immediately, and make a run for the Arkansas River, three hundred miles distant. The aptly named State Line Road, which ran north-south along the boundary between Missouri and Kansas, was the most direct route back to the Confederacy and safety, but in order to get there Price first had to force his way past Curtis's right. At first light he advanced a brigade on Independence Road to demonstrate in front of Main Ford, where Curtis happened to be, and sent everyone else in a southerly direction up the east side of the Big Blue. Shelby's battered division led the way, followed by Major General James F. Fagan's division. The rebel horsemen were to ride around the right flank of the Union position or, failing that, locate an undefended ford and get across the Big Blue before Curtis grasped what was happening. Marmaduke's division remained in Independence as rear guard, a hazardous assignment with Pleasonton now only a few miles behind.[39]

Curtis quickly recognized the "very feeble demonstration" on Independence Road for what it was, a feint, but he was slow to react to what was obviously some kind of misdirection on Price's part. Most of the morning passed before Curtis learned to his satisfaction that an enemy column was moving south across his front, almost certainly seeking a way around his position. About eleven o'clock, having failed to locate the end of the Union line, Shelby and Fagan became impatient. They turned west and tried to smash their way across the Big Blue at Byram's Ford, a heavily used and thus heavily defended position only six miles south of Main Ford. The Confederates frittered away several hours making costly frontal assaults before they stumbled upon an unguarded cattle crossing nearby. This allowed them to outflank the Union defenders and seize the ford. As the rebels poured across the Big Blue, the Union right fell back toward Kansas City like a swinging door. Organization broke down on both sides and the fighting degenerated into a confused swirl of small-unit encounters. Few regiments had flags or other means of identification; many combatants, both Union and Confederate, wore civilian clothes. To make matters even more confusing, if that was possible, thousands of rebels were dressed in captured blue uniforms.[40]

Curtis learned of the Confederate breakthrough at Byram's Ford between two and three o'clock in the afternoon. Why it took so long for such vital information to reach him is not known, but he realized at once that the Union position along the Big Blue was untenable. He directed Blunt and the cavalry to contain the breach as best they could, then he, Dietzler, and the infantry hurried back to the inner ring of defensive works around Kansas City. For a time the Confederate onslaught seemed unstoppable. "We could see the prairie covered with rebs as far as the eye could reach," recalled a dispirited Colorado cavalryman. Fortunately, Blunt was at his best in desperate situations. He quickly organized a series of bold counterattacks that slowed and eventually halted the rebel advance. Late in the afternoon his First Division established a new defensive line along the bluffs on the north side of Brush Creek, immediately south of Westport. The rebels withdrew to the bluffs on the south side of the stream. The opposing positions were roughly parallel and extended east-west for several miles between the Big Blue and the Kansas-Missouri line. Darkness brought an end to the fighting.[41]

As the Army of the Border fell back from the Big Blue, it pivoted to the right to conform to the altered tactical situation. By sunset on October 22 the Federals faced south instead of east. The ninety-degree change of front had important consequences. The new Union position still shielded Kansas City and most of Kansas, but it no longer barred access to State Line Road. During the afternoon and evening hours Price got his entire force across the Big Blue—a good thing, too, because Pleasonton was closing fast. His cavalry division, seven thousand men and ten guns, routed Marmaduke's rear guard at Independence and reached Byram's Ford not long after the last of the rebels had crossed. Later that evening Pleasonton notified Curtis that he was on the field and would cross the Big Blue in the morning. It was the first direct communication between the two generals. The Confederates had escaped one trap but were hardly in the clear. They now were outnumbered, outgunned, and, as would soon become apparent, outgeneraled.[42]

Curtis established his headquarters in a Kansas City hotel called the Gillis House. He stayed up until three o'clock in the morning conferring with his staff and seeing that everyone, both soldiers and militiamen, received rations, water, ammunition, and such medical care as was available. The day had not gone as he had hoped, but most of his men had performed well and appeared ready to resume the struggle in the morning. The Confederates, by contrast, seemed interested mostly in escaping. Prisoners and deserters confirmed that Price's train was hastening away to the south. Curtis concluded that Kansas was no longer in the rebel crosshairs and that the time had come to seize the initiative, just as he had done under somewhat similar circumstances at Pea Ridge. "Price retreats southward," he telegraphed the War Department that night. "I am preparing to renew the attack and pursue at daylight with all my available cavalry." Curtis directed Blunt and Dietzler to concentrate their forces south of Westport and make a "united, powerful attack" as soon as it was light enough to see. Then he turned in for a few hours of much-needed rest.[43]

A few days earlier Curtis had jotted down a tentative plan of action and sent it to Rosecrans: "I must confront Price, checking his [westward] progress as best I can, till he develops a movement southward." That scenario was now playing out word for word.[44]

• • •

The Army of the Border went on the offensive just before dawn on October 23. Curtis was delayed leaving Kansas City, so Blunt got the climactic Battle of Westport off to a rousing start. Union troops descended the bluffs on the north side of Brush Creek, passed through the woods bordering the stream, and ascended the bluffs on the opposite side. As soon as they emerged from the cover of the trees they came under heavy fire from the waiting Confederates, most of whom were arrayed behind stone walls that were proof against small-arms fire. The rebels easily repulsed the Union attack. Blunt regrouped and tried again but with the same result. Stymied, he rode to nearby Westport and climbed to the top of Harris House, a three-story hotel with a flat roof and a commanding view of the rolling countryside. Curtis reached Westport around eight o'clock and joined Blunt on the roof. The two generals studied the Confederates, who were "deployed in endless lines on the open prairie" to the south. They decided to wait for the rest of the militia to arrive from Kansas City before making another attempt to dislodge the rebels from their ready-made defenses.[45]

Curtis accompanied Blunt back to Brush Creek, where they began moving batteries forward to provide close artillery support for the next attack. The guns would knock down the stone walls and open lanes for the cavalry and infantry. Curtis intended to direct the assault, but fate intervened in the person of a local farmer named George Thoman. The elderly German immigrant approached Curtis to complain in heavily accented English that the Confederates had stolen his favorite mare. Curtis commiserated with Thoman but said there was nothing he could do. Then, out of the blue, Thoman offered to show Curtis a way around the Confederate position. Instead of assigning a staff officer to accompany Thoman, as was the usual practice, Curtis decided to investigate the matter himself.[46]

Thoman led Curtis, his escort company with two mountain howitzers, and a six-gun battery up the winding valley of Brush Creek. Near the state line the Federals turned southwest into a narrow defile carved by Swan Creek. A short while later they emerged onto high ground several hundred yards behind the Confederate line. The little cavalcade had passed completely across the front and around the left flank of Shelby's division without being detected. Curtis instructed the artillerymen to open fire and sent a courier racing back the way they had come with orders for more guns to ascend the bluffs. The rebels were thrown into confusion by the barrage of shot and shell from their left rear and did not recover in time to resist the third and final Union assault, which Blunt set in motion during Curtis's absence.[47]

It was now late morning. Curtis watched the battle unfold from his unusual vantage point on the Confederate side of the field. Blunt's First Division emerged from the woods on the Union left and surged up the bluffs, followed by Dietzler's Second Division on the right, nearer to Curtis. The Union commander had never seen the militia in action and watched closely as the Kansans came "swarming out of the forest, displaying a length [of line] and strength of numbers that surprised me." He described the militia's movements as "steady, orderly, and gallant" and thought they might have passed for veteran soldiers had they been properly uniformed. Two weeks of drill had clearly made a difference in the militia's ability to execute orders on the battlefield. Satisfied that events were moving his way, Curtis thanked Thoman for his patriotism, then hurried away to resume tactical command of the Army of the Border.[48]

The Battle of Westport lasted about two hours. The fighting was particularly chaotic and intense on the Union left, where the Confederates occupied a jumble of small fields and narrow lanes bordered by stone walls. When a Union battery was manhandled to within musket shot early in the contest, several hundred rebels leapt over the walls they were sheltering behind and rushed forward to capture the guns. "I tell you the rebs came on in good style," wrote a Union cavalryman supporting the battery. "When they got within fifty paces we opened on them with our Carbines and pistols, give them four or five volleys, drew sabres and charged them. Such a cut up I never saw. In about ten minutes who was not killed and cut to pieces was taken prisoner." Scenes like this were repeated dozens of times as Union forces surged forward from one shattered wall to the next, gaining ground in fits and starts. Confederate resistance crumbled along with the walls.[49]

By noon the Federals were converging on the Confederates from north and east. While Curtis and Blunt pushed Shelby and Fagan back from Brush Creek, Pleasonton forced Marmaduke away from Byram's Ford and crossed the Big Blue. The problem now facing the rebels was how to disengage and get away, no easy task with Union forces approaching from two directions. Price departed in haste, leaving his subordinates to organize a withdrawal as best they could. The result was predictable. A few Confederate units fell back in a disciplined fashion, but most did not. Curtis described the disorderly rebel retreat as a "complete rout."[50]

The Confederates had given Curtis the slip after Pea Ridge; he was determined not to let that happen again. He ordered a general pursuit and enjoyed the splendid sight of his and Pleasonton's victorious troops—cavalry, artillery, and even some infantry—streaming southward after the flying foe. "We steadily advanced all arms over a beautiful prairie, where both armies were in full view," he wrote. The rebels remained in sight but just out of reach for the rest of the day. An hour into the chase Curtis paused to scribble an exultant message to the War Department: "We have driven the enemy seven or eight miles south of Westport. Our success is glorious. We are still in hot pursuit." The fight for Kansas was over. The race to the Arkansas River was beginning.[51]

13

RACE TO THE ARKANSAS

THE CHASE CONTINUED ALL AFTERNOON. CURTIS, BLUNT, Dietzler, and Pleasonton gathered at a farmhouse on Indian Creek around two thirty, for what Curtis called "dinner and consultation." They were soon joined by Carney, Lane, and other political figures. Introductions and congratulations were followed by a spirited exchange of views on what to do next. Carney, Lane, and Dietzler pressed Curtis to lift martial law and demobilize the militia. Curtis was agreeable, up to a point. He restored civil authority in most of Kansas and dismissed the militia from the northern counties, but he kept the militia from the still-endangered southern counties in service a bit longer. "The enemy are repelled and driven south," he announced to the newspapers. "Our success is beyond all anticipation."[1]

After the politicians hurried away to oversee demobilization and resume electioneering, the generals turned their attention to military matters, particularly the vexing question of who was in charge. Curtis was the senior officer present but he was outside his department. He had, in fact, been outside his department for more than a week, but that did not become an issue until Pleasonton arrived. After some discussion, Pleasonton consented to follow Curtis's orders until Rosecrans arrived or the War Department decreed otherwise. Curtis found that acceptable for the moment and reorganized the Army of the Border accordingly. He consolidated the remaining soldiers and militiamen from the Department of Kansas in Blunt's First Division and incorporated Pleasonton's troops from the Department of the Missouri into a new Second Division. Everyone understood this to be a temporary arrangement. Curtis later explained, "I expected General Rosecrans to reach the front and take command," but Rosecrans never showed up. As a result, for the next few days Curtis was in nominal command of a mixed force of soldiers and militiamen from two departments. The awkward arrangement quickly proved unworkable.[2]

Curtis declared his intention to keep after Price. Blunt growled his approval, but Pleasonton objected. He argued that the campaign was over, despite the continued presence of a Confederate army on Missouri soil. Pleasonton had performed capably up to this point, pursuing the rebels from Jefferson City to Westport and pitching into their rear guard at every opportunity. Now he switched off. Curtis later confided to Belinda that Pleasonton was "especially satisfied" with his performance at Westport and thought he "had done enough and ought to stop." When Curtis rejected that argument, Pleasonton changed tack, claiming that his men and animals were worn to a frazzle after their long ride from Jefferson City and could go no farther. Curtis still refused to abandon the chase but agreed, reluctantly, to slow the pace. He told Halleck that the rebels were "in full retreat and much demoralized," but that many of his own men and animals, meaning Pleasonton's division, were "much exhausted and must have a little rest." The Federals halted for the night near Little Santa Fe, a hamlet on the state line a dozen miles south of Westport.[3]

Curtis's immediate concern was the safety of Fort Scott, which lay in the path of the fleeing rebel army. He instructed the garrison to hold on. "Stand," he ordered. "The enemy is flying, closely pursued. Your only safety is to remain and keep everything in the fort." Blunt, too, was concerned about Fort Scott and dashed off a message in his singular style: "Have had a hard day's fighting, but we have broke [Price] up in business. We have been pressing his rear hard, and shall continue to do so until the end." Blunt advised the garrison that if Price approached "you must fight him to the last extremity. We will be close upon his heels."[4]

The next day, October 24, the Federals continued south along the state line in a loose formation several miles wide. Curtis was in a good mood and summarized his progress as follows: "Everything goes on gloriously; my troops are doing splendidly; we are taking many prisoners." Curtis advised Rosecrans that he and Pleasonton had joined forces, urging him to hurry forward and take charge. He stressed that the pursuit "must be pressed day and night if we expect to capture Price and his forces." Rosecrans, however, showed no interest in catching up or taking command. He seemed content to follow at a safe distance and let Curtis handle the rebels. Around noon Curtis informed the War Department that Price was still hurrying toward the Arkansas River, but "dead horses and other debris show his demoralized and destitute condition and my probable success in overhauling him." The Federals stopped for the night near the burned-out hamlet of West Point, fifty miles from Westport. Curtis, Blunt, and Pleasonton crowded into an ambulance to escape a steady rain and enjoyed a "sumptuous supper" of boiled chicken.[5]

Any chance that Price might escape with his army and train intact evaporated the following morning, October 25, when Union troops struck the Confederates in their soggy camps along the Marais des Cygnes River. The rebels put up only slight resistance before continuing southward toward Mine Creek. Price and Shelby crossed the stream and rode ahead to reconnoiter Fort Scott, while Fagan and Marmaduke remained behind to safeguard the train. Two of Pleasonton's brigades, led by Colonel John F. Philips and Lieutenant Colonel Frederick Benteen (of Little Bighorn fame), were in the lead and caught the Confederates straddling Mine Creek. Pleasonton had fallen from his horse and was riding in an ambulance several miles to the rear, so the two colonels attacked on their own. The Federals drove hundreds of rebels into the rain-swollen stream in the wildest disorder and seized nearly half of the teams and wagons. The battle was over before Pleasonton reached the scene, though Curtis arrived in time for his staff and escort to help round up prisoners.[6]

During the chaotic encounter, a wounded Iowa cavalryman named James Dunlavy single-handedly captured Marmaduke and presented the Confederate general to Curtis. The Union commander had nothing to say to Marmaduke beyond an exchange of pleasantries, but he chatted amiably with Dunlavy. Fighting was still going on only two hundred yards away, but Curtis seemed unperturbed. Speaking loudly to be heard over the racket, he told Dunlavy that he knew his father, an Iowa attorney and legislator with whom he had campaigned in the 1860 election, and asked after his health. Before riding off, Curtis gave Marmaduke's pistol to the young cavalryman as a trophy and ordered him to seek medical attention for his injury.[7]

Mine Creek was the largest and most decisive cavalry engagement west of the Appalachian Mountains. More than 1,300 Confederates were killed, wounded, or captured in the brief but violent affair. Among the prisoners taken were two generals (one of them Marmaduke) and three colonels. The Federals also seized eight artillery pieces and more than a hundred wagons, many still packed with plunder. There were fewer than eighty Union casualties. Curtis described Mine Creek as a "complete victory" and praised Philips and Benteen for their initiative. Curtis believed Mine Creek validated his policy of close, dogged pursuit. As for Price, he was so shaken by the disaster that he turned away to the southeast, all thought of attacking Fort Scott forgotten.[8]

• • •

For a brief time it appeared Curtis might achieve the holy grail of Civil War generals, the capture of an enemy army, but it was not to be. The Federals were undone by an administrative fiasco of their own making. It seems obvious in retrospect that when Price crossed the Arkansas River in September, Grant should have appointed a temporary commander for the entire trans-Mississippi, an officer with authority over all forces engaged or likely to become engaged with the Army of Missouri. The obvious candidate was Rosecrans, the senior general in the three affected departments, but Grant disliked Rosecrans, doubted his ability, and refused to put him in charge. Grant was right about Rosecrans but wrong to do nothing. His uncharacteristic failure to act led to a lack of cooperation and coordination among Rosecrans,

Curtis, and Steele that allowed Price to make his way across half of Arkansas and most of Missouri against little or no opposition.

Grant compounded his error after Curtis and Pleasonton joined forces at Westport. The awkward situation cried out for some sort of temporary unified command, but again, Grant did nothing. To be fair to Grant, he could not have made such a mess of things without Halleck's help. He had assigned Halleck the task of shielding him from nonessential communications. This Halleck did by providing Grant with summaries of the many messages pouring into the War Department each day from far-flung commands, but in the process he often altered content to reflect his personal views. During the Missouri Expedition, for example, Halleck routinely criticized Rosecrans (which was often justified) and belittled or ignored Curtis (which was not). Curtis rightly suspected Halleck was doctoring and deleting his dispatches. "I had to report [to Grant] through Halleck who hates me as the Devil does holy water," he told Henry. Because of Halleck's editorial efforts, Grant never had an accurate understanding of what was happening in the distant trans-Mississippi. This may help to explain why he waited so long to intervene.[9]

• • •

Curtis was dissatisfied with the Army of the Border's loose, straggling approach to Mine Creek. After the battle he gathered his troops into a more orderly formation before resuming the pursuit. For a time he and Pleasonton, the latter apparently restored to health, rode at the head of the massed regiments and batteries as if on review. Curtis was something of a military romantic; he frequently turned in his saddle to watch the thousands of Union troops "spread over vast prairies, some moving at full speed in column, some in double lines, and others as skirmishers." It was, he declared, the "most extensive, beautiful, and animated view of hostile armies I have ever witnessed." The Federals had no difficulty following the trail left by the Confederates. Curtis wrote that "our way over the prairie was plainly, graphically marked by the scattered equipments, wagons, guns, utensils, and animals left by the rebels, and the fire and smoke created by their burning of the hay and grass along their route." Hundreds of dead, wounded, exhausted, dispirited, and unhorsed rebels, some of them scorched by the flames, dotted the prairie. The constant need to maneuver around the fires gradually broke up the Union formation.[10]

Late that afternoon the Confederates slowed to cross the Marmiton River near the hamlet of Charlot. The Federals reached the scene in considerable force and skirmished until dark but did not press the issue. Pleasonton had been looking for an excuse to break off the chase for two days and now he found one. When the shooting stopped, he learned that he was only five miles from Fort Scott and ordered his division to proceed in that direction. He did not inform Curtis or seek permission to abandon the pursuit. He simply left. Curtis arrived at the Marmiton just in time to see the greater part of his army turn west, away from the retreating Confederates. He hurried forward and confronted Pleasonton. Exactly what was said between the two generals is not known. Curtis wrote only that "contrary to my wishes" Pleasonton sought "rest and subsistence" at Fort Scott, but he clearly was upset by Pleasonton's disregard of his orders and disruption of his plans. "It was my earnest desire to rest on the field, sending to Fort Scott for food and forage," Curtis later explained.[11]

Curtis had initially envisioned the defense of Kansas as a series of delaying actions. He expected to fight and fall back from one defensive position to another, drawing ever closer to his principal supply depot at Fort Leavenworth. His line of communications would shorten, not lengthen, as the campaign progressed. Everything changed when Price abruptly turned south toward the Arkansas River. Curtis's decision to follow was correct but it played havoc with his logistical arrangements. After Westport the Army of the Border moved rapidly away from, not toward, its base of supplies. Quartermaster, commissary, and ordnance departments scrambled to reorient, reorganize, and expand their efforts, but inevitably there were delays and shortages. By the time the Federals reached the Marmiton late on October 25 they were low on food, forage, and ammunition and anxiously looked forward to whatever Fort Scott had to offer.

Following his contretemps with Pleasonton, Curtis hurried ahead to Fort Scott. He was back in the Department of Kansas and exercised his authority to the fullest. Some of his staff went to work distributing the supplies stockpiled at the post, while others prepared for the arrival of a train from Fort Leavenworth, reported to be only hours away. A weary but exultant Curtis informed the War Department of the day's dramatic events. He summarized the fights at Marais de Cygnes, Mine Creek, and the Marmiton and reported that he now was in possession of all but three of Price's guns. He also explained his tenuous logistical situation in some detail but promised to "proceed in the pursuit with all the forces I can keep on the way." Later that night he learned that the rebels were burning wagons filled with ammunition a dozen miles east of the fort. At some point in that busy evening Curtis lifted martial law in southern Kansas and released the remaining Kansas militia. That night he slept in a bed for the first time since leaving the Gillis House in Kansas City.[12]

Curtis awoke early the next morning, October 26, and wrote a long letter home. "I had a good nights sleep and [was] comfortable," he assured Belinda. Curtis complained about Pleasonton and his officers, most of whom continued to grumble loudly about the prolonged and, in their minds, unnecessary pursuit: "I have trouble with officers who want to halt their commands but I hope to keep them on the war path." The officers in question continued to claim that their mounts were worn out, but Curtis declared that "as long as horses can stand on their feet they must be considered fit for duty." On a more positive note, he told Belinda that "our military family," that is, his staff, was "all well and all laboring as mortals never did before" to insure that everyone received sufficient rations to keep them going for a few more days. To Curtis's immense relief, the expected supply train arrived on schedule. The wagons were unloaded in less than an hour by thousands of willing hands and sent back empty to Fort Leavenworth. "In this way," Curtis wrote, "my troops may be fed while Prices must starve if they are pressed into the Country they are now going to." The syntax was garbled but the meaning was clear.[13]

The unplanned detour to Fort Scott allowed the Confederates to open up a small lead; there were no clashes for the next twenty-four hours. Upon picking up Price's trail at the Marmiton, Curtis reported that the path of the rebel army was, as usual, "strewn with all sorts of supplies, and [we] continue to take his weary straggling rebel followers." Pleasonton provided the big news of the day. He granted himself medical leave and departed for St. Louis, ostensibly because of his "injury" but actually because he felt he had achieved a suitable amount of personal glory at Westport and saw no point in continuing. Pleasonton had the gall to assure Curtis that his "hearty cooperation" would continue even in his absence. He directed his officers to follow Curtis's orders until Rosecrans issued instructions to the contrary. Curtis had already grown tired of Pleasonton and shed no tears over his departure. He did not know that Pleasonton had sent a letter to Rosecrans in which he grossly inflated his role at Westport and characterized the subsequent pursuit of Price as a colossal waste of resources.[14]

Blunt's First Division, now in the lead, hurried across the southwestern corner of Missouri and caught up with Price at Newtonia late on October 28. Blunt thought it likely the Confederates would break and run as they had done at Mine Creek, so he made an immediate attack with his relatively small force. To his surprise, the rebels stood their ground and even counterattacked. Fighting flared until dark, when the enemy again withdrew. The Federals suffered over one hundred casualties; Confederate losses were slightly lower. Curtis came up with the Second Division just as the firing died down. He described the second battle of Newtonia as a "severe engagement" between "greatly disproportioned forces," praising Blunt for his boldness, if not his judgment. The Federals had closed the gap and were once again within striking distance of the Confederates.[15]

During the rapid march to Newtonia, Curtis was stricken with a familiar pain in his shoulders and back. He was unable to stay in the saddle for any length of time and spent the remainder of the campaign in an ambulance. He did not mention any of this in his letters home or in his official correspondence, but Sam remembered years later that the lengthy pursuit was hard on his father: "The rapid decay of his vital forces was plainly visible from this time forward until his death."[16]

The next day, October 29, Rosecrans finally bestirred himself—with predictably disastrous results. Convinced by Pleasonton's poison pen that the campaign had run its course, Rosecrans ordered his forces to cease cooperating with Curtis, let Price go, and return to their home districts in Missouri. Pleasonton, of course, had already departed for St. Louis, but now his men left as well. "I was astonished and sorely disappointed," exclaimed Curtis. That was an understatement. He was beside himself with rage and frustration at Rosecrans's deliberate sabotage—there is no other word—of an ongoing military operation. He informed the War Department of what Rosecrans had done and announced that, since he had only Blunt's division (now reduced to the size of a small brigade) under his immediate command, he was throwing in the towel: "Deeming it improper to continue a pursuit in another department, suspended by its proper commander, I shall return by slow marches to my proper department command." Curtis and slightly more than one thousand horsemen, all that remained of the Army of the Border, retraced their steps a dozen miles to Neosho, Missouri, and stopped for the night. Price continued on toward the Arkansas River at a more leisurely pace, hardly able to believe his good fortune.[17]

Curtis installed himself at the kitchen table of an abandoned house in Neosho and wrote a strongly worded message to the War Department describing his situation. "From the commencement of my efforts in this campaign," he explained, "I have had to occupy a debatable position as to my authority over troops." The Kansas militia "caviled" about crossing state lines, but that was nothing compared to the behavior of Rosecrans, Pleasonton, and other officers ("except one or two") in the Department of the Missouri who repeatedly "expressed a conviction that they had done enough." Curtis said he had used "argument, expostulation, and orders" to keep everyone focused on the task at hand: "The necessity of pushing Price's forces beyond the Arkansas is so obvious I have not hesitated to disregard department lines." He expressed his amazement that Rosecrans and Pleasonton could not see that necessity as well. He described how Pleasonton, "without consulting me," diverted his force to Fort Scott and "insisted that farther pursuit was needless." Then Rosecrans, far to the rear and ignorant of conditions at the front, unilaterally withdrew his forces from the fight. At that point, Curtis explained, he gave up the pursuit: "I saw no alternative and with mortification turned from the retreating foe."[18]

Shortly after Curtis sent off the above dispatch, a courier arrived from Fort Scott with an urgent telegram from the War Department: "General Grant directs that Price be pursued to the Arkansas River, or at least till he encounters Steele or Reynolds." Curtis immediately sent couriers racing after Pleasonton's troops (though not Pleasonton himself) with copies of Grant's order and an order of his own to reassemble at Cassville and resume the pursuit. Curtis then informed Rosecrans that, in accordance with orders from the general in chief, he was going after Price with all available troops, regardless of departmental affiliation.[19]

Unfortunately, Grant's order was flawed. The author of the dispatch (presumably Halleck, in light of the wording) did not specify who was to be in charge of the pursuit or what troops he was to command. The author probably assumed Rosecrans and Curtis would continue with whatever command arrangement they had put in place, unaware that there was no formal arrangement between the two department commanders, only an informal and short-lived understanding between Curtis and Pleasonton. Curtis may or may not have noticed the omission, but Rosecrans did. Instead of seeking clarification from the War Department, Rosecrans declared Grant's order invalid and instructed everyone in his department to ignore it and any orders from Curtis as well.

As far as Rosecrans was concerned, the campaign was over and Curtis was on his own.[20]

Meanwhile, back at the kitchen table, a weary Curtis wrote to Belinda. He described the campaign as "laborious and exciting" and explained that he looked a mess because his baggage had been misplaced: "I am now troubled only with the clothes I had on when I started." He related his difficulties with Pleasonton and his moment of disbelief when Rosecrans shut down his pursuit of Price: "I had to give up the chase just when the enemy had received the hardest blow and was again in close proximity in full range. *I was never more disgusted*." He told Belinda of Grant's recently arrived order and his faint hope that it would get things back on track.[21]

Curtis reckoned that Rosecrans's blundering cost the Federals at least forty-eight hours, but he believed he could make up the lost time and inflict additional damage on Price before he crossed the Arkansas River. If he could achieve that, Curtis was certain the Confederates would "never be anxious to try another mission to Missouri." He also believed a strong Union finish would convince the guerrillas traveling with Price to stay away as well: "We are driving most of the bushwhackers in the great herd of Price, and I hope to get them so far away they will trouble us no more forever."[22]

The only Union detachment to rejoin Curtis was Benteen's brigade, which had been assigned to a different department and was no longer subject to Rosecrans's orders. The additional manpower increased the size of the Army of the Border to about 2,800 cavalry and a dozen guns. That was sufficient for Curtis. The Federals hurried south on Telegraph Road, the same rocky thoroughfare Curtis had traveled in his pursuit of Price and the Missouri State Guard in 1862. "Price retreats rapidly but I am gaining on him again," Curtis reported. The next day, November 1, the Federals crossed into northwestern Arkansas. A few miles down the road Curtis traversed a familiar landscape. "The old battle ground of Pea Ridge was shrouded with snow and looked cold bleak and sorrowful," he told Henry. Memories of the battle and of Sadie's death depressed him: "My heart was pressed down with sadness and my eyes dimmed with tears as [I] passed this scene of my greatest and most distinguished of my victories."[23]

The weather deteriorated and the Federals were forced to stop, first at Little Sugar Creek then at Cross Hollows, and wait out a fierce winter storm. "We had incessant snow and rain," Curtis later reported, "and being without tents we suffered severely." From the relative comfort of his ambulance, Curtis wrote to Rosecrans and offered him one last chance to redeem himself, but to no avail. Rosecrans was already on his way back to St. Louis. Curtis shared his gloomy thoughts with a colleague at Fort Scott: "It was a great misfortune that the Missouri troops were withdrawn [by Rosecrans] from Price's pursuit. It has so detained and weakened my forces I cannot accomplish my hopes or much for our cause." This was the lowest point of the campaign for Curtis.[24]

While the Army of the Border huddled at Cross Hollows, a second courier arrived and handed Curtis another telegram from the War Department. This time Grant (or Halleck) got it right. The new order specifically placed Curtis in command "of all troops belonging to the Department of the Missouri and now serving on the western border of that State," and directed him to carry out Grant's previous order to pursue Price to the Arkansas. Curtis immediately sent another wave of couriers racing after Pleasonton's now impossibly distant troops. Incredibly, Rosecrans refused to recognize Curtis's expanded authority despite a direct order to that effect from the general in chief. He again instructed his troops to return to their home districts and stay there.[25]

Curtis threw off his dark mood: "I shall leave [my] trains and push forward with all speed and caution" with the troops at hand. By keeping up the pressure on Price, he hoped "to scare the rebels away from Fort Smith and save our comrades there." The Federals clattered down Telegraph Road and steadily gained ground on the fleeing Confederates. Curtis wrote that the pursuit across northwestern Arkansas "was conducted most vigorously, in great part without a commissary train, the troops living on fresh beef, abandoned by the retreating foe, or gathered in the country."[26]

The much-reduced Army of the Border reached Fayetteville on November 4. The Union outpost had been established during the Prairie Grove campaign and existed in an almost constant state of siege. Desperate to close out his raid with a victory, any victory, Price detached Fagan to capture the town and its tiny garrison, but word of Curtis's rapid approach drove the Confederates away. Fagan's troops departed in such haste they left behind a trophy, the flag of Blunt's escort company that had been nearly wiped out at Baxter Springs thirteen months earlier. For Curtis, the faded banner was a sad memento of his son's murder. Fayetteville had little to offer in the way of creature comforts except hardtack, forage, and shelter, but that was much appreciated by the hungry, ragged, and frostbitten newcomers.[27]

The Federals left Fayetteville the following day, passed over the Prairie Grove and Cane Hill battlegrounds, and entered the Indian Territory. The Confederates, now only a few hours ahead, picked up the pace, shedding men, firearms, artillery, camp equipment, and vehicles (including Price's carriage) at an unprecedented rate. Curtis described their flight as "hasty and terrified." Late on November 7 the dissolving Army of Missouri splashed across the Arkansas River twenty-five miles above Fort Smith. The pursuing Federals, with Benteen's command in the lead, arrived the next morning. "My wearied troops drew rein on the north bank of the Arkansas River," was how Curtis described the moment. Artillerymen fired dozens of rounds across the river to hasten the rebels on their way, but Curtis made no attempt to follow. The Westport campaign was over.[28]

That night a "most terrific thunder-storm and a deluging rain" pounded the Union camp. Curtis sat in his ambulance and tried to keep his paperwork dry. He issued an order thanking his men for their courage, patriotism, and, above all, endurance. He also prepared a report for the War Department in which he stated that Price "carried nothing of consequence" across the Arkansas River except a rabble of demoralized and disorganized survivors, many without arms, ammunition, shoes, or mounts and all without food. He declared Kansas, Missouri, northern Arkansas, and the Indian Territory safe from Price's "starving hordes" for the foreseeable future. Curtis also addressed a pointed note to Rosecrans in which he described his success in driving thousands of "half-starved bushwhackers and brutish vagabonds" back into the Confederacy. The next day he dissolved the Army of the Border. The Federals followed various routes home to allow for more effective foraging, but all suffered serious hardships. Curtis himself returned to Fort Leavenworth by way of Fort Gibson and Fort Scott, the reverse of the route he had followed earlier in the year.[29]

The 1864 Missouri Expedition lasted two months, covered 1,500 miles, and involved more than fifty thousand soldiers, militiamen, and guerrillas, a significant percentage of the male population of the trans-Mississippi. Not a day went by without at least one battle, skirmish, raid, or random act of violence. Hundreds of homes and businesses were looted, vandalized, or destroyed. Bridges were burned, telegraph lines wrecked, and banks robbed. Thousands were killed, wounded, or captured, but it seems impossible to come up with reliable figures, given the nature of the opposing forces. All that can be said with certainty is that Confederate casualties outstripped Union losses by a wide margin. Curtis and Price battled their way across parts of three states and the Indian Territory during the final weeks of the operation. When they reached the Arkansas River and parted ways, the Army of Missouri was a shambles and the conflict in the trans-Mississippi was effectively over. Few other Civil War campaigns were as decisive.[30]

Curtis was the architect of the Union victory. He recognized the danger to Kansas early on, assembled an army from scratch, overcame a host of difficulties, and won the largest battle fought west of the Mississippi River. He was the driving force behind the relentless pursuit after Westport that sealed the victory. For most of the campaign Curtis received only limited cooperation from the adjacent Department of the Missouri. Toward the end he received none at all. Curtis triumphed over Price in spite of Rosecrans and Pleasonton.

General and Mrs. Curtis attended a "grand reception" in the city of Leavenworth on November 18 to celebrate the deliverance of Kansas. Curtis noticed that among the applauding attendees were some of the very people who had undercut him at every turn. He and Belinda smiled and enjoyed the gala event. Over the next few weeks Curtis stayed close to home. He was not surprised to learn that a free-for-all for public recognition and government favor was underway in St. Louis. Rosecrans and Pleasonton showed more energy in their quest for preferment and position than they ever did in the campaign against Price. Curtis told Henry that "great efforts were made by General Rosecrans and his associated officers in St. Louis to steal the honors of my victories just as other Generals sought to absorb the glory of my former campaign against Price," a swipe at Sigel's behavior after Pea Ridge. Curtis did not think the fracas in St. Louis would affect his standing in Kansas: "This does me no harm here where the facts are well known and my achievements will be as enduring as the history of this great growing western portion of our continent."[31]

A hint of Curtis's altered feelings toward Rosecrans is evident in his response to a Missourian who complained about the presence of rebels in his neighborhood. "But you must look to General Rosecrans," Curtis replied. "He must attend to his own department. What I have done in Missouri seems to provoke my foes to continual slanders by the St. Louis press, and I get no thanks from those who ought to recognize my earnest exertions to cooperate with them." He said he did not feel bound to become involved "where my neighbors hold command and find fault with what I do at their request." If Rosecrans wanted any help in the future, he was not going to find it at Fort Leavenworth.[32]

A month or so after returning to Kansas, Curtis provided Henry with a capsule account of his role in the Westport campaign: "I contended against a thousand difficulties. A powerful force approached. Political excitement caused distrust, and doubt and indifference. My regular volunteers were few and widely distributed and the militia unorganized and unarmed. In the face of all dangers on the tenth of October I called out the militia, organized, armed, rallied, took them into Missouri, and fortified them." He then summarized events from Lexington to Westport: "I gained a complete victory, which I followed up for near three hundred miles concluding my pursuit on the banks of the Arkansas." He assured Henry that the "plain simple facts will be fully presented in my report and cannot fail to interest you and others who may cast a glance at western warfare." Curtis boasted that "my health was excellent and my powers of endurance equal to the strongest of my men." That was the only untruth in the account.[33]

Curtis sometimes carped about the Kansas State Militia in private, but in public he had nothing but praise for the thousands of citizen-soldiers who "left their homes and served faithfully in checking the enemy." Most of the men in the ranks fought well despite "indifferent equipments and doubtful pay," and dozens were killed or wounded, mostly in the chaotic retreat from Byram's Ford. In his official report Curtis declared that the "militia of Kansas behaved nobly and saved their State from devastation." No other Union general was compelled to rely so heavily on an armed citizenry to repel a Confederate threat.[34]

Curtis recognized that the Missouri Expedition was only a "side act in the great drama" of the Civil War, but he was content to have done his duty and made another contribution to the downfall of the rebellion in the West. He regretted that his hard-fought engagements during the Westport campaign did not receive the newspaper coverage he thought they deserved, but he tried to look on the bright side. Price was gone, the bushwhackers were (mostly) gone, and the war now seemed far away. The Department of Kansas, he wrote, was in a condition of "profound peace and quiet." That, of course, had always been his goal.[35]

• • •

After ten months of nearly constant duty in the field, Curtis welcomed the opportunity to settle quietly into a comfortable routine of office work, social events, and family activities. When his daily duties failed to fill the available time, he resumed conserving his official papers, a process he had initiated the previous year in St. Louis. He told Henry, "I am saving a vast amount of manuscripts in the way of scraps pasted in large scrapbooks, but hardly expect to find time or inclination during some years to come to even read them over. But they are important items in the history of this country west of the Mississippi, and may after I am gone be interesting to the millions that will inhabit the soil." Curtis filled five more scrapbooks with hundreds of documents that might otherwise have been lost and shipped them to Keokuk.[36]

Curtis tried to keep up with the war in the East and occasionally discussed Grant's operations with Henry. Having backed the Confederates into the defenses of Richmond and Petersburg after a costly overland campaign, Grant was gradually extending his lines around the immobilized rebels. Curtis struggled to understand what was happening from the sketchy coverage in the newspapers. He concluded that Grant, and Sherman in Georgia, had pinned in place the only two rebel armies of consequence. "We are therefore gaining if we merely hold on both at Richmond and Atlanta," he told Henry. "The struggle must bear more heavily on our enemies than on us." He believed it was only a matter of time before the Confederacy collapsed.[37]

Curtis also followed the 1864 fall elections. He was pleased at Lincoln's re-election and positively overjoyed by radical Republican victories in Missouri and Kansas. "There never was such a clean sweep," he exulted. Curtis wondered if Lincoln now regretted his misguided courtship of Gamble's conservative faction in Missouri, a faction that had moved heaven and earth to oust Curtis from department command. "I was in the midst of that fight," Curtis reminded Henry, "and my judgement prevailed." In other words, he had been right all along.[38]

• • •

While Federals and Confederates battled it out along the Kansas-Missouri line in the fall of 1864, the clash of cultures on the Great

Plains intensified. How Curtis might have responded is unknown, because the Missouri Expedition compelled him to turn his attention eastward. When he announced in mid-October that "Price is now the dangerous foe" and called on Blunt to help him fend off the Confederates, it signaled a reorientation of military priorities within the Department of Kansas. Curtis informed Colorado Territorial Governor John Evans that he would have to use his own judgment and resources in dealing with hostile Indians. "You must act on your own authority and discretion in calling out militia," wrote Curtis. "I hope you will do so and allow the Federal troops to come forward [to Kansas] soon." Indian raids tapered off with the onset of cooler weather, but Curtis warned Evans that the Natives only wanted a respite from fighting so they could accumulate enough food to survive until spring: "All they fear is winter approaching and therefore they [pretend to] desire peace, which they cannot have at present." Curtis was fair and even generous to Indians who gave up raiding, but he had no patience with those who murdered innocents.[39]

Curtis dispatched similar advice to Colonel John M. Chivington, commander of the rough-and-tumble Colorado territorial militia. Chivington was a difficult character who chose to interpret orders freely, but his initiative had helped turn back a Confederate invasion at Glorieta, New Mexico, two years earlier and he was a hero to many Coloradans. At one time Curtis even told Halleck that Chivington was the "best man" to defend Colorado, a vote of confidence he came to regret.[40]

Curtis strove to get his stern, but fair, Indian policy across to Evans, Chivington, and other civil and military officials in the western reaches of his vast department. In letter after letter he insisted that "wild" Indians "must be kept at arm's length" until they changed their behavior. The Indians had learned to bend government policy to their advantage; that would no longer be tolerated. "The old and infirm and lazy will come in" to the forts and agencies, as reservations were then called, to receive their allotments of beef, blankets, and bullets, "while the wicked are allowed to go on with their devilment." To insure that a uniform approach was instituted and enforced throughout the department, Curtis ordered that "no peace must be made without my directions." He insisted that Indians must return hostages and stolen stock before peace talks could begin. At the same time, he stressed that negotiating was preferable to campaigning. Evans and Chivington, however, believed it was better to exterminate than negotiate. They deliberately misinterpreted Curtis's words to mean they had carte blanche to operate as they saw fit.[41]

While Curtis and Blunt had their hands full with the Confederates, Evans and Chivington launched a campaign of extermination against any and all Indians within their reach. On November 29, 1864, Chivington and a large force of undisciplined Colorado militiamen and civilian volunteers overran an encampment of Cheyennes and Arapahoes at Sand Creek in the southeastern corner of the territory. No soldiers were involved. Casualties among the Indians, especially women and children, were heavy. Chivington claimed victory and vengeance, but as details of the incident emerged, public condemnation mounted. Upon orders from the War Department, Curtis opened an investigation that placed the blame for the horrific affair squarely on Chivington, who resigned his militia commission and left the territory to escape punishment.[42]

Had Price not threatened Kansas when he did, Curtis would not have recalled Blunt, and the history of that time and place would have turned out differently. Unlike Chivington, who viewed "colored" peoples as savages or worse, Blunt was a committed abolitionist and an ardent advocate for African-American and Indian soldiers. He spent much of the Civil War in the Indian Territory working with Native peoples and helping to organize the Union Indian Brigade. It seems safe to say that if Blunt had remained in charge of military affairs on the central plains in the fall of 1864, there would have been no Sand Creek.

• • •

In December 1864 Curtis learned of the latest round of administrative changes in the trans-Mississippi. He grabbed pen and paper to inform Henry that both Rosecrans and "that scoundrel Steele" had been removed from their commands. He remarked that Lincoln was "evidently waking up," but it was Grant who engineered the changes. Curtis did not yet know that he, too, was destined for a change of scenery.[43]

14

PEACEMAKING

GRANT DID NOT GET AROUND TO REORGANIZING THE TRANS-
Mississippi until nearly two months after the close of the Missouri Expedition. He merged the Department of Kansas back into
the Department of the Missouri, then consolidated the enlarged
Department of the Missouri and the Department of the Northwest into a new entity, the Military Division of the Missouri. He
elevated Pope to overall command, placed Major General Grenville M. Dodge in charge of the Department of the Missouri, and
transferred Curtis to the Department of the Northwest. Having
gotten rid of Rosecrans and Steele, Grant wanted to remove Curtis as well, citing his "inefficiency" as the reason, but the Iowa
general's military accomplishments and political connections
made that impossible. Shunting Curtis to the sidelines was the
best (or worst) Grant could do. Why he did it remains a mystery.[1]

Curtis learned of his new assignment on January 31, 1865. The
Department of the Northwest consisted of Iowa, Minnesota, and
Wisconsin, an expanse of prairies, woodlands, and bogs extending from the Great Lakes to the Great Plains and north to Canada. It was as far from the Confederacy as it was possible to get
in the trans-Mississippi; Curtis recognized that what appeared to
be a lateral transfer from one department command to another
was actually a form of exile. The victor of Pea Ridge and Westport was out of the war. Curtis informed Belinda that he had
been "switched off into a very quiet corner," but he was more
forthcoming with Henry. "I confess I feel myself *shelved*," he
wrote. "All this does not seem to me right." Nevertheless, Curtis approved of Grant's long-overdue decision to place the trans-

Mississippi under a single commander. Had Grant done this six months earlier, the Missouri Expedition would have followed a different course.[2]

Saying goodbye to the tight-knit Fort Leavenworth community proved painful for Curtis. "I did not know how hard it was to leave [the] Kansas department till I began to say farewell to my friends on the bank of the Missouri," he confessed to Belinda. "The whole years' service has been a continual ovation or active campaigning and I [left] so sudden I had hardly time to reflect on the *persons and scenes* that had surrounded me. It is a brilliant page in my eventful life, and in looking back I shall remember with the strongest affection the friends and incidents that have transpired." His stay in Kansas, he added, would live in his memory "as a gem in the ocean of time."[3]

Curtis reached Milwaukee and assumed command on February 13, 1865. He called on Pope at his home and found him "very polite and agreeable." (The Pope he remembered from Missouri in 1861 had been insufferably arrogant.) Pope warned his successor that the Department of the Northwest had "barely force sufficient for absolutely necessary defensive purposes," but that was an old story for Curtis. He had been outnumbered since the war began. The generals exchanged information and parted on good terms. Pope soon left for his new posting in St. Louis while Curtis moved into a hotel and explored his surroundings. "The town is [in] every way good looking but very quiet," he informed Belinda. "There is no sound of bugle, drums, or martial tread." Curtis looked into renting a house along the lakefront, but he was shocked at the cost and decided to remain in the hotel. He did not need much space and, with the war winding down, he did not think he would be long in Milwaukee. The February weather was cold and dreary; he advised Belinda to remain in Iowa and visit Wisconsin in the summer, "if it pleases Providence and Mr. Lincoln to keep me in the upper country."[4]

The Department of the Northwest was quiet during the winter months. Curtis spent several hours per day preparing his report on the Westport campaign. He was appalled by the number of omissions, exaggerations, distortions, and outright lies in the reports submitted by Rosecrans, Pleasanton, and other officers in the Department of the Missouri. He vowed to Henry that his version of the truth would be as accurate as he could make it: "I shall try to place matters right in my report without such a *suppression* [of the facts] as Generals nearby have done to their eternal shame." Members of his staff trickled in, but there was little for them to do. That was fine with Curtis. After a trying year spent largely in the saddle, he was content to take things "very easy."[5]

Military celebrities were few and far between in wartime Wisconsin; Curtis found himself embraced by a "fashionable circle" of the "most wealthy and agreeable people" in Milwaukee. He was invited to plays, operas, and dinners, but his evenings out with the local glitterati made him conscious of his worn attire. "I am growing shabby," he confessed to Belinda. He had new clothes made but balked at spending the "monstrous sum" of $100 on a stylish overcoat. He continued to wear his frayed and faded army greatcoat.[6]

While Curtis enjoyed the high life in Milwaukee, Belinda, Caddie, and Julia reestablished themselves in Keokuk. Belinda, as usual, made all the travel arrangements and supervised the packing and shipping of the family's clothes, furnishings, and household goods from Kansas back to Iowa. It is unclear what arrangements, if any, she had made regarding occupancy or upkeep of the family home during their time at Fort Leavenworth, but she was unhappy with the building's "dilapidated" condition. She informed her husband that they would surely lose their place in Keokuk's social pecking order unless something was done about the sagging porch and peeling paint. Curtis reminded Belinda that "our position in society depends only on our rank and good character. We can live just as plain as we please." Besides, he added, our house "is far better than that occupied by Mr. Lincoln and probably far better than other Presidents have enjoyed." He considered it "madness" to spend money refurbishing their "comfortable house" while the war still raged. The Curtis estate remained in its weather-beaten state.[7]

Curtis was in Keokuk when Lee surrendered at Appomattox in April 1865. Other capitulations followed as the southern rebellion sputtered to a close. His reaction to these momentous events was muted. "It has been a costly struggle in a thousand ways," he wrote to Sam. "Let us hope that our posterity will appreciate and profit by it." Thoughts of Henry and Sadie must have weighed heavily on his mind. The news of Lincoln's murder arrived a week later. Curtis was "terribly shocked" by the "infamous assassination" and delivered a memorial address for the fallen president in St. John's Episcopal Church. Speaking at length, Curtis "very plainly" expressed his uncompromising views on slavery, secession, rebellion, emancipation, and retribution. He declared that Jefferson Davis should be hanged for treason and was pleased to see that his remarks upset the "copperheads that infest our Congregation."[8]

Curtis returned to Milwaukee just as a handful of Sioux went on a rampage and murdered an isolated pioneer family. The incident generated widespread alarm in a region where memories of the Sioux Uprising were still vivid. "The terrors of 1862 are not yet subsided here," he explained to Belinda. "They tell awful stories of the horrible massacre." Responding to the uproar, Curtis directed his principal subordinates, Brigadier Generals Henry H. Sibley and Alfred Sully, to take all necessary measures to "check the Indians and allay the public anxiety." Both officers had served in their current positions for years and knew their business. Curtis did not think they would benefit from his presence, so he remained in Milwaukee.[9]

A flurry of overheated newspaper editorials and a mounting public furor compelled Curtis to take the field, much against his better judgment. As soon as the ice melted he traveled by train and steamboat to Fort Snelling, near St. Paul, Minnesota, to confer with Sibley and to be seen taking charge of the situation. Sibley feared the exaggerated stories of Indian depredations would trigger a "universal stampede." He suggested building a line of small military posts along the frontier to calm the populace. Curtis disapproved. He did not want a "multiplicity of little forts" separated by creeks, lakes, and bogs. He proposed instead that Minnesotans demonstrate some initiative and construct "neighborhood forts," that is, Kansas-style blockhouses, where they could congregate and defend themselves in times of danger. Neither plan was put into effect.[10]

Curtis and Sibley eventually decided on a modest show of force to cow the Indians and calm the public. A column of soldiers marched out of Fort Snelling and beat the bushes for several weeks but failed to locate any Natives. The Sioux, innocent and guilty alike, fled north to Canada or west onto the Great Plains, beyond the army's reach. Pope did not think the loss of a single family necessitated the expense of a prolonged campaign and made his displeasure known. Exasperated at being pulled in two directions, Curtis informed Minnesota state officials that his troops had done all they could to counter the "supposed danger." It was time, he wrote, for the citizenry to shoulder more of the burden of local defense. "The settlements must be self-reliant," he declared.[11]

• • •

Back in Milwaukee, Curtis contemplated his future. The huge volunteer force that had fought and won the Civil War was melting away, but what Sherman termed the "future army" was still a work in progress. The postwar military establishment would have to carry out occupation duty in the defeated but unreconstructed South, an area comprising nearly one-third of the nation. It also would have to defend the Atlantic and Pacific coasts and increase the level of security in the West, an immense and inhospitable region where the Native population was anything but welcoming. Questions abounded. How large would the new army be? How would it be organized? Where would it be deployed? Who would be in charge?[12]

Curtis warned Sam that "our occupations as soldiers is nearly played out and we must save our means and arrange our affairs for private economical living." He advised his son to consider the law as a livelihood. Belinda received a similar letter discussing the likelihood of career changes and the necessity of fiscal responsibility. "I see the great *probability* of our being thrown out of our income and will have to save all I can to aid us in starting [a] new business to meet necessary demands," he wrote. "We must keep the matter of reduction of the army in view, and prepare for the cessation of our present ample income by strict economy of our *dimes*." Curtis had gotten used to a regular paycheck and did not look forward to depending on his "daily labor" for a living. When Henry asked whether he had put aside enough money to live comfortably after the war, Curtis admitted that he had not: "All I have saved has gone to pay debts, taxes, and plant out my vinyards." Henry must have groaned.[13]

Curtis recognized that his age worked against him. In 1865 he was fifty-eight years old on paper, sixty in reality. He also suspected that his four years of military service west of the Mississippi River did not count for much in postwar Washington: "Those who have served nearest General Grant, and nearest to Headquarters, are most likely to be retained in preference to those kept on the frontier as I have been. Still I am disposed in this as in other matters concerning my duty, to leave it to my superiors to say when my services seem unnecessary." But while Curtis was inclined to await developments, others were not. Several of his staff officers, including some who had been with him from the beginning, wished to remain in the army. They feared, as Curtis explained to Henry, that a "rush from other quarters will crowd me out of the army carrying my staff with me and such I suppose is very probable."[14]

After waffling for several weeks, Curtis made up his mind. "I desire to remain in the Army," he informed Pope. He was reluctant to become involved in the unseemly scramble for preference taking place at the War Department, so he fell back on a letter-writing campaign. He asked Henry and other prominent Republicans to communicate with Stanton on his behalf. He even provided talking points: "I am about the eighth in rank and have during the war constantly commanded independent first class commands—expeditions, armies, and departments.

I think always successfully." He wanted his supporters to write to Grant as well but admitted, "I do not know how to get at him." Given Grant's antipathy, a handful of letters would not have done much good.[15]

As spring became summer, Curtis spent much of his time revisiting the past and reflecting on the future. He basked in the glow of his soldierly accomplishments and was comforted by the thought that, no matter how things turned out, "nothing can deprive me of a glorious record which has been furrowed deep in the virgin soil of the country west of the Mississippi." At other times he smoldered at the unfair treatment he had received from Halleck and others in the military establishment. Curtis had been in uniform "from the beginning of the strife to the end," but despite a sterling record he felt he had not been properly appreciated or rewarded. He was especially unhappy that certain officers "much my inferior in age, experience, and in my judgement also in desserts" had received preferential treatment. There were days when Curtis was not sure he wanted to stay in an organization that seemed not to want him.[16]

If Curtis was certain about anything, it was that he did not want to command occupation forces in the former Confederacy. "I have no personal desire to press my way into administrative duties [in the] South, where my reputation is sure to suffer," he informed Belinda. He had struggled in the "tarnishing toilsome field of controversy between traitors and true men" since his days as a congressman, and was sick and tired of dealing with rebels, secessionists, secessionist sympathizers, slave owners, proslavery advocates, and Democrats in general. He expected reconstruction would be a "great and difficult task" and was not optimistic about the result. He was especially concerned about the fate of the freedmen. In unusually blunt language, he wrote that the newly liberated slaves must not be allowed to slip back under the control of "insolent revengeful masters, as they certainly will be, if chicken hearted officials administer the affairs of the rebel states." He lambasted "our truckling pro-slavery heartless commanding officers," a swipe at Halleck, Schofield, Steele, and other opponents or lukewarm supporters of emancipation.[17]

In June Curtis made what he thought would be a quick trip home to Iowa, but while walking back from a neighbor's house on a "dark stormy night" he tripped over a flower box in his front yard. He broke one arm and sprained the other, and he was "laid up" under Belinda's care for several weeks. Curtis did not request medical leave because he feared it would provide Grant with a pretext to remove him, so he had staff officers shuttle between Milwaukee and Keokuk once a week to keep the paperwork flowing.[18]

Weeks passed without a word from Washington. Curtis began to fret: "I almost wish they would muster me out and make it my necessity to go and plow for a living." In July he returned to Milwaukee, one arm in a sling, and informed Belinda that he expected to "be relieved or get orders very soon." On July 25 the War Department announced the merger of the Department of the Northwest into the ever-expanding Department of the Missouri. Curtis was instructed to return to Keokuk and await orders. "Things seem to work just about as much against me as they can," he told his wife. "I do not expect much more than an honorable discharge in due time." His military career appeared to be over. Then, ten days later, Curtis received a telegram directing him to report in person to the War Department for an important assignment. He set out for Washington the next morning.[19]

• • •

Curtis reached the capital city and rented a room in Mrs. Joy's now very familiar boardinghouse. The next day he went to the War Department and was warmly received by Secretary Stanton. The two men walked to the White House to meet with President Andrew Johnson and the rest of the cabinet. Secretary of State William H. Seward congratulated Curtis on his wartime record, while others around the table, including Johnson, expressed their admiration for his years of public service. Secretary of the Interior James Harlan, a friend and fellow Iowa Republican, then got down to business. Harlan reviewed the unsettled situation on the Great Plains following the Sand Creek affair, announcing that the administration wanted to offer the Indians an olive branch. He asked if Curtis would serve as the military representative on a diplomatic mission to the tribes on the northern plains, principally the Sioux. The administration, Harlan explained, desired a major general who knew something about the Plains Indians and who could be spared from his current assignment. The position seemed designed with Curtis in mind, as likely it was. "I readily accepted," Curtis told Henry. "The service is important and may be agreeable."[20]

By the summer of 1865 it was clear that most of the Indians on the Great Plains were determined to defend their traditional hunting grounds and way of life. It was also apparent that a military conquest of such a vast region would be slow, difficult, and costly. The War Department and the Bureau of Indian Affairs (part of the Department of the Interior) had long been at odds over the best way to deal with "wild" Indians, but under prodding from the White House they grudgingly agreed to work together. The result of that collaboration was the Northwest Treaty Commission of 1865–66, commonly called the Indian peace commission. The commission was tasked with reducing the potential for violence on the northern plains by convincing the Indians to relocate to remote regions of their own choosing, far from trails, railroads, and settlements, where they might gradually adopt a settled way of life. There was to be no coercion. Other prominent members of the commission included the superintendent of Indian affairs and the governor of the Dakota Territory.[21]

Curtis was unfamiliar with the land and peoples north of the Platte River, so he bustled around Washington collecting maps from the War Department and reports from the Bureau of Indian Affairs. He hoped to better understand "what the Indians desire and the government can do." The appointment allowed Curtis to retain his military rank and salary for another six to twelve months while engaging in a matter of national importance. Equally significant in his mind, it meant that he was still well regarded by officials at the highest levels of the government.[22]

While waiting for the paperwork to go through, Curtis squeezed in a bit of private business. He visited the Supreme Court (then located in the Capitol building) to pay court costs from the case of *Brown v. Curtis*, the everlasting Omaha property dispute. The court had finally settled the case in June by ordering the two sides to divide the disputed properties in a mutually satisfactory fashion, something Curtis had been trying unsuccessfully to get Brown to do for years. Curtis was satisfied with the settlement, as it allowed him to claim "more lots than I anticipated." Heeding his own advice to watch every dime, Curtis wrote a draft to the court for $135.15 then wasted no time asking Henry to reimburse him for half that amount ("I have the receipt").[23]

While in the Capitol, Curtis called on Chief Justice Salmon P. Chase, who had served as secretary of the treasury in Lincoln's cabinet. The two men chatted about old times; Curtis was pleased to learn that Chase was one of several cabinet officers who had urged the president—unsuccessfully—to allow Curtis and Flag Officer Davis to take Vicksburg by storm in August 1862. After leaving Chase, Curtis bumped into Joseph Holt, judge advocate general of the army, who asked him to serve as a judge in the trial of Henry Wirz, Confederate commandant of the notorious Andersonville prison camp. Curtis politely declined, explaining that he had just accepted a position on the Northwest Treaty Commission. Curtis would not have accepted the offer in any case. He believed Holt had behaved badly during the Helena inquiry and wanted to have nothing more to do with him. To top off a busy day, Curtis dined with Secretary Harlan and discussed the progress of the Union Pacific in some detail, a conversation that would have important consequences.[24]

The next night a crowd of enthusiastic Republicans, complete with a brass band, serenaded Curtis at his boardinghouse. Called on to make a speech, he stepped outside and praised the Republican Party for its patriotism and vision. He then issued a "cordial invitation to partake of his hospitality." Party members, bandsmen, and passersby surged inside and enjoyed what Curtis described as a "collation of fruit and cake and wine and whiskey which I had requested Mrs. Joy to provide," an acknowledgment that the noisy affair was not exactly spontaneous. "The whole matter went off very satisfactory to my friends," Curtis concluded. No wonder he informed Belinda that he had received a "very hearty reception from old friends" and made "some very valuable new ones" during his stay in Washington. He seemed to be easing back into national politics.[25]

Curtis did not see Grant, but by this time he had learned that the general in chief did not want him in the postwar army. His political connections, not his military achievements, were responsible for his appointment to the Indian peace commission. Curtis suspected, correctly, that it would be his last assignment in uniform. Sam chose this inopportune moment to ask his father to help him obtain a place in the postwar army. Curtis did not think his son was serious about a military career, but he promised to do what he could: "After this hurly-burly is over, if I survive in my position, [it] will enable me to do more for you in some way." Curtis then wrote to Pope, requesting that Sam be put in charge of the peace commission's military escort. Pope agreed. Father and son would go west together.[26]

It was customary for the government to provide Indians with gifts—that is, bribes—during negotiations, so Curtis made a quick trip to New York City to purchase hats, clothes, blankets, knives, needles, fishhooks, pots, ladles, and other practical items. "We worked hard all day hunting up all sorts of goods and buying some ten or fifteen thousand dollars worth," Curtis told Belinda. He shipped the goods ahead, then allowed himself a day to explore Manhattan. He strolled along Broadway and Wall Street and enjoyed a "splendid ride" through newly completed Central Park. He hoped to see the *Great Eastern*, the largest vessel yet constructed, but that behemoth was still out in the Atlantic laying an undersea telegraph cable between Europe and North America, a project Curtis described as a "great point in the history of the world." On August 26, after nearly three weeks on the East Coast, he boarded a train and headed home.[27]

· · ·

In late September 1865 the Indian peace commissioners assembled at various points along the Missouri River and awaited the arrival of a pair of chartered steamboats. Curtis and Sam boarded the sternwheeler *Calypso* at Omaha and proceeded up the shallow, winding stream. Curtis spent much of the trip in a chair on the upper deck, watching the world go by. For the first time in ages he had nothing to do. "I have had more real rest from labor for the three past days than I have had for four years past," he wrote. "I have only to care for myself. No letters to answer. No orders to give. No duties to perform and no company to entertain."[28]

It took the commissioners nearly a week to reach the Yankton Agency in present-day South Dakota. Three thousand Yanktonai Sioux eked out a living around the agency. They struck Curtis as a "peaceable, poor, and very sad looking crowd." When the commissioners learned that the Indians were on the verge of starvation because promised government rations had not arrived, they distributed thousands of pounds of bacon, hard bread, and flour from their own stores. Curtis was incensed at the callousness and incompetence of the Bureau of Indian Affairs. "Negligence and failures in treaty matters and injustice on the part of Government is very great and very mortifying," he reported. While Sam assumed command of the commission's military escort (twenty men and a pair of mountain howitzers) from nearby Fort Randall, Curtis wandered through the Yanktonai encampment and described what he saw to Belinda. The teepees, he wrote, were "beautifully tanned and sewed very strong." He poked his head into several teepees and found the interiors to be "about as well arranged and comfortable as our ordinary frontier cabins; and warm and comfortable in times of cold and storm." He concluded that they made "first rate houses." The *Calypso* was quieter than usual that night, because Sam and the other soldiers were ashore "sparking the Sioux girls."[29]

Curtis took advantage of the peace and quiet to pen a thoughtful letter to Belinda about their future. He reminded her that the three farms outside Keokuk, purchased nearly two decades earlier, were the key to her security: "If I were to die they are the best of property for you during life and our children after." The numerous other properties were also valuable: "We have only to hold on and pay taxes to save ample means for our old age and our children after." What triggered this sudden urge to discuss financial security is not known.[30]

Low water brought the boats to a temporary halt a short distance above the Yankton Agency, so the commissioners completed the final seventy miles of their journey jolting across the prairie in army ambulances. On September 26 they finally reached Fort Sully, a square enclosure of log buildings just below present-day Pierre, South Dakota. Curtis outranked the post commander and was treated accordingly: "I am his special guest he having given me his bed, and placing me at his right hand at the board." Life at the isolated outpost was far from idyllic. "Fleas and bugs are terrible in this dry country and rats also seem formidable," Curtis observed stoically. The riverside marshes bred mosquitoes as well.[31]

The commission remained at Fort Sully for three uncomfortable weeks, meeting leaders from several Sioux tribes. First to arrive was a party of Miniconjous. Curtis described them as "very large men, well dressed in skins highly ornamented with beads, quills, and other trinkets." Several had scalps attached to their clothes. Despite this grisly display, Curtis felt some sympathy for them. The Indians, he told Belinda, are being "driven from pillar to post by our various military expeditions and none of them seem to know what they should do." The meetings took place just outside the fort in a large wall tent furnished with a table, chairs, and rugs. Curtis wore his full-dress uniform, complete with sash and sword, and opened each session with a prepared statement. During the subsequent speechmaking, he took careful notes. The Sioux invariably brought out a "medicine pipe" and everyone took turns smoking. This posed a problem for Curtis: "As I am no smoker my comrades were amused at my efforts to 'draw fire' but by hard sucking and puffing I went through the performance to the amusement of all present white and red men."[32]

All sides were on their best behavior, and the meetings went well. The Miniconjous pledged to forgo attacks on settlers and travelers but were unwilling to abandon their nomadic traditions. Curtis observed, sadly but succinctly, that "they prefer to follow the Buffalo and perish with them." The Indians promised to return in the spring for additional talks. Much to the commission's embarrassment, the steamboats carrying the goods purchased in New York were delayed by low water. The disappointed Miniconjous left Fort Sully empty-handed.[33]

The Brules arrived next and participated in the same ceremonial negotiations, with essentially the same outcome. They stayed a little longer, hoping the boats and their gifts would arrive, then they rode away as well. Before the Brules departed, Curtis twice visited their camp. He was accompanied only by a junior officer from the garrison and apparently did not feel uncomfortable surrounded by "hostiles." During one visit he attempted to take photographs but discovered the Natives were "so shy of such novelties I do not succeed very well." On another occasion he chanced to meet a "modest pretty girl" about thirteen years of age who reminded him of Caddie. He urged her parents to send her to the nearest agency or mission school but confided to Belinda that he did not think that would happen. "Her destiny cannot be changed from her savage obscurity," he wrote, "Whatever her fate, little White Cloud deserves our sympathy."[34]

Curtis believed the Sioux, or most of them, wanted a permanent peace, but neither he nor anyone else could see a way to make that happen. He expected westward emigration to increase after the Civil War and bring an end to the Indians' way of life within a decade or two. If conflicts erupted, and Curtis believed they would, he had no doubt about the outcome. The Indians were wily, bold, and brave, but he did not think any individual tribe was strong enough to defeat a "good Regiment of Cavalry with two or three light pieces of Artillery."[35]

After the Miniconjous and Brules departed, the commissioners waited to see whether any more Indians would make an appearance. The weather was turning colder and no one wanted to spend the winter snowed in at Fort Sully. Curtis whiled away the time botanizing, much as he had done in Mexico. He tramped up and down the riverbank searching for new varieties of plants. He was surprised by a nearly total solar eclipse that swept across the Dakota Territory on October 19. "We had no notice of its coming and I could not imagine for some time what made it so dark," admitted Curtis. It was by all accounts the most exciting moment of the expedition.[36]

Shortly after the eclipse, delegations of Yanktonai, Two Kettles, Sans Arc, Santee, and Hunkpapa Sioux arrived at Fort Sully and conferred with the peace commissioners. Like the Miniconjous and Brules before them, they agreed to stop their attacks and promised to return in the spring. By this time the much-delayed steamboats had arrived and the latecomers had a field day picking through crates and barrels filled with household goods. The peace commission met with about 130 Indian leaders altogether. How many others failed to attend cannot be determined.[37]

Their mission accomplished, the peace commissioners left Fort Sully at the end of October. Curtis submitted lengthy reports to Stanton and Harlan wherein he recommended that the government hold a second round of talks with the Sioux in the spring, a position the entire commission strongly seconded. Curtis also urged the secretaries to address the "eternal bickering" between army officers and Indian agents. The public squabbles confused the Natives and threatened to undermine treaty arrangements. By the middle of November 1865 a weary Curtis was back in Keokuk enjoying the comforts of home.[38]

• • •

Six months passed before the Northwest Treaty Commission's next diplomatic mission. During that time Curtis's military career came to a close. His last day of service as a major general of U.S. Volunteers was April 30, 1866. He had been in uniform one month short of five years, longer than all but a handful of volunteer officers. Curtis wondered how his altered status would affect his role on the peace commission. He raised that issue in a letter to Secretary Harlan: "Clothed as I was last year with military rank, I could secure many accommodations from that branch of the service, and have more influence with the Indians." That, obviously, no longer was the case. In the same letter he complained that his civilian salary was not "adequate compensation for the toil, exposure, and mortifications which will attend the journey." Nevertheless, he stated, "It is my duty to go, and I will try, as on former occasions, to secure a success."[39]

Curtis knew that he was not the only high-ranking victim of military retrenchment, but his unceremonious return to civilian life left him melancholy and depressed. An unusually somber tone is evident in his correspondence at this time, including a note in which he advised Henry to put his financial papers in order: "We cannot expect to live a great many years; and we better keep our matters as plain as possible, to avoid trouble to our successors." It seems almost unnecessary to add that Curtis failed to follow his own advice.[40]

Curtis's second and final mission to the Indians began on June 10, 1866. He reached Sioux City, the rendezvous point on the Missouri River, a day early and settled into a hotel. That evening he confessed to Belinda that he regretted the "many years of dangers and separations" they had endured while he pursued his civil and military careers: "I get the blues occasionally and dread my long absence from home and family which lies before me." He wrote that he wished he was back in Iowa watching over his garden. "I would like to go round with you and see how the vines and shrubs and flowers and vegetables are progressing during the past weeks," he wrote. "Home sick you say? Yes a little home sick. Well 'go where duty calls' is all we can do and a kind providence must provide for all of us."[41]

The next day Curtis walked down to the waterfront and discovered that none of the other commissioners had arrived. Annoyed, he boarded the chartered steamboat *Ben Johnson* and set out alone for the Yankton Agency. Unseasonably low water forced him ashore short of his destination, so he sent the boat back to Sioux City and traveled by hired wagon to the agency. He saw Indians planting corn along the river, a development he found encouraging. After a brief stop at Yankton Curtis continued overland to Fort Sully, as he had done the previous September. This time, however, he had no military escort and was accompanied only by a driver and an interpreter. The travelers slept on the open prairie without tents.[42]

The little party was almost within sight of Fort Sully when it passed a Brule encampment and Curtis saw the girl named White Cloud. He stopped and presented her with a dress he had brought from Keokuk for just such an unlikely occurrence. "Just think," Curtis wrote to Belinda that night, "a wild Indian child with a dress and silk mantle." The girl ran off to show the dress to her friends, and Curtis resumed his journey. He never saw her again. Curtis was remarkably unconcerned about his personal safety on his jaunts into Indian country. "I have more fear of snakes than Indians and see no danger at present of either," he told Belinda. "The Indians have kept their [side of the] treaty much better than we have done."[43]

With every passing day Curtis seemed to become more sympathetic toward the Indians. "It is painful to witness so much wretchedness," he confessed to Belinda. "I see no one that *feels* as I do that their wants deserve earnest efforts of relief, and no one labors so hard and I hope so efficiently as I can, and do, for their welfare." He believed he still had enough influence with Secretary Harlan and others in Washington to make a difference: "I may be mistaken but I think I am saving human life and human suffering however little credit or compensation I may receive."[44]

Curtis reached Fort Sully on June 25 but could do nothing substantive until the other peace commissioners arrived. He occupied a small room with a good bed and consumed a monotonous diet of bacon, bread, and coffee, occasionally enlivened by a side of potatoes. "I have no reason to complain now of hard fare," he quipped. Curtis estimated there were two thousand Indians around the fort, with more arriving every day. All were waiting for the peace talks to begin so they could receive their gifts. Curtis feared "their expectations are vastly greater than our supplies." He met on his own with several Sioux leaders, men he remembered or who remembered him from the first round of meetings. He told Belinda, "I am not conscious of being very tired and my health never was better, but I am gradually approximating to Indian style having acquired nearly their complexion." No longer in uniform, he wore moccasins and decorated his hat with feathers. He attended a sun dance, which he described as a "terrible exhibition of heathenish devotions." Curtis predicted that if he stayed on the plains much longer "I will become Sioux all over." The only fly in the ointment was the quality of life at Fort Sully, which had not improved since his previous visit: "This is a dirty dusty little fort and I will be tired enough of it before the boat comes."[45]

The boat in question, the *Ben Johnson*, arrived two weeks later with the other peace commissioners and several tons of stores and gifts. The familiar talks resumed, additional agreements were made, and gifts were distributed. Fort Sully was only the first stop. The commissioners continued up the Missouri River to Forts Rice, Berthold, and Union, the last located on the edge of the Montana territory. The journey was tedious, because the river was low and the boat was frequently forced to stop and wait for a freshet. Curtis sometimes went ashore and walked along the bank, easily keeping pace with the boat and occasionally firing at deer browsing in the gallery forests. One day he walked fifteen miles. "I am as usual in excellent health," he boasted to Henry.[46]

As the commissioners pushed deeper into the interior of the continent, they came across new groups of Indians, including Arikara, Assiniboine, Blackfoot, Crow, and Mandan. These tribes did not get along with the Sioux or with each other, and difficulties abounded. Curtis was in a meeting with Arikara leaders at Fort Berthold when a Sioux war party brazenly attempted to run off the Arikara horse herd. A fight erupted and Curtis reported that five Sioux were "killed, scalped, and cut to pieces." None of the commissioners was hurt, but it took some time to get the exultant Arikaras back into the bullet-riddled tent. On another occasion he noted that the Arikaras vociferously objected to a Bureau of Indian Affairs proposal to ban whiskey.[47]

When not conferring with the Indians, Curtis marveled at the immensity of the Great Plains and the land's unlimited potential. "I am better pleased with the whole country than I expected to be," he remarked to Belinda. In his mind's eye he saw the rolling grasslands transformed into a landscape of productive farms, prosperous towns, and busy railroads. He was more convinced than ever that his decision to cast his lot in the West had been correct.[48]

The members of the Northwest Treaty Commission concluded their labors at the end of July and made their way back down the Missouri. Reports and recommendations were prepared, submitted, read (presumably), and filed, but little changed on the northern plains in the short run. The talks were tentative and did not lead to a permanent peace, but they did no harm and demonstrated that many Indians were tired of conflict and were willing to negotiate. The commissioners and tribal leaders had made a start, nothing more. It would be up to others to continue the process. As for Curtis, he would spend the final months of his life working on the railroad.

15

UNION PACIFIC

SHORTLY AFTER RETURNING FROM HIS FIRST PEACEMAK-
ing mission in December 1865, Curtis was summoned back to
Washington by Secretary of the Interior Harlan. The purpose
of this trip, however, was not peace with the Indians but oversight of the Union Pacific. When Curtis gave up his congressional seat in 1861 he had asked Harlan, then a senator from Iowa,
to assume sponsorship of his Pacific railroad bill. Harlan did so.
Now, with rebellion crushed and railroad construction underway, Harlan returned the favor. He asked Curtis to serve on a
three-member board of commissioners tasked with inspect-
ing the bed, track, trestles, tunnels, switches, tanks, and other
engineering features of the immense transcontinental undertaking. Curtis leapt at the chance to be on the commission, not
just because of his enthusiasm for the project but also because
the job would provide a salary "when my official military head
comes off," which happened a few months later. "There will be
no need of our starving next year," he told Belinda.[1]

As on previous visits to the capital, Curtis stayed at Mrs. Joy's,
which he now called "my old Washington home." He met with
the other two commissioners, Colonel James H. Simpson of the
Corps of Engineers, one of his West Point classmates, and Dr.
William M. White, a civilian physician. He also dined with Harlan and with members of Congress, including Senator John Sherman of Ohio, the general's younger brother. Curtis and Sherman
had known each other since the mid-1830s, when they worked
together on the Muskingum River project. They reminisced about
old times in Ohio and congratulated themselves on how far they—

and the country—had come. Curtis described his social outings to Henry and quipped, "So you see I am busy."[2]

While Curtis was in Washington, Sam was in New York preparing to sail for Europe. He had been discharged from the army while still on escort duty with the peace commission. The experience had soured him on the military and he decided to see a little of the world before choosing a career in civilian life. Curtis encouraged his son to make the most of his travels and showered him with advice: "It will not do to idle away time when it is so expensive and when there is so much to see." He advised Sam, who was a bit rough around the edges, to acquire presentable clothes, learn some French phrases, and remember to remove his hat when meeting ladies. Good manners, he intoned, "cost very little and in refined society always mark good breeding." Predictably, Curtis also cautioned Sam to watch his expenses and avoid over-tipping. ("Economy must be rigidly observed.") Sam wrote home regularly and described his European experiences in detail. Curtis enjoyed the letters so much he had them published in the *Keokuk Gate City*.[3]

Sam experienced a romantic disappointment before setting out for the Old World. Details are lacking, but he was quite disheartened. Curtis did not approve of a grown man moping around and encouraged Sam to pull himself together. "There is no need of overdoing love affairs," he wrote. "You have position and means and you have acquired them mainly by your own exertions. You are well informed and able to find a companion every way agreeable." As generations of parents have done in similar circumstances, Curtis pointed out the obvious: "When there is one bright flower, you may also find others just about as sweet. Do not lavish your affections when they are not reciprocated. Excuse my intermeddling." Then, without warning, Curtis abruptly changed the subject: "I have labored and fought for position in the highest circles, and I expect my children to occupy my place." That outburst may have been the most revealing sentence he ever wrote.[4]

Curtis returned to Keokuk after Christmas, thoroughly satisfied with the result of his latest trip to Washington. "My official life still continues," he told Henry. In the first week of January 1866, after only a few days at home, Curtis set out for Omaha to join his new colleagues and inspect the initial forty miles of Union Pacific track. Despite snow, sleet, and howling winds, the commissioners completed their assignment on schedule. Simpson and White headed home, but Curtis remained in Omaha for a few days to check on his private interests.[5]

At the beginning of February 1866 Harlan called Curtis back to Washington to deal with a serious issue affecting both the Union Pacific and its far western counterpart, the Central Pacific. In the rush to get the transcontinental railroad up and running, no system-wide standards for construction, operations, and maintenance had been officially established. Harlan asked the board of commissioners to preside over a weeklong conference in the capital to rectify this oversight. Participants included government officials, company directors, engineers, manufacturers, and outside consultants, among them such prominent engineers as Herman Haupt and Benjamin H. Latrobe. The conference produced requirements, regulations, and guidelines for every imaginable situation builders and operators might encounter. Curtis was in the thick of things. He told Henry, "I have been here nearly a week and during that period I have done a months labor." On February 24 commissioners and conferees submitted a fifty-page report to Harlan, who had it printed and distributed. The new standards made the railroad safer and more efficient.[6]

Despite his busy work schedule, Curtis maintained a full social calendar during his four-week stay in Washington. On February 5 he attended a soiree and chatted with the Grants. He told Belinda that Julia Grant asked after her ("Says she remembers you very well"), but he did not relate anything the general in chief might have said. The following evening he went to a levee at the White House, mingling with President Johnson and other political figures. Two nights later he enjoyed a performance of *The Magic Flute*. A week after that he barely avoided an awkward encounter with the Fremonts at yet another party. He did not exaggerate when he reported, "Washington is very gay." Curtis may have felt guilty about enjoying himself; in his letters to Belinda he frequently stated that he was living "very economically" in a "very cold and indifferent" room. He returned to Keokuk in early March, just in time to prepare for his second round of meetings with the Indians on the Upper Missouri, as described in the previous chapter.[7]

• • •

Following the close of his second and final peacemaking mission in August 1866, Curtis went directly to Washington and submitted his reports, recommendations, and receipts to Stanton and Harlan. This concluded his yearlong stint on the Northwest Treaty Commission. While in the capital he caught up on reconstruction politics, which had taken an acrimonious turn since his last visit. Curtis was dismayed by the uproar over the status and rights of freedmen. He condemned the demagoguery and hypocrisy displayed by both parties. "I get out of patience with the whole concern," he told Belinda. "Suffrage should be as universal as possible." To escape the turmoil, Curtis made a quick trip to New York, where he busied himself "either attending to business or sight seeing." He did not identify what business he attended to or sights he saw. He was soon back in Keokuk for a welcome rest.[8]

About this time Curtis had an opportunity to act on his convictions. The family renting one of his three Keokuk farms moved out and a Black family applied for the vacancy. Curtis turned them down. "I fear the neighbors might be hostile," he explained to Belinda. "It is a pretty bad neighborhood. Then I suppose we would have to furnish teams and other stock as the family is probably very poor." Curtis may have felt he had already done his part in bringing forth a new birth of freedom, or even that he was protecting the Black family from insult or injury, but the evasive tone of his remarks is all too evident.[9]

In late September Curtis returned to Omaha to resume his new role as a railroad commissioner. He told Belinda that, as he walked the familiar streets, he was struck by the thought that "only a few of our seven dear children remain to witness a realization of our pioneer efforts in all the West." His depression deepened as he passed places associated with his deceased son: "Poor Henry was so identified with everything about me, that his amiable spirit seems to have been ingrained on every object." He suggested that they vacation in Omaha the following year and revisit the places "where we used so much to enjoy ourselves." Then, perhaps recognizing the melancholy tone of his letter, he added that Omaha was booming and property values seemed certain to increase "for a century to come."[10]

The next morning Curtis and the other railroad commissioners assembled at the new Union Pacific station and rattled west on a hot, dusty, and overcrowded train. Curtis described the 480-mile, round-trip journey as "pretty hard," but stated that the Union Pacific seemed to be doing "all in their power to make us comfortable so we have no reason to complain." The tracks ended in west-central Nebraska, just past the one hundredth meridian, though the unfinished earthen roadbed continued on to the horizon.[11]

The commissioners were satisfied with the quality of the engineering work they examined, but they were positively dazzled by the ingenious logistical arrangements that allowed the railroad to go forward, mile after mile, even as the distance to foundries, mills, and factories "back east" steadily increased. The commissioners were paid on a per diem basis by the Union Pacific, so the company naturally encouraged them to complete their work as quickly as possible in order to keep costs down. This penny-pinching irritated Curtis. "I have protested against needless haste," he told Belinda. "We are paid by the day and I do not propose working every night and every Sunday" in order to save the Union Pacific a few dollars. Their job done in their own good time, the commissioners returned to Omaha, where they completed their report and received their salary. "My pay is very fair," Curtis confided coyly to Henry, "and I have made satisfactory settlements all round."[12]

Curtis got back to Keokuk in time to vote the Republican ticket in the 1866 midterm elections. A few days later he received a request from the Corps of Engineers regarding navigation on the Mississippi River. The corps wanted his advice on how best to overcome the Des Moines Rapids, the shallow stretch of water above Keokuk that had bedeviled river-men and engineers for decades. Curtis must have snorted in amusement. Since arriving in Iowa he had consistently advocated digging a bypass canal along the west bank of the Mississippi to avoid the rapids, but his proposal had been ignored, denounced as a boondoggle, or rejected because of the cost. Others had tried to implement less expensive measures, but all had failed. The government's request was a tacit acknowledgment that Curtis had been right all along, but he no longer seemed to care. He confessed to Henry, "I am weary of the subject of the rapids, having exhausted the assignment years ago." The corps persisted; he finally agreed to send a copy of his old proposal to Washington. The bypass canal Curtis first envisioned in the 1840s was finally completed in 1877, a decade after his death. It was partially submerged by the construction of Lock and Dam No. 19 in the early twentieth century.[13]

For years Curtis had urged Henry to visit Keokuk. Now he did. In November 1866 Henry and wife, Elizabeth, arrived for an extended stay. Hosmer had moved to Keokuk some time earlier, so the three aging brothers were together for the first time in years. Curtis organized a tour of the town and a visit to his farms. Henry could not help but notice his younger brother's worn appearance and uncertain step and asked about his health. Curtis reluctantly acknowledged an "increasing debility" in his physical condition but insisted he was still sound overall and perfectly capable of performing the duties of a railroad inspector. Henry let the matter drop.[14]

After bidding his brother and sister-in-law farewell, Curtis prepared for his next Union Pacific inspection trip. It was mid-December, and the rolling prairie "never looked more cold and dreary." Curtis reached Omaha several days ahead of his colleagues. He tramped around the town, met with attorneys and business associates, spoke with locals (by now he was almost one himself), paid his property taxes, and generally took the economic pulse of the region. Commerce, he reported to Henry, was thriving: "Business is brisk and preparations for building next year are being extensively made." He was excited to learn that the Union Pacific was planning to construct a railroad bridge over the Missouri River. In the meantime the ferry company was about to acquire another boat to handle the increase in traffic. Curtis thought the company was "doing business on a pretty fair scale."[15]

Curtis wrote to Belinda nearly every day. In one letter he expressed his unhappiness with Caddie's blossoming social life. Apparently, his daughter (now fourteen) enjoyed dances and parties. "I hope Caddie will settle down to her studies," Curtis huffed, "and not engage in any more fandangoes during the holiday season except to have a merry Christmas and New Year." Demonstrating the selective memory for which older people are justly famous, Curtis declared that things were different when he was a youngster in Ohio: "Some amusement each day and a little relaxation Saturday afternoon, was all children required when we were learning." This from the fandango king of Licking County, who nearly caused his parents and siblings to despair![16]

Simpson, Curtis, and White gathered for the last time at the Union Pacific station in Omaha on December 22. The track now extended three hundred miles west to North Platte; simply getting to the newly laid rails was a twelve-hour journey each way. Curtis dreaded the trip, but he and his colleagues were in for a pleasant surprise. The company had recently acquired a special railroad car built for Abraham Lincoln. The president had never used the car in life, but it famously carried his coffin from Washington to Springfield for burial. The Lincoln Car, as it was known, was one of the most elegantly appointed vehicles on the continent; the commissioners traveled in unprecedented luxury. They had the car to themselves and were spared the "bustle and trouble which have attended former trips on this road." They were also the beneficiaries of special meals. "We fared sumptuously," Curtis recorded. The inspection went off without a hitch. Curtis assured Belinda that he was in "excellent health," despite the busy schedule and cold weather. In fact, he had only three days to live.[17]

While at North Platte, Curtis wrote an unusual letter to the *Keokuk Gate City*. It was both a progress report on the Union Pacific and a preview of what the completed railroad would mean for the Hawkeye state. Curtis began by declaring that he was writing from the "very end of the last rail," an astonishing seven hundred miles west of Keokuk: "This is realizing all my hopes, and accomplishing wonders for Iowa." He outlined the economic benefits the railroad would bring—indeed, was already bringing—to the state and the nation, benefits he had predicted in countless addresses and essays over the years. "I am more than ever convinced of our superior advantages and prospects," Curtis concluded, "and rejoice in my home in Iowa, on the banks of our bright and beautiful Mississippi." As a valedictory statement it could not have been improved upon.[18]

The commissioners left North Platte on Christmas Eve and returned to Omaha the next morning. After receiving their pay (a whopping $900 each), they decided to stay in town for the Christmas holiday and depart the following day. They checked into the Herndon House and prepared their report. Curtis dashed off a hasty letter to Belinda in which he explained where he was, expressed his regrets at missing another Christmas at home with family and friends, and announced that he had a "pocket full of green backs." He also revealed a newfound desire "to spend some money on a porch and other outside finish to our house," a statement that must have caused Belinda to jump for joy. Just before closing, Curtis mentioned that he was going to have Christmas dinner at the home of the publisher of the *Omaha Republican*. "I wish it was at our little round table," he added wistfully. Those were the last of the thousands of words he wrote to Belinda.[19]

The next morning, December 26, 1866, the commissioners took a carriage down the western bank of the Missouri River to a point opposite Council Bluffs. The river was frozen over, but Curtis thought the ice looked "somewhat doubtful." He suggested they walk across and have the carriage follow behind. It was a blustery day and the footing was poor, but everyone reached the eastern bank without any apparent difficulty. The commissioners climbed back into the carriage and set out for the nearest railroad station, twenty-two miles to the east, where they intended to catch the afternoon train to Des Moines. The carriage traveled only a few hundred feet before Dr. White noticed that Curtis was very pale. He asked if Curtis was all right but received no answer. A moment later, Curtis toppled over. Simpson and White took him to a nearby home and summoned two physicians from Council Bluffs, but nothing could be done. Curtis was dead at the age of sixty-one, most likely the victim of a stroke, then termed apoplexy. There had been no sign that something was amiss. Simpson informed Belinda that Curtis on his last morning was "in fine health and very lively, and had been for some time."[20]

• • •

Curtis's remains were taken by train to Keokuk. Union Pacific officials and prominent citizens from Omaha and Council Bluffs escorted the coffin. In Chicago, where a change of trains was made, an impromptu honor guard of former Union officers attended the transfer at the station. The funeral was held in Keokuk on December 30, 1866. It was an elaborate affair filled with pomp and circumstance. Businesses were closed and lampposts, storefronts, and residences were draped in black. U.S. flags were everywhere. Church bells tolled and an artillery salute of thirteen guns, appropriate for a major general, was fired as the procession wended its way from the Curtis home on High Street to Chatham Methodist Episcopal Church and from there to Oakland Cemetery. The Knights Templar and other Masonic orders turned out in full force and regalia to escort the hearse. Veterans of the Second Iowa followed behind, as did city officials, the Young America Fire Company, and a number of civic organizations.[21]

The winter sky was "bleak" and "cold winds swept the streets, making the day one of the most disagreeable of the season," but the frigid conditions failed to deter hundreds of people from joining the somber procession and crowding into the cemetery.

Curtis was interred in the family plot next to four of his children. Belinda later had a handsome granite obelisk placed over the grave. Henry made certain the monument displayed his brother's correct date of birth.[22]

• • •

Belinda outlived Samuel by more than two decades. In 1880 she applied for a widow's pension on the grounds that her husband's death was a direct result of the "exertions and anxieties" he had experienced during the Civil War. Sam, her attorney, argued that his father's parents and siblings had all lived exceptionally long and healthy lives, and that his death at the relatively youthful age of sixty-one was caused by the "hardships and exposure" he had endured in a series of long and difficult campaigns against rebels and Indians. Sam made the case that Curtis was as much a casualty of the war as any soldier struck down by a bullet. By a special act of Congress, Belinda was awarded $50 a month dating from the time of her husband's death, a substantial sum. The pension, combined with proceeds from the farms and the occasional sale of properties, provided her with a comfortable income. She died on February 3, 1888, aged seventy-six, and was buried alongside her husband.[23]

16

MEMORY

CURTIS COMPILED A LIST OF SUPERLATIVES ("FIRST," "FAR-thest," "longest") matched by few other Union generals. From the beginning of 1862 to the end of 1864, his name and image appeared regularly in newspapers across the North. Hardly had the war ended, however, before he and his accomplishments, civil and military, began to fade into the shadows.

Many of those who served with Curtis attempted to restore him to his rightful place in history. The most prominent was Philip Sheridan, a future general in chief of the army, who wrote in his autobiography, "I was always convinced that Curtis was deserving of the highest commendation, not only for the skill displayed on the field, but for a zeal and daring in campaign which was not often exhibited at that early period of the war." Sheridan was not alone in his opinion. Grenville Dodge, who gained fame and fortune after the war as the chief engineer of the Union Pacific, closely followed the course of Civil War historiography and was puzzled by the treatment accorded Curtis, his one-time commanding officer. "I have never thought that General Curtis has received the credit he was entitled to," Dodge wrote.[1]

The men in the ranks echoed their superiors. Richard Hinton served with Curtis in Kansas and produced the best participant account of the Westport campaign. "No officer in the army deserves greater credit than General Curtis, for the uniform success and devotion he has won and shown," Hinton declared. An Iowa artilleryman who took part in the Pea Ridge campaign felt much the same way. "I desire to say in just praise of Gen. Curtis that he fully merited the high esteem and respect entertained for him by his soldiers," wrote Samuel Black. "He was ever watchful for the welfare of his troops. He would frequently ask when riding along our line of march: 'Boys how are you? How are you standing the march?' He will not be forgotten by the boys in blue who followed him through the perils and hardships of that long and trying campaign." Dozens of other Union veterans, high and low, expressed similar sentiments, but their efforts had little effect.[2]

In a certain sense, Curtis cooperated in his own diminishment. He disliked promoting himself. For most of his life he naively believed he would be recognized and rewarded in proportion to his achievements, without the need for a public relations campaign. His early death in 1866 was another factor. Curtis did not live long enough to participate in the postwar squabbles among Civil War commanders. He wrote no memoir endorsing his own actions and disparaging those of others. His voice was stilled only eighteen months after the close of hostilities, which allowed puffed-up poseurs like Sigel, Schofield, and Pleasonton to produce self-serving accounts of the war in the West that slighted or ignored his role. Finally, his abolitionist sentiments and practices alienated many who strove to erase him from the history books.[3]

Curtis also was a victim of geography. He spent the entire war in the trans-Mississippi, a region too often dismissed, then and now, as being of little importance. Halleck, Grant, Sherman, Sheridan, and Schofield, among others, started out on the west side of the Mississippi River but eventually made their way to the east side, where opportunities for preference, promotion, and public recognition were greater. Curtis remained in the trans-Mississippi, far from the centers of power and publicity. Perhaps he preferred it that way. The West was his home. Like tens of thousands of other Union soldiers who served beyond the Great River, he fell victim to a sort of national amnesia.

And then there is the puzzling matter of Grant's animosity, evident as early as the fall of 1861 but never explained. Curtis was mystified by Grant's hostile attitude—the two men barely knew each other—and he eventually gave up trying to understand it. A possible explanation is that Grant, who was notorious for nursing slights and holding grudges, identified Curtis as a competitor for favor and promotion when both men served in the same department in 1861–62, and thereafter acted to check him at every opportunity. A less likely scenario is that Grant, a one-time regular officer, had it in for amateur soldiers, especially so-called political generals. But Curtis was a West Pointer and Mexican War veteran like Grant, and Grant would have gotten nowhere without the support of his own political patron, Illinois congressman Elihu B. Washburne. Neither explanation seems satisfactory. The mystery remains.

Only in Iowa was Curtis's memory, and the memory of his accomplishments, kept alive with monuments and memorials. In 1898 the state dedicated the Soldiers' and Sailors' Monument on the capitol grounds in Des Moines. The impressive neoclassical structure honors the more than seventy-six thousand Iowans who served in the Union army and navy during the Civil War. The base of the monument supports equestrian statues of Iowa's four most prominent military leaders: Curtis, Dodge, John M. Corse, and Marcellus Crocker. The statuary was the work of the distinguished Danish sculptor Carl Rohl-Smith. After a century of exposure to polluted air the monument was restored to its former glory in 1999.[4]

The citizens of Keokuk also remembered their most famous Civil War soldier. The state offered a duplicate casting of each statue on the Soldiers' and Sailors' Monument to the community most closely associated with the historical figure. The Gate City obtained a copy of the Curtis statue and purchased a tall granite pedestal from a quarry in Vermont. Keokuk lacks a town square, so the statue was initially placed at the intersection of Third and Main Streets in the center of the business district. A large crowd attended the dedication on July 4, 1898. Inevitably, the statue became an impediment to twentieth-century automobile traffic; in 1939 it was moved to Victory Park in Keokuk's historic waterfront district. Handsomely restored in 2019, the statue remains in the park today, only a few steps from the spot where Curtis first set foot on Iowa soil.[5]

Perhaps the most appropriate memorial to Curtis the soldier is Pea Ridge National Military Park in Arkansas, the site of his signature victory in the Civil War. In recent years the National Park Service has restored the historic landscape and introduced a new interpretive scheme that places Curtis at the center of events. The park visitor center displays the uniform coat and sword Curtis wore during the battle. But while the Pea Ridge battleground has survived in nearly pristine condition, the Westport battleground has not. Nearly all of the historic terrain and the memory of what Curtis achieved there have been lost to urban expansion and public indifference. Fortunately, the uniform coat worn by Curtis at Westport is preserved at Wilson's Creek National Battlefield in Missouri.

Curtis the engineer left his mark—literally—across the middle of the country. In addition to his home in Keokuk, he designed and constructed railways, roads, bridges, canals, locks, dams, dikes, sewers, and wharves on both sides of the Mississippi River. He even altered the course of the river itself at St. Louis. An array of plaques, markers, exhibits, and publications record his accomplishments. Finally, he was as much as anyone the father of the transcontinental railroad. No one worked longer or harder or in so many different roles to promote a connection with the Pacific Coast. He lived just long enough to see his vision becoming reality. In an interesting juxtaposition of time and place, the Union Pacific Railroad Museum in Omaha displays the swallowtail uniform coat Curtis wore as colonel of the Third Ohio in the Mexican War.

At one time or another Curtis was an engineer, architect, attorney, businessman, politician, soldier, and diplomat. In most of these endeavors he achieved a substantial measure of success. His personal life, however, was marred by repeated tragedy. He and Belinda enjoyed a warm and lasting relationship, but they endured long separations and suffered the loss of five of their seven children, all but one struck down by the dreadful epidemics that ravaged the United States in the nineteenth century.

Curtis left behind a substantial documentary trail. His voluminous papers are preserved in archives, libraries, and museums across the country from Connecticut to California. Readers interested in discovering more about Curtis and his place in American history, especially his role in preserving the Union, will find no shortage of information.

NOTES

Abbreviations

ALPL   Abraham Lincoln Presidential Library
BBC   Belinda Buckingham Curtis
HBC   Henry Barnes Curtis
HL   Huntington Library
HWH   Henry W. Halleck
LC   Library of Congress
MHMA   Missouri History Museum Archives
NARA   National Archives and Records Administration
NYHS   New-York Historical Society
OHCA   Ohio History Connection Archives
OR   U.S. War Department, *The War of the Rebellion*
ORN   U.S. Department of the Navy, *Official Records of the Union and Confederate Navies in the War of the Rebellion*
SHSI   State Historical Society of Iowa
SRC   Samuel Ryan Curtis
UA   University of Arkansas

1. Beginnings

1. Johnston, *Record of Connecticut Men*, 281; *Biographical Encyclopedia of Ohio*, 236; HBC deposition, May 11, 1880, Curtis Pension File, Veterans Administration, NARA.

2. *Biographical Encyclopedia of Ohio*, 236; *Biographical Record of Knox County*, 18. The settlement of early Ohio is described in Hurt, *Ohio Frontier*. The four Curtis daughters were Eunice, Eliza, Sarah, and Violette.

3. Hill, *History of Knox County*, 242, 644–46; John W. Warden to SRC, July 10, 1823, Curtis Papers, Yale; Smucker, *Centennial History of Licking County*, 68.

4. HBC to SRC, January 10 and 25, 1824, Curtis Papers, Yale.

5. HBC to SRC, July 12, 1824, Robert McComb to SRC, February 14, SRC to Hosmer Curtis, [February 15], and Hosmer Curtis to SRC, February 18, 1825, Curtis Papers, Yale.

6. Robert McComb to SRC, April 8, 1825, Curtis Papers, Yale. McComb was said to have a "deep sympathy with young men who were struggling to gain a foothold in life, and assisted many of them on the upward climb." Taylor, *Centennial History of Columbus*, 624–25.

7. Hosmer Curtis to SRC, June 2, HBC to SRC, July 24, and Amos H. Caffee to SRC, April 11, 1825, Curtis Papers, Yale.

8. [?] to SRC, June 4, 1830, and Zarah and Phally Curtis to SRC, January 9, 1826, Curtis Papers, Yale.

9. HBC to SRC, November 30, 1826, Curtis Papers, Yale.

10. HBC to SRC, November 30, 1826, Curtis Papers, Yale; *Register of the Officers and Cadets*, 15.

11. HBC to SRC, November 30 and December 12, 1826, Curtis Papers, Yale.

12. Ambrose, *Duty, Honor, Country*, 62–124; Hosmer Curtis to SRC, January 1, 1828, Curtis Papers, SHSI.

13. Burkard, "Edge of Glory," 3–6; Ambrose, *Duty, Honor, Country*, 62–124; HBC to SRC, July 22, 1827, Curtis Papers, Yale.

14. SRC to HBC, January 20, 1828, Curtis Papers, HL; SRC to Hosmer Curtis, January 12, 182[8], Curtis Papers, SHSI. Professor Charles Davies, Curtis's instructor, was widely considered to be the finest mathematician in the country.

15. Hosmer Curtis to SRC, March 2, and HBC to SRC, July 26, 1828, Curtis Papers, Yale; SRC to HBC, January 27, 1831, Gilder-Lehrman Collection, NYHS.

16. SRC to Hosmer Curtis, January 12, 182[8], and Hosmer Curtis to SRC, January 1, 1828, Curtis Papers, SHSI.

17. Chance, *Mexico Under Fire*, 100.

18. Chance, *Mexico Under Fire*, 99–100; SRC to [?], January 30, and to Samuel C. Ridgely, March 5, 1831, Curtis Papers, Yale. Curtis was replaced as superintendent of the mess hall in his final year. He wrote, but did not send, a strong note of protest.

19. Hosmer Curtis to SRC, April 5, and HBC to SRC, May 31, 1829, Curtis Papers, Yale; Chance, *Mexico Under Fire*, 100.

20. HBC to SRC, March 2, 1830, Curtis Papers, Yale.

21. HBC to SRC, November 13, 1830, Curtis Papers, SHSI.

22. HBC deposition, May 11, 1880, Curtis Pension File, Veterans Administration, NARA.

23. SRC to HBC, January 27, 1831, Gilder-Lehrman Collection, NYHS.

24. *Register of the Officers and Cadets*, 7; Cullum, *Biographical Register*, 491. Military academy graduates were required to serve four years on active duty beginning in 1838.

25. Hosmer Curtis to SRC, April 17, 1831, Curtis Papers, Yale; Agnew, *Fort Gibson*, 29–113.

26. BBC deposition, July 21, 1880, Curtis Pension File, Veterans Administration, NARA; Chance, *Mexico Under Fire*, 6. Phally Yale Curtis died on August 15, 1831, and was buried in Mound View Cemetery in Mount Vernon, Ohio.

27. Agnew, *Fort Gibson*, 29–113; HBC to SRC, November 30, 1826, Curtis Papers, Yale.

28. SRC to Luther M. Kennett, July 19, 1850, Curtis Papers, Yale.

29. SRC to Luther M. Kennett, July 19, 1850, Curtis Papers, Yale. A good introduction to the subject with much information on Ohio is Raitz, *National Road*.

30. December 24, 1859, Curtis Journal, ALPL; Rosenberg, *Cholera Years*, 13–98. Amanda died on June 1, 1834, and was buried in Mansfield, Ohio.

31. SRC to BBC, September 4, 1836, Curtis Papers, Yale.

32. SRC to BBC, September 4, 1836, Curtis Papers, Yale.

33. Shaw, *Canals for a Nation*, 126–59; Hosmer Curtis to SRC, April 17, 1831, Curtis Papers, Yale.

34. Andrews, *History of Marietta*, 272; Huntington and McClelland, *History of the Ohio Canals*, 27; *In Memoriam*, 54.

35. SRC to BBC, December 27–29, 1839, Curtis Papers, Yale. A skeleton map displays details of a road, canal, stream, or other feature but leaves the rest of the map blank.

36. SRC to BBC, September 4, 1836, Curtis Papers, Yale.

37. Chance, *Mexico Under Fire*, 100; SRC to Luther M. Kennett, July 19, 1850, Curtis Papers, Yale.

38. Scheiber, *Ohio Canal Era*, 110–12, 122–27.

39. Scheiber, *Ohio Canal Era*, 110; Huntington and McClelland, *History of the Ohio Canals*, 40.

40. American Society of Civil Engineers, "Muskingum River Navigation System."

41. SRC to Luther M. Kennett, July 19, 1850, Curtis Papers, Yale; *In Memoriam*, 54, 64–65.

42. SRC to Luther M. Kennett, July 19, 1850, Curtis Papers, Yale; *In Memoriam*, 54; "Profile of the Muskingum Valley Turnpike," Curtis Papers, OHCA; Curtis, *Muskingum Valley Turnpike*.

43. SRC to Luther M. Kennett, July 19, 1850, Curtis Papers, Yale; *Wooster Democrat*, July 17, 1845; Douglas, *History of Wayne County*, 293. A long-running advertisement on the front page of the *Wooster Democrat* informed readers that Curtis's law office was "two doors west of the American Hotel."

44. SRC to Luther M. Kennett, July 19, 1850, Curtis Papers, Yale.

45. Lee, *History of the City of Columbus*, 2:16. Ohio abolished the moribund state militia in 1844 and made the "volunteer militia" responsible for local defense and civic order. *Acts of a General Nature*, 42:53–60.

46. "Early Life of Major General Curtis" and "Unfinished Autobiography," Curtis Papers, Yale; *In Memoriam*, 55; Lee, *History of the City of Columbus*, 2:394.

2. Mexico

1. Winders, *Mr. Polk's Army*, 10–11, 74; Bauer, *Mexican War*, 69–72; "Early Life of Major General Curtis," Curtis Papers, Yale; Ryan, "Ohio in the Mex-

ican War," 280. A total of 7,857 Ohioans served in the Mexican War, 2,321 in the regular army and 5,536 in the volunteer regiments authorized by the president.

2. SRC to BBC, June 2, 1846, Curtis Papers, Yale. Curtis served as Ohio adjutant general from May 20 to June 24, 1846.

3. SRC to BBC, May 20 and 23, 1846, Curtis Papers, Yale.

4. Ryan, "Ohio in the Mexican War," 280; SRC to BBC, May 20, 21, and 23 and June 2, 1846, Curtis Papers, Yale.

5. Lee, *History of the City of Columbus*, 2:16–19; SRC to D. D. Tompkins, June 10, and to BBC, June 12 and 16, 1846, Curtis Papers, Yale.

6. SRC to BBC, June 16, 1846, Curtis Papers, Yale.

7. SRC to BBC, June 8, and John E. Wool to SRC, June 7–10, 1846, Curtis Papers, Yale.

8. SRC to HBC, July 5, 1846, Curtis Papers, HL; Chance, *Mexico Under Fire*, 3, 212.

9. *Columbus Ohio State Journal*, July 9, 1846.

10. Bauer, *Mexican War*, 32–84. An excellent study of these events is Murphy, *Two Armies on the Rio Grande*.

11. Chance, *Mexico Under Fire*, 4–5; SRC to HBC, July 5, 1846, Curtis Papers, HL; SRC to BBC, July 5, 1846, Curtis Papers, Yale.

12. Chance, *Mexico Under Fire*, 5–6.

13. Chance, *Mexico Under Fire*, 6.

14. SRC to BBC, July 11, 1846, Curtis Papers, Yale; Chance, *Mexico Under Fire*, 7.

15. SRC to HBC, July 11, 1846, Curtis Papers, HL; SRC to BBC, July 11, 1846, Curtis Papers, Yale; Chance, *Mexico Under Fire*, 7.

16. Chance, *Mexico Under Fire*, 8–10.

17. SRC to HBC, July 20, 1846, Curtis Papers, HL. Brazos Island was an island only at high tide. At low tide it was a peninsula that extended north from the mouth of the Rio Grande.

18. Chance, *Mexico Under Fire*, 98; Bauer, *Mexican War*, 83–84.

19. SRC to BBC, July 20 and 25, 1846, Curtis Papers, Yale; Chance, *Mexico Under Fire*, 12–15.

20. Chance, *Mexico Under Fire*, 16.

21. Chance, *Mexico Under Fire*, 22; Winders, *Mr. Polk's Army*, 84–87.

22. Bauer, *Mexican War*, 57–58, 83.

23. Chance, *Mexico Under Fire*, 22.

24. Chance, *Mexico Under Fire*, 27–31; SRC to BBC, December 22, 1846, Curtis Papers, Yale.

25. Chance, *Mexico Under Fire*, 31–34; SRC to BBC, September 10 and 19, 1846, Curtis Papers, Yale; SRC to HBC, September 7, 1846, Curtis Papers, HL.

26. Chance, *Mexico Under Fire*, 24–25, 34–35, 39; Winders, *Mr. Polk's Army*, 139–57; SRC to HBC, September 7, 1846, Curtis Papers, HL.

27. Chance, *Mexico Under Fire*, 42–43; SRC to HBC, December 31, 1846, Curtis Papers, HL.

28. Bauer, *Mexican War*, 87–101. The standard account of the Monterrey campaign is Dishman, *Perfect Gibraltar*.

29. Chance, *Mexico Under Fire*, 47–54; SRC to BBC, October 21 and November 16, 1846, Curtis Papers, Yale.

30. Chance, *Mexico Under Fire*, 43–44; SRC to BBC, October 21 and November 4, 1846, and February 16, 1847, Curtis Papers, Yale. The "horned frog" was still alive in March 1847.

31. SRC to BBC, October 18, 1846, and April 19, 1847, Curtis Papers, Yale.

32. SRC to BBC, January 6, 1847, Curtis Papers, Yale; Chance, *Mexico Under Fire*, 46, 64, 74.

33. Chance, *Mexico Under Fire*, 84–85.

34. Chance, *Mexico Under Fire*, 85–86.

35. Chance, *Mexico Under Fire*, 96.

36. Chance, *Mexico Under Fire*, 88–89; SRC to HBC, December 31, 1846, Curtis Papers, HL.

37. Bauer, *Mexican War*, 232–38; Johnson, *Gallant Little Army*, 14–18; Chance, *Mexico Under Fire*, 101.

38. Chance, *Mexico Under Fire*, 92, 110; SRC to HBC, January 27, 1847, Curtis Papers, HL.

39. Chance, *Mexico Under Fire*, 108–10; SRC to HBC, January 27, 1847, Curtis Papers, HL.

40. Bauer, *Mexican War*, 204–6; Chance, *Mexico Under Fire*, 113–23; SRC to HBC, January 27, 1847, Curtis Papers, HL; SRC to BBC, February 12, 1847, Curtis Papers, Yale.

41. Chance, *Mexico Under Fire*, 122–23; SRC to BBC, February 12, 1847, Curtis Papers, Yale.

42. Chance, *Mexico Under Fire*, 122–26; SRC to BBC, February 12, 1847, Curtis Papers, Yale.

43. SRC to BBC, February 16 and 25, 1847, Curtis Papers, Yale.

44. Chance, *Mexico Under Fire*, 127; SRC to BBC, February 25, 1847, Curtis Papers, Yale; SRC to HBC, February 17, 1847, Curtis Papers, HL.

45. SRC to BBC, February 16 and 25, 1847, Curtis Papers, Yale.

46. Bauer, *Mexican War*, 218–19; Chance, *Mexico Under Fire*, 133–40; SRC to BBC, February 26 and March 2, 1847, Curtis Papers, Yale.

47. Bauer, *Mexican War*, 219–20; Chance, *Mexico Under Fire*, 112–13, 141–42; Chaffin and Cohen, *Correspondence of James K. Polk*, 12:108; SRC to BBC, March 3, 1847, Curtis Papers, Yale. Surgeon Nathan S. Jarvis carried the letter to Washington. He also carried a box containing Curtis's watch and second journal, which he mailed to Wooster. The watch belonged to Major General Mariano Arista, the officer who had opposed Taylor at Palo Alto and Resaca de la Palma. It was described as a "splendid old fashioned gold watch said

to have cost five hundred dollars." The Spanish consul in Matamoros presented the watch to Curtis. SRC to BBC, January 6, 1847, Curtis Papers, Yale.

48. Quaife, *Diary of James K. Polk*, 2:434–38, 451–52.

49. The best account of the battle is Lavender, *Climax at Buena Vista*.

50. SRC to BBC, March 3 and 12, 1847, Curtis Papers, Yale; SRC to HBC, March 24, 1847, Curtis Papers, HL; Chance, *Mexico Under Fire*, 150.

51. Chance, *Mexico Under Fire*, 157–60, 162–64; SRC to BBC, March 19, 1847, Curtis Papers, Yale; SRC to HBC, March 24, 1847, Curtis Papers, HL.

52. Chance, *Mexico Under Fire*, 164–65.

53. Chance, *Mexico Under Fire*, 164, 166; SRC to BBC, April 7, 1847, Curtis Papers, Yale.

54. Chance, *Mexico Under Fire*, 175–77; SRC to HBC, March 24, 1847, Curtis Papers, HL.

55. Chance, *Mexico Under Fire*, 185–86; SRC to BBC, April 7, 1847, Curtis Papers, Yale; SRC to HBC, March 24, 1847, Curtis Papers, HL.

56. Chance, *Mexico Under Fire*, 189–93.

57. Chance, *Mexico Under Fire*, 185–86; SRC to HBC, June 1, 1847, Curtis Papers, HL; SRC to BBC, May 2, 1847, Curtis Papers, Yale.

58. Chance, *Mexico Under Fire*, 186–93; SRC to HBC, May 25, 1847, Curtis Papers, HL; SRC to BBC, May 21, 1847, Curtis Papers, Yale.

59. Chance, *Mexico Under Fire*, 194–95; SRC to HBC, June 1, 1847, Curtis Papers, HL; SRC to BBC, June 2, 1847, Curtis Papers, Yale.

60. Chance, *Mexico Under Fire*, 188–89.

61. Chance, *Mexico Under Fire*, 199–208; SRC to BBC, June 10 and 11, 1847, Curtis Papers, Yale.

62. SRC to BBC, July 20, 1847, Curtis Papers, Yale; SRC to HBC, August 1, 1847, Curtis Papers, HL.

63. Chance, *Mexico Under Fire*, 208–9.

64. SRC to HBC, August 1, 1847, Curtis Papers, HL.

3. Engineering

1. SRC to HBC, November 14, 1847, Curtis Papers, HL. The Treaty of Guadalupe Hidalgo, which ended the war, was signed on February 2 and ratified on May 30, 1848. Bauer, *Mexican War*, 378–88.

2. Hubler, "Des Moines River Navigation," 287–94.

3. *Report of the Board of Public Works*, 6.

4. *Report of the Board of Public Works*, 6; SRC to HBC, November 14, 1847, Curtis Papers, HL.

5. SRC to HBC, November 14, 1847, Curtis Papers, HL; SRC to BBC, November 26 and December 3, 1847, Curtis Papers, Yale.

6. SRC to BBC, December 11, 1847, Curtis Papers, Yale. Curtis wrote that the "rapids are not such as to offer picturesque scenery. It is merely a long rough rocky ripple, so shallow that boats cannot get over it."

7. SRC to BBC, December 11, 1847, Curtis Papers, Yale.

8. SRC to BBC, December 11, 1847, Curtis Papers, Yale.

9. SRC to BBC, December 11 and 22, 1847, Curtis Papers, Yale.

10. SRC to BBC, January 9, 184[8], Curtis Papers, Yale. Curtis incorrectly dated this letter 1847.

11. SRC to BBC, December 22, 1847, and January 9, 184[8], Curtis Papers, Yale.

12. SRC to BBC, January 9, 1848, Curtis Papers Yale.

13. SRC to BBC, February 28 and March 8, 1848, Curtis Papers, Yale.

14. Curtis, "Engineer's Report, No. 1," *Journal of the House of Representatives*, 94–99; *Report of the Board of Public Works*, 8.

15. Douglas, *History of the Lawyers*, 302–3; Cullum, *Biographical Register*, 419; *Keokuk Dispatch*, July 2, 1850.

16. SRC to BBC, February 28, 1848, Curtis Papers, Yale; Curtis, *Engineer's Report No. 1*; Clemens, *City of Keokuk*, 30.

17. Curtis, "Engineer's Report, No. 2," *Journal of the House of Representatives*, 124–200.

18. National Register of Historic Places, "Gen. Samuel R. Curtis House"; February 4, 1851, Curtis Journal, MHMA.

19. SRC to HBC, July 22, 1849, Curtis Papers, HL; National Register of Historic Places, "Gen. Samuel R. Curtis House."

20. SRC to HBC, July 22, 1849, Curtis Papers, HL. Zarah Curtis died on June 7, 1849, and was buried alongside his wife in Mound View Cemetery in Mount Vernon, Ohio.

21. SRC to HBC, July 22, 1849, Curtis Papers, Yale; Rosenberg, *Cholera Years*, 101–20.

22. Hubler, "Des Moines River Navigation," 295–306; *Keokuk Dispatch*, July 16, 1850; BBC to SRC, July 3, 1849, Curtis Papers, Yale; SRC to HBC, July 22, 1849, Curtis Papers, HL.

23. Curtis, "Engineer's Report, No. 3," *Journal of the Senate*, 86–89. The pamphlet version is Curtis, *Engineer's Report, No. 3*.

24. Swisher, "Des Moines River Improvement Project," 142–80.

25. SRC to HBC, July 22, 1849, December 9, 1850, and January 7, 1852, Curtis Papers, HL.

26. SRC to Henry Z. and Samuel S. Curtis, March 16, and BBC to same, March 19, 1850, Curtis Papers, Yale.

27. SRC to Henry Z. and Samuel S. Curtis, March 16, and BBC to same, March 19, 1850, Curtis Papers, Yale.

28. SRC to HBC, July 22, 1849, Curtis Papers, HL.

29. Dietzler, "Major General Samuel Ryan Curtis," 356–58.

30. SRC to Luther M. Kennett, July 19, 1850, Curtis Papers, Yale; *Revised Ordinances*, 182.

31. Dietzler, "Major General Samuel Ryan Curtis," 358; Freeman, *R.E. Lee*, 1:140–58, 170–83.

32. December 27 and 31, 1850, and April 22, 1851, Curtis Journal, MHMA.

33. May 28–31 and June 1–11, 1851, Curtis Journal, MHMA.

34. SRC to city council, July 22, 1851; undated clipping from *St. Louis Republican*; January 24 and February 5, 1852, Curtis Journal, MHMA.

35. SRC to city council, August 13, 1852; undated clipping from *St. Louis Republican*; March 14, 1852, Curtis Journal, MHMA.

36. Dietzler, "Major General Samuel Ryan Curtis," 356–57; Christensen, "Henry Kayser," *Dictionary of Missouri Biography*, 446; Stevens, *St. Louis*, 1:264–65.

37. October 20 and December 20 and 24, 1850, February 21 and 27, 1851, Curtis Journal, MHMA.

38. SRC to BBC, November 2, 1850, Curtis Papers, Yale; undated clipping from *St. Louis Intelligencer*; April 17, 1851, and 14 and 27 February 1852, Curtis Journal, MHMA. Washington Square was obliterated when a new city hall was constructed on the site in 1904.

39. SRC to BBC, November 2 and December 17, 1850, and February 8 and March 21, 1851, Curtis Papers, Yale; December 12, 25, and 27, 1850, Curtis Journal, MHMA.

40. SRC to HBC, December 9, 1850, Curtis Papers, Yale; October 26, 1850, Curtis Journal, MHMA.

41. March 17, 1851, Curtis Journal, MHMA; Rosenberg, *Jenny Lind in America*, 181–89.

42. October 8, 1850, and April 11 and 24, May 16 and 23, June 13, and July 4–5, 1851, Curtis Journal, MHMA. Yale and Bucky were buried in the Curtis family plot in Oakland Cemetery in Keokuk.

43. July 12 and 14, 1851, Curtis Journal, MHMA; SRC to BBC, September 8, 1851, Curtis Papers, Yale.

44. October 20 and December 16, 1851, and January 19, 1852, Curtis Journal, MHMA; SRC to HBC, January 7, 1852, Curtis Papers, Yale.

45. SRC to HBC, January 7, 1852, and August 30, 1853, Curtis Papers, Yale; January 16, 1852, and enclosed bill for piano lessons dated December 29, 1852, Curtis Journal, MHMA.

46. SRC to HBC, January 7 and December 15, 1852, Curtis Papers, Yale; August 30, 1851, and January 24, 1852, Curtis Journal, MHMA.

47. SRC to HBC, January 7 and December 15, 1852, Curtis Papers, Yale.

48. SRC to HBC, August 30, 1853, Curtis Papers, Yale; Tarver and Cobb, "Philadelphia, Fort Wayne and Platte River," 367.

49. SRC to Erasmus Gest, August 30, 1853, Gest Papers, OHCA.

50. SRC to HBC, August 30, 1853, Curtis Papers, Yale.

51. SRC to HBC, August 30, 1853, Curtis Papers, Yale; Curtis, *Proceedings of a Pacific Railroad Convention*, 3–14; *History of Madison County*, 387; SRC

to Erasmus Gest, January 30, February 4 and 24, March 11 and 17, and August 8, 1854, Gest Papers, OHCA; SRC to Henry Z. Curtis and Samuel S. Curtis, February 24 and March 15, 1854, Curtis Papers, SHSI.

52. SRC to Erasmus Gest, February 24, March 27, and April 3, 1854, Gest Papers, OHCA; SRC to Henry Z. Curtis, March 27, 1854, Curtis Papers, SHSI.

53. SRC to Henry Z. Curtis and Samuel S. Curtis, August 31, 1851, and March 15, 1854, and to Henry Z. Curtis, March 3, 1854, Curtis Papers, SHSI.

54. SRC to Erasmus Gest, March 11, April 26, and October 20, 1854, Gest Papers, OHCA; SRC to Henry Z. Curtis, February 2 and October 22, 1854, Curtis Papers, SHSI.

55. SRC to HBC, August 30, 1853, Curtis Papers, Yale; SRC to Erasmus Gest, November 16, 1853, Gest Papers, OHCA.

56. Curtis, "Habits of Missouri River," 383–87.

57. Curtis, "Habits of Missouri River," 383–87; May 22, 1852, Curtis Journal, MHMA.

58. SRC to Thomas B. Cuming, May 10, 1851, Cuming-Hamilton Collection, Joslyn Art Museum.

59. Curtis, "Desmoines Valley," 187–90; SRC to Erasmus Gest, December 4, 1853, Gest Papers, OHCA.

4. Business and Politics

1. SRC to Henry Z. Curtis, May 15, 1854, Curtis Papers, Yale.

2. SRC to Henry Z. Curtis, May 15, 1854, Curtis Papers, Yale.

3. SRC to Henry Z. Curtis, May 15, and to HBC, March 1 and May 25, 1855, April 22 and August 15, 1856, and August 16, 1857, Curtis Papers, Yale; Enos Lowe to SRC, September 29, 1855, and January 23, 1856, Cuming Papers, Nebraska State Historical Society; *Laws, Resolutions and Memorials*, 448.

4. SRC to HBC, February 5 and March 1, 1855, and March 6 and August 15, 1856, and Henry Z. Curtis to SRC, January 30, 1859, Curtis Papers, Yale; SRC to HBC, August 14, 1857, Curtis Papers, HL; SRC to HBC, February 24, 1856, Henry Barnes Curtis Papers, OHCA.

5. SRC to BBC, March 10 and 15, Henry Z. Curtis to BBC, September 15, Samuel S. Curtis to BBC, November 12 and 24, 1854, and SRC to HBC, April 22, May 17, and August 31, 1856, Curtis Papers, Yale; SRC to HBC, February 24, 1856, Henry Barnes Curtis Papers, OHCA; SRC to Henry Z. Curtis and Samuel S. Curtis, March 15 and October 22, 1854, Curtis Papers, SHSI; Griswold, *Pictorial History*, 435–36.

6. SRC to HBC, August 15, 1856, August 11, 1859, and April 12 and December 12, 1861, Curtis Papers, Yale; SRC to HBC, February 24, 1856, Henry Barnes Curtis Papers, OHCA; Cole and Ebersole, *Courts and Legal Profession*, 2:759, 769.

7. SRC to HBC, January 7, 1852, Curtis Papers, Yale.

8. National Register of Historic Places, "Gen. Samuel R. Curtis House"; SRC to Henry Z. Curtis, May 15, 1855 and August 31, 1857, Curtis Papers, Yale; SRC to HBC, August 14, 1857, Curtis Papers, HL. The addition altered the roofline and changed the footprint of the house from an L to a near-square.

9. SRC to HBC, March 11, May 25, and December 8, 1855, January 9, 1856, and September 9 and 20, 1857, Curtis Papers, Yale.

10. SRC to HBC, November 18, 1860, Curtis Papers, Yale.

11. December 22, 1850, and January 5, 1851, Curtis Journal, MHMA.

12. The emergence of the Republican Party is presented in Rosenberg, *Iowa on the Eve of the Civil War*.

13. *Keokuk Daily Post*, April 8, May 16, and August 21, 1856; SRC to HBC, April 22, 1856, Curtis Papers, Yale; *Keokuk Dispatch*, May 13, 1856; Clemens, *City of Keokuk in 1856*, 4–14; Roberts and Moorhead, *Story of Lee County*, 1:145; Twain, *Life on the Mississippi*, 404.

14. SRC to BBC, July 27, 1856, Curtis Papers, Yale; Rosenberg, *Iowa on the Eve of the Civil War*, 12–16, 137–38, 145.

15. Stiles, *Recollections and Sketches*, 131; *Keokuk Daily Post*, September 21, 1856; SRC to HBC, August 15, 1856, Curtis Papers, Yale; Rosenberg, *Iowa on the Eve of the Civil War*, 142. The description of Curtis dates from his 1860 re-election campaign, but I have taken the liberty of placing it here.

16. SRC to HBC, September 20, 1856, Curtis Papers, Yale; Chaffin, *Path-finder*, 435–48.

17. SRC to Henry Z. Curtis, January 18, 1857, Curtis Papers, Yale.

18. SRC to Henry Z. Curtis, January 18, 1857, Curtis Papers, Yale.

19. SRC to Henry Z. and Samuel S. Curtis, February 5, 1858, and to HBC, September 9 and 20, 1857, and November 18, 1858, Curtis Papers, Yale; SRC to HBC, December 15, 1857, Curtis Papers, HL. On one occasion Curtis estimated his monthly expenses at $115, on another at $135. I have averaged the two figures.

20. SRC to HBC, December 15, 1857, Curtis Papers, HL; SRC to Henry Z. and Samuel S. Curtis, April 3, 1858, Curtis Papers, Yale.

21. SRC to HBC, June 22, 1856, and June 27, 1857, Curtis Letters, Yale; Samuel S. Curtis to HBC, June 2 and July 8, 1857, Curtis Papers, HL.

22. Samuel S. Curtis to HBC, June 2, 1857, Curtis Papers, HL; SRC to HBC, June 27, 1857, Curtis Papers, Yale.

23. Henry Z. Curtis to SRC, October 24, 1857, and SRC to Henry Z. Curtis, September 9 and October 24, 1857, Curtis Papers, Yale; SRC to HBC, August 4 and December 15, 1857, Curtis Papers, HL. The causes and consequences of the crash are described in Huston, *Panic of 1857*.

24. SRC to Henry Z. and Samuel S. Curtis, October 12, 1857, Curtis Papers, Yale.

25. Samuel S. Curtis to Henry Z. Curtis, August 9, 1857, Henry Z. Curtis to SRC, September 18 and October 25, 1857, and SRC to HBC, September 20, 1857, Curtis Papers, Yale; SRC to HBC, August 14, 1857, Curtis Papers, HL.

26. SRC to Henry Z. and Samuel S. Curtis, October 24, and to HBC, August 31 and September 20, 1857, Curtis Papers, Yale.

27. SRC to John B. Floyd, January 29, to HBC, January 7, and to Henry Z. and Samuel S. Curtis, February 5, 1858, Curtis Papers, Yale; Curtis, *Central American Question*; Curtis, *Remarks*.

28. SRC to Henry Z. and Samuel S. Curtis, February 5, and to HBC, January 7, 1858, Curtis Papers, Yale.

29. SRC to HBC, June 4, 1858, Curtis Papers, Yale.

30. Sparks, "Iowa Republicans," 274–75, 284; Rosenberg, *Iowa on the Eve of the Civil War*, 146–47, 178.

31. Sparks, "Iowa Republicans," 284; SRC to HBC, January 13, 1859, and April 20, 1860, Curtis Papers, Yale.

32. SRC to Samuel S. Curtis, October 21, and to HBC, November 18, 1858, and August 11, 1859, Curtis Papers, Yale.

33. SRC to HBC, January 9, 1860, Curtis Papers, Yale; Smiley, *Semi-Centennial History*, 1:233–37; Colton, "Irrepressible Conflict," 36. Sam named Curtis Street and Curtis Park for himself. The Curtis Park neighborhood is now a trendy residential and commercial area in central Denver.

34. Dudley, "Notes on the Early Military History," 166–96; Thayer, "Pawnee War," 231–46.

35. SRC to HBC, December 4, 1859, Curtis Papers, Yale; December 7 and 17, 1859, Curtis Journal, ALPL.

36. December 5, 1859, Curtis Journal, ALPL; SRC to BBC, December [25], 1860, Curtis Papers, Yale.

37. SRC to HBC, December 4 and 8, 1859, and November 18, 1860, Curtis Papers, Yale; December 5 and 6, 1859, Curtis Journal, ALPL.

38. December 8, 12, 20, 23, and 24, 1859, and January 4, 10, and 19, 1860, Curtis Journal, ALPL.

39. December 17, 1859, Curtis Journal, ALPL.

40. SRC to BBC, June 22, and to HBC, June 16 and 18, July 27, September 30, and November 18, 1860, Curtis Papers, Yale; November 6–12, 1860, Curtis Journal, ALPL; Curtis, *To the People*; Sparks, "Iowa Republicans," 284; Rosenberg, *Iowa on the Eve of the Civil War*, 222.

41. SRC to BBC, December 3 and [25], and to HBC, December 4, 1860, Curtis Papers, Yale.

42. SRC to BBC, December 30, 1860, Curtis Papers, Yale.

43. SRC to BBC, December [25], 1860, Curtis Papers, Yale; December 5, 1860, Curtis Journal, ALPL.

44. SRC to HBC, December 5, and Committee Invitation, December 27, 1860, Curtis Papers, Yale; December 5–28, 1860, and January 11–18, 1861, Curtis Journal, ALPL.

45. Davis, *Union Pacific Railway*, 90–95; January 23, February 3 and 27, March 1–10, May 14 and 24, and December 19–20, 1860, Curtis Journal, ALPL.

46. Davis, *Union Pacific Railway*, 95; January 5 and 9, February 1, 4, 7, 12, and 14, and March [3], 1861, Curtis Journal, ALPL.

47. SRC to HBC, January 11, February 12, and April 1, 1861, Curtis Papers, Yale; January 10–11, February 3, 15–16, and 21, and March 4, 1861, Curtis Journal, ALPL.

48. Colton, "Irrepressible Conflict," 36; SRC to HBC, April 1, 1861, Curtis Papers, Yale; Curtis, "Army of the South-West," 628.

5. General

1. Colton, "Irrepressible Conflict," 24.

2. Colton, "Irrepressible Conflict," 40–41; Curtis, "Army of the South-West," 628–29.

3. SRC to Sarah B. Curtis, April 22, 1861 (two letters), Curtis Papers, Yale; Colton, "Irrepressible Conflict," 40–42; Curtis, "Army of the South-West," 629.

4. Butler, *Butler's Book*, 199–200.

5. Colton, "Irrepressible Conflict," 43–44; Curtis, "Army of the South-West," 630. The incredulous commissary officer was Lieutenant Colonel Joseph P. Taylor, who had been appointed to that position in 1829.

6. Colton, "Irrepressible Conflict," 46; *Keokuk Gate City*, May 24, 1861. Keokuk was selected because it was the southernmost Iowa town on the Mississippi River, not because Curtis lived there.

7. Colton, "Irrepressible Conflict," 46.

8. Colton, "Irrepressible Conflict," 54.

9. Parrish, *History of Missouri*, 3:1–29.

10. Colton, "Irrepressible Conflict," 56.

11. Colton, "Irrepressible Conflict," 56.

12. Curtis, "Report on Operations of Iowa Troops," 358–67; SRC to BBC, June 16, 1861, Curtis Papers, Yale; *Keokuk Gate City*, January 27, 1863; Curtis, "Army of the South-West," 631–33; Piston and Hatcher, *Wilson's Creek*, 47–59.

13. Colton, "Irrepressible Conflict," 57–58.

14. Colton, "With Fremont in Missouri," 106–8.

15. SRC to HBC, July 23, 1861, Curtis Papers, Yale; Curtis, "Army of the South-West," 634. The battle is ably recounted in Hennessy, *First Battle of Manassas*.

16. SRC to HBC, July 23, 1861, Curtis Papers, Yale.

17. SRC to HBC, July 23, 1861, Curtis Papers, Yale; Colton, "With Fremont in Missouri," 114–17.

18. Colton, "With Fremont in Missouri," 113–16.

19. SRC to HBC, July 23, 1861, Curtis Papers, Yale.

20. Colton, "With Fremont in Missouri," 117–20.

21. Gen. Orders No. 1, August 12, 1861, Curtis File, Adjutant General's Office, NARA; Colton, "With Fremont in Missouri," 120–22; Winter, *Civil*

War in St. Louis, 5–7. Jefferson Barracks County Park preserves several of the original buildings.

22. Winter, *Civil War in St. Louis*, 73–75. Fremont named the new post for Senator Thomas H. Benton, his deceased father-in-law. Fairground Park occupies much of the site today.

23. Colton, "With Fremont in Missouri," 128–32.

24. Gen. Orders No. 1, September 8, 1861, Curtis File, Adjutant General's Office, NARA; SRC to HBC, August [3] and October 1, 1861, Curtis Papers, Yale; Colton, "With Fremont in Missouri," 127–32.

25. Colton, "With Fremont in Missouri," 132; SRC to HBC, October 1, 1861, Curtis Papers, Yale.

26. Piston and Hatcher, *Wilson's Creek*, 44–47, 72–91.

27. Piston and Hatcher, *Wilson's Creek*, 92–118.

28. Piston and Hatcher, *Wilson's Creek*, 118–21; SRC to HBC, August [3], 1861, Curtis Papers, Yale.

29. Piston and Hatcher, *Wilson's Creek*, 138–313; Colton, "With Fremont in Missouri," 122–23.

30. Piston and Hatcher, *Wilson's Creek*, 313–16; Colton, "With Fremont in Missouri," 126, 136.

31. Chaffin, *Pathfinder*, 455–73; Colton, "With Fremont in Missouri," 126.

32. Basler, *Collected Works of Abraham Lincoln*, 4:550–51.

33. OR, 3:540–42.

34. Colton, "With Fremont in Missouri," 139–42.

35. SRC to HBC, October 12, 1861, Curtis Papers, Yale; SRC to HBC, December 1, 1861, Curtis Papers, HL; Colton, "With Fremont in Missouri," 119; Curtis, "Army of the South-West," 635.

36. Basler, *Collected Works of Abraham Lincoln*, 4:562–63.

37. Basler, *Collected Works of Abraham Lincoln*, 4:562–63; Colton, "With Fremont in Missouri," 151.

38. Basler, *Collected Works of Abraham Lincoln*, 4:563; OR, 3:559.

39. Colton, "With Fremont in Missouri," 152–56, 161.

40. OR, 3:560, 569; Colton, "With Fremont in Missouri," 163–64, and "Frontier War Problems," 303–4; SRC to HBC, December 1, 1861, Curtis Papers, HL.

41. "Military Service," 3, Curtis Papers, SHSI; Simon, *Papers of Ulysses S. Grant*, 3:177.

42. OR, 3:567, 8:368–69. The best Halleck biography is Marszalek, *Commander of All Lincoln's Armies*, but it has relatively little to say about his time in St. Louis or his relationship with Curtis.

43. Shea and Hess, *Pea Ridge*, 3; SRC to HBC, December 1, 1861, Curtis Papers, HL. The Planters' House was located next to the Old Courthouse on Fourth Street between Chestnut and Pine. It was demolished in 1891.

44. Shea and Hess, *Pea Ridge*, 3–5.

6. Ozarkia

1. December 27 and 28, 1861, Curtis Journal, ALPL; Curtis, "Army of the South-West," 641; OR, 8:473. Belinda, Sadie, and Carrie moved into a boardinghouse in St. Louis after leaving Benton Barracks.

2. Hess, "Sigel's Resignation," 5–17. The standard Sigel biography is Engle, *Yankee Dutchman.*

3. Colton, "Frontier War Problems," 306–7; December 31, 1861, Curtis Journal, ALPL.

4. Shea and Hess, *Pea Ridge,* 7–9; SRC to HBC, January 30, 1862, Curtis Papers, HL.

5. SRC to HBC, February 25, 1862, Curtis Papers, HL; OR, 8:490, 513–14; Shea and Hess, *Pea Ridge,* 10–11; January 12 and 19, 1862, Curtis Journal, ALPL; Sheridan, *Personal Memoirs,* 1:127–28; Special Orders No. 15, January 4, 1862, General Orders, and HWH to SRC, February 12, 1862, Letters Received, NARA.

6. Shea and Hess, *Pea Ridge,* 11; SRC to Francis J. Herron, January 12, 1862, Herron Papers, NYHS.

7. January 6–7, 1862, Curtis Journal, ALPL.

8. SRC to HBC, January 30, 1862, Curtis Papers, HL. An adjutant managed the flow of paperwork (orders, reports, correspondence) in and out of a military headquarters.

9. Shea and Hess, *Pea Ridge,* 9–10; OR, 8:472.

10. Shea and Hess, *Pea Ridge,* 9–10; January 1, 1862, Curtis Journal, ALPL; OR, 8:490.

11. Shea and Hess, *Pea Ridge,* 10; January 13, 1862, Curtis Journal, ALPL; OR, 8:499, 506.

12. Shea and Hess, *Pea Ridge,* 12–14; OR, 8:488–89, 499, 528.

13. OR, 8:540; Franz Sigel to SRC, January 28 and February 2, 1862, Letters Received, and SRC to Alexander S. Asboth, February 1, 1862, Letters Sent, NARA.

14. Curtis, "Army of the South-West," 676; OR, 8:527.

15. SRC to HBC, January 30 and February 25, 1862, Curtis Papers, HL; Sheridan, *Personal Memoirs,* 1:129.

16. Curtis, "Army of the South-West," 679–81; Shea and Hess, *Pea Ridge,* 14; SRC to HBC, January 30, 1862, Curtis Papers, HL.

17. Shea and Hess, *Pea Ridge,* 14.

18. OR, 8:544, 514; SRC to HBC, January 30, 1862, Curtis Papers, HL.

19. Shea and Hess, *Pea Ridge,* 25–27.

20. Shea and Hess, *Pea Ridge,* 28.

21. SRC to HWH, February 13, 1862, Letters Sent, and Alexander S. Asboth and Eugene A. Carr to SRC, both February 13, 1862, Letters Received, NARA; Curtis, "Army of the South-West," 725–27.

22. Shea and Hess, *Pea Ridge,* 29–30.

23. OR, 8:556, 596.

24. Shea and Hess, *Pea Ridge*, 30–34.

25. Shea and Hess, *Pea Ridge*, 34–36; SRC to HBC, February 25, 1862, Curtis Papers, HL; OR, 8:558.

26. Shea and Hess, *Pea Ridge*, 39; OR, 8:560.

27. Shea and Hess, *Pea Ridge*, 39–44.

28. Shea and Hess, *Pea Ridge*, 44. This engagement is also known as Dunagin's Farm.

29. Shea and Hess, *Pea Ridge*, 46; OR, 8:559.

30. Shea and Hess, *Pea Ridge*, 45–50.

31. Shea and Hess, *Pea Ridge*, 50–51; OR, 8:562.

32. Shea and Hess, *Pea Ridge*, 51–53.

33. Shea and Hess, *Pea Ridge*, 52.

34. Shea and Hess, *Pea Ridge*, 52–53.

35. John Miller to SRC, February 25, and Proclamation, March 1, 1862, Curtis Papers, SHSI.

36. SRC to HBC, February 25, 1862, Curtis Papers, HL.

37. Shea and Hess, *Pea Ridge*, 52–53.

38. OR, 8:577, 588–89.

39. Shea and Hess, *Pea Ridge*, 19–25, 55–58.

40. Shea and Hess, *Pea Ridge*, 59.

41. Shea and Hess, *Pea Ridge*, 62–65.

42. Shea and Hess, *Pea Ridge*, 65–66; OR, 8:592.

43. Shea and Hess, *Pea Ridge*, 66; OR, 8:592.

44. Shea and Hess, *Pea Ridge*, 67–68; OR, 8:198.

45. Shea and Hess, *Pea Ridge*, 68–70.

46. Shea and Hess, *Pea Ridge*, 70–77.

47. Shea and Hess, *Pea Ridge*, 78–84.

48. Shea and Hess, *Pea Ridge*, 84–87.

7. Pea Ridge

1. Shea and Hess, *Pea Ridge*, 88–89. Pea Ridge National Military Park preserves the entire battleground in a nearly pristine condition.

2. Shea and Hess, *Pea Ridge*, 89.

3. Shea and Hess, *Pea Ridge*, 90.

4. Shea and Hess, *Pea Ridge*, 91–93.

5. Shea and Hess, *Pea Ridge*, 93–120.

6. Shea and Hess, *Pea Ridge*, 151–67.

7. Shea and Hess, *Pea Ridge*, 168; OR, 8:199.

8. Shea and Hess, *Pea Ridge*, 119–20.

9. Shea and Hess, *Pea Ridge*, 120; OR, 8:199.

10. Shea and Hess, *Pea Ridge*, 105, 146–48; OR, 8:200.

11. Shea and Hess, *Pea Ridge*, 120.

12. Shea and Hess, *Pea Ridge*, 147, 204–5; OR, 8:200.

13. Shea and Hess, *Pea Ridge*, 215–16; OR, 8:201.

14. Shea and Hess, *Pea Ridge*, 217–18; Grenville M. Dodge to A. P. Wood, [n.d.] 1866, Dodge Papers, SHSI.

15. Shea and Hess, *Pea Ridge*, 223–38.

16. Shea and Hess, *Pea Ridge*, 223–38.

17. Shea and Hess, *Pea Ridge*, 238.

18. Shea and Hess, *Pea Ridge*, 238; OR, 8:202.

19. Shea and Hess, *Pea Ridge*, 243–54; SRC to HBC, March 13, 1862, Curtis Papers, HL; SRC to BBC, March 10, 1862, Curtis Papers, SHSI.

20. SRC to HBC, March 13, 1862, Curtis Papers, HL.

21. Shea and Hess, *Pea Ridge*, 254–57; SRC to BBC, March 10, 1862, Curtis Papers, SHSI.

22. Shea and Hess, *Pea Ridge*, 257–58; OR, 8:598; SRC to HWH, March 10, 1862, Curtis Papers, SHSI.

23. OR, 8:191–93.

24. Shea and Hess, *Pea Ridge*, 270–71.

25. Shea and Hess, *Pea Ridge*, 167; Curtis, "Army of the South-West," 154.

26. Shea and Hess, *Pea Ridge*, 167, 238; SRC to HBC, March 13, 1862, Curtis Papers, HL.

27. SRC to BBC, March 10, 1862, Curtis Papers, SHSI.

28. SRC to BBC, March 10, 1862, Curtis Papers, SHSI; SRC to HBC, March 13, 1862, Curtis Papers, HL.

29. Shea and Hess, *Pea Ridge*, 271–75. Cross Timbers is four miles north of Cross Timber Hollow.

30. Shea and Hess, *Pea Ridge*, 279–82; SRC to BBC and to HWH, both March 10, and Grenville M. Dodge to SRC, April 5, 1862, Curtis Papers, SHSI; SRC to George E. Waring, March 24, and to HWH, April 11, 1862, Letters Sent, NARA.

31. SRC to HWH, March 10, 1862, Curtis Papers, SHSI.

32. Robert Allen to SRC, April 25, 1862, Letters Received, NARA.

33. SRC to HWH, March 10, and to BBC, March 21, 1862, Curtis Papers, SHSI; Sheridan, *Personal Memoirs*, 1:127–35; Dodge, "Biography," Dodge Papers, SHSI.

34. Shea and Hess, *Pea Ridge*, 277; SRC to HWH and to W. R. English, both March 22, 1862, Letters Sent, NARA.

35. SRC to BBC and to Sadie B. Curtis, March 21 and 26, 1862, Curtis Papers, SHSI; March 25, 1862, Curtis Journal, ALPL.

36. March 27, 1862, Curtis Journal, ALPL.

37. SRC to BBC, March 21, 1862, Curtis Papers, SHSI; SRC and Henry Z. Curtis to BBC, both March 27, 1862, Curtis Papers, Yale. Curtis wrote a chatty, four-page letter to Sadie on the day she died. SRC to Sadie B. Curtis, March 26, 1862, Curtis Papers, SHSI.

38. Chapman S. Charlot to SRC, April 18, 1862, Curtis Papers, SHSI; SRC to HBC, November 21, 1862, Curtis Papers, HL.

39. *Keokuk Gate City,* March 31 and April 5, 1862; April 24, 1862, Curtis Journal, ALPL; SRC to BBC, March 27, 1862, Curtis Papers, Yale; SRC to HBC, April 11, 1862, Curtis Papers, HL; OR, 8:662.

8. March to the Mississippi

1. Shea and Hess, *Pea Ridge,* 290–91; SRC to Jefferson C. Davis, April 4, 1862, Letters Sent, NARA. A detailed account of Union movements between Pea Ridge and Helena is Schultz, *March to the River.*

2. Shea and Hess, *Pea Ridge,* 291–92; SRC to Frederick S. Winslow, April 17, 1862, Letters Sent, NARA; April 24 and 27, 1862, Curtis Journal, ALPL; OR, 13:363–64.

3. SRC to Sadie B. Curtis, March 26, 1862, Curtis Papers, SHSI; April 25, 1862, Curtis Journal, ALPL. The unfortunate officer was Lieutenant W. A. Heacock, Fourth Iowa Cavalry.

4. Shea and Hess, *Pea Ridge,* 286–92.

5. Shea and Hess, *Pea Ridge,* 292; Curtis, "Army of the South-West," 117–18.

6. SRC to HWH, April 28, 1862, Letters Sent, NARA.

7. June 11, 1862, Curtis Journal, ALPL.

8. Shea and Hess, *Pea Ridge,* 292.

9. May 3, 14, and 17, 1862, Curtis Journal, ALPL; SRC to Frederick Steele, May 6, 1862, Letters Sent, NARA; SRC to Sadie B. Curtis, March 26, 1862, Curtis Papers, SHSI.

10. Shea and Hess, *Pea Ridge,* 292–95; OR, 13:369–70.

11. Shea and Hess, *Pea Ridge,* 295; OR, 13:374–75.

12. Shea and Hess, *Pea Ridge,* 295–96.

13. OR, 8:665, 679, 13:363–64.

14. Shea and Hess, *Pea Ridge,* 297; SRC to Sempronius H. Boyd, May 11, and to Peter J. Osterhaus, May 13, 1862, Letters Sent, NARA.

15. Shea, *Fields of Blood,* 1–9; Shea and Hess, *Pea Ridge,* 296–98; SRC to HBC, June 18, 1862, Curtis Papers, HL.

16. Shea and Hess, *Pea Ridge,* 298–99; SRC to Peter J. Osterhaus, May 20, 1862, Letters Sent, NARA.

17. Shea and Hess, *Pea Ridge,* 299.

18. Shea and Hess, *Pea Ridge,* 299–300; May 20, 1862, Curtis Journal, ALPL; SRC to Sempronius H. Boyd, May 28, 1862, Letters Sent, NARA.

19. SRC to HBC, April 11, 1862, Curtis Papers, HL.

20. Shea and Hess, *Pea Ridge,* 300; May 30, 1862, Curtis Journal, ALPL.

21. OR, 13:448.

22. Shea and Hess, *Pea Ridge,* 300; SRC to John M. Schofield, June 26, 1862, Letters Sent, and Gen. Order 21, May 28, 1862, General Orders, NARA.

23. Shea and Hess, *Pea Ridge,* 301; SR to HBC, June 18, 1862, Curtis Papers, HL. Author's italics.

24. Shea and Hess, *Pea Ridge*, 301; Powell Clayton to SRC, July 4, 1862, Letters Received, NARA.

25. Shea and Hess, *Pea Ridge*, 301–2; Special Orders, March 26 and 27 and April 2, 1862, General Orders, NARA.

26. OR, 13:756; May 21, 1862, Curtis Journal, ALPL; Teters, *Practical Liberators*, 36–38.

27. Shea and Hess, *Pea Ridge*, 302–3; July 7, 1862, Curtis Journal, ALPL; SRC to HWH, July 14, 1862, Letters Sent, NARA. A detailed account of the engagement at Cache River (also known as Cotton Plant) is Shea, "Confederate Defeat."

28. Shea and Hess, *Pea Ridge*, 303; July 9, 1862, Curtis Journal, ALPL.

29. Shea and Hess, *Pea Ridge*, 303–4; "Military Service," 12, Curtis Papers, SHSI.

30. SRC to HWH, July 14, 1862, Letters Sent, NARA; ORN, 23:260; OR, 13:469.

31. OR, 13:477, 524–25. Brigadier General Alvin P. Hovey's newly arrived command became the army's Fourth Division.

32. The strategic situation in the Mississippi Valley in the latter half of 1862 is described in Shea and Winschel, *Vicksburg Is the Key*, 1–45.

33. Shea and Winschel, *Vicksburg Is the Key*, 1–45.

34. ORN, 23:260, 273, 288–89, 294–97, 305.

35. OR, 13:172, 240, 519–20; Curtis, "Army of the South-West," 219–20.

36. OR, 13:240.

37. ORN, 23:281, 286; OR, 13:541; Niven, *Chase Papers*, 1:361.

38. Shea and Winschel, *Vicksburg Is the Key*, 38–55.

39. OR, 13:544, 546; Niven, *Chase Papers*, 358–59, 363–64; "Military Service," 15–16, Curtis Papers, SHSI.

40. Beale, *Diary of Edward Bates*, 283; Christ, *Civil War Arkansas*, 88–144. Fort Curtis was demolished after the war. A modern reconstruction is located near the original site.

41. OR, 13:541, 553, 571, 22:10–11.

42. The Union occupation of Helena is ably discussed in Hess, "Confiscation."

43. Teters, *Practical Liberators*, 12–16; OR, 13:524–25.

44. Hess, "Confiscation," 62–63.

45. OR, 13:775, 22:10–11; Hess, "Confiscation," 65–68.

46. SRC to HWH, July 28, 1862, Curtis Papers, ALPL; OR, 22:15–16.

47. Hess, "Confiscation," 69–74; Chernow, *Grant*, 231–36; Marszalek, *Sherman*, 188–94.

48. General Orders Nos. 35 and 40, July 30 and August 25, and Norton P. Chipman to Abraham Lincoln, November 10, 1862, Curtis Papers, ALPL; OR, 13:553.

49. OR, 13:553; SRC to HBC, September 4, 1862, Curtis Papers, HL; "Military Service," 13–14, Curtis Papers, SHSI.

9. Missouri

1. Davis, *Union Pacific Railway*, 103; OR, 13:553, 556; SRC to HBC, September 4, 1862, Curtis Papers, HL.

2. Davis, *Union Pacific Railway*, 110–11; *New York Times*, September 2 and 3, 1862; SRC to HBC, September 4, 1862, Curtis Papers, HL; SRC to BBC, August 21, 1865, Curtis Papers, SHSI.

3. SRC to HBC, September 4, 1862, Curtis Papers, HL; OR, 13:553; SRC to BBC, August 21, 1865, Curtis Papers, SHSI.

4. *Keokuk Gate City*, September 10, 1862; SRC to HBC, September 4, 1862, Curtis Papers, HL.

5. OR, 13:240, 653, 656.

6. Shea, *Fields of Blood*, 18–20; OR, 13:646.

7. OR, 13:544–45, 560, 671.

8. The Department of the Missouri was reestablished on September 19, 1862, three days before Halleck telegraphed Curtis to assume command. Parrish, *Turbulent Partnership*, 90, 101.

9. OR, 13:666; October 2, 1862, Curtis Journal, ALPL.

10. The Colorado and Nebraska territories were added to the Department of the Missouri on October 11, 1862. OR, 13:729.

11. Shea, *Fields of Blood*, 16–17; OR, 13:654, 667, 718–19.

12. OR, 13:674.

13. Shea, *Fields of Blood*, 26–27; OR, 13:673, 712.

14. SRC to BBC, October 5 and 26, 1862, Curtis Papers, Yale.

15. SRC to HBC, September 4, 1862, Curtis Papers, HL.

16. OR, 13:739, 761–63.

17. Shea, *Fields of Blood*, 28; OR, 13:715–16.

18. Shea, *Fields of Blood*, 22–26, 29.

19. OR, 13:723.

20. Shea, *Fields of Blood*, 28–30.

21. Shea, *Fields of Blood*, 34–67.

22. Shea, *Fields of Blood*, 48–50; *Fairfield Ledger*, October 30, 1862.

23. Shea, *Fields of Blood*, 50–51; OR, 13:762–63.

24. Shea, *Fields of Blood*, 51; OR, 13:761–62, 778.

25. Shea, *Fields of Blood*, 63–67; OR, 13:781; SRC to John M. Schofield, November 13, 1862, Curtis Papers, SHSI.

26. Shea, *Fields of Blood*, 61–127; "Military Service," 22, Curtis Papers, SHSI.

27. Shea, *Fields of Blood*, 114–15; OR, 22(1):789.

28. Shea, *Fields of Blood*, 114–15, 128–44; OR, 22(1):806.

29. OR, 22(1):816.

30. Shea, *Fields of Blood*, 145–252.

31. Shea, *Fields of Blood*, 261–62.

32. Shea, *Fields of Blood*, 254–55; SRC to James G. Blunt, December 10, 1862, Herron Papers, NYHS; OR, 22(1):68–69, 22(2):11.

33. Shea, *Fields of Blood*, 268–82; OR, 22(1):167; SRC to James G. Blunt and Francis J. Herron, December 29, 1862, Curtis Papers, SHSI.

34. Shea, *Fields of Blood*, 73–74, 265.

35. Shea, *Fields of Blood*, 255–56, 285–86; OR, 22(1):853. Schofield's self-serving autobiography, *Forty-Six Years in the Army*, is filled with derogatory remarks about Curtis, Blunt, and Herron.

36. SRC to HBC, December 14, 1862, Curtis Papers, HL.

37. Bradbury, "'This War Is Managed Mighty Strange,'" 28–31; OR, 13:702, 746; Frederick Steele to HWH, November 1, 1862, Steele Papers, Stanford; John M. Schofield to Frederick Steele, September 18, 1862, Schofield Papers, Library of Congress.

38. Bradbury, "'This War Is Managed Mighty Strange,'" 31–32; OR, 13:702, 782, 793–94; Frederick Steele to HWH, November 1, 1862, Steele Papers, Stanford.

39. Bradbury, "'This War Is Managed Mighty Strange,'" 28–37; OR, 13:670–71, 729–30.

40. OR, 22(2):82, 92.

41. OR, 22(2):42–43, 68.

42. OR, 22(2):158–59, 176–77.

43. SRC to Abraham Lincoln, December 2, 1862, Curtis Papers, SHSI.

44. SRC to BBC, April 27, 1863, Curtis Papers, Yale.

45. OR, 13:688–89; "Military Service," 27, Curtis Papers, SHSI.

10. Inquisition and Interlude

1. Parrish, *Turbulent Partnership*, 106–7; Boman, *Lincoln's Resolute Unionist*, 189.

2. Boman, *Lincoln's Resolute Unionist*, 178; *St. Louis Missouri Republican*, October 13, 1862.

3. Parrish, *Turbulent Partnership*, 110.

4. Parrish, *Turbulent Partnership*, 108; Boman, *Lincoln's Resolute Unionist*, 193–95.

5. Gerteis, *Civil War St. Louis*, 182–84; Pitcock and Gurley, *I Acted from Principle*, 16–17.

6. Gerteis, *Civil War St. Louis*, 184–85; Parrish, *Turbulent Partnership*, 110–13; Boman, *Lincoln's Resolute Unionist*, 190–92; OR, 22(2):6–7, 25–26.

7. OR, 22(2):17–18.

8. OR, 22(2):42–43.

9. Gerteis, *Civil War St. Louis*, 270–74; OR, 22(2):147.

10. Gerteis, *Civil War St. Louis*, 275–76; Samuel W. Sawyer to H. W. Hunt, September 1, 1864, Sawyer Letter, Indiana Historical Society.

11. OR, 22(2):25–26.

12. OR, 13:726–28, 756; SRC to Thomas C. Hindman, October 10, 1862, Alexander Papers, Columbia.

13. SRC to HBC, December 14, 1862, Curtis Papers, HL.

14. OR, 13:800, 812–13.

15. SRC to HBC, November 5 and 17, 1863, Curtis Papers, HL.

16. OR, 22(2):152; "Military Service," 25–26, Curtis Papers, SHSI; SRC to HBC, May 6, 1863, Curtis Papers, HL; Beale, *Diary of Edward Bates*, 294.

17. OR, 22(2):157, 215–16, 277; SRC to HBC, May 18, 1863, Curtis Papers, HL.

18. OR, 22(2):277, 290–93.

19. Abraham Lincoln to SRC, November 6, 1862, Curtis Papers, SHSI. A keen analysis of the Curtis court of inquiry is Beckenbaugh, "War of Politics."

20. SRC to HBC, November 21, 1862, Curtis Papers, HL; SRC to Abraham Lincoln, November 9, 1862, Curtis Papers, SHSI; OR, 13:83–84.

21. SRC to Abraham Lincoln, November 9, 1862, Curtis Papers, SHSI.

22. SRC to HBC, November 21, 1862, Curtis Papers, HL.

23. SRC to HBC, November 21, 1862, Curtis Papers, HL.

24. OR, 13:683, 751–52.

25. OR, 13:683, 577.

26. OR, 13:751–52; Beale, *Diary of Edward Bates*, 276, 279.

27. Richard R. Ballinger to Henry Z. Curtis, December 1, 1862, Curtis Papers, Yale; James M. Ruggles to [SRC], December 16, 1862, Curtis Papers, ALPL.

28. Beckenbaugh, "War of Politics," 50–51.

29. Beckenbaugh, "War of Politics," 51–74.

30. Rasmussen, "Spoils of the Victors," 169–70; SRC to HBC, January 9, 1863, Curtis Papers, HL.

31. SRC to HBC, May 18, 1863, Curtis Papers, HL; "Journal of Passing Events," 21–22, Curtis Papers, SHSI.

32. SRC to HBC, June 22 and September 20, 1863, Curtis Papers, HL.

33. Stuart, *Iowa Colonels*, 49–50.

34. SRC to HBC, June 1, July 2, and September 20, 1863, Curtis Papers, HL; *Keokuk Gate City*, August 17, 1863.

35. OR, 22(2):215–16.

36. SRC to HBC, July 2 and September 20, 1863, Curtis Papers, HL.

37. Norton P. Chipman to SRC, June 10, 1863, Curtis Papers, SHSI.

38. Abraham Lincoln to SRC, June 8, 1863, Curtis Papers, SHSI; *Keokuk Gate City*, July 1, 1863.

39. "Military Service," 30, Curtis Papers, SHSI; SRC to HBC, November 24 and December 9 and 18, 1863, Curtis Papers, HL; SRC to [William K. Strong], [1863], Curtis Letter, MHMA; SRC to Cadwallader C. Washburn, February 3, 1863, Washburn Papers, State Historical Society of Wisconsin; OR, 22(2):92–93.

40. SRC to HBC, July 2, October 15 and 19, and November 17, 1863, Curtis Papers, HL.

41. Beckenbaugh, "War of Politics," 74–77; SRC to HBC, November 21, 1862, and May 6 and 18 and June 1, 1863, Curtis Papers, HL; "Military Service," 30, Curtis Papers, SHSI. Several officers, including Curtis's son Henry, were

found to have dabbled in cotton trading on a small scale, but the court was not interested in such small fry. The only officer who seems to have really lined his pockets was Captain Ferdinand Winslow, Sheridan's successor as quartermaster, who made wagons and steamboats available to traders for a price, but the court was not interested in him either. Rasmussen, "Spoils of the Victors," 161–79.

42. Joseph Holt to Edwin M. Stanton, August 8, 1863, Records of the Judge Advocate General's Office, NARA.

43. SRC to Abraham Lincoln, November 8, and Norton P. Chipman to Abraham Lincoln, November 10, 1863, Curtis Papers, ALPL.

44. SRC to HBC, June 1 and September 20, 1863, Curtis Papers, HL; Norton P. Chipman to SRC, October 10, 1863, Curtis Papers, Yale; John W. Boynton to SRC, May 25, 1865, Curtis Papers, SHSI; Castel, *Frontier State at War*, 158–61; Burkard, "Edge of Glory," 189.

45. SRC to HBC, October 15, 1863, Curtis Papers, HL.

46. SRC to HBC, October 15 and 19, 1863, Curtis Papers, HL; *Keokuk Gate City*, October 16, 1863.

47. "Journal of Passing Events," 21, Curtis Papers, SHSI; SRC to Samuel S. Curtis, November 4, 1863, Curtis Papers, Yale.

48. SRC to HBC, November 17 and December 18, 1863, and January 3, 1864, Curtis Papers, HL; Burlingame and Ettlinger, *Inside Lincoln's White House*, 127.

11. Fort Leavenworth

1. OR, 34(2):7; Simpson and Berlin, *Sherman's Civil War*, 580. The original Department of Kansas was merged into the Department of the Missouri in November 1861.

2. SRC to HBC, January 3, 1864, Curtis Papers, HL; January 2–16, 1864, "Journal of Passing Events," Curtis Papers, SHSI.

3. January 16, 1864, "Journal of Passing Events," Curtis Papers, SHSI; SRC to HBC, January 19, 1864, Curtis Papers, HL.

4. SRC to HBC, January 19, 1864, Curtis Papers, HL; *Leavenworth Conservative*, January 10, 1864; *Leavenworth Daily Times*, January 20 and 22, 1864; OR, 34(2):301–2; January 21, 1864, "Journal of Passing Events," Curtis Papers, SHSI.

5. HBC to SRC, January 8 and 25, 1864, and numerous other letters and telegrams in Curtis Papers, SHSI.

6. BBC to SRC, January 14, 1864, and January 26, 1864, "Journal of Passing Events," Curtis Papers, SHSI.

7. Castel, *Frontier State at War*, 17–36; SRC to HBC, January 19, 1864, Curtis Papers, HL.

8. January 3, 1864, "Journal of Passing Events," Curtis Papers, SHSI.

9. OR, 34(2):162–64, 169–70, 446–47, 652.

10. January 1, 1864, "Journal of Passing Events," Curtis Papers, SHSI.

11. "Military Service," 107, and January 30–31 and February 2–3, 1864, "Journal of Passing Events," Curtis Papers, SHSI; OR, 34(2):339–40; SRC to HBC, February 20, 1864, Curtis Papers, HL. Fort Scott National Historic Site preserves much of the original post.

12. SRC to HBC, February 20, 1864, Curtis Papers, HL; BBC to SRC, February 26, 1864, Curtis Papers, SHSI.

13. SRC to HBC February 20, 1864, Curtis Papers, HL.

14. OR, 34(2):281–82, 301–2, 329–30, 460–62, 538. The standard account of the Indian Home Guard is Britton, *Union Indian Brigade*.

15. OR, 34(2):557–58.

16. OR, 34(2):581, 292–93, 339–40, 753–54, 34(3):178, 192, 240. Some features of the original Fort Smith are preserved in Fort Smith National Historic Site.

17. BBC to SRC, February 4, 6, and 26, 1864, Curtis Papers, SHSI: SRC to HBC, February 20 and April 8, 1864, Curtis Papers, HL.

18. "Military Service," 107, Curtis Papers, SHSI; February 11 and 20, 1864, "Journal of Passing Events," Curtis Papers, SHSI; OR, 34(2):375–76.

19. February 21–24, 1864, "Journal of Passing Events," Curtis Papers, SHSI; *Lawrence Kansas State Journal*, February 25, 1864; OR, 34(2):443–44. The reference is to the 1857 Sepoy Mutiny in India.

20. OR, 34(2):460–61. The actual distance traveled was nearly nine hundred miles.

21. OR, 34(2):377, 384–85. Rosecrans was appointed commander of the Department of the Missouri on January 28, 1864.

22. OR, 34(2):168–69, 805, 34(3):199, 302, 34(4):72.

23. OR, 34(4):338, 446, 41(2):127.

24. OR, 34(2):652.

25. February 27, 1864, "Journal of Passing Events," Curtis Papers, SHSI; OR, 34(2):338–40, 462–63, 669–70.

26. OR, 34(3):288–89, 465–67, 502, 34(4):71, 134.

27. OR, 34(3):200.

28. OR, 34(3):162–64, 178, 192, 751; SRC to James G. Blunt, January 29, 1864, Curtis Papers, SHSI.

29. April 1–2, 1864, "Journal of Passing Events," Curtis Papers, SHSI; SRC to HBC, April 8 and June 27, 1864, Curtis Papers, HL; OR, 34(3):199.

30. SRC to HBC, June 7, 1864, Curtis Papers, HL; March 8, 1864, "Journal of Passing Events," Curtis Papers, SHSI.

31. SRC to HBC, June 7, 1864, Curtis Papers, HL.

32. SRC to Montgomery C. Meigs, June 16, 1864, Curtis Collection, University of Kansas; Basler, *Collected Works of Abraham Lincoln*, 4:473.

33. SRC to Merritt H. Insley, May 18, 1864, Curtis Papers, SHSI.

34. SRC to HBC, April 8 and June 7, 20, and 27, 1864, Curtis Papers, HL.

35. SRC to HBC, June 7 and 27, 1864, Curtis Papers, HL; May 31, 1864, "Journal of Passing Events," Curtis Papers, SHSI.

36. "Military Service," 109–10, Curtis Papers, SHSI.

37. OR, 41(1):49, 52–53, 41(2):145, 156, 159, 174–75, 185, 187–88, 191.

38. OR, 41(1):251, 253, 511.

39. Utley, *Frontiersmen in Blue*, 281–88; OR, 41(2):368, 378, 484; *Leavenworth Daily Times*, July 29, 1864.

40. Utley, *Frontiersmen in Blue*, 287–88; OR, 41(2):314, 315, 322, 332–33, 379. Fort Riley remains an active military base.

41. OR, 41(2):428.

42. OR, 41(2):629–31; SRC to BBC, July 28, 1864, Curtis Papers, Yale. A historical marker on U.S. 56 identifies the site of Fort Zarah.

43. OR, 41(2):629–31; SRC to James G. Blunt, January 29, 1864, and March 14, 1864, "Journal of Passing Events," Curtis Papers, SHSI.

44. OR, 41(2):413, 445–46.

45. OR, 41(1):188–90, 41(2):483–85. Nearly all of the original post is preserved in Fort Larned National Historic Site.

46. Utley, *Frontiersmen in Blue*, 288–89; Potter, *Standing Firmly by the Flag*, 140–43; Hagerty, "Indian Raids Along the Platte and Little Blue," 176–86, 239–52.

47. Potter, *Standing Firmly by the Flag*, 143–46; OR, 41(2):661, 691; "Military Service," 112, Curtis Papers, SHSI.

48. OR, 41(2):610–11.

49. OR, 41(2):720; SRC to HBC, August 17, 1864, Curtis Papers, HL.

50. Potter, *Standing Firmly by the Flag*, 146–48; OR, 41(2):763, 775, 789, 808, 826, 864, 914–15, 944, 965. Fort Kearney State Historical Site preserves the location of the original post but not much else.

51. OR, 41(2):856–57, 914–15, 41(3):294.

52. Hagerty, "Indian Raids Along the Platte and Little Blue," 253–60; OR, 41(2):789, 41(3):36, 98, 112, 180, 234, 236, 244; Curtis Pension File, Veterans Administration, NARA. Curtis marked the routes of his 1864 Kansas and Nebraska expeditions and his 1865–66 Northwest Treaty Commission travels on a "Military Map of Nebraska and Dakota," Curtis Papers, SHSI.

53. "Military Service," 112, Curtis Papers, SHSI; OR, 41(1):244–47, 41(3):112, 180, 262.

12. Westport

1. OR, 41(3):180. Lause, *Collapse of Price's Raid*, and Sinisi, *Last Hurrah*, are comprehensive accounts of the Missouri Expedition. Monnett, *Action Before Westport*, focuses on the battle proper.

2. Sinisi, *Last Hurrah*, 1–47; Monnett, *Action Before Westport*, 18–19; OR, 41(2):1040. The best account of the Red River campaign is Joiner, *Through the Howling Wilderness*.

3. OR, 41(3):234–35, 312.

4. *OR*, 41(3):290, 291, 371–72.

5. Sinisi, *Last Hurrah*, 49–109; January 23, 1864, "Journal of Passing Events," Curtis Papers, SHSI. Battle of Pilot Knob State Historic Site preserves the battleground.

6. Sinisi, *Last Hurrah*, 111–38, 143–45; *OR*, 41(1):729.

7. Sinisi, *Last Hurrah*, 138–43.

8. *OR*, 41(1):467, 41(3):311, 350, 369, 377, 398, 673, 751, 41(4):92.

9. *OR*, 41(3):398, 571, 673–74.

10. *OR*, 41(3):593–94, 650, 713.

11. *OR*, 41(1):465, 657.

12. *OR*, 41(3):650–51, 657.

13. *OR*, 41(3):769.

14. *OR*, 41(3):713, 725.

15. Sinisi, *Last Hurrah*, 152–57; *OR*, 41(1):465, 468–70, 41(3):736, 751; *Leavenworth Daily Times*, October 5, 1864.

16. Sinisi, *Last Hurrah*, 147–57; *OR*, 41(1):470–71.

17. *OR*, 41(3):734, 761, 762.

18. *OR*, 41(1):479, 41(3):763, 764, 765, 794; Blunt, "General Blunt's Account," 252–53.

19. *OR*, 41(3):821, 822, 868, 895.

20. *OR*, 41(3):793, 821, 822.

21. SRC to BBC, October 13, 1864, Curtis Papers, Yale.

22. *OR*, 41(3):867, 41(4):464, 479. As many as sixteen thousand Kansas militiamen may have turned out in some fashion, but not all crossed into Missouri or engaged the Confederates. Hinton, *Rebel Invasion*, 44–48.

23. SRC to HBC, October 14, 1864, Curtis Papers, HL; *OR*, 41(1):536, 41(3):870.

24. *OR*, 41(3):822; SRC to HBC, October 14, 1864, Curtis Papers, HL.

25. *OR*, 41(3):872–73, 41(4):473.

26. *OR*, 41(3):870.

27. *OR*, 41(3):860, 41(4):52, 98, 474.

28. *OR*, 41(1):434–39, 41(3):826, 860, 867, 41(4):15; Curtis, "Cruise on the Benton," Curtis Papers, SHSI.

29. BBC to SRC, October 19, 1864, Curtis Papers, Yale.

30. *OR*, 41(3):899, 41(4):190.

31. Monnett, *Action Before Westport*, 47–55; Sinisi, *Last Hurrah*, 171–80; Lee, *Gettysburg of the West*, 32; "Military Service," 114–15, Curtis Papers, SHSI; Hinton, *Rebel Invasion*, 134.

32. Hinton, *Rebel Invasion*, 51–52, 62–66; Kitts, "Civil War Diary," 331; *OR*, 41(4):115, 117, 473.

33. *OR*, 41(4):115, 141, 142–43, 144, 145, 150, 164, 478–79; "Military Service," 115, Curtis Papers, SHSI.

34. Sinisi, *Last Hurrah*, 181–85; *OR*, 41(4):145.

35. Monnett, *Action Before Westport*, 56–68; Sinisi, *Last Hurrah*, 185–91; Hinton, *Rebel Invasion*, 96–99, 102; OR, 41(1):525, 41(4):163, 165; Blunt, "General Blunt's Account," 254–57.

36. Monnett, *Action Before Westport*, 69–76; Sinisi, *Last Hurrah*, 194–97; OR, 41(4):165, 166; Blunt, "General Blunt's Account," 257–59.

37. Monnett, *Action Before Westport*, 92–94; OR, 41(4):164.

38. Monnett, *Action Before Westport*, 69–76; SRC to Kersey Coates, October 21, 1864, Curtis Papers, Yale; OR, 41(4):164, 165.

39. Monnett, *Action Before Westport*, 77–78.

40. Monnett, *Action Before Westport*, 78–85; Hinton, *Rebel Invasion*, 134; OR, 41(4):189, 195. The Byram's Ford battleground is preserved in Big Blue Battlefield Park, part of the Kansas City municipal park system.

41. Monnett, *Action Before Westport*, 78–85; H. A. Seiffert to Andrew McMahon, November 11, 1864, Lighton Family Papers, UA.

42. Monnett, *Action Before Westport*, 85–90; OR, 41(4):189, 193, 195.

43. Monnett, *Action Before Westport*, 91–96; OR, 41(1):485, 41(4):189.

44. OR, 41(4):142.

45. Monnett, *Action Before Westport*, 98–103; OR, 41(4):208, 485; Curtis, "Cruise on the Benton," Curtis Papers, SHSI.

46. Monnett, *Action Before Westport*, 103–4; Sinisi, *Last Hurrah*, 227–28; OR, 41(1):486.

47. Monnett, *Action Before Westport*, 104; Sinisi, *Last Hurrah*, 227–28; OR, 41(1):486.

48. OR, 41(1): 486.

49. H. A. Seiffert to Andrew McMahon, November 11, 1864, Lighton Family Papers, UA.

50. Monnett, *Action Before Westport*, 104–22; "Military Service," 116–17, Curtis Papers, SHSI; OR, 41(1):486.

51. Hinton, *Rebel Invasion*, 161, 164; OR, 41(1):486, 41(4):208.

13. Race to the Arkansas

1. Sinisi, *Last Hurrah*, 255–56; OR, 41(1):491; Hinton, *Rebel Invasion*, 176.

2. OR, 41(4):208; "Military Service," 119, Curtis Papers, SHSI.

3. OR, 41(4):208; SRC to BBC, October 30, 1864, Curtis Papers, Yale.

4. OR, 41(4):193, 194, 209.

5. Sinisi, *Last Hurrah*, 259–72; Buresh, *October 25th*, 66–68; OR, 41(4):211, 229.

6. Buresh, *October 25th*, 89–134; OR, 41(1):494, 41(4):242; "Military Service," 118–19, Curtis Papers, SHSI. Mine Creek Civil War Battlefield State Historic Site preserves the battleground.

7. Bryant, "Capture of General Marmaduke," 251–56; Harvey Dunlavy to SRC, October 29, and SRC to Harvey Dunlavy, November 28, 1864, Curtis Papers, SHSI.

8. Buresh, *October 25th*, 134; Sinisi, *Last Hurrah*, 288–89; OR, 41(1):494.

9. SRC to HBC, December 12, 1864, Curtis Papers, HL.

10. Sinisi, *Last Hurrah*, 294–99; OR, 41(1):497, 503.

11. Sinisi, *Last Hurrah*, 299–305; "Military Service," 120, Curtis Papers, SHSI; OR, 41(1):503.

12. OR, 41(4):256; "Military Service," 120, Curtis Papers, SHSI.

13. SRC to BBC, October 26, 1864, Curtis Papers, Yale.

14. Sinisi, *Last Hurrah*, 303–4, 311; OR, 41(1):510–11, 41(4):286–87; SRC to BBC, October 30, 1864, Curtis Papers, Yale.

15. Sinisi, *Last Hurrah*, 307–22; "Military Service," 121, Curtis Papers, SHSI; Blunt, "General Blunt's Account," 262–63. The first battle of Newtonia, fought on September 30, 1862, was the opening round of the Prairie Grove campaign.

16. Curtis Pension File, Veterans Administration, NARA.

17. "Military Service," 122–23, Curtis Papers, SHSI; OR, 41(4):318, 507. A different take on the Curtis-Rosecrans controversy is presented in Lamers, *Edge of Glory*, 429–34.

18. "Military Service," 122–23, Curtis Papers, SHSI; OR, 41(4):301, 330, 331–33.

19. SRC to BBC, October 30, 1864, Curtis Papers, Yale.

20. OR, 41(4):330–31.

21. SRC to BBC, October 30, 1864, Curtis Papers, Yale (author's italics).

22. SRC to BBC, October 30, 1864, Curtis Papers, Yale; OR, 41(4):336.

23. Sinisi, *Last Hurrah*, 327–28; SRC to HBC, December 12, 1864, Curtis Papers, HL; OR, 41(4):394, 401.

24. OR, 41(4):401, 406, 515.

25. "Military Service," 123–24, Curtis Papers, SHSI; OR, 41(4):420.

26. OR, 41(4):421; SRC to HBC, December 12, 1864, Curtis Papers, HL; Samuel P. Curtis to SRC, July 9, 1863, and "Military Service," 125, Curtis Papers, SHSI.

27. Sinisi, *Last Hurrah*, 329–31; OR, 41(1):517.

28. Sinisi, *Last Hurrah*, 334–36; OR, 41(1):517, 41(4):496; "Military Service," 127, Curtis Papers, SHSI.

29. "Military Service," 124, Curtis Papers, SHSI; OR, 41(1): 496, 530.

30. "Military Service," 127, Curtis Papers, SHSI.

31. SRC to HBC, December 12, 1864, Curtis Papers, HL.

32. OR, 41(4):659.

33. SRC to HBC, December 12, 1864, Curtis Papers, HL.

34. OR, 41(1):491.

35. SRC to HBC, December 12, 1864, Curtis Papers, HL; "Military Service," 128, Curtis Papers, SHSI.

36. SRC to HBC, September 20, 1863, and December 12, 1864, Curtis Papers, HL.

37. SRC to HBC, August 17, 1864, Curtis Papers, HL.

38. SRC to HBC, August 17 and December 12, 1864, Curtis Papers, HL.

39. *OR*, 34(2):742–43, 34(4):353, 41(2):484.

40. *OR*, 22(2):123–24; Convery, "John M. Chivington," 149–73.

41. *OR*, 41(3):462, 525, 571, 41(4):751, 771–72.

42. *OR*, 34(4):421–22. Hoig, *Sand Creek Massacre*, is the standard account. Sand Creek Massacre National Historic Site preserves the battleground.

43. SRC to HBC, December 16, 1865, Curtis Papers, HL.

14. Peacemaking

1. *OR*, 41(4):716, 717, 784–85, 48(1):686.

2. SRC to HBC, February 13, 1865, Curtis Papers, HL; SRC to BBC, May 3, 1865, Curtis Papers, Yale; *OR*, 48(1):747–48.

3. SRC to BBC, February 11, 1865, Curtis Papers, Yale; *OR*, 48(1):769–70.

4. *OR* 48(1):762–63, 780–81, 835, 845, 48(2):50; SRC to BBC, February 11, 13, and 21, 1865, Curtis Papers, Yale.

5. SRC to HBC, January 7 and February 13, 1865, Curtis Papers, HL; SRC to BBC, March 11, 1865, Curtis Papers, Yale.

6. SRC to BBC, February 24 and 28, 1865, Curtis Papers, Yale.

7. SRC to BBC, February 28 and May 16, 1865, Curtis Papers, Yale; SRC to HBC, April 21, 1865, Curtis Papers, HL.

8. SRC to HBC, April 21, 1865, Curtis Papers, HL.

9. Utley, *Frontiersmen in Blue*, 322–23; SRC to HBC, May 22, 1865, Curtis Papers, HL; SRC to BBC, April 27 and May 15, 1865, Curtis Papers, Yale.

10. Utley, *Frontiersmen in Blue*, 322–23; SRC to HBC, May 22, 1865, Curtis Papers, HL; SRC to BBC, April 27 and May 15, 1865, Curtis Papers, Yale.

11. *OR*, 48(1):924–25, 48(2):471; SRC to HBC, July 6, 1865, Curtis Papers, HL.

12. *OR*, 48(2):1050.

13. SRC to Samuel S. Curtis, April 10, and to BBC, May 3 and 16, 1865, Curtis Papers, Yale; SRC to HBC, May 22, 1864, Curtis Papers, HL.

14. SRC to HBC, May 22, 1864, Curtis Papers, HL; SRC to BBC, May 3, 1864, Curtis Papers, Yale.

15. *OR*, 48(2):741; SRC to HBC, May 22, 1865, Curtis Papers, HL; SRC to BBC, May 3 and June 18, 1865, Curtis Papers, Yale. In a subsequent letter Curtis stated he was tenth in rank.

16. SRC to BBC, May 3, 1865, Curtis Papers, Yale; SRC to HBC, May 22, 1865, Curtis Papers, HL.

17. SRC to BBC, February 25, 1866, Curtis Papers, Yale.

18. SRC to HBC, July 6, 1865, Curtis Papers, HL; SRC to John Pope, June 24, and to Henry H. Sibley, July 3, 1865, Curtis File, Adjutant General's Office, NARA.

19. Special Order No. 118, July 22, 1865, Curtis File, Adjutant General's Office, NARA; *OR*, 48(2):1125; SRC to HBC, July 24 and August 3 and 6, 1865, Curtis Papers, HL; SRC to BBC, May 3, 15, and 21 and July 14, 20, 22, 25, and 26, 1865, Curtis Papers, Yale.

20. SRC to HBC, August 11, 1865, Curtis Papers, HL; SRC to BBC, August 15, 1865, Curtis Papers, Yale.

21. Utley, *Frontiersmen in Blue*, 309–10, 336–38; Sievers, "Westward by Indian Treaty," 82–83; SRC to Grenville M. Dodge, September 18, 1865, Curtis Papers, Yale; James Harlan to SRC, August 22, 1865, Curtis Papers, SHSI.

22. James Harlan to SRC, August 17, and SRC to BBC, August 15 and 18 and October 12, 1865, Curtis Papers, Yale.

23. SRC to HBC, August 23, 1865, Curtis Papers, HL; SRC to BBC, June 18, 1865, Curtis Papers, Yale.

24. SRC to BBC, June 15 and 21 and August 23, 1865, Curtis Papers, Yale; Niven, *Salmon P. Chase Papers*, 3:285.

25. *Washington Daily National Republican*, August 18, 1865; SRC to BBC, August 18, 1865, Curtis Papers, Yale.

26. SRC to BBC, August 11, and to Samuel S. Curtis, August 21, 1865, Curtis Papers, Yale.

27. SRC to BBC, August 15, 26, and 27, 1865, Curtis Papers, Yale.

28. Athearn, *Forts of the Upper Missouri*, 202–10; SRC to BBC, September 22 and October 12, 1865, Curtis Papers, Yale; SRC to Chapman S. Charlot, September 18, 1865, Curtis Papers, SHSI.

29. SRC to BBC, September 28, 1865, Curtis Papers, Yale; SRC to James Harlan, September 28, and to commandant at Fort Randall, September 29, 1865, Curtis Papers, SHSI.

30. SRC to BBC, September 29, 1865, Curtis Papers, Yale.

31. SRC to BBC, October 6, 1865, Curtis Papers, Yale. Fort Sully was demolished shortly after Curtis visited. The site of the fort is preserved in Farm Island Recreation Area.

32. Sievers, "Westward by Indian Treaty," 85–86; SRC to BBC, October 6 and 10, and to James Harlan, October 10, 1865, Curtis Papers, Yale; SRC to HBC, October 12, 1865, Curtis Papers, HL.

33. SRC to BBC, October 10, 1865, Curtis Papers, Yale; "Notes of Meetings with Indian Leaders," October 28, [1865], Curtis Papers, SHSI.

34. SRC to BBC, October 16 and 20, 1865, Curtis Papers, Yale.

35. SRC to James Harlan, October 10, and to Edwin M. Stanton, October 11, 1865, Curtis Papers, Yale.

36. Sievers, "Westward by Indian Treaty," 86; SRC to BBC, October 12 and 20, 1865, Curtis Papers, Yale.

37. Athearn, *Forts of the Upper Missouri*, 208–9; SRC to BBC, October 20, 1865, Curtis Papers, Yale.

38. SRC to James Harlan, October 20, and to Edwin M. Stanton, October 11, 20, and 25, 1865, Curtis Papers, Yale.

39. SRC to James Harlan, May 4, 1866, Curtis Papers, Yale.

40. SRC to HBC, June 5, 1866, Curtis Papers, HL.

41. SRC to BBC, May 11 and 15 and June 10, 1866, Curtis Papers, Yale.

42. SRC to BBC, May 18 and 23, 1866, Curtis Papers, Yale; SRC to HBC, June 5, 1866, Curtis Papers, HL.

43. SRC to BBC, May 23, 1866, Curtis Papers, Yale.

44. SRC to BBC, June 10, 1866, Curtis Papers, Yale.

45. SRC to BBC, May 25 and June 10, 1866, Curtis Papers, Yale.

46. Sievers, "Westward by Indian Treaty," 84, 86; SRC to BBC, June 6, 10, 20, and 22 and July 1, 1866, Curtis Papers, Yale; SRC to HBC, June 5, 1866, Curtis Papers, HL.

47. Sievers, "Westward by Indian Treaty," 86; SRC to BBC, July 13 and 26, 1866, Curtis Papers, Yale.

48. SRC to BBC, July 10, 1866, Curtis Papers, Yale.

15. Union Pacific

1. James Harlan to SRC, November 16, 1865, and SRC to BBC, February 17, 1866, Curtis Papers, Yale.

2. SRC to BBC, December 13, 1865, and James Harlan to SRC, March 3, 1866, Curtis Papers, Yale; SRC to HBC, December 16, 1865, Curtis Papers, HL.

3. SRC to Samuel S. Curtis, December 22, 1865, and to BBC, February 20, 1866, Curtis Papers, Yale.

4. SRC to Samuel S. Curtis, December 22 and 23, 1865, and to BBC, February 20, 1866, Curtis Papers, Yale.

5. SRC to HBC, December 16, 1865, Curtis Papers, HL; SRC to BBC, January 8, 1866, Curtis Papers, Yale; *Omaha Herald*, January 7, 1866.

6. SRC to HBC, February 7, 1866, Curtis Papers, HL; SRC to BBC, February 2, 1866, Curtis Papers, Yale; "Pacific Railroad Convention," 156–57; *Report of Board Convened to Determine on a Standard*, 6–50.

7. SRC to BBC, February 6, 7, and 20, 1866, Curtis Papers, Yale; SRC to HBC, February 7, 1866, Curtis Papers, HL.

8. SRC to BBC, February 25 and September 14, 18, and 25, 1866, Curtis Papers, Yale; SRC to HBC, August 25, 1866, Curtis Papers, HL.

9. SRC to BBC, February 10, 1866, Curtis Papers, Yale.

10. SRC to BBC, September 28, 1866, Curtis Papers, Yale.

11. SRC to HBC, August 25, 1866, Curtis Papers, HL; SRC to BBC, October 2, 1866, Curtis Papers, Yale.

12. SRC to BBC, October 2, 1866, Curtis Papers, Yale.

13. SRC to HBC, November 15, 1866, Curtis Papers, HL; Wilson, "Des Moines Rapids Canal," 117–32.

14. HBC deposition, May 11, 1880, Curtis Pension File, Veterans Administration, NARA.

15. SRC to BBC, December 16 and 19, 1866, Curtis Papers, Yale; SRC to HBC, December 22, 1866, Curtis Papers, HL.

16. SRC to BBC, December 10–11, 1866, Curtis Papers, Yale.

17. SRC to BBC, December 16, 21, 23, and 25, 1866, Curtis Papers, Yale.

18. *Keokuk Gate City*, December 29, 1866.

19. *In Memoriam*, 6; SRC to BBC, December 25, 1866, Curtis Papers, Yale.

20. James H. Simpson to BBC, December 26, 1866, Curtis Collection, Louisiana State Museum; *In Memoriam*, 6–10, 63. Dr. John F. Sanford, Curtis's personal physician, believed a ruptured aneurysm was the cause of death.

21. *In Memoriam*, 24–62; *Keokuk Daily Gate City*, December 28, 1866, and January 1, 1867.

22. *Keokuk Gate City*, January 1, 1867.

23. Curtis Pension File, Veterans Administration, NARA.

16. Memory

1. Sheridan, *Personal Memoirs*, 1:132; Dodge, *Battle of Atlanta*, 31, 33; Dodge, *Fiftieth Anniversary*, 61–64.

2. Hinton, *Rebel Invasion*, 341; Black, *Soldier's Recollections*, 18.

3. Sigel, "Pea Ridge Campaign," and Schofield, *Forty-Six Years in the Army*, contain numerous examples.

4. Noun, "Iowa Soldiers' and Sailors' Monument"; Weed, *Hand Book for Iowa Soldiers' and Sailors' Monument*.

5. Grace, "General Curtis Monument."

BIBLIOGRAPHY

Archives and Manuscript Materials

Cadwallader C. Washburn Papers. State Historical Society of Wisconsin, Madison.

Campaign Book of the Army of the Border. Kansas State Historical Society, Topeka.

Cuming-Hamilton Collection. Joslyn Art Museum, Omaha.

Erasmus Gest Papers. Ohio History Connection Archives, Columbus.

Francis J. Herron Papers. New-York Historical Society, New York.

Frank J. North Papers. Nebraska State Historical Society, Lincoln.

Frederick Steele Papers. Stanford University, Palo Alto CA.

General Orders 1861–1862. Army of the Southwest, Records of the War Department, RG 393. National Archives and Records Administration, Washington DC.

Gilder Lehrman Collection. New-York Historical Society, New York.

Hamilton Rowan Gamble Papers. Missouri History Museum Library, St. Louis.

Henry Barnes Curtis Papers. Ohio History Connection Archives, Columbus.

John M. Schofield Papers. Library of Congress, Washington DC.

Letters Received 1861–1862. Army of the Southwest, Records of the War Department, RG 393. National Archives and Records Administration, Washington DC.

Letters Sent 1862. Army of the Southwest, Records of the War Department, RG 393. National Archives and Records Administration, Washington DC.

Lighton Family Papers. University of Arkansas, Fayetteville.

Peter W. Alexander Papers. Columbia University, New York.

Samuel Ryan Curtis Collection. Louisiana State Museum Historical Center, New Orleans.

Samuel Ryan Curtis Collection. University of Kansas, Lawrence.

Samuel Ryan Curtis Diaries and Papers. University of California, Berkeley.

Samuel Ryan Curtis File. Adjutant General's Office, Records of the War Department, RG 94. National Archives and Records Administration, Washington DC.

Samuel Ryan Curtis Investigation File. Judge Advocate General's Office, Records of the War Department, RG 153. National Archives and Records Administration, Washington DC.

Samuel Ryan Curtis Letter and Journal. Missouri History Museum Library, St. Louis.

Samuel Ryan Curtis Papers. Abraham Lincoln Presidential Library, Springfield IL.

Samuel Ryan Curtis Papers. Huntington Library, San Marino CA.

Samuel Ryan Curtis Papers. Ohio History Connection Archives, Columbus.

Samuel Ryan Curtis Papers. State Historical Society of Iowa, Des Moines.

Samuel Ryan Curtis Papers. Yale University, New Haven.

Samuel Ryan Curtis Pension File. Veterans Administration, Records of the War Department, RG 15. National Archives and Records Administration, Washington DC.

Samuel W. Sawyer Letter. Indiana Historical Society, Indianapolis.

Special Orders 1861–1862. Army of the Southwest, Records of the War Department, RG 393. National Archives and Records Administration, Washington DC.

Thomas B. Cuming Papers. Nebraska State Historical Society, Lincoln.

Published Works

Acts of a General Nature Passed by the State of Ohio. Columbus: Medary, 1844.

Agnew, Brad. *Fort Gibson: Terminal on the Trail of Tears.* Norman: University of Oklahoma Press, 1980.

Ambrose, Stephen E. *Duty, Honor, Country: A History of West Point.* Baltimore: Johns Hopkins University Press, 1966.

American Society of Civil Engineers. "Muskingum River Navigation System." May 2015. http://www.asce.org/about-civil-engineering/history-and-heritage/historic-landmarks/muskingum-river-navigation-system.

Andrews, Martin R., ed. *History of Marietta and Washington County, Ohio, and Representative Citizens.* Chicago: Biographical, 1902.

Athearn, Robert G. *Forts of the Upper Missouri.* Englewood Cliffs NJ: Prentice Hall, 1967.

Basler, Roy P., ed. *The Collected Works of Abraham Lincoln.* 9 vols. New Brunswick NJ: Rutgers University Press, 1953.

Bauer, K. Jack. *The Mexican War, 1846–1848.* New York: Macmillan, 1974.

Beale, Howard K., ed. *The Diary of Edward Bates, 1859–1866.* Washington DC: U.S. Government Printing Office, 1933.

Beckenbaugh, Terry L. "The War of Politics: Samuel Ryan Curtis, Race, and the Political/Military Establishment." PhD diss., University of Arkansas, 2001.

The Biographical Encyclopedia of Ohio of the Nineteenth Century. Cincinnati: Galaxy, 1876.

The Biographical Record of Knox County, Ohio. Chicago: Lewis, 1902.

Black, Samuel. *A Soldier's Recollections of the Civil War*. Minco OK: Minstrel, 1912.

Blunt, James G. "General Blunt's Account of His Civil War Experiences." *Kansas Historical Quarterly* 1 (1932): 211–65.

Boman, Dennis K. *Lincoln's Resolute Unionist: Hamilton Gamble, Dred Scott Dissenter and Missouri's Civil War Governor*. Baton Rouge: Louisiana State University Press, 2006.

Bradbury, John F., Jr. "'This War Is Managed Mighty Strange': The Army of Southeastern Missouri, 1862–1863." *Missouri Historical Review* 89 (1994): 28–47.

Britton, Wiley. *The Union Indian Brigade in the Civil War*. Kansas City: Franklin Hudson, 1922.

Bryant, Thomas J. "The Capture of General Marmaduke by James Dunlavy an Iowa Private Cavalryman." *Iowa Journal of History and Politics* 11 (1913): 248–57.

Buresh, Lumir F. *October 25th and the Battle of Mine Creek*. Kansas City: Lowell Press, 1977.

Burkard, Dick J. "The Edge of Glory: The Civil War Career of Samuel Ryan Curtis." Master's thesis, Southern Illinois University, 1984.

Burlingame, Michael, and John R. T. Ettlinger, eds. *Inside Lincoln's White House: The Complete Civil War Diary of John Hay*. Carbondale: Southern Illinois University Press, 1997.

Butler, Benjamin F. *Butler's Book*. Boston: Thayer, 1892.

Byers, Samuel H. M. *Iowa in War Times*. Des Moines IA: Condit, 1888.

Castel, Albert. *A Frontier State at War: Kansas, 1861–1865*. Ithaca NY: Cornell University Press, 1958.

Chaffin, Tom. *Pathfinder: John Charles Fremont and the Course of American Empire*. Norman: University of Oklahoma Press, 2014.

Chaffin, Tom, and Michael D. Cohen, eds. *Correspondence of James K. Polk*. 13 vols. Knoxville: University of Tennessee Press, 1969–.

Chance, Joseph E., ed. *Mexico Under Fire: Being the Diary of Samuel Ryan Curtis, 3rd Ohio Volunteer Regiment, during the American Military Occupation of Northern Mexico, 1846–1847*. Fort Worth: Texas Christian University Press, 1994.

Chapman, Frederick W. *The Buckingham Family: Or, the Descendants of Thomas Buckingham, One of the First Settlers of Milford, Conn.* Hartford CT: Case, Lockwood and Brainard, 1872.

Chernow, Ron. *Grant*. New York: Penguin, 2017.

Christ, Mark K. *Civil War Arkansas, 1863: The Battle for a State*. Norman: University of Oklahoma Press, 2010.

Christensen, Lawrence O., et al., eds. *Dictionary of Missouri Biography*. Columbia: University of Missouri Press, 1999.

Clemens, Orion. *City of Keokuk in 1856*. Keokuk IA: Clemens, 1856.

Cole, Chester C., and Ezra C. Ebersole. *The Courts and Legal Profession of Iowa.* 2 vols. Chicago: Cooper, 1907.

Colton, Kenneth E., ed. "Frontier War Problems: The Letters of Samuel Ryan Curtis." *Annals of Iowa* 24 (1943): 298–315.

——— . "The Irrepressible Conflict of 1861: The Letters of Samuel Ryan Curtis." *Annals of Iowa* 24 (1942): 14–59.

——— . "With Fremont in Missouri in 1861: The Letters of Samuel Ryan Curtis." *Annals of Iowa* 24 (1942): 105–67.

Convery, William J. "John M. Chivington." In *Soldiers West: Biographies from the Military Frontier,* edited by Paul A. Hutton and Durwood Ball, 149–73. Norman: University of Oklahoma Press, 2009.

Crawford, Samuel J. *Kansas in the Sixties.* Chicago: McClurg, 1911.

Cullum, George W. *Biographical Register of the Officers and Graduates of the U.S. Military Academy.* Boston: Houghton Mifflin, 1891.

Curtis, Samuel P. "The Army of the South-West, and the First Campaign in Arkansas." *Annals of Iowa* 4 (1866): 625–45, 673–88, 721–37; 5 (1867): 769–85, 817–33, 865–76, 917–33; 6 (1868): 1–12, 69–84, 141–60, 249–70; 7 (1869): 1–20, 113–32, 209–25.

Curtis, Samuel R. *The Central American Question.* Washington DC: Buell and Blanchard, 1858.

——— . "The Desmoines Valley." *The Western Journal, and Civilian* 10 (1853): 187–90.

——— . "Engineer's Report, No. 1" and "Engineer's Report, No. 2." In *Journal of the House of Representatives of the Second Regular Session of the General Assembly of the State of Iowa, 1848.* Fort Madison IA: Statesman, 1849.

——— . *Engineer's Report No. 1: To the Directors of the Navigation and Hydraulic Company of the Mississippi Rapids, December 1, 1849.* Cincinnati: Tagart, 1849.

——— . "Engineer's Report, No. 3." In *Journal of the Senate of the Third General Assembly of the State of Iowa.* Iowa City: Palmer and Paul, 1850.

——— . *Engineer's Report, No. 3, to the Board of Public Works, on the Improvement of the Desmoines River.* Dubuque IA: Miners Express, 1849.

——— . "Habits of Missouri River—Harbor of St. Joseph." *The Western Journal, and Civilian* 10 (1853): 383–87.

——— . *The Mormon Rebellion and the Bill to Raise Volunteers: Speech of Hon. Samuel R. Curtis, of Iowa.* Washington DC: n.p., 1858.

——— . *Muskingum Valley Turnpike. Notice to Contractors.* Marietta OH: Intelligencer, 1839.

——— . *Proceedings of a Pacific Railroad Convention at Lacon, Illinois: With the Address of Col. Samuel R. Curtis.* Cincinnati: Thorpe, 1853.

——— . *Remarks of Hon. Samuel R. Curtis, of Iowa, on the Bill Creating Pensions to Soldiers Who Served in the Last War with Great Britain and the Indian Wars Preceding.* Washington DC: Buell and Blanchard, [1858].

———. "Report on Operations of Iowa Troops in Missouri in June, 1861." *Annals of Iowa* 8 (1908): 358–67.

———. *To the People of the First Iowa District.* Keokuk IA: n.p., 1859.

Davis, John P. *The Union Pacific Railway: A Study in Railway Politics, History, and Economics.* Chicago: Griggs, 1894.

Dietzler, John P. "Major General Samuel Ryan Curtis—City Engineer." *Missouri Historical Review* 51 (1957): 354–61.

Dishman, Christopher D. *A Perfect Gibraltar: The Battle for Monterrey, Mexico, 1846.* Norman: University of Oklahoma Press, 2010.

Dodge, Grenville M. *The Battle of Atlanta and Other Campaigns.* Council Bluffs IA: Monarch, 1911.

———. *Fiftieth Anniversary: Fourth Iowa Veteran Infantry, Dodge's Second Iowa Battery, Dodge's Band.* Council Bluffs IA: Monarch, 1911.

Douglas, Ben. *History of the Lawyers of Wayne County, Ohio, from 1812 to 1900.* Wooster OH: Clapper, 1900.

———. *History of Wayne County, Ohio, from the Days of the Pioneers and First Settlers to the Present Time.* Indianapolis: Douglass, 1878.

Dudley, Edgar S. "Notes on the Early Military History of Nebraska." *Transactions and Reports of the Nebraska State Historical Society* 2 (1887): 166–96.

Engle, Stephen D. *Yankee Dutchman: The Life of Franz Sigel.* Fayetteville: University of Arkansas Press, 1993.

Freeman, Douglas S. *R.E. Lee: A Biography.* 4 vols. New York: Scribner's, 1934–35.

Gallaher, Ruth A. "Samuel Ryan Curtis." *Iowa Journal of History and Politics* 25 (1927): 331–58.

Gerteis, Louis S. *The Civil War in Missouri: A Military History.* Columbia: University of Missouri Press, 2012.

———. *Civil War St. Louis.* Lawrence: University Press of Kansas, 2004.

Grace, Mary. "The General Curtis Monument." *Keokuk Confluence* 6 (2012): 14–16.

Griswold, Bert J. *The Pictorial History of Fort Wayne, Indiana.* Chicago: Law, 1917.

Hagerty, Leroy W. "Indian Raids Along the Platte and Little Blue Rivers, 1864–1865." *Nebraska History* 28 (1947): 176–86, 239–60.

Hennessy, John J. *The First Battle of Manassas: An End to Innocence, July 18–21, 1861.* Mechanicsburg PA: Stackpole, 2015.

Hess, Earl J. "Confiscation and the Northern War Effort: The Army of the Southwest at Helena." *Arkansas Historical Quarterly* 44 (1985): 56–75.

———. "Sigel's Resignation: A Study in German-Americanism and the Civil War." *Civil War History* 26 (1980): 5–17.

Hill, Norman N. *History of Knox County, Ohio, Its Past and Present.* Mount Vernon OH: Graham, 1881.

Hinton, Richard J. *Rebel Invasion of Missouri and Kansas and the Campaign of the Army of the Border.* Chicago: Church and Goodman, 1865.

The History of Madison County, Iowa. Des Moines IA: Union Historical, 1879.

Hoig, Stan. *The Sand Creek Massacre.* Norman: University of Oklahoma Press, 1961.

Hubler, Dave. "Des Moines River Navigation; Great Expectations Unfulfilled." *Annals of Iowa* 39 (1968): 287–306.

Hudson, David, et al. *The Biographical Dictionary of Iowa.* Ames: University of Iowa Press, 2009.

Huntington, Charles C., and Cloys P. McClelland. *History of the Ohio Canals.* Columbus: Ohio Historical Society, 1905.

Hurt, R. Douglas. *The Ohio Frontier: Crucible of the Old Northwest, 1720–1830.* Indianapolis: Indiana University Press, 1998.

Huston, James L. *The Panic of 1857 and the Coming of the Civil War.* Baton Rouge: Louisiana State University Press, 1987.

In Memoriam. Maj. Gen. Samuel Ryan Curtis. Died December 26th, 1866. Keokuk IA: Rees, 1867.

Johnson, Timothy D. *A Gallant Little Army: The Mexico City Campaign.* Lawrence: University Press of Kansas, 2007.

Johnston, John P. *The Record of Connecticut Men in the Military and Naval Service during the War of the Revolution, 1775–1783.* 3 vols. Hartford CT: Case, Lockwood and Brainard, 1889.

Joiner, Gary D. *Through the Howling Wilderness: The 1864 Red River Campaign and Union Failure in the West.* Knoxville: University of Tennessee Press, 2006.

Kitts, John H. "The Civil War Diary of John Howard Kitts." *Collections of the Kansas State Historical Society* 14 (1918): 318–32.

Lamers, William M. *The Edge of Glory: A Biography of General William S. Rosecrans, U.S.A.* Baton Rouge: Louisiana State University Press, 1961.

Lause, Mark A. *The Collapse of Price's Raid: The Beginning of the End in Civil War Missouri.* Columbia: University of Missouri Press, 2016.

Lavender, David. *Climax at Buena Vista: The Decisive Battle of the Mexican-American War.* Philadelphia: Lippincott, 1966.

Laws, Resolutions and Memorials, Passed at the Regular Session of the First General Assembly of the Territory of Nebraska. Omaha: Sherman and Strickland, 1855.

Lee, Alfred E. *History of the City of Columbus, Capital of Ohio.* 2 vols. New York: Musell, 1892.

Lee, Fred L. *Gettysburg of the West: The Battle of Westport, October 21–23, 1864.* Independence: Two Trails, 1996.

"Major H. Z. Curtis." *Portrait Monthly of the New York Illustrated News* 1 (1863): 94.

Marszalek, John F. *Commander of All Lincoln's Armies: A Life of General Henry W. Halleck*. Cambridge MA: Harvard University Press, 2004.

———. *Sherman: A Soldier's Passion for Order*. New York: Free Press, 1993.

Michael, Steven B. "Ohio and the Mexican War: Public Response to the 1846–1848 Crisis." PhD diss., Ohio State University, 1985.

Monnett, Howard N. *Action Before Westport, 1864*. Boulder: University Press of Colorado, 1995.

Morrison, James L., Jr. *"The Best School in the World": West Point, the Pre–Civil War Years, 1833–1866*. Kent OH: Kent State University Press, 1986.

Murphy, Douglas A. *Two Armies on the Rio Grande: The First Campaign of the US-Mexican War*. College Station: Texas A&M University Press, 2014.

"Museum Notes." *Annals of Iowa* 38 (1968): 238–40.

National Register of Historic Places. "Gen. Samuel R. Curtis House." https:// npgallery.nps.gov/NRHP/AssetDetail/d2b5e4d2-744e-43aa-a3c2 -99dff1bd6a13.

Nichols, Bruce. *Guerrilla Warfare in Civil War Missouri, 1862–1865*. 4 vols. Jefferson NC: McFarland, 2004–13.

Niven, John, ed. *The Salmon P. Chase Papers*. 5 vols. Kent OH: Kent State University Press, 1993–98.

Noun, Louise R. "The Iowa Soldiers' and Sailors' Monument." *Palimpsest* 67 (1986): 80–93.

"Pacific Railroad Convention." *American Railroad Journal* 22 (1866): 156–57.

Parrish, William E. *A History of Missouri*. 3 vols. Columbia: University of Missouri Press, 1971–74.

———. *Turbulent Partnership: Missouri and the Union, 1861–1865*. Columbia: University of Missouri Press, 1963.

Piston, William G., and Richard W. Hatcher III. *Wilson's Creek: The Second Battle of the Civil War and the Men Who Fought It*. Chapel Hill: University of North Carolina Press, 2000.

Potter, James E. *Standing Firmly by the Flag: Nebraska Territory and the Civil War, 1861–1867*. Lincoln: University of Nebraska Press, 2013.

Quaife, Milo M., ed. *The Diary of James K. Polk*. 4 vols. Chicago: McClurg, 1910.

Raitz, Karl B., ed. *The National Road*. Baltimore: Johns Hopkins University Press, 1996.

Rasmussen, Anders B. "The Spoils of the Victors: Captain Ferdinand Winslow and the 1863 Curtis Court of Inquiry." *Annals of Iowa* 76 (2017): 161–79.

Register of the Officers and Cadets of the U.S. Military Academy. New York: n.p., 1831.

Report of Board Convened to Determine on a Standard for Construction of the Pacific Railroad. Washington DC: Government Printing Office, 1866.

Report of the Board of Public Works, on the Improvement of the Des Moines River. December 1, 1848. Iowa City: Palmer and Paul, 1848.

The Revised Ordinances of the City of St. Louis. St. Louis: Chamber and Knapp, 1850.

Roberts, Nelson C., and Samuel W. Moorhead, eds. *Story of Lee County, Iowa.* 2 vols. Chicago: Clarke, 1914.

Rosenberg, Charles E. *The Cholera Years: The United States in 1832, 1849, and 1866.* Chicago: University of Chicago Press, 1962.

Rosenberg, Charles G. *Jenny Lind in America.* New York: Stringer and Townshend, 1851.

Rosenberg, Morton M. *Iowa on the Eve of the Civil War: A Decade of Frontier Politics.* Norman: University of Oklahoma Press, 1972.

Ryan, Daniel J. "Ohio in the Mexican War." *Ohio Archeological and Historical Publications* 21 (1912): 277–95.

Scheiber, Harry N. *Ohio Canal Era: A Case Study of Government and the Economy, 1820–1861.* Athens: Ohio University Press, 1968.

Schofield, John M. *Forty-Six Years in the Army.* New York: Century, 1897.

Schultz, Robert G. *The March to the River: From the Battle of Pea Ridge to Helena, Spring 1862.* Iowa City: Camp Pope Publishing, 2014.

Shaw, Ronald E. *Canals for a Nation: The Canal Era in the United States, 1790–1860.* Lexington: University Press of Kentucky, 1993.

Shea, William L. "The Confederate Defeat at Cache River." *Arkansas Historical Quarterly* 52 (1993): 129–55.

———. *Fields of Blood: The Prairie Grove Campaign.* Chapel Hill: University of North Carolina Press, 2009.

Shea, William L., and Earl J. Hess. *Pea Ridge: Civil War Campaign in the West.* Chapel Hill: University of North Carolina Press, 1992.

Shea, William L., and Terrence J. Winschel. *Vicksburg Is the Key: The Struggle for the Mississippi River.* Lincoln: University of Nebraska Press, 2003.

Sheridan, Philip H. *Personal Memoirs of P.H. Sheridan.* 2 vols. New York: Webster, 1888.

Sievers, Michael A. "Westward by Indian Treaty: The Upper Missouri Example." *Nebraska History* 56 (1975): 77–107.

Sigel, Franz. "The Pea Ridge Campaign." In *Battles and Leaders of the Civil War,* edited by Robert U. Johnson and Clarence C. Buel, 314–34. 4 vols. New York: Century, 1884–87.

Simon, John Y., ed. *The Papers of Ulysses S. Grant.* 31 vols. to date. Carbondale: Southern Illinois University Press, 1967–2012.

Simpson, Brooks D., and Jean V. Berlin, eds. *Sherman's Civil War: Selected Correspondence of William T. Sherman, 1860–1865.* Chapel Hill: University of North Carolina Press, 1999.

Sinisi, Kyle. *The Last Hurrah: Sterling Price's Missouri Expedition of 1864.* Lanham MD: Rowman and Littlefield, 2015.

Smiley, Jerome C. *Semi-Centennial History of the State of Colorado.* 2 vols. Chicago: Lewis, 1913.

Smucker, Isaac. *Centennial History of Licking County, Ohio.* Newark OH: Clark and Underwood, 1876.

Sparks, David S. "Iowa Republicans and the Railroads." *Iowa Journal of History* 53 (1955): 273–86.

Stevens, Walter B. *St. Louis: The Fourth City.* 2 vols. New York: Clarke, 1911.

Stiles, Edward H. *Recollections and Sketches of Notable Lawyers and Public Men of Early Iowa.* Des Moines IA: Homestead, 1916.

Stuart, Addison A. *Iowa Colonels and Regiments: Being a History of Iowa Regiments in the War of the Rebellion.* Des Moines IA: Mills, 1865.

Swisher, Jacob A. "The Des Moines River Improvement Project." *Iowa Journal of History and Politics* 35 (1937): 142–80.

Tarver, Micajah, and Henry Cobb. "Philadelphia, Fort Wayne and Platte River Airline Railroad." *The Western Journal, and Civilian* 14 (1855): 367.

Taylor, Hawkins. "Gen. Curtis." *Iowa Historical Record* 3 (1887): 561–67.

Taylor, William A. *Centennial History of Columbus and Franklin County, Ohio.* Chicago: Clarke, 1909.

Teters, Kristopher A. *Practical Liberators: Union Officers in the Western Theater during the Civil War.* Chapel Hill: University of North Carolina Press, 2018.

Thayer, John M. "The Pawnee War of 1859." *Proceedings and Collections of the Nebraska State Historical Society* 5 (1902): 231–46.

Twain, Mark. *Life on the Mississippi.* Boston: Osgood, 1883.

U.S. Department of the Navy. *Official Records of the Union and Confederate Navies in the War of the Rebellion.* 30 vols. Washington DC: Government Printing Office, 1894–1922.

U.S. War Department. *The War of the Rebellion: A Compilation of the Official Records of the Union and Confederate Armies.* 128 vols. Washington DC: Government Printing Office, 1880–1901.

Utley, Robert M. *Frontiersmen in Blue: The United States Army and the Indians, 1848–1865.* New York: Macmillan, 1967.

Warren, Steven L. *The Second Battle of Cabin Creek: Brilliant Victory.* Charleston SC: History Press, 2012.

Weed, Cora C. *Hand Book for Iowa Soldiers' and Sailors' Monument.* [Des Moines]: [State of Iowa], 1898.

Wilson, Ben H. "The Des Moines Rapids Canal." *Palimpsest* 5 (1924): 117–32.

Winders, Richard B. *Mr. Polk's Army: The American Military Experience in the Mexican War.* College Station: Texas A&M University Press, 1997.

Winter, William C. *The Civil War in St. Louis: A Guided Tour.* St. Louis: Missouri Historical Society Press, 1994.

INDEX